MEYER WEISGAL . . . SO FAR

To my newly found friend
Shablai
With warm regards.
Meyer W.

Jan 9/73

MEYER WEISGAL
... SO FAR

An Autobiography

Weidenfeld and Nicolson

Weidenfeld and Nicolson
5 Winsley Street London W1

Weidenfeld and Nicolson Jerusalem
19 Herzog Street Jerusalem

Designed by Alex Berlyne

Frontispiece courtesy Gershon Dror

ISBN 0 297 99373 9

Printed in Israel by Keter Press; bound by Wiener Bindery, Jerusalem, 1971

To Shirley,
who bore all this and more

Acknowledgments

Somewhere in sacred Jewish writings it is said that he who gives credit where credit is due is helping to bring redemption to the world. I should like these acknowledgments to hasten the arrival of the Messiah, if only by a few hours.

It has been a universal custom for an author to put his wife's name at the end of the list of those to whom he is indebted—as a climax, presumably: and a pious tribute to the long-suffering woman, etc. I choose to begin with my wife, Shirley. In addition to her natural endowments—which are considerable—she was a more than competent part-time secretary. She could decipher and rewrite the scrawls which I myself could not read twenty-four hours after I had written them. Wherever and whenever we were in the same part of the world and I was inspired, she was ready, able and willing, not without a few mild groans, to take down in longhand my reminiscences and musings, beginning in 1953 in La Croix in the south of France, where I was ill, and afraid I would leave the world without having said my piece. But I recovered and abandoned the piece for another fourteen years. From page twenty-one on, the reader will see in more detail what she has been to this life and this book about this life. And God knows, she knows and I know. So let it be.

Now for my daughter Helen Amir (whose name has been distorted in Hebrew into Chaya) of whom it can be said that were it not for her the book not only would never have been written, but would have been finished five years ago. I don't regret the delay. Chapter Twenty-Four illustrates both points, and a great deal more, for instance that the real 'culprit' behind Helen was George Weidenfeld. Anyway, fourteen years after La Croix, she started putting the first draft together, writing and rewriting, discovering long forgotten letters and speeches, adding to, expunging from, and editing deathless prose.

It was Joseph Brainin who pulled this first draft to pieces. He and Maurice Samuel were closer to me than any other two people in the world for more than fifty years. The first draft went to Joe, my adviser and severest critic. His remembrances of things past matched and collided with my own, and his inborn Viennese sensitivity was ruffled by my free and easy-going style. Then he, Helen and I picked up the pieces and put them together again. Alas, early in 1970 Joe died. On the day of his funeral Maurice said to me, 'We were three and now we are only two. Who knows how far we have yet to travel? But I would like to take over with your manuscript where Joe left off.' I would never have dared ask him to do this—deeply involved as he always has been with his own program of writing (he was on his twenty-seventh or twenty-eighth book). But of course I accepted his generosity, with a plea, 'Please Moish, don't reduce me or elevate me to the purity of your English style.' He accepted this limitation, but the manuscript nevertheless was subjected to his scrupulous ministration and his passionate dedication to precision.

Amos Elon, an eminent Israeli writer and journalist, rescued me from many pitfalls and made valuable suggestions. My secretary, Joseph Eligouloff, typed and retyped, and retyped the thing, enduring without a murmur (or so it seemed) my indecipherable scrawl. For the index, general checking of facts and spellings, and stylistic 'improvements'—weeding out some of my purple passages—I owe, and present, my gratitude to Helene Hughes Fineman.

I wish to express my profound gratitude to my dear friend Reuven Rubin for the drawing which opens this book.

If I have in any way offended anyone by omission or commission, I beg forgiveness.

In accordance with the time-honored rule, I finish with an unequivocal 'I, and no one else, am responsible for everything in this book.'

M.W.W.

Contents

'The only shield to a man's memory is the rectitude and sincerity of his actions.'

Winston Churchill

'Jews recited the Psalms . . . while their goats nodded in affirmation'; specially drawn for this book by Reuven Rubin.

I The Beginning

Like most Jews I was born in Kikl.

Whenever I mention the little place that gave me to the world, mildly astonished looks are turned on me: 'Is there really such a place?' and I have to answer: 'I'm not at all sure anymore.' Memory tells me that indeed there was a Kikl once upon a time, somewhere in the province of Plotsk, in the Poland that was part of the Russian Empire. But like Chelm or Kasri-elevky, geography was never its strong point. More than a town, or a village, or even a hamlet, Kikl was a state of mind. Its real boundaries were not in space but in time. It was an abstract of Jewish history which can only be located in the memory, the literature, and the folklore of the Jews. Of course it had a specific longitude and latitude, but that is irrelevant. It was a place where Jews recited the Psalms over and over again and praised God for the bounty that filled their souls, while their goats nodded in affirmation. That their stomachs were empty was never a bone of contention with Him. For this they could blame their relatives. It was one of those tattered and bedraggled pockets of Jewish life thickly strewn over Eastern Europe at the turn of the century, where a pious father prayed more for his sons' education and his daughters' marriages than for the wherewithal to make them possible. And everyone was overjoyed but no one surprised when the prayers were answered. Take my father, for example. Shloyme Chaim Weisgal was the *chazan* of Kikl—cantor you would say today. He never had a penny to his name, yet one of my brothers, the oldest, studied music in Breslau, another took up engineering in Plotsk, the capital of the province, a third attended a *yeshivah* under the illustrious Rabbi Reines of Lida, all this while we were in Kikl. We younger ones went to *cheder*.

We were poor, of course—so was everybody else in Kikl—but we were among the poorest. We were largely dependent on the bounty of an uncle whose house we shared; he occupied the ground floor, we the upper. Uncle Getzel was the village *katzev*, or butcher, and also the village *g'vir*. *Katzev* by association means ignoramus and in this respect Uncle Getzel conformed to type. As *g'vir*, or man of wealth, and leader of the community, he conformed less adequately. The most that could be said of him was that as long as the Kiklites ate, Uncle Getzel had an income. And the best that could be said of him was that as long as he had an income, we too ate. In his relationship to my father I learned very early the meaning of the old Hebrew saying: 'If a man dedicates himself to the service of God, others will attend to his worldly wants.'

My father was universally venerated and if Uncle Getzel assumed part of the burden of his life, it was only proper. My father did not feel that he was under any obligation. On the contrary, it was Getzel who was beholden. Besides, the man was childless; what good was his 'wealth' to him?

My father came from a long line of rabbis. He had *smicha* and *kabolah*, that is rabbinical ordination and attestation, from the great Reb Yeshuele Kutner, a distant relative of ours, known as the Vilner Gaon of Poland after one of the greatest Jewish scholars of all time. Nothing more need be said on that point. It was like saying 'a graduate of Harvard Law School' or 'legal secretary to Justice Holmes.' Your reputation was made without test. But despite his ordination and his profound piety, my father did not enter the rabbinate. His ruling passion, his life's preoccupation was music—a remarkable thing considering the time and the circumstances of his early years. There was certainly no music school in nearby Sherpce where he had grown up—although Sherpce was a metropolis in comparison with Kikl. All of his musical education was acquired by what we might call today a correspondence course—except that there were no correspondence schools either. Choir leaders and even choir boys from various synagogues were accustomed to conduct enormous correspondences with their peers in other places, exchanging their musical compositions by mail, handwritten of course. Traveling *meshorrerim*, or singers, carried new melodies from place to place. Many of them passed through Kikl on their way to Germany in pursuit of solid musical education. Since my father was a *chazan* of some renown, our house was a way station for these wandering minstrels, an impromptu stage for their 'auditions.' Father was somewhat suspicious of these visitors who were not noted for their religious dependability but he enjoyed their music.

From the days of my earliest childhood until his death in America in 1921 I remember him poring over his vast tomes and making musical notations.

The music sheets were somehow or other always next to a Talmudic Tractate. I have the impression that he went from one to the other: he would leave a piece of music to pursue some problem in the Tractate and then a phrase in the Tractate would set him off composing. In the absence of radios, phonographs and local opera houses, he 'heard' his music in books and I have a well-founded suspicion that he sometimes scanned non-devotional scores. Once, during a Friday evening service—many years later, in the Bronx—he was suddenly carried away into a rendition of *Lecho Dodi*, the traditional welcome to the Sabbath, which bore a strange resemblance to 'Rachel, Quand Du Seigneur' from Halevi's *La Juive*, enhanced by *chazonishe* trills and roulades. When I asked him, slyly, if this was a new composition of his, he confided: 'Don't tell anyone, I read it in a book.' Even if there had been an opera house in the vicinity of Kikl, my father would not have dreamed of patronizing so pagan an institution. Only once, towards the end of his life in America, did I succeed in breaking down his resistance and dragging him to hear Caruso. It was a matinée and the opera was Bizet's *The Pearlfishers*. When Caruso sang that famous aria 'Je crois entendre encore,' with its curious echo of the *chazan's* wail, I glanced at my father, sitting there in his Prince Albert and skullcap. There were tears streaming down his face. As we walked out I asked him: 'So, father, what do you think of this *goy?*' He replied: '*Alle chazonim megen a kapore zayn far im.*' This can be only feebly rendered in English by 'Now that I've heard him, all the world's *chazonim* can bury themselves alive.'

Naturally my father did not only sing and write liturgical music. He was prolific in other directions. He was the *shochet* or ritual slaughterer of Kikl, the *mohel*, circumciser of newborn males, he had two wives—not, God forbid! at the same time—and produced eleven children. Chronologically I was the fourth son and fifth child of my father's first wife and I came into the world with a twin sister. My mother died giving birth to her sixth child but not before she called in her sixteen year old niece, my cousin Lodzia, and bestowed upon her the inheritance: a husband, fifteen years her senior, and six children, three of whom, myself included, were under three years of age. Poor girl! She could not have been less suited by temperament or inclination for the job. But the hand of my dead mother was heavy on her. Lodzia was exceptionally beautiful, temperamental, a reader of forbidden books, and given to writing revolutionary poetry. She was a rebel, and marriage didn't change her. She continued to rebel— against her husband, against the role assigned her as wife of the *chazan*, against her environment, against the system.

I don't remember my own mother, but certainly as far as I was concerned Lodzia stepped into the breach with utter devotion. She rearranged the household: my three older brothers were away from home most of the time, and Lodzia sent my twin sister Chaya and my youngest brother, Sam, to live downstairs with Uncle Getzel; I remained with her, she doted on me, and I ruled the roost.

The situation was not a happy one for my father; there was constant friction between him and Lodzia as to my upbringing. He was a loving father, and if he had any worldly ambition it was to give his sons a good education. But he was strict in his outlook and an old-fashioned disciplinarian in his methods. When I received a slap, Lodzia would take me in her arms and turn on him with, 'What do you want of the child?'

But this was only a minor disagreement. My father was quite incapable of understanding Lodzia and her ways. Young as she was, Lodzia had already been engaged for some time in the activities of the Bund, the Jewish revolutionary organization, and she had made up her mind that marriage —even to the *chazan* of Kikl—was not going to interfere with them. Her revolutionary ardor continued unabated, and when I was old enough she used me as a messenger to her comrades in arranging illegal meetings or lectures, usually on the Sabbath. When my father left for *shul* Lodzia would keep me behind on some pretext or other, with the promise to send me on in a few minutes. And so she did, but I was always told to make my way to the synagogue by way of so-and-so's house, and to repeat certain words to him. I naturally had not the slightest idea of what it was all about, but I was thrilled by the secrecy of it. When I finally arrived at the synagogue I took my place next to my father, right on the *bima*, the platform, a much coveted place, and innocently joined in the services.

My brothers and I had good voices—mine was an unusually limpid alto—and singly, in pairs, or three at a time depending on how many were at home, we made up part of my father's synagogue choir. When we returned from services on the Sabbath, Lodzia always had an extra piece of cake waiting for me. My father uneasily allowed this curious indulgence; only Lodzia and I knew the reason for it. One way or another, Sabbath was easily the best day of the week for me, as for all Jews, young and old.

I must have been about seven when Lodzia arranged her biggest clandestine meeting ever. The great Charney Vladeck was coming all the way to Kikl. In those days Vladeck was known as the Yiddish Lassalle; in his later years he settled in America and became the managing editor of the *Jewish Daily Forward*, the foremost Yiddish newspaper of America and the organ of the socialist movement. In 1933 we became friends, and although

at opposite poles, he a socialist, I a Zionist, did considerable business together. At the time I was producing a mammoth Jewish spectacle, *The
Romance of a People*, and Vladeck took three performances under the
patronage of the *Forward*. It was a great attraction for the Jews of New York
and whether or not it contributed to socialism, it certainly increased the
circulation of the paper. In my childhood days he was a remote and legendary figure, and his arrival in the backwater of Kikl was an extraordinary
event. The meeting was naturally held on a Saturday, the one workless
day of the week, and on this occasion Lodzia made especial use of me:
like a juvenile Paul Revere, I was dispatched to sound the alarm, that is,
to round up the class conscious for the meeting in the forest.

A secret in Kikl, like anywhere else, lasted about forty-eight hours. It
became known that the *chazente*, the *chazan's* wife, had been one of the
leading spirits in the conspiratorial meeting in the forest, and that furthermore it was by no means her first offence: she had been haunting the groves
in the company of shady characters for a long time. Rumors, wild and
tantalizing, spread like wildfire, and ended in the flat accusation that she
was having a love affair with one of the revolutionaries. Now a love affair
in Kikl was not what is understood by a love affair in sophisticated society;
it meant a walk in the meadows holding hands with someone not your
husband; it meant a mild flirtation and an exchange of covert glances. But
even this kind of love affair, coupled as it was with godless revolutionary
activities, was an unheard of affront to the pious of Kikl on the part of the
chazan's wife. And, Lodzia, far from seeking to allay the rumors, fed them.
One day, to the utter chagrin, I might almost say the despair of my father,
and to the horror of all Kikl, she appeared in the village streets in her own
hair! As is generally known, when a pious Jewish woman married in those
days—and the custom still prevails among the ultraorthodox—she cut off
her hair and covered her head with a *sheytl* or wig. The origins of the
custom are obscure. Some authorities claim that it goes back to the Middle
Ages, when the lord of the manor had the *jus primae noctis*, the right of the
first night, with every newly married bride on his desmesne; and Jewish
women bought themselves out of this humiliation by sacrificing their
crowning glory and bringing the proceeds to their lord. Others assign a
less picturesque origin: the *sheytl* was simply a 'keep off' sign; it indicated
the lady's marital status and while advertising her unavailability diminished
her attractiveness. Whatever its origins, the *sheytl* of the married woman
had tremendous sanctity, and when Lodzia appeared in the streets of
Kikl, or what passed for streets in Kikl, with her own gold-flaming hair
in full view, a visible shudder ran through the village. She was not only

defying tradition; she was mocking her husband and practically confirming the worst that rumor told of her. Actually Lodzia did not have the courage to discard the *sheytl*—that came much later. She simply combed part of her hair over the *sheytl* giving the impression that she wore none. Sufficient of a mortal sin to condemn her to the stake. And it was not all.

About that time, and perhaps in connection with the tense situation, Lodzia staged another rebellion. Since most of the women of Kikl were as illiterate as they were pious, it was the duty of the *chazente* to read the prayers aloud in the women's section of the synagogue, and the women would repeat them after her. One Sabbath Lodzia struck: she refused to perform this chore. It may have been her way of getting even with the gossips. There was no one with the knowledge and practiced skill to replace her, and her refusal was tantamount to apostasy; certainly she was abandoning the women of Kikl to their ignorance. For two Saturdays the women sat in mute testimony to the great heresy. Kikl was in an uproar; deputations came and went; the air was sulphurous with threats and my father's livelihood trembled in the balance. Somehow, the dust settled on the third Sabbath, and everything was back to normal. The *chazente* returned to her flock and the women of Kikl regained their voices.

These extraordinary doings did not exactly enhance my father's prestige and probably contributed not a little to our eventual departure for America; yet it must be said to Lodzia's credit that she proved resourceful and diplomatic in other fields pertaining to the family fortunes.

Now I know it doesn't sound credible but all historians of early Kikliana agree that I was a very beautiful child. My stepmother who had a great fondness for me, enhanced that beauty with clothes remade from her old dresses or father's discarded silken *kopote*. My black curls were allowed to grow freely, even beyond the age considered proper for a boy in Kikl. Whenever the 'pantry' was empty, which was often, Lodzia would deck me out in my finery and send me down to Uncle Getzel, ostensibly to sing for him, for he was very fond of my solos, but actually to extract some money for bread or milk. He knew it was a ruse but he was a willing victim. He used to mark down these 'gifts' on the wall with a piece of white chalk and watch the column mount till the day when he would have a reckoning with my father.

This became a pattern with him, but its effectiveness was at the mercy of my twin sister, Chaya, who lived with him, and who would, in his absence, mount a chair and erase the record. Then, when he returned, we would suddenly hear a great roaring and bellowing, which went on for several minutes while Uncle Getzel restored the record from memory. After a while the tumult would subside, Uncle Getzel looking at the writing on the wall and muttering to himself, 'What am I doing? He can't pay me anyway. Why use up good chalk?' With a grand gesture and a swish of his sleeve he himself would wipe the slate clean. Peace was restored to his soul and to the household. Feeling himself to be the great benefactor, he would mount the stairs as if nothing had happened, and if father was in would invariably ask him, 'Got a new melody for the coming Sabbath of the New Moon?' My father rarely reacted. He would bury his face in a folio of the Talmud, reluctant to waste time on Uncle Getzel, the ignoramus.

On such occasions Lodzia would save the situation. She knew all my father's compositions even better than the choir (my father contemptuously referred to its members as 'wooden logs') and she had an excellent singing voice. She would pick up the score and regale Uncle Getzel with a full preview of the coming New Moon Sabbath service. The impromptu session ended in an all round reconciliation, and Uncle Getzel, besides having wiped out the national debt, threw a couple of rubles into the bargain. But his parting shot was always the same, addressed to my father: '*Mach mir nisht treyf di beheyme morgen*, Don't tell me again tomorrow that the new-slaughtered ox is not kosher enough.' This was an allusion to my father's strictness as a *shochet*, and carried with it a not too subtle hint of bribery. In effect he was saying: 'Look how generous I am with my rubles, why can't you be generous with my oxen?'

My father was meticulous in the performance of his religious functions and nobody appreciated this less than Uncle Getzel. All of Kikl held its breath when the lungs of the cow or the ox were inflated for the examination. The slightest defect might render the animal non-kosher. That would be a day of mourning for Uncle and for the community; the former lost money, the latter were without meat for the Sabbath. And even though his own family was involved in the general disaster, my father would not swerve by a hair's breadth from the strict interpretation of the law. When an animal was declared '*treyf*'—not kosher—Uncle Getzel became unapproachable. He got the feeling that his status and his entire economic position were being undermined by this silly business of a *p'gima*, a stain on the lung of the cow. And for us it meant not only a meatless Sabbath, it meant also the drying up of the sluices of Uncle Getzel's generosity.

In such crises, which were not infrequent, Lodzia rose to the situation. She had a remarkable gift for borrowing—all the more remarkable in view of her reputation as a rebel. But curiously enough on these occasions she, who could not have cared less about the whole business of *kashrut*, became a flaming defender of the faith. The sanctity of ritual slaughter, to hear her tell it, was the center of gravity of Jewish law, the sustaining power of the Jewish people. The dumbfounded Kiklites listened to the impassioned words flowing from Lodzia's lips, and loved every minute of it. Even Uncle Getzel had to retreat before her.

And now I come to the incident which towers above all my other childhood memories. My oldest brother, Abba, had left Kikl when I was eight years old. I had at that time the impression that he was a full-grown man. Today, still hale, hearty and active as a cantor, he claims that he is only five years my senior which makes him either a fibber or a genius for at the time he had a job as choir leader in a distant town of respectable size, an extraordinary achievement for a *bar mitzvah* boy. When he celebrated his 'eightieth' birthday, he admitted to me that five years may have gotten lost in the course of his various migrations. Anyway, he was suddenly inspired to send for his little brother in Kikl, with an offer to keep me for the summer and the High Holidays as one of his soloists.

It was a tremendous event for Kikl, and the inhabitants turned out *en masse* to bid me farewell. Their feelings were mixed; they were proud that Kikl was sending its second musical contribution into the great world, and at such an early age; they lamented that on the approaching High Holidays they would not hear my plaintive tones. But from the send-off it would seem that pride outweighed regret.

Travel in those days and in those parts was pretty much as Sholem Aleichem describes it in *Tevye the Dairyman*. After a day and a night of trundling in one of the uncovered wagons then in use, I arrived at Nyesheve, the city of my brother's triumph.

Nyesheve was very different from Kikl. It lay smack on the German border and had something of German style to it. It had a veneer of *Kultur*, very thin to be sure, but enough to take in the eye at first glance. On the Sabbath the Jews wore 'stove pipes' and frock coats, unheard of in Kikl. The daughters of the well-to-do spoke Polish, while Yiddish was reduced to something that passed for *Mittelhochdeutsch*, what we used to call Yiddish with a *passach*, because of the tendency to turn every vowel sound into a broad *a*. There were other differences. Kikl had neither streets nor avenues nor pavements, and not even dirt roads; it was a cloud of dust in the summer and a quagmire in the winter. Nyesheve had cobblestone streets and sidewalks of a sort—that is to say, a strip raised above the level of the gutter. Altogether Nyesheve impressed me as a great city.

No one came to meet me, for how was anyone to know when my wagon would arrive? I was simply put off by the drayman in front of the *chazan's* house, my presence being loudly announced before the drayman drove off. The *chazan* came out, a handsome young man with a fine blond beard and a rather forbidding mien. His Yiddish was strange to me. The Yiddish of Kikl was intimate and affectionate; his sounded at once richer, affected and deliberately gruff. His first impulse, probably, was to give me a couple of slaps to establish his authority; but he restrained himself and instead handed me over to his wife, who gave me something to eat and put me to bed.

My brother did not come over till late in the day; when he arrived he immediately got down to business with the *chazan* and the *chazente*. 'Where will he eat? Where will he stay?' I listened in a daze, vaguely aware of names and days being shuffled around, and I was terrified to find myself the subject of so grave and protracted a discussion. Somewhat later I realized what it was all about; I was being apportioned, meal by meal, nightly bed by nightly bed, among the various *baalebatim*, or householders, of Nyesheve, with due regard for those who were too high in the social scale to be approached and those who were too low to be solicited on behalf of the provincial boy.

The next morning I discovered that only the theory and tactics had been discussed, for my brother took me on the rounds ostensibly to show me off but actually to put into effect the arrangements that had been so laboriously worked out the previous evening. It was made to seem very casual. His arm about me, he directed my steps over the billeting route: 'You must meet Yankel *shnayder* (the tailor), or Mottel *balagole* (the drayman), or Itzik *bodner* (the cooper).' Once inside the house I was introduced as the little brother, the 'soloist.' Abba would inquire after the members of the household, trade gossip with the wife, pinch the baby's cheek, and any other cheeks, anterior or posterior, available. If the master of the house was home he would disappear with him, leaving me, somewhat forlorn, to soften the heart of the *baaleboste*, or housewife. Outside the negotiations were conducted long and earnestly, and eventually I was set in regard to my 'days'—Monday with this one, Tuesday with that one, Wednesday with the other one—for the duration. Always it was made to appear that I had been invited. Thus I learned, at the age of seven or eight, the meaning of the old Yiddish custom of *essen teg*, or 'eating days,' as if they were edible things. Tens of thousands of wandering *yeshivah* boys have been its beneficiaries in past generations: at times its martyrs, giving rise to the phrase '*essen teg un shlingen treren*, to eat days and gulp down tears.'

Thus my summer was provided for, and all went well until a week or two before *slichos*, the penitential period of prayer which precedes the New Year by about a week. The choir was gathered for rehearsal and I, who had been imported with such fanfare, stood ready for the usual solo. The signal came, I opened my mouth, and nothing came out. I tried again; still nothing. A few moments of appalled silence; the choir was paralyzed; the cantor turned on me, livid: 'A whole summer we fed you, coddled you, fattened you like a goose before Passover—and now! No solo for the High Holidays?' He carried on for several minutes, raving like a maniac, and, to everyone's relief, burst from the room. When he returned, he carried a bundle which he proceeded to untie, spreading the contents on the table: a pair of new boots and a quilted coat, or *burke*, as we called it—my pay for the six months of service. 'You see these beautiful boots?' he shouted. I nodded dumbly. 'You see this magnificent *burke?*' I nodded again. 'All this was made for you! That is, if you sing. And if you don't sing'—dramatic pause—'if you don't sing, it all goes back where it came from.'

I found my voice—but not to sing. The ducts opened and a great wailing issued from my throat. My brother, who was after all responsible for me, had been standing by and had not uttered a single word during all of these proceedings. He looked as if a curse from heaven had fallen upon him. He would have liked the earth to open there and then and swallow him.

I cannot imagine how this would have ended if it hadn't been for the *chazente*, my good angel. She had listened to everything, and at the crucial moment she tore into the room like one of the furies. 'Stop braying like an ox!' she hissed at her husband. 'Shouting won't bring back the child's voice. Give him to me, do you hear? Give him to me, and he'll sing.' There was such authority and assurance in her rage that her husband fell back before her, and all of us, including my unhappy self, were convinced that she knew what she was about.

She took me out of the room, together with the boots and the *burke*. Me she put to bed; the *burke* and the boots she placed on a chair where I could gaze on them all day long. She gave me milk and honey, raw eggs, and various concoctions of her own devising. For a week I was pampered like a crown prince. The next Saturday afternoon the miracle took place. The dulcet tones of my alto came back with a freshness and a vigor that astonished even me. The *chazan*, hearing me, almost danced for joy; he was for dragging me off to rehearsals that very moment. The *chazente* wouldn't hear of it. 'Let him rest,' she commanded. 'He'll be all right tonight.'

'Tonight,' it should be explained, meant the darkness before the dawn, for the penitential *slichos* prayers are recited and sung in the synagogue well before daylight arrives. At three o'clock in the morning I was awakened and given a final dose of milk and honey; then I was bundled up in a huge blanket and the baritone carried me through the sleeping streets to the synagogue. When my turn came to lift up my voice, I felt a pair of pleading eyes on me, and turning mine toward the women's gallery I saw Chana the *chazente* leaning over the balustrade, pleading dumbly with me, 'Don't let me down.'

'*Haneshomo loch vehaguf sheloch*, Man's soul is Thine and so is his body' came out sweet and clear with all the trills and roulades that had been drilled into me all summer until the moment of my collapse. The *chazan* followed with a fugue an octave higher; then I repeated my part according to instructions, the *chazan* repeated his, and then the choir came in:

HANESHOMO LOCH

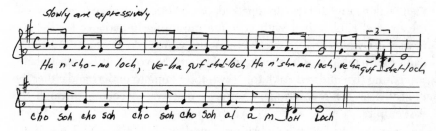

Chana the *chazente* wept for joy. All the other women in the gallery wept with her, but for quite other reasons. One is supposed to weep when the mournful *slichos* notes float past the flickering candles into the darkness and then up to heaven; one weeps even if one doesn't understand the words, as was mostly the case with the women. For these are the days and nights preceding the judgment in heaven and the closing of mortal accounts.

I need hardly say that my brother was ecstatic. I had made my debut as a singer in Israel—and I had been a 'smash hit.'

After the High Holidays I returned to Kikl, carrying my booty—the new *burke* and the new boots. My return as a conquering hero was an even greater event than my departure. Boots and *burke* were placed on display, to be examined and, of course, evaluated: ten rubles, twenty, thirty! Fantastic figures were mentioned while I beamed. My father was genuinely moved—I think he foresaw in me one of the great *chazonim* who were the wonders of their generation. I was asked over and over again to repeat the melodies I had learned in Nyesheve, and I was ready to perform on any and all occasions. I have remained so until this day, frequently to the annoyance of my friends, particularly the professional singers and musicians—of whom there is a whole stable in my family. It was different in Kikl; there they could not have enough of me. I sang every one of my Nyesheve songs, keeping *haneshomo loch vehaguf sheloch* till the end as my *pièce de résistance*. And I never sang without drawing tears from my audience. Once my maternal grandfather, who always sat silently in a corner taking it all in, called me over: 'Come here, my child, you have given me new life,' and he stuck a coin in my hand.

The furor settled down, more or less; the town which had somehow survived my absence again became accustomed to my presence. The winter rains began, and Kikl turned into a vast, shallow pond interspersed with muddy islands between which we navigated. It was the same old Kikl, and yet not the same. There were subtle changes which I could not define. And then certain familiar faces disappeared, one by one. A strange tension was in the air, and Kikl waited with new and mounting impatience for the one newspaper which arrived every Friday and which was passed from hand to hand. Something was happening in the outside world, in Russia-Poland, something that affected Kikl, too. I was too young to understand either the pogroms or the revolutionary upsurge that was sweeping through the vast empire.

But one thing became increasingly evident. In 1903–4 Kikl was thinning out considerably. So were all the Kikls in Russia and Poland. Jews were fleeing—from pogroms, from the fear of pogroms, from poverty, from humiliation. They were fleeing *en masse* to the New World, to the *goldene medina*, the golden land. The stories of the fabulous riches waiting to be picked up on the streets of New York and Chicago inflamed everyone's imagination, everyone's, that is, but my father's. Whether the stories were true or not mattered little to him: to him America was *treyf*, and he would have none of it. He was not going to consign his children to apostasy and damnation. Not even the founding of a Kikl *shul* in Chicago impressed him. He had seen pictures which told the real story: Jews who had cast off the ancient caftan, or gaberdine of the pious, and had adopted the short jacket of the atheistic modernists; Jews clean shaven, Jews hatless. No, America was not for my father, and he was not to be budged.

Such was his resolve; but within one year a concatenation of events swept even him away in the tide.

My brother Leybish, the second oldest, was in Plotsk, studying engineering. He had a talent for gadgets, and once, before he left, he built an iron bed for us. It was one of the marvels of Kikl, a masterpiece of engineering and craftsmanship. It had taken half the Jewish community and several friendly *goyim* to install the bed in the house, and it became a showpiece for all visitors. In Plotsk, Leybish did well at school, but like many young men of that period became involved in the revolutionary movement and before long ended up in jail. Because it was his first offence, and because his relatives guaranteed that he would not offend again—and also because of a number of bribes judiciously distributed—he was let out. He repaid the efforts and sacrifices of his relatives by getting himself rearrested within a few weeks. This time the going was harder. As a second offender he was to be sent to the big jail in Warsaw. That was where the distinguished revolutionaries went, not the amateur rabble rousers; from Warsaw one graduated to Siberia.

With the news of the second arrest came a warning to father from his relatives in Plotsk; nothing but immediate escape from the Plotsk jail and flight from the country could save Leybish. Local authorities could always be bribed, but once Leybish was in the central jail there was no hope. The money was raised, the officials were reached; all that remained was to get a promise from Leybish that he would clear out of the country. Leybish balked; his conscience forbade him to abandon his comrades, it was a betrayal of the revolution. My father went to him, storming; and even the revolutionary Lodzia added her pleas; our relatives were unanimous in urging discretion on Leybish, and they finally succeeded.

My father was secretly proud of his son's revolutionary spirit; at the same time he was deeply distressed for his own peculiar reasons. If his son remained in jail, where would he get kosher food? And would he be allowed to keep his *tefillin?* It simply did not occur to my father that Leybish had long since given up both.

Finally Leybish was released and crossed the border to the city of Thorn, in Upper Silesia, where he waited till the steamship tickets arrived from relatives in Chicago. My father went to Thorn to bid him farewell, believing that this was the last time he would set eyes on his second oldest son. Heavy-hearted, he returned to Kikl, there to be confronted with the second in the series of events. This one concerned my third brother, Joshua, who was studying at the *yeshivah* in Lida, and was entitled to wear the uniform of a gymnasiast. Joshua had done something even more revolutionary than anything reported of Leybish: he had slapped the face of the son of Rabbi Reines, head of the *yeshivah* and founder of the Mizrachi, the religious sector of the Zionist movement. The slap resounded far and wide, and its reverberations were heard in Kikl. I remember the horror that descended on my father and on the inhabitants of Kikl; it was almost as if Joshua had slapped the Rabbi himself. Somehow, I do not know how, the business was patched up, Joshua was not expelled; but it was clear that his rabbinical career—if ever he had hoped for one—was irreparably compromised. (Some thirty years later I fully exonerated my brother, when I met this son of a Rabbi, who all his life had been trying to live on the reputation of his father. I remembered the slap, and I must confess I was tempted to deliver one on my own account.)

The third, and really decisive event centered on my father. The Jewish population of Kikl was shrinking at a terrifying rate. Even before the exodus began, it had been difficult to keep body and soul together; now, even with the help of Uncle Getzel, it was becoming impossible. And just at this time my father received an invitation to become the *chazan* of a much larger community called, if I remember correctly, Mlava, or maybe it was Retchoyns. He snatched at the opportunity.

Naturally he was called in for a hearing, that is, for a sample Sabbath performance, and from all accounts it was of exceptional quality. It was said of him *er hot marish oylem geven*, which in faithful idiomatic translation is 'he took the town by storm.' Immediately after the *havdale*, the home ceremonial ushering out the Sabbath, the *baalebatim* came together and unanimously elected him the *chazan* of Mlava. Nothing remained for him but to return to Kikl the next day and wind up his affairs. It was early summer, and he was to enter on his duties well before the High Holidays. All was settled, the terms agreed upon, the mutual congratulations exchanged. The next morning, while bidding him farewell, the president of the community asked my father casually, 'What kind of chassid are you?', that is to say of what particular chassidic rabbi was my father the follower. In those days, it will be remembered, chassidic rabbis still had their courts, their followers and their rivalries. To the president's casual inquiry my father answered as casually: 'Alexander.' Little did he know what that single word was to mean to him and to the Weisgal family.

Once back in Kikl, my father dutifully set about finding a replacement; but while the search went on rumors began to reach Kikl of strife and dissension in Mlava over the choice of the new *chazan*. At first they were not taken seriously; no *chazan* was ever elected in a Jewish community without violent protests from the partisans of disappointed candidates. But the rumors gathered volume; they grew more persistent, and soon eyewitnesses came to Kikl and told of the 'civil war' in Mlava. How could a chassid of the Alexander Rabbi be *chazan* in Mlava when the Mlavites were overwhelmingly followers of the Gerer Rabbi? It was useless to argue that my father's particular chassidic loyalty had not the slightest influence on the character of his services. Sure enough, a letter arrived from Mlava with bitter news: inasmuch as the *baalebatim* of Mlava had taken it for granted, in view of my father's stainless piety, his religious ardor and the intimacy of his devotional approach to the Almighty, that he was a Gerer chassid, they had been profoundly shocked that he was in fact an Alexander chassid; it was therefore unthinkable that he would become the messenger before the Throne for the Jews of Mlava. Were the *baalebatim* who had endorsed his candidacy to insist on the contract, there would be no peace in Mlava, and surely my father would not want to fan the flames of warfare between brethren. Therefore the *baalebatim* of Mlava asked my father to release them from their pledge. At least, so they said: in reality they were not asking—they were telling him.

This letter was the real turning point in our lives. My father was a changed man. For days on end he sat and brooded. Despite, or perhaps because of his piety, my father was by nature an exuberant man. He danced with the Lord. Whenever he came to the lectern his features were transformed by an inward illumination. Prayer had never been a routine with him; always he felt that on the efficacy of his entreaties rested the fate of the community. Very often we children in the choir wept with him when, on the Day of Atonement, he began the *hineni heoni mimaas*, 'behold me, poor in good deeds . . .' His were real tears, not the simulated ones you get from the modern cantor.

The days passed, and my father did not recover his spirits. Friends came to comfort him, but to no avail; the shock of disappointment had been too deep. How deep we did not guess, as we did not guess what there was behind his brooding. Without confiding in anyone, not even his wife, he had written to Leybish that he was ready to come to America, and only on the day the great big envelope came with the steamship tickets was the decision revealed, and all Kikl learned and gasped: Shloyme Chaim *der chazan* is going to America.

2 Farewell to Kikl

The immediate reason for my father's change of heart about America did not appeal to Kikl's collective imagination. The blame for his decision was laid squarely at Lodzia's door. It was inconceivable that he should have taken such a step of his own free will. She must have beguiled him and would yet lead him to apostasy. But if Kikl was irritated, confused, and otherwise incredulous at his decision to emigrate, the *landsleit* in New York and Chicago were staggered. As one old Kiklite in New York put it: 'If Shloyme Chayim is coming to America, there is hope for the Messiah too.' Well, my father arrived and the Messiah is still on his way.

With his departure the house seemed to empty out, even with a new crop of children, the first three of Lodzia's eventual five. Our home had always been what is called in Hebrew *beis havad lechochomim*—a kind of meeting place for intellectuals. Apart from the Kiklites of the upper strain, i.e. those who knew how to discuss a tractate in the Talmud or argue the meaning of a certain phrase in Maimonides' *Guide to the Perplexed*, it was a haven for all sorts of visitors passing through Kikl: rabbis, students, singers, bride-seekers, or their agents, *shadchonim*. The Kiklites would just drop in whenever the urge for disputation came upon them. The itinerants arrived by a more circuitous route. They would go first to the synagogue, just as today a visitor to a strange town goes first to a hotel. When the prayers were over, the more respectable and solid *baalebatim* would linger a while, sizing up the visitors before inviting them to their various homes. My father needed a cooling off period after performing the services and he would seat himself in the back of the *shul* for ten or fifteen minutes. By the time he was ready to leave, the synagogue was empty of Kiklites, and the more promising or at least the more impressive look-ing of the visitors had already been snatched up. Those who remained waited hopefully for the *chazan* to catch his breath. It was inconceivable that he should ignore their presence and thus consign them to the *hekdesh* or communal lodging house. And they were right. He would ask, 'Where do you come from? How long are you staying? What is your purpose?' Whatever the mission, one or more of these perambulating worthies would be brought home *epis toiem tzu zein*, that is, for a bite to eat. We didn't have enough for ourselves but that made little difference. As our folk-sayings have it: one must not humiliate a Jew, and besides there is no reason to feel ashamed because of a little more water in the soup. If the visitor proved interesting and knew something about the big world, my mother would take center stage and display her own erudition; the visitor was not to think she was the average *chazente*. Then all was well and the evening passed off cheerily. But if he turned out to be a *nebechl*, a dreary bore, there was hell to pay. The scene would not occur at once; Lodzia was too civilized for that. But once the guest had been bedded down in our guest house—one of Uncle Getzel's empty stables—it was always a toss-up which way the evening would end and the drama of it made life interesting.

With father gone, life became drab. Lodzia was considered an *almonah*, a widow, or at best an *aguna*, an abandoned wife. We children were regarded as orphans. We became full-fledged objects of charity, wholly dependent upon Uncle Getzel, without chalk and without scenes. Our only function was to wait for the *shifskarten* which, we were told, might take a year or two.

I must confess that at first I did not quite grasp the full implications of my father's move. I thought it was like another version of my own trip to Nyesheve. But only one week after his departure I was made dramatically aware of the fact that things had indeed changed. I was without warning and—it seemed to me—without reason evicted from my place of honor on the *bima* during the Sabbath service. I went weeping to Uncle Getzel, who tried to explain to me that I had, alas, come down in the world. I was, so to speak, no longer the son of Shloyme Chaim the *chazan;* I was the son of Shloyme Chaim who had gone to America. I did not realize at first that my father had departed Kikl for ever—it was unnatural. Nevertheless my new and diminished status was slowly but surely made clear to me and I had to look for ways of restoring it, for turning my disadvantage to good account. On Sabbath mornings, no longer privileged to sit at the *chazan's* side, I spent more of the time with the children outside the synagogue, and there I became an expert on American affairs. I must have had some talent both as an inventor and a raconteur, because the children listened with bated breath. What I spun out of my imagination I don't remember; I only recall the intensity of the interest I aroused. America! The magic word. My credentials were obviously unassailable: my father and brother were there and I was going to join them.

During that waiting period a notable event occurred: our house burned down. Of course in our Kikl, as in all other Kikls, it happened in the middle of the night. I am told I was rolled up in a blanket and thrown from an upper window. We were carted away on a wagon to a nearby meadow where we could watch the glorious blaze to our hearts' content. That I remember distinctly. Where we went from there, how we reestablished our household—all this is vague. The next thing I recall is living in a place that used to belong to a certain Pan Prozhamovsky.

Prozhamovsky, however, I remember very clearly, both as a person and legend. He was a former Polish landowner who had been separated from his money and his estates by cards and women, mostly the latter. Destitute, he had moved smack into the middle of Jewish Kikl, occupying part of a run-down house formerly his, now the property of a Jew, and living there, the story ran, rent free. This act of grace on the part of the Jewish landlord Prozhamovsky had earned honestly enough; in the days of his affluence he, unlike most of the members of his class, had shown consistent goodwill toward the Jews. He had been generous; he used to walk through the alleys of Kikl distributing small coins to the Jewish children. Despite his comedown in the world he never appeared in public save in a frock coat; true, it was densely inhabited by the fleas which had migrated into it from the huge dogs which seemed to be as inseparable from him as the frock coat. It was said that the dogs slept with him, and I wondered whether he also slept in the frock coat, refusing to part, waking or asleep, from the testimonies to his former grandeur.

He and his dogs lived in a garret at the top of the house in which we were temporarily installed, and we became great friends—that is with Prozhamovsky. His dogs were not permitted to enter our room. We didn't mind the fleas.

I suppose that I remember him so clearly because much later, in America, whenever I appeared looking particularly elegant someone in the family was sure to call out: 'Here comes Prozhamovsky.'

When I was about ten, the tickets for America arrived and preparations for the voyage began. Abba and Joshua were to remain in Europe to continue their studies while Chaya, my twin sister, and Sam, my younger brother, were to stay behind with Uncle Getzel. This arrangement was necessary as there were only five tickets in the envelope. They joined us, as did Joshua and Abba, in the course of time. So we were five, Lodzia and I and three small ones, Mendel, Rose and Jack. As the 'man' of the family, I had certain responsibilities: I carried one of them in my arms all the way. The usual weeping of friends and relations sent us on our way to the German border by horse and wagon, whence to Bremen and the SS. *Kronprinzessin Caecilia*, New York-bound. The fate of this boat during the First World War had a certain bearing on my life in America, and led to my acquaintance with one of the outstanding personalities of the generation, which is probably why I remember it.

My recollections of the voyage are sketchy. I remember of course the dirt, the squalor, the stench, the three-layer berths, the queuing up for meals of the steerage passengers. I even recall sneaking up to First Class and being given an orange by an old lady. I had never seen an orange before, and proceeded to eat it—peel and all. But what has stuck in my mind all these years with a particular horror was something that preceded the actual voyage—the 'delousing' process in Bremen. Males and females were separated and told to undress. Naked, we were herded into a room, fifty or a hundred at a time. The steam pipes began to hiss and we were swallowed in a huge cloud of steam, while our clothes were being similarly fumigated. I suppose that these sanitary measures were demanded by the American immigration authorities. But what left a scar on my memory was the way it was done—the grim efficiency of the Germans, their treatment of us as cattle, their utter lack of feeling for human dignity. Decades later, in the days of the Hitler holocaust and the death chambers, the memory of the 'delousing' process in Bremen came back to me, like a prophetic foreboding, a rehearsal.

There is a German saying, 'Nothing is as certain as the accidental.' What if Leybish had not gone to Plotsk to become an engineer? Would he have become involved in the revolutionary movement and been forced to flee to America? Who can say? What if the Gerer chassidim had been a bit more tolerant and elected my father *chazan* of Mlava? Would we have remained in Eastern Europe? Probably. Our fate, my fate, could have been the fate of the six million who perished. But no. It was otherwise. I was plucked from the burning, consigned to life, not by any grand universal design but by indifferent chance.

There is that passage in the Passover Haggadah: 'In every generation it is incumbent upon each to regard himself as if he himself had gone forth from Egypt.' This is part of the tragic, prophetic wisdom of Israel, the core, perhaps, of Jewish existence. And the great wide world has never ceased to repeat the lesson, lest we, the Jews, forget.

After fifteen weary days of tossing and crossing we came in sight of the Statue of Liberty—which may sound a little more romantic than it really was. The bulk of the passengers in steerage were never aware of it, and if the rumor of it reached some of them, they could not *see* the lady with the lamp, jammed together as they were into the bowels of the ship. Nor was the experience of Castle Gardens—this was the immigration depot later replaced by Ellis Island—a compensation for missing the Statue of Liberty, at least as far as I was concerned. I had to look after three little children, one of whom could hardly walk. I had to help collect and count the bundles; for it must not be imagined that we traveled with neatly packed trunks and valises. Three-quarters of our possessions, clothes, pillows, pots, pans, were wrapped up in shawls, table-cloths, sacking—bundles large, small, middle-sized, all of them precious, and all moving with us from stage to stage so that we could keep track of them. I had little energy for impressions, and those that filtered through to me were bad.

Before we were let loose on unsuspecting America we were put into a huge cage for what seemed hours. We were looking out of the cage for father and he, no doubt, was looking in for us. When we finally spotted him among the mass of fathers, sons and husbands come to 'redeem' their families, there was nothing we could do except wave to attract his attention. I remember this upset me very much. I didn't think it was just, or that the organization was proper. (My penchant for organization manifested itself early.) He finally spotted us, and things became somewhat more tolerable. I didn't recognize him; that is, I did, but he looked different to me. I had remembered him with a long beard, a long silk caftan with a black *gartel*, or girdle, its two ends dangling on each side, and a *straimel*—a broad-brimmed furred hat. All this was gone. The beard, though still of respectable size, was neatly trimmed. The black caftan was replaced by a formal Prince Albert, the *straimel* by a black derby. To me it seemed the height of elegance. I was sure my father had become a millionaire. Who else would wear such a fancy rig? I soon found out that it was merely his Sabbath outfit, the uniform of his profession.

After the reunion and the mopping up operations we were on our way, by ferry and then horse car, to the lower East Side of New York: 99 Cannon Street to be exact. Geographically, Cannon Street was about 4,000 miles from Kikl; structurally or architecturally, despite the ugly tenement houses, about 100 years ahead of Kikl; spiritually, intellectually, and socially it was identical with Kikl. I might say a clean shaven, or trimmed Kikl, but often not even that.

Friends, *mishpocha*, *landsleit* came in droves to greet us. Nine-tenths of them were unknown to me or known only through hearsay or rumor. 'Meyer, meet Avrom, Sarah Rochel's son. Here they call him Abe. This is Mortche, Leah Dvosse's son. Here they call him Max.' That established the identity. These visits didn't last very long, and in a day or two the hordes had melted: everybody had to go back to work, my father among them. As for me, I became an *habitué* of Cannon Street, made my own acquaintances, and picked up some English.

Opposite 99 Cannon Street stood a big synagogue. I think it was called the *Galitzianer shul*. The basement of the *shul* had a *mikveh* or ritual bathing pool over whose destiny an old couple presided; i.e. the woman did the work and the old man with a patriarchal beard and long *tzises*—ritualistic fringes—sat on a little stool near the entrance exchanging pleasantries with the passersby. Most of the social activities of Cannon Street revolved around the synagogue and *mikveh*. Like most of the youngsters on the block, I too gravitated towards the environs of the synagogue. The old man sitting on the stool liked children, but loved to tease them. But not a word of English ever passed his lips. In Yiddish, of course, I was in my element.

Every other day or so, his granddaughter from Pitt Street would be brought over. She was five or six years old, dark, enchantment itself, with big brown eyes, and elegantly dressed—'upper class.' The grand-father was immensely proud of the little girl, and bounced her on his knee most of the time. Now, if I were to tell the reader that then and there I fell in love with this little girl, made up my mind to marry her, and was prepared to wait sixteen years for the privilege he wouldn't believe me. Nor would I. It was only after we had been married for ten years that we accidentally reconstructed our early acquaintance.

Our sojourn in Cannon Street lasted only a few weeks. As far as I was concerned, Cannon Street wasn't the real America, the America I had heard about or conjured up in my day dreams. It was just a more crowded, more intensive Kikl with the same language, the same gossip, the same people. Only in Kikl you could escape to the meadow or even as far as the lake. Here you were hemmed in between two rows of tenement houses on a narrow strip called 'the street.' I felt that Cannon Street at best was only the anteroom to the real America and I was vindicated as soon as we made our first move. It was a big move, all the way 'up north'—to the Bronx! My father had secured a position there as *chazan* in a *shul*, with side duties as ritual slaughterer in the chicken market. To me our second 'aliya' was far more exciting than the first even though we were spared—for reasons which were beyond my comprehension at the time—the formalities of delousing. Crossing the Atlantic bottled up in the steerage of the *Kron-prinzessin Caecilia* simply couldn't hold a candle—for thrills—to riding the elevated from Houston Street. The journey past 8th Street, 14th Street, 23rd Street to 156th Street represented to me the progress of society in the New World. There was no doubt about it. This time we were really taking the plunge into the vast sea of America, there to be sucked into the waters of the new civilization. Caldwell Avenue embraced us. It was goodbye forever to Kikl and its Cannon Street annex.

3 The Greening of an American

The distance between Cannon Street and Caldwell Avenue didn't turn out to be all that great; the gentiles were certainly more in evidence, but the Jews were settled in such thick clusters that the *goyim* were largely irrelevant to our daily lives. Yiddish was still the language of our home, of social intercourse, commerce, industry and the arts, and the pattern of our lives underwent little change.

Still, it was the beginning of our Americanization. Four months elapsed between our arrival in Caldwell Avenue and my enrolment in school when the system reopened after Labor Day. I spent those weeks playing in the streets and acquiring local color. By the time school started I was sufficiently assimilated to enter my name on the rolls as Max Weisgal—Max Winifred Weisgal yet. I can understand how Meyer became Max—that was the common practice; how Velvel became Winifred still baffles me. I do not remember, either, the source of this happy inspiration; but I do remember the reaction of my father when I proudly announced it. Enraged, he gave me a hearty slap, and told me to resume my original Jewish identity the very next day, quoting to me the relevant passage of the circumcision ritual: 'His name in Israel shall be . . .'

When I look back, after almost seventy years, at that attempt at instant Americanization, I still cannot untangle my motives. I certainly was not aware of any wish to play down my Jewishness; at age ten I did not harbor such precocious ambitions. Perhaps the elegance of the sound, Max Winifred, seduced me—especially the Winifred, which I did not know was a female name, confusing it, I suppose, with its first cousin Winfred.

After the confusion and excitement of the new migration, our home life slipped back into its familiar pattern. Still, there were changes. Leybish, who had preceded us to America, lived with us, and his earnings, added to my father's salary, enabled us to get along without an Uncle Getzel.

Leybish, by the way, had become Leo before we arrived; it was too late for my father to slap him back into his 'natural' name. One feature of our life remained true to the Kikl tradition: my father still brought home, after the Friday evening services, a variety of dinner guests, and Lodzia still reacted as she had in Kikl. It did not trouble her if she had to stretch the meal for an extra guest or two; what mattered was the quality of the entertainment the guest or guests provided. A bit of intellectual stimulation did wonders for her.

Perhaps it did too much; she was susceptible to all noble and progressive ideals. In Kikl she had been an intransigent Bundist—and Bundism was anti-Zionist. In the Bronx she became an intransigent Zionist, an intransigent Communist, an intransigent Socialist. Sometimes she managed to hold all views simultaneously, sometimes she focused on one of them. It all depended on whom she was arguing with, who was holding a meeting that night or which of her children she was at the moment trying to 'encourage.' She was deeply attached to all of them, those she 'inherited' and those she bore my father—the last two of them, Esther and Isaac, in America.

Although I cannot pin-point the exact dates, our first sojourn in the Bronx was of short duration. We moved to Chicago. Why Chicago? For some reason or other the first Kiklites to migrate had chosen that city, and in time set up a Kikl synagogue there. It so happened that the *gabbai*, or 'president,' of that synagogue, was Lodzia's father; but even without that I dare say that the Kikl community in Chicago would have invited my father to be its cantor. It was not difficult to convince him that among his own he would be happier than among the strangers in the Bronx. And so, Leo having preceded us and gone into business in Chicago, we followed and established ourselves in the vicinity of the Tell Place Synagogue, Kikl's contribution to American Jewish history.

My father's official introduction to his new-old congregants was painful and embarrassing—also touching. We arrived, according to the usual arrangement, a little before the High Holidays, so that he might prepare for his ordeal. There was much happiness in the Tell Place Congregation; the old days were back again, the tradition had been reestablished, *Chazan* Shloyme Chaim Weisgal was once more among his own. And then, on the great day, something unforeseeable and terrifying happened; my father lost his voice—exactly as I had done in Nyesheve! He opened his mouth, and what came out was the croaking of a frog. For a few moments the congregation was appalled, then it recovered. It began to hum along with him and when he tried to reach a high note raised its voice and covered his pathetic effort. His courage and the loving sympathy of the audience made that Rosh Hashonah into a memorable occasion. In the nine day interval before Yom Kippur my father recovered his voice, and the performance he then gave was, he always thought, the greatest in his life.

My own activities in Chicago were, surprisingly enough, recorded for posterity. There is extant a photograph of me as a vendor of matches. The picture doesn't quite tell all: I also sold fly-paper. Nevertheless, many people have questioned the authenticity of this photo, or conversely, the authenticity of my humble beginnings. Who ever heard of a match-boy posing—and the pose is almost regal—for his portrait? The fact is that I was trying to sell a box of matches to a photographer on Milwaukee Avenue who was just too cheap to lay down cash on the table. He offered to take my picture instead. He was a very enterprising young man because by the time he printed the picture I was not only out of the match business, I was out of Chicago and back in the Bronx. But honest he was and delivered it to my relatives. I saw it for the first time in 1919, eight years later, when I was in Chicago covering the Zionist Convention for the *Maccabean*. I had a partner in the match and fly-paper business, which did not last long, because we had an argument as to who did more business; we began by counting the matches and ended up by throwing them at each other. Somehow one of them ignited and the partnership went up in flames.

My father would not take a penny of my earnings. He told me to save them up, and so I did, adding pennies and nickels to a growing little hoard in a box on the mantlepiece. One day the contents of the box, and my brother Leo, disappeared. He had received a tempting business offer from an auctioneering firm in New York, and in desperation had helped himself to my 'capital.' This was not really Leo: he was, all his life, the best and the most devoted member of the family, always helped to hold it together, and took everyone's troubles on himself. Naturally I was overwhelmed at the the time, but he repaid me a thousandfold over the years.

I may have been *bar mitzvah* in Chicago, I really don't remember. In those days it was nothing to get excited about; it was simply a chore. You had to get up earlier on the day of your thirteenth birthday to go to *shul* and do it. If it happened Monday or Thursday, one 'became a man' before going to school. Anyway, in those days of no records, one was approximately, not specifically thirteen. I was only invested with a definite birthday when I went into the army. Since my father remembered that I was born a few weeks after Simchas Torah, the Day of the Rejoicing of the Law, he chose November 10th. I, for my part, when I had to register army inductees who were as vague about their birthdays as I was about mine, developed what I still consider a simple but ingenious system. Today there are probably some hundreds of veterans—they were mostly recently arrived Poles or southern negroes—who proudly celebrate their birthdays on July 4th or December 25th. It all depended on whether they answered 'summer' or 'winter' to my question: 'When were you born?'

But I am ahead of my story. For the moment we are still in Chicago, and father is more and more unhappy. He had been warmly received by the congregation, but Kikl on Lake Michigan was not Kikl in Poland. True, the money was better than in Kikl, and even better than in the Bronx, but what my father might have put up with in strangers he could not bear to see in his compatriots—the slow erosion of their piety, the intrusion of brash newcomers, the general deterioration of old world Jewish ways. He decided to leave.

We returned to New York in 1911, again to the Bronx, and I enrolled in Morris High School. If there is any one time in my life to which I can point and say with certainty, 'That was the beginning of my ruination,' it is while I was at Morris High, when I got bitten by the bug of Zionism. That in itself was not too bad: young people tend to become afflicted with impossible causes; but I got convinced at the same time that I was a budding literary genius as well—a deadly, though not disastrous, combination.

It took a little time to realize that I was 'hooked.' I could not know then that Zionism was going to be my full-time occupation, my vocation, avocation, obsession—my monomania—for the rest of my life. In the interim I made a few more ventures into the business world, and even had a final fling as a professional singer.

Like all able-bodied immigrant boys I spent my after-school hours on one job or another; for example, I cleaned fish across the street from our home on Brook Avenue. I cleaned it with industry but, it seems, with a certain lack of skill; I was fired by popular demand when all the baalabostes on Brook Avenue complained that their gefilte fish tasted of gall. I transferred my services to the liquor business, where, oddly enough, I was 'rediscovered' as a singer.

My status in the liquor business was a lowly one: I was a delivery boy. The area assigned to me was a section of Harlem, and my equipment was a bicycle cart into which I packed the bottles of beer and liquor. Lenox Avenue and 114th Street was in those days the citadel of the Jewish upper middle class, and those big apartment houses represented the highest ambition to our immigrant world. My technique was simple; I would park the bicycle cart outside, take the order into the basement, and ring the dumb-waiter bell or shout up the shaft. When the answer came and the dumbwaiter was lowered, I would hoist up the bottles and wait for the 'empties.'

One day I heard a muffled shout from above. The man was taking his time in working the contraption, and I had nothing better to do than sing. I had chosen, out of my extensive repertoire, one of the very popular Yiddish songs of that day—and it is still popular—called *Unter di Grininke Beymelech*, 'Under the Little Green Trees,' by the greatest Hebrew poet of modern times, Chaim Nachman Bialik. I suppose that the dumbwaiter shaft magnified and deepened my voice, for the mysterious person upstairs let me sing to the very last trill and then called down, '*Yingele, kum aroyf*, Sonny, come around.' The dumbwaiter descended, I sent up the liquor, and went round to the entrance, at 110th Street and Seventh Avenue, to one of the most elegant houses in Harlem, facing Central Park.

He turned out to be Platon Brunoff, the composer of the melody to which the words were set. He expressed, in the most extravagant terms, his admiration of my musical gifts, and I drank in his words blissfully, profoundly convinced of *his* gifts as a critic: somewhat older now, and a more experienced student of human nature, I am inclined to think that his admiration had more to do with the accidental choice of the music than with the intrinsic quality of my rendition. I got to know Platon Brunoff quite well. He was a big man with broad shoulders and long flowing hair, and he wore an opera cape in all seasons. He was a Russian Jew who spoke only a broken Yiddish and he had a tremendous *basso profundo*.

He asked me what I did and what my father did. Then he made me sing again for him. I was in seventh heaven, and he behaved as if he had discovered another Caruso. He arranged an audition for me with the great Yossele Rosenblatt, and I left his apartment treading on air.

It wasn't until I got downstairs that I remembered the bicycle cart, with the precious load. It was gone, the load was gone, the empty bottles as well as the full bottles. And my job was gone. My boss could hardly be expected to be exhilarated by this event; he had an unusually wide range of maledictions, but no appreciation at all of the higher things of life.

On Brunoff's recommendation Rosenblatt sent me to his choir leader, who hired me for the High Holidays. The *shul* on 116th Street and Fifth Avenue, where the incomparable Yossele Rosenblatt performed, was to the Jews of New York what the Metropolitan was, and still is, to the rest of the population. I was paid a munificent $100 for my services, and I have a strong suspicion now that Brunoff made up part or most of it from his own pocket. But that one brilliant episode saw the end of my musical ambitions. My voice had begun to change, and, to be truthful, my interest in music as a career had been marginal.

During my last year in high school I had a job as a fur examiner. This is—or was—a highly skilled and interesting profession. You blow into the fur and where you see a hole in the skin you stick in a piece of paper. I immediately became an expert. I was also in charge of the packaging and helped the boss with the bookkeeping. Beyond that I also became, in a private capacity, his expert on *chazonim* and *chazones:* he was the President of the Henry Street synagogue, and he was so impressed by my general knowledge of *chazones* that he never hired a cantor without my approval or at least my opinion.

I got along so well with him that my family already saw me as a success-ful and opulent furrier. A good job was waiting for me as soon as I left high school; and my salary which was already an unbelievable $18 a week would even be raised. But this was not to be. I had little interest in music as a profession, and less in furs. Zionism, and my growing love affair with the English language, were simply too much competition. I purchased in ten-cent weekly installments the two-volume Funk and Wagnall's Dictionary. Its excitement, for me, was enhanced by the lectern that came with it; and I used to stand over it at night, like a *yeshivah bocher* over his Talmud. I think it was the lectern that really sold me, for the posture had a haunting familiarity: thus my father, and my father's father, had studied the huge folios of the Tractates, so brilliantly described in one of Bialik's most famous poems, *The Masmid:*

> Mark well the swaying shadow and the voice:
> It is a *Masmid* in his prison-house,
> A prisoner, self-guarded, self-condemned,
> Self-sacrificed to study of the Law . . .

To account for the Zionist passion which took hold of me at that time I need look no further than my home and its two dominant spirits, my father and Lodzia. In all literate Jewish homes, causes and movements flourished naturally; in ours, it seems, more than in others. My father did not belong to any Zionist Organization, not even the Mizrachi: but his Zionism was deep rooted and articulate. I was told—I did not witness it myself, though I was ten years old at the time—that when the news of Theodor Herzl's death reached my father, he sat *shiva* (seven-day mourn-ing) for him. (That may have been the year he arrived in America.) Lodzia, we have seen, was hospitable to the most contradictory causes; her en-thusiasm for Zionism was not dampened by her belief in the impending world revolution: she was a loyal Labor Zionist while she contributed poems to the *Morgen Freiheit*, the Communist Yiddish daily. Leo remained a radical even while achieving a successful business career; my younger brother Emanuel was the head of the Young People's Socialist League (YPSL) in the Bronx during its heyday; my twin sister Chaya—Helen— was an uncompromising Zionist.

Our house was for years something of a 24-hour debating society. It continued even after I had left high school. Maurice Samuel, the writer, my friend in the Zionist movement, thus describes us in the retrospect of more than fifty years: 'The Weisgal family was a fascinating phenomenon. More a *shtetl* than a family, it was magnified in the visitor's imagination by the abounding vitality of its members, its noisy, affectionate, disputations—a tribal hullabaloo in which no personality was repressed; and there was no lack of personalities. There was in it the vivacity of Catfish Row shot through with the cultural standards of the Jewish tradition.'

I was still in high school when I became a member of an élite Yiddish- and Hebrew-speaking Zionist society called Hashachar—'the Dawn.' One has to conjure up a vanished world to realize how insane that kind of group looked to outsiders—young people playing with the idea of a Jewish homeland in Palestine, but playing in earnest, really believing in the pos- sibility, and, therefore, really insane. We had next to nothing in Palestine; fewer than a hundred thousand Jews, a handful of colonies and a townlet called Tel Aviv north of Jaffa.

It was a fellow student of mine at Morris High, Shimon Halkin, who introduced me first to his family and then to Hashachar. I was delighted, captivated, and astonished by the family—it was Hebrew-speaking! I had never met a family in which Hebrew was the language of daily con- verse. Such families are rare in America even today—in those days they were unheard of. But even with all of our Zionist faith, nobody would have dreamed that one day Shimon would be professor of poetry at a Hebrew University in the Jewish State. A distinguished Hebrew poet, yes; there have been great Hebrew poets throughout the long history of the disper- sion—but not professors at Hebrew universities.

Another member of that unusual Bronx Zionist Society had in a way an even more curious career. He settled in Palestine shortly after the Balfour Declaration, changed his name from Zusmanovitch to Yekutieli and became—of all things—a customs inspector. From professor and poet to customs inspector is a far cry, but I must say that when, on one of my visits to Palestine, it fell to Yekutieli to inspect my bags I was infinitely more moved than by any encounter with a prince of literature. We stood staring at each other like two lunatics and then exploded into wild laughter.

Yekutieli became, eventually, a dignified burgher of the city of Haifa and only recently died.

I return to the Hashachar days and the paths, unpredictable but I suppose inevitable, that led me into the Zionist orbit.

Shortly before my graduation from Morris High School we were reading in class *The Merchant of Venice*. I sat in the first row, and immediately behind me sat a fellow who muttered 'Jew bastard' every time Mr. Shylock's name was mentioned. This went on for several periods and I got madder and madder. Finally I went to the teacher and told him that the fellow behind me had absolutely no understanding of Shakespeare. My teacher generously suggested that I write out my thoughts on the subject. I was enchanted by the idea, and went to work for at least a month. I read widely, and I remember that George Brandes was one of my sources. I wrote and rewrote till my fingers were numb, and when I was convinced that I could not improve on the product I did something unusual for those days: I had the manuscript typed. I brought it to my teacher who suspended class while he read it rapidly; then he said, to my confusion and delight: 'Weisgal, read it to these morons,' while to the class he said: 'Remember, you so-and-so's, his accent is not on the paper.' This was not all. He sent me to the principal, Mr. Newman, not a Jew by the way, who read it and asked me to read it before the school assembly; then it was published in the school magazine and awarded the annual literary prize.

So much for the 'Shylock episode' in my school career. It made me, for a short time, a celebrity among the Bronx Zionists. I was regarded as *the* representative of Anglo-Saxon culture in the Hashachar. I was invited to give a lecture, and after laborious preparation did so, with resounding success. My father and Lodzia both attended, and sat there bursting with pride. I was later elected secretary to the Society.

I do not know how much either my father or Lodzia understood of my lofty English style, but my friend Zusmanovitch, whose ignorance of Shakespeare was equalled only by his ignorance of the English language, proclaimed my piece on Shylock a literary masterpiece, worthy of the Bard himself. Naturally I was impressed by the opinion of so exalted a critic. 'You must take this essay,' he said, 'and remember to call it an essay, to Mr. Lipsky, who will surely publish it in *The Maccabean*.' This was the publication of the American Zionist movement and Lipsky was its editor. The 'essay' never saw the light. But I did, for I met Louis Lipsky.

Here I must pause in the personal narrative and fill in some of that background without which the personal is unintelligible. But how can I evoke that background as a living thing for those who know it, if at all, as something remote, heard of, told of and imperfectly remembered? Today the name of Shmaryahu Levin is, for Israelis, a street in Tel Aviv behind the Habimah Theatre; tomorrow the name of Brandeis will be merely that of a university in Massachusetts. As for Louis Lipsky, how will he be remembered after his generation?

In their day these were powers in the evolving Zionist movement and I, a neophyte, watched them as they guided it out of its inchoate beginnings toward a place of leadership in Jewish life. In 1912–13 Zionism was—to change the figure—still in its swaddling clothes. Until the advent of Louis D. Brandeis, the Federation of American Zionists was a loosely linked chain of societies like the Hashachar, Yiddish speaking for the most part, East European in origin. In 1912 Hadassah, now a formidable force in American Jewish life, was a year old, a handful of enthusiastic women gathered round Henrietta Szold. That was the year that Nahum Sokolow came to America and, with Jacob de Haas, converted Brandeis to Zionism.

Brandeis was regarded by many as the greatest legal mind in America and his open acceptance of the Zionist program was a stunning event for us, giving stature, respectability, prestige. But if Brandeis performed this public relations service, it was Shmaryahu Levin who brought to the movement a renewed fervor and a deepened insight.

This extraordinary man, who had been both a leading European Zionist and a member of the Second Russian Duma before its dissolution in 1907, had come to America shortly before the outbreak of the First World War to win support for the recently established Haifa Technical School, now the famous Technion. His mission completed, he set out for Europe again two days before the declaration of war. He traveled on the *Kronprinzessin Caecilia*—my *Kronprinzessin Caecilia*—but unlike me, not in steerage. He described somewhere the manner in which he became aware of a change in his destiny. It was dinner time and he sat at table engaged in conversation. Suddenly he noticed that the moon, which had been shining in through the windows on his right was shining in from the windows on his left. It took him a few minutes to realize that this was not an optical illusion. Without notice to the passengers, the captain had turned the direction of the ship through an angle of one hundred and eighty degrees: war had broken out. He had been instructed by radio to return to New York. It was thus that Shmaryahu Levin was 'marooned' in America for the duration. American Zionism was by no means the loser.

In those days the majority of American Jews spoke Yiddish; the *Jewish Daily Forward* had a circulation of over 200,000, and *The Day* and *The*

Morning Journal were not far behind. There was a lively Yiddish theatre and a dynamic Yiddish intellectual life. Into that life Shmaryahu Levin, undoubtedly the foremost Yiddish orator of his day, came like a tornado. He didn't like the term 'orator'—that was reserved for Zvi Hirsch Masliansky, a speaker of an entirely different mould. Whenever a notice appeared, containing only two words '*Masliansky Yedaber*, Masliansky will speak,' the streets were black with Jews. Shmaryahu Levin had a masterly command of Yiddish and a mordant wit; he combined a thorough Jewish education in Bible and Talmud with a wide range of modern learning. His public addresses were always on a high intellectual level, filled with talmudic, midrashic and biblical quotations and allusions and leading always into the contemporaty Jewish scene. He never spoke down to an audience and wherever he went he was an enormous attraction. Chaim Weizmann, who was very close to him, has written that he could always put Shmaryahu Levin in a rage by asking with pretended innocence, 'Shmarya, are you making a speech tonight,' and Shmarya would answer hotly: 'I don't make speeches, I give lectures.' Be it said of Shmaryahu Levin that he educated a generation of American Jews in Zionism: the children and grandchildren of that generation are also, whether they know it or not, his beneficiaries.

The transformation of the Zionist movement in America was symbolized by the change of address. When I was still at high school the Federation of American Zionists had its offices on Henry Street, on the Lower East Side. By 1914 the offices of the Zionist Organization of America—that was the new name—were at 44 East 23rd Street. The change of name also indicated an important change of structure. The ZOA was a national membership organization, and its energies were focused on the gathering of political support for what emerged in 1917 as the Balfour Declaration. What we aimed at was nothing less than the creation of a political protectorate which would foster the development of a Jewish Homeland in Palestine. In the movement it was a time of unity, harmony and singleness of purpose—admirable characteristics which the Zionist movement soon after, and the State of Israel much later, seemed to find somewhat less than indispensable. The leadership was vested in a group of outstanding people: Louis D. Brandeis, Stephen S. Wise, Julian W. Mack, Louis Lipsky, Jacob de Haas (who later became Brandeis' spokesman when his accession to the Supreme Court sealed his lips politically), Felix Frankfurter (who, though not active publicly, was considered by some the movement's *éminence grise*), Richard Gottheil, Professor of Semitics at Columbia, and Henrietta Szold.

It was to Louis Lipsky that I went on that summer day in 1914 with my essay under my arm. Lipsky's official role was that of Secretary for Organization; actually he was of incomparably greater importance. He was then, and remained until his death, the foremost articulator, in English, of American Zionist thought. He was born in Rochester, he was as American as baseball or Coca-Cola. He developed an exceptional style both as writer and speaker, yet he gravitated not toward the assimilationist element in Jewish life, but toward the Yiddish theatre and Yiddish literature, toward the warmth and excitement of New York's Lower East Side. He loved the Yiddish language, but in spite of arduous efforts he never mastered it sufficiently to speak it freely. Shmaryahu Levin, with his magic command of Yiddish, was his hero.

I knew Lipsky from a distance. He had come a number of times to address the Hashachar and I had listened to him with awe. How could anyone, I wondered, above all a Zionist, express such beautiful thoughts in such beautiful English? His speeches were all grace, clarity, economy, with none of the uncontrolled ebullience which distinguished our fiery East Side Yiddish orators. He would carry us to action on the inner glow of his spirit. If Shmaryahu Levin was the educator of a Yiddish-speaking generation of Zionists, Louis Lipsky performed the same service for its younger, English-speaking contemporaries.

So there I was, almost twenty, just out of high school (my American education started late), a fur examiner by occupation, a Zionist by persuasion and infection, a Kiklite by birth, a Bronxonian by adoption—in short a provincial greenhorn, standing in the corridors of the Zionist Organization waiting to be admitted into the sanctum. Now one simply didn't march into the office of the man one wanted to see. First, one stood around for an hour or so waiting, absorbing the atmosphere. So I stood around and absorbed and I was captivated; I was utterly and completely overwhelmed; I was a lost man. The place was full of people who looked as if the destiny of the world hung upon their words. There was an assortment of girl secretaries and they all looked beautiful, to me at least. The air was thick with smoke and thicker with meaning and I ached to be part of it. Had someone asked me then and there to throw up my $18-a-week job in order to wash windows and clean floors for the Zionists—without pay—I would have answered at once, 'Yes.'

4   Novitiate in Zion

And that is more or less what happened. To be sure, I was not asked to throw up my $18-a-week job; I threw it up freely and joyously. I was not asked to work for nothing, only for next to nothing: the precise figure was $4 a week. I was not set to floor-washing and window-cleaning, but at the outset my duties, never very clearly defined, were of no very exalted order.

What Louis Lipsky saw in me at our first interview I do not know; but what he soon discovered in me he has himself recorded. He describes me as 'a breezy, aggressive, argumentative youth, neither subdued by authority, nor respectful toward law and order [who was] taken into the Zionist offices on trial as handyman, free to find his own destiny in the maze of Zionist activity.' If I made the impression of breeziness and aggressiveness, I was not aware of it. It was not at all the way I felt inside. I was a novice, and knew it. I wanted to serve and the only payment I sought was to breathe the heady air generated by the activity of the Zionist office. I suppose it was this eagerness, coupled with my utter Jewishness, that moved Lipsky to give me a trial. Of the Shylock essay which was supposed to be my entry into the higher echelons of the movement nothing more was ever heard. Lipsky took it from me and 'filed it away'—literally and figuratively.

As to the impression Lipsky made on me, I must say that my first feelings of awe and gratitude were too powerful for detailed observations to register. Gradually, as I saw him more clearly, and as I learned to know him over the years, I distinguished those characteristics that made up his remarkable personality. I knew him at first as my boss, but almost immediately I was aware of a kind of father and son relationship, with its familiar pattern—father admonishes, son does not listen, etc. My admiration for him was boundless. Though I sometimes struggled, I tried to emulate him, in particular to adopt his literary style, in which I was quite unsuccessful. When, later, I worked under him, or rather with him—one did not work 'under Lipsky'—on *The Maccabean* and *The New Palestine*, he was forever warning me against the excessive use of the adjective. 'Be sparing of your adjectives' he would say, as he slashed ruthlessly at one of my pieces, blood spouting from every line. 'You're a good editor, but a lousy writer'—which was true. I comforted myself that it was cause and effect: one had to be a lousy writer to be a good editor. But—and here was one measure of the man—he was as ruthless with his own creations as with mine. Throwing an editorial on my desk he would say: 'Do what you want with it.' Later he would invariably comment: 'I think you made it better,' never a groan or a burst of resentment over the omission of some cherished phrase; and what a contrast that was to many a Zionist leader who, not having written his piece in the first place, was ready to spill the last drop of my blood on the altar of his 'ghost'!

As Secretary for Organization—a key position in any movement—Lipsky was in the front rank of the leaders of Zionism, but there was a strange dissonance between his role and his character. The quality of leadership may be an admirable thing, but it is grounded in a dilemma, the conflict between the good and the expedient. Expediency may be given the respectable name of necessity, and the conflict is sharpened by the kind of vanity which rises from over-anxiety to seem to be in the right. But Lipsky was without any of these weaknesses. His thought was always for the good of the movement. He never wittingly sought position or power; he had a majestic indifference to the pomp and circumstance of leadership. He compelled without conscious effort the attention and admiration of thousands who looked to him, through many decades, as *the* leader of American Zionism.

Within the organization Lipsky was known as the master parliamentarian, the presiding genius of Zionist conventions—and one had indeed to be a parliamentary genius to maintain any order at all at these annual convulsions. He was cool in the midst of fury, level-headed in the midst of confusion, quick with the right word. To a notorious bore who appealed to him as chairman to get him the attention of the audience, he once said: 'My dear sir, if you cannot hold the attention of the audience, I cannot do it for you.' To another who was explaining how cleverly he had rectified one of his own mistakes, he said: 'Sir, the adroitness with which you have extricated yourself from that position does not excuse the clumsiness with which you involved yourself in it.'

Man of organization as he was, Lipsky had in him a streak of the bohemian. Tall, gaunt, with a sharp Indian face, keen, handsome, usually impassive, and with his careless clothes, he would have passed for a playwright or an actor. He had been, before he entered the Zionist Organization, a journalist and dramatic critic. At one time he had been the associate editor of *The American Hebrew* with Harry Sherman, who later founded the Book-of-the-Month Club. For years he was the dramatic critic of the *Daily Telegraph*, which had a large circulation because it ran the racing forms. The theatre and especially the Yiddish theatre—on which he was the leading authority—was his second love. I think he was never more relaxed than when, on free evenings and late into the night, he would sit among his followers at the Tip Toe Inn, a rather pale imitation of Berlin's Romanische Café, for all the world like a chassidic rebbe among his chassidim, holding forth on the Yiddish Rialto, its leading figures, its history, its successes and failures.

Underneath his reserve, Lipsky was such a complex personality that it took me some time to discover what had pulled him into the Zionist movement. It was, in the end, really very simple—he loved Jews. By this I mean 'real' Jews, Jews who spoke Yiddish. I can only guess that it derived from his deep devotion to his Yiddish-speaking mother. His father had been something of a scholar, religious, and steeped in the classical Hebrew elements of the Jewish tradition. Lipsky once described him as 'cold and remote.' Whether this pocket analysis is correct or not, Lipsky had, all his life, a distaste for synagogues, rabbis and religion. To the Hebrew language he was cold: strange, to say the least, for a man who devoted his life, or certainly the mass of its energies, to the recreation of a Jewish Homeland, part of which was to be effected through the revival of Hebrew. Somehow the paradox was resolved by Lipsky's self-identification with the Zionism of Chaim Weizmann and Shmaryahu Levin, the Yiddish speaking *folksmenschen* of the movement. They, like their European colleagues, were in fact Hebraists. Lipsky was not anti-Hebrew; he simply found it irrelevant to his Zionism. For that matter he never succeeded in mastering Yiddish; but that was where his heart lay. When I come to tell the story of the struggle between Brandeis and Weizmann, between 'Brandeis Zionism' and 'Weizmann Zionism,' we shall find Lipsky deeply and intuitively committed to Weizmann and 'Weizmann Zionism.' On the surface it should not have been so, particularly when one considered a certain similarity, in personal austerity and intellectual precision, between Brandeis and Lipsky: but we shall see that something deeper than form, or political theory, decided Lipsky's role in that profoundly important struggle of half a century ago.

'I also sold fly-paper.' Chicago, *ca.* 1909 (see page 25)

My father, Shlomo Chaim, the cantor

My mother, Lodzia, the revolutionary

above My brother Abba. As a young man he 'looked, dressed and comported himself like Kaiser Wilhelm.' At 80 plus he is still singing
below My brother Josh today. A fugitive from the rabbinate, 1911

above Apprentice in Zion, in an 'intellectual' posture. *below left* Camp Hancock, Georgia, 1917–19, helping to 'redress the balance' (see page 47). *below right* On the 'bum' after being rejected, temporarily, by Shirley

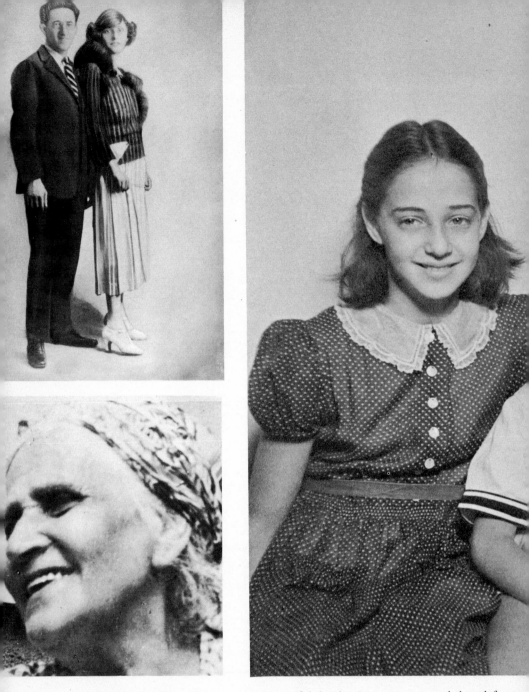

above, left With Shirley, my beautiful bride, June 10, 1923. *below left* 'Shirley's mother stood the test' (see page 63)

My beautiful bride—15 years later, with Helen, David and Mendy

The Editor, *ca.* 1925

Meanwhile I am still the brash, breezy, argumentative, awed, timid and worshipful youth of nineteen wild with joy at having landed a job with the Zionist Organization at $4 a week. When I came home that first day and told my father of my unbelievable good luck, he looked at me long and hard, and these were his words: '*Meyle, got vet helfen!* So be it, God will help us out! Let us not worry, my son. You want to go to the Zionists, go.' That was his attitude and it was wonderful. And it wasn't easy for him to accept. My contribution to the family income had been the largest; I don't think my father made more than $14 a week. Leo too encouraged me; if life had forced him to abandon his great dreams and sink to the world of business, he saw no reason why I should suffer the same fate.

The one man who raised the roof about my decision was my boss. First he stormed, then he broke down and wept. He was a bachelor, and his only living relative was a maiden sister. He had counted on me to become his partner and then his heir—the sole legatee. Not only was I leaving him in the lurch; I was throwing away the opportunity of a lifetime. But when I told him what my new salary was, a peculiar look came into his eyes; he was still disconsolate, but it seemed to be dawning on him that there was a fatal flaw in my character, and that I would never be a businessman. He was right. As I recall those remote days, it occurs to me that the $18 a week he paid me was part of his strategy to make me his partner and heir; $8 a week would have been a more likely salary for a junior employee. Evidently he liked me.

Lipsky's recollection that I was free to find my own destiny was accurate, and I found it very quickly. For a few weeks I was simply an errand boy, carrying proofs between the office and the printer, and running off the wrappers for *The Maccabean*. But once I had been exposed to that great seducer, the print shop, I was a lost man. I finally discovered that printer's ink ran in my veins. Not a single aspect of the production process was devoid of charm for me. Instead of hanging around idly waiting for the printer's devil to pull off the galleys or page proofs, I watched at close quarters, and with considerable envy, the earnest young men who marked proofs at the Grayzell Press on Lafayette Street. I recall them as young men —in fact they were considerably my seniors, and some of them have honorable places in the early history of American Zionism. There was Baruch Zuckerman, who was to become the leader of American Labor Zionism and is now a distinguished elder statesman living in Jerusalem. There was the late Abe Goldberg, the editor of *Dos Yiddishe Folk*, the Yiddish counterpart of *The Maccabean*, a dark, tiny man with fiery eyes and curly hair, a brilliant and dynamic Yiddish speaker.

But the man I watched with such special intensity that he began to shy away from me was the managing editor of *The Maccabean*. He was a man called Hyman R. Segal, a poet of some merit. His brother was the inventor of what came to be called the Segal lock, and for some reason he decided that he could not make a business of it without the help of his poetical brother. However ungracious it may sound, I must say that if Hyman R. Segal was no better as a businessman than as an editor, he was not much of an acquisition to the Segal Lock Company. In any case, he handed in his resignation in 1916, became a businessman and continued to write poetry. Before he left he wrote a letter, about which I knew nothing at the time, to Brandeis, who was the Zionist President. It read in part: 'We have a young man here who acts as sort of factotum and I would suggest that he be given the opportunity to run this paper because I think he is qualified to do so.' My qualifications consisted of the fact that he did not know any Yiddish and I did. True, I had by that time caught on to the mechanical side of production—specifications for the blockmaker, type faces, type sizes, fillers. I began to help Segal paste up the pages. As a matter of fact I went even further: I offered him advice—free of charge and frequently— on ways of improving the paper, all of which he ignored. But my chief qualification was my command of Yiddish. Every time his attention was called to some world-shaking item in the Yiddish press, he would call me in to translate it for him.

The importance of the Yiddish press in the Jewish world of those days can hardly be exaggerated. It was the sole source of Jewish news to English readers, for there was no Jewish news agency. Hence, on an Anglo-Jewish publication anyone who was bilingual even in an elementary way was an indispensable expert, and my knowledge of both languages was sound enough. *The Maccabean* was not the only Anglo-Jewish paper which depended on me for Jewish news. I like to remember that Jacob de Haas, who was the publisher-editor of *The Boston Jewish Advocate*, used to pay me $2.00 a week for being his 'New York correspondent,' that is, for sending him regularly translations of news items from *The Jewish Morning Journal*.

I also like to remember that this expertise of mine was responsible for my first intimate contact with Shmaryahu Levin, and my first literary assignment. Shmarya (as we used to call him affectionately) had published a collection of his newspaper pieces under the name of *Milchome Tseiten*, 'In War Time.' I was the only one around the office who could both read the book in Yiddish and write about it in English, and Segal asked me to do a review and an interview with Shmarya all in one. When I handed in my assignment Segal offered me either $5 or a byline. I took the byline.

There was, I am happy to say, no struggle around my promotion. Brandeis' reply to Segal's recommendation was terse and unambiguous: 'I agree.' That was it: I became the secretary of the editorial board.

Which brings me to a small matter of historical record. I am not altogether blind to my defects and I do not see myself as a soft-spoken, gentle, obliging, easy-going, even-tempered human being; but I wonder why it is that people derive a special joy from exaggerating my shortcomings. Even Lipsky, my master, teacher and guide, fell prey to the legends that sprang up round me in those early days at the Zionist office. He wrote of me that I 'discovered the way to the vacant chair of the migratory editor of *The Maccabean* . . . , took possession of it without authority, and held it against all invaders.' How now? My rise from errand boy to editor after only two years was authorized by a future Justice of the U.S. Supreme Court. What greater authority hath man?

Anyway, as soon as I was in 'possession' I ran off to Columbia to take a course in journalism. I had a burning desire to make something of that stodgy little monthly.

Before my promotion, and after it, my activities were not limited to the production and mailing of *The Maccabean*, which consisted of eight pages, sometimes twelve, occasionally sixteen. Young idealists drawing 'salaries' from public funds had to look for various ways of making themselves useful. I became among other things an organizer of open-air meetings, my principal duty consisting of carrying the soap box, and my principal orator being Maurice Samuel. I had run into him somewhere in the corridors of the ZOA late in 1914; he was a few months younger than I; we took to each other at once—a sort of love-at-first-sight—and have never since lost sight of each other. We have been close friends for almost sixty years. Samuel, or Moish, as our inner circle has always called him, spoke English like an Englishman, which is not surprising since he came from Manchester, England, where he had known Weizmann. I, with my traceable accent, considered this nonetheless an enormous distinction. I can still see and hear him expounding Zionism at Madison Square, opposite our offices, or at other nearby points, where garment workers and office help used to come to eat their midday sandwiches. I used to set up the stand and mumble a word or two of introduction; then Moish would take over. We had competitors, for Madison Square was New York's Hyde Park, and as often as not we would end the session in a fight with the Young Socialists across the street. My younger brother Emanuel would occasionally turn up as a heckler, or even as the rival orator. Each of us was saving the Jews in his own way, but as is always the case, a common objective pursued by different methods bred more hostility than diametrically opposed objectives.

From the beginning, our friendship flowed over from the professional to the personal. One of our plans was to read through the whole of Shakespeare together; the purpose was to improve my knowledge of the English language. We started with Hamlet—typical Jewish *chutzpe*—and worked at it so thoroughly that we never got any further. At the Hashachar Society, which Moish soon joined, he became a great attraction as our own dispenser of Anglo-Saxon culture. I acted as his impresario and assigned various roles to him on the cultural evenings which we arranged at a Masonic lodge on Boston Road. On one occasion, as I remember, Moish, slender, handsome, with luxuriant brown curls, much admired by the younger female members of Hashachar, played the mandolin and followed it by a recitation of *The Raven*. Neither the musical pieces nor the poem had any connection with Zionism—they were glimpses into the outside world: but they warmed up the atmosphere. These preliminaries over, we plunged into Zionism in Yiddish and English. A much more significant evening was one at which the immortal Sholem Aleichem recited his own works. That was in 1916, shortly before his death. His appearance at the Hashachar was among his last, and by a peculiar quirk of memory I can recall what he read that evening: it was the story of two Jews in a railroad carriage who were dying to play cards but could find no other 'table' than the stomach of a priest who had stretched himself out on the opposite bench and was snoring away happily; the game was going well until, in the excitement of the moment, one of the players slapped down his card with such enthusiasm that the slumbering cleric awoke. (What odd things we find in the storeroom of memory!)

It was at that evening that Maurice Samuel, the aspiring young novelist and essayist—his first novel *The Outsider* was already burning in his bosom—became infatuated with Sholem Aleichem. He denies it, but I know better. His infatuation turned into a life-long love affair with Sholem Aleichem's genius. When Moish came to America in 1914 his Yiddish was practically nonexistent. It was at best a kind of Rumanian gibberish. From that moment he determined to master the language and his success had enormous consequences for English literature. What had been hitherto an unlocked treasure—an untranslatable body of great art—he transmuted in his *The World of Sholem Aleichem* into an English classic. He had the wit, and the wisdom, not to translate Sholem Aleichem. He transported his spirit, his wit, his tragic overtones of Jewish life into an English idiom unsurpassed to this day. In later years he translated many Yiddish classics, opening up a new world to American readers and writers.

My first thought on 'usurping' the secretaryship of *The Maccabean's* editorial board was how to get rid of that august body. Editorial boards in general and editorial boards of house organs in particular are usually collections of would-be writers and organizational hatchetmen whose function it is to thwart the efforts of the editor to put out a decent journal. With Lipsky to guide me, the other members of the board were simply dead weight. *The Maccabean*, when I inherited it, was an unobtrusive, amateurish, half-educated Jewish publication whose greatest selling point was that it appeared regularly. Fortunately the Zionist Organization did not have to sell it; it came free with the dues. I decided that the editorial board had to be allowed to wither away, and I made it a matter of policy to consult it as infrequently as possible.

I began by changing the cover and livening up the format; but of course my main problem was to improve the quality of the contents, to make the paper more readable, or I should say, readable, controversial, and maybe even exciting. With no budget for writers' fees I had to use such volunteer talent as I could find. Surprisingly enough a considerable quantity of it was available in the Organization, but had never been tapped. Lipsky himself, for example; he had advised, edited, censored on *The Maccabean;* he had never written for it. I got him to write. I enlisted Maurice Samuel, Max Heller, the Reform Rabbi of New Orleans and a fine writer, and Bernard G. Richards. Richards, a member of the editorial board of little use in that capacity, was the author of a charming book, *The Discourses of Kiedansky*. He was soon to become the secretary general of the American Jewish Congress, but he continued as a contributor to *The Maccabean*. I too took an occasional crack at the business with an editorial. I also managed to get Boardman Robinson, cartoonist of *The New York Morning Telegraph*, to caricature some intramural issues of the American Jewish scene—and that almost brought my editorial career to an end before it was properly started. Robinson was a radical, and he portrayed some of the members of the American Jewish Committee as typical overfed capitalists. The American Jewish Committee was the American Jewish 'establishment' of those days and it was composed entirely of German Jews. No East European Jew —until recently—could cross its threshold or enter the holy precincts of its exclusive Harmonie Club on 60th Street. The ZOA was very much at odds with the American Jewish Committee at the time—and for a long time after—but the leaders and supporters of Zionism did not particularly take to this disparagement of moneyed men as such. I was ordered to drop Robinson, and I was threatened with dismissal; but I was not intimidated. To begin with, I did not like taking orders; I also didn't approve of this kind of censorship; and finally I felt instinctively that whatever aroused my colleagues to such a frenzy of interest was good for the paper. The dispute was settled by Boardman's voluntary retirement. He withdrew to devote himself to painting, in which he made a distinguished career.

In the early part of 1917 I was compelled to supplement my activities as journalist by those of newspaper-vendor. This combination, somewhat less irrational than matches and flypaper, came about as follows: my older brother Josh, it will be remembered, had remained behind in Poland to complete his rabbinical training. By 1912, when he joined us, he was a full-fledged rabbi by European, though not by American, standards. He could only qualify for the American rabbinate by further training at the Jewish Theological Seminary—which meant that he was supposed to begin from scratch and go formally over old ground. Josh submitted, but after a short time dropped out, from sheer boredom. From the Seminary at 123rd Street he moved a few blocks down to Columbia. This too was short-lived, for during his studentship he was given the franchise for a newsstand at the corner of Broadway and 116th Street, university property, through the intervention of Professor Gottheil, and found it a full-time job. He even had to take a partner, Herman Mankiewicz, who later became a very successful script writer. The newsstand thrived, and when, at the beginning of 1917, Josh was called up to the army—he had taken out his first papers—there could be no thought of relinquishing so promising an enterprise. I took over.

My days were a bit crowded. I would get up at three in the morning and bicycle down to the newsstand and attend to all the preliminary chores. From there it was only a few steps to Columbia. But from 116th Street to the new Zionist office at the corner of Fifth Avenue and 12th Street was a longer ride, which I retraced in the evening to look after the newsstand again. Then came the ride home, a hasty supper and my study period, which I got through by the time-honored device, dear to the memory of *yeshivah* boys, of keeping my feet in a bucket of cold water so as not to fall asleep. I made the four trips a day on my bicycle because four nickels (the subway fare in those days) mounted up to twenty cents, which I felt I could not afford. I preferred to run—or rather ride—myself ragged. Fortunately my bicycle was stolen and my idiotic false economy came to an end; I could not find the energy—or the money—for another bicycle.

This hectic editor-student-newsvendor interlude was cut short by the American government. My brother Leo was in the Navy, Josh in the Army. Washington considered that this was not enough to convince the Germans that their case was hopeless. Or perhaps it had got wind of the fact that a fourth Weisgal, my oldest brother, Abba, was fighting on the other side, with the Austrian Empire. If so, it wanted every American Weisgal of military age to help redress the balance, and I was called up. My induction into the American Army took place just as I was about to join the Jewish Legion for Palestine which had been organized in the excitement and wake of the Balfour Declaration.

The Balfour Declaration! November 2, 1917! Of those who were old enough to grasp the meaning of this historic document at the time of its issuance by the British War Cabinet, only a fast diminishing number are still living. Between then and now other fateful events have occurred in Jewish life, some that are remembered with horror, others that lift up the heart. Possibly time has erased in the memory of the survivors the thrill that ran through the Jewish people at the time; possibly, again, remembering how long it took to awaken 'the Jewish people' to action after the Balfour Declaration, it was only the Zionist minority of those days that was sent into an ecstasy of hope. Famous as the Declaration now is, it must be repeated here:

'His Majesty's Government view with favour the establishment in Palestine of a National Home for the Jewish people, and will use their best endeavours to facilitate the achievement of this object, it being clearly understood that nothing shall be done which may prejudice the civil and religious rights of the existing non-Jewish communities in Palestine or the rights and political status enjoyed by Jews in any other country.'

We, the Zionists, knew at the time that the document was a compromise; the British propensity to be vague about promises balked at clear support of our aspirations. But this was the first time in modern history that a great power had expressed recognition, however obliquely, of the right of the Jewish people to reconstitute itself as a nation in Palestine. Why the British went even this far cannot be explained simply; the motives were confused and sometimes contradictory. The British were interested in winning Jewish support in America and Russia for the war effort; some of them believed that a measure of restitution was due to the Jews for anti-Semitism, of which Britain itself was not wholly free; there were also those, in the government and elsewhere, who sympathized with Zionism as an ideal. All these factors were present, and more; but on one particular factor history speaks with a single voice: without Chaim Weizmann, who charmed, cajoled, instructed, persuaded and pressed members of the British government, there would have been no Balfour Declaration.

It was as near as we could come in those days to what Theodor Herzl had dreamed of—a 'charter' for Palestine. In that sense, it was what we had been waiting and working for; it gave clear form to strivings that had been inchoate till then; it delineated our political program. That it was only a document, that it could be given a wide range of interpretations, was clearly understood by those who had helped to bring it to birth—Weizmann, Sokolow, Brandeis and others. Nevertheless, for large numbers of Jews all over the world it was the first rumblings of the Messiah. The war which up to that time had merely been 'to save the world for democracy,' took on a special meaning for the Jewish people, which now had its stake in the outcome. We did not, at the moment, foresee the long, bitter struggle that lay before us; it seemed to us, the Zionists, that if we could help secure Palestine for the British, our troubles would be over, and we felt with the poet:

> Bliss was it in that dawn to be alive.
> But to be young was very heaven.

President Wilson forestalled by a few days my plan to get into the Jewish Legion. Some weeks before there had come down from Montreal a young man by the name of Joe Brainin; his mission was to recruit volunteers for the Legion, and we formed a friendship ended only by his recent death, early in 1970; and I cannot imagine ever becoming accustomed to his absence. Joe's life had been a colorful one. He was born in Vienna, raised in Berlin, Switzerland and Belgium and as a youth had settled in Canada. His father, Reuben Brainin, was one of the leading Hebrew writers of his day, and one of the principal modernizers of Hebrew style, but like most Hebrew writers he earned a livelihood from Yiddish journalism, a characteristic of the time when Hebrew was struggling to re-establish itself as a language of daily discourse. Joe 'inherited' neither Yiddish nor Hebrew from his father; his languages were French, German and English, and in the last he had an impeccable style. He spent most of his life in America, but till the end he remained a European at heart, with the *feinshmekerai*, as we say in Yiddish, the delicate esthetic taste, of the Viennese salon. On his arrival in New York he linked up with two other men in a remarkable trio within the Legion. The first was Gershon Agronsky from Philadelphia, then the editor of *Dos Yiddishe Folk*, the Yiddish counterpart of *The*

Maccabean. Agronsky settled early in Palestine and founded *The Palestine Post*, now *The Jerusalem Post*, Israel's only English language daily; he went on to become the Mayor of Jerusalem in the State of Israel. The second was Louis Fischer, another Philadelphian. He had been a Hebrew teacher, and became a famous foreign correspondent, for a time strongly attracted by the Russian Revolution. Joe oscillated from Zionism to Communism, to journalism, and back again. I was friendly with all three, but most of all I was drawn to Joe, who all his life tormented me about having nearly spilled his blood in the liberation of Palestine. I remember sitting in Camp Hancock shortly after my induction and bursting with envy when I read in the Yiddish papers: *Brainin's zihn flien iber Haifa un varfen bombes*, Brainin's sons (Joe and his brother Moe) fly over Haifa and drop bombs. There is no historical record that either Joe or Mo ever fired a shot in the First World War; nor did two other stalwarts of the Jewish Legion in Palestine, David Ben Gurion, later Israel's first Prime Minister, and Yitzhak Ben-Zvi, Israel's second President, though they made valorous contributions to the war in other directions.

With the same regard for history, I must record that my own military career was not exactly heroic. But while my fellow-Zionists were at least on the spot when the liberation of Palestine took place, I was in Camp Hancock in Georgia. Nevertheless I made my little contribution toward the advancement of the Jewish cause. Very soon after our company was properly constituted we were taken out into the field for a briefing in the dos and don'ts of soldierly deportment. The first lieutenant, to whom this duty was entrusted, told us that we were always to salute the British flag, the French flag, and the flags of all the other Allies. When the question period came I raised my hand and asked, in all innocence: 'What about the Jewish flag?' There was nothing facetious about my question. After the Balfour Declaration and the formation of the Jewish Legion I believed, as thousands of other Jews did, that we were now to be counted among the Allies. In response to my question a couple of dozen Irishmen (I don't know why I had the impression that they were all Irishmen) spontaneously pulled out dollar bills and began to wave them, to my confusion and resentment.

The lieutenant (I afterwards discovered he was a professor at the University of Pennsylvania) called me out to front center and told me to explain my viewpoint to the men. I did this with enthusiasm and some degree of eloquence. I told them about the Balfour Declaration, about the Jewish Legion, about our struggle to regain our ancestral home. When I was done, the lieutenant issued an order that whenever an American soldier passed the Jewish flag, which I had described, he was to salute it exactly as he would salute the American flag or the flag of any of the other Allies.

I was tremendously elated at this 'historic' decision and at once sent off a long report to Mr. A. H. Fromenson, in charge of Public Relations at the Zionist Organization, to the effect that the American Army had recognized the Jewish State. Fromenson was as profoundly impressed as I and he issued a release proclaiming this great political triumph to a breathless world. Two years later, long after I was out of the army, I happened to pick up a paper called *The Jewish Messenger of Shanghai*, edited by a man called Ben Ezra and carrying on its masthead the legend 'Published Spasmodical-ly.' There, as if it were the latest news, was a full page story of our recognition by Camp Hancock. It had taken two years for this good news to reach the Jews of China!

I was in the army for a year and a half during which I saw action on a variety of fronts, none of them very far from Camp Hancock. One day it was discovered that I could type. I was immediately promoted to corporal and attached to some major as his orderly. My fringe duties were to shine his shoes and keep the place clean. These completed, the major would begin to dictate to me the orders of the day. Most of them he turned into complicated literary creations which always began with a statement of the purpose of the war and ended with an appeal to every man to do his duty. At every sitting he would pace the room in deep thought, as if he were rewriting the Declaration of Independence. On the third day I said to him: 'Sir, you don't have to dictate. I know what you want to say. I can do it myself.' That was the end of my corporalship. I was demoted, my stripes were removed and I was sent back to my company in disgrace.

This was by no means the end of my military career, for the war was not yet over. One day I was called in by the captain. He barked at me (in the army oral orders are not spoken), 'You are leaving for New York within forty-eight hours to make speeches for Liberty Bonds.' I was out of the camp within four, most of which I spent with a friendly supply sergeant improving my military appearance. My fastidiousness about clothes was already highly developed and I was not at all happy with the sartorial standards of Camp Hancock. Generally speaking, the American uniforms of the First World War—I am speaking of the ranks—were not the last word in style, and there was not much room for personal improvements. However, since I was about to appear before civilian audiences as the autho-rized representative of the armed forces, the sergeant was ready to accede to two modest demands: one, spiral leggings (really quite smart if you are not bowlegged, and my legs stood the test), and two, a small cap worn akimbo instead of the broad-brimmed affair which was standard. These items were issued to me on condition that I keep them in my duffle bag until I arrived in New York. My trip had been arranged through the Jewish Section of the Liberty Bonds, and for six weeks, during which I made speeches, I was provided with a beautiful—and patriotic—motor corps girl to drive me around.

It goes without saying that a visit to the Zionist offices in my spiral leggings was a must. They were housed at that time in a huge loft on the fifth floor of 55 Fifth Avenue—a succession of 'fives' into which numerologists read various portents. On one side there was a long corridor, on the other the executive offices. They were divided in the center by a wire cage containing the general staff, dominated, in the middle, by the membership department. Over this department presided a gentleman bearing the distinguished name of Mervin Isaacs. The name used to annoy me; I thought it was pretentious and artificial—Mervin didn't belong with Isaacs. Moreover, I did not like the article thus labeled; he was the epitome of the petty bureaucrat who takes himself with enormous seriousness. Unfortunately I had to pass through his little empire in order to make my grand entry into Lipsky's office, and so I was compelled to stop, shake hands and exchange a few pleasantries.

Sitting next to Isaacs was a lovely dark-haired girl, well dressed, and obviously his secretary. I found myself lingering at Mr. Isaac's desk somewhat longer than I had intended; I also found myself hoping that my uniform was making some kind of impression. I further found myself wondering how I could make this more than a fleeting encounter, and suddenly I ventured, 'Could I take you out to lunch?' Mervin Isaacs undertook to speak for her. Scornfully he advised me, 'Don't waste your time. She wouldn't even talk to you.' He was right—up to a point. But after four and a half years of sustained effort I succeeded in wearing down her resistance and she married me. Her name was Shirley Hirshfeld, and she was the little girl on grandfather's knee in front of the Cannon Street *mikveh*.

My stint with Liberty Bonds was to terminate a few days before Rosh Hashanah, and it occurred to me that as I was in New York it would be absurd for me not to spend the High Holidays with my family. The only thing I lacked was permission from the army. To bridge this gap I wired Headquarters in Georgia: 'Needed here another few days—if I don't hear to the contrary will take it for granted that leave is O. K.' I did not hear anything to the contrary until I got back to Camp Hancock ten days later. My reception was warm, but hardly cordial, in fact my sergeant was livid. 'Where the hell have you been?' he roared. I looked at him uncomprehendingly: 'But I sent you a telegram.' From the convulsive expression on his face I judged that he could not decide whether I was a fraud or an idiot. Then he found his tongue, and in ten minutes of army eloquence made it clear that he considered me both. I stood and took it meekly—what else could I do?—and when he wound up with a despairing: 'Get to hell out of here, you dumb bastard!' I made what is called in Yiddish a *vayivrach*, a speedy departure.

Armistice Day came soon after, but it took nearly five months to de-mobilize me. But life was never dull. On weekends the Jewish boys would go into nearby Aiken, South Carolina, which had a thriving Jewish com-munity which in some odd way reminded me of Kikl. We soldiers were well received, taken into Jewish homes, and called up to the reading of the Torah when we attended the Sabbath services. We were appreci-ative, and I decided to do something for the community. I organized a soldier choir to sing in the *shul* on Sabbath. This was not very difficult to arrange, for there were over a thousand Jewish soldiers in Camp Hancock. Our performance was an immense success, and everyone was happy except the *chazan*, who was also the *shammes* (beadle and superin-tendent), the *shochet*, the *mohel* and father confessor to the congregation. In addition, he operated a grocery store. We had made it all too obvious that his talents belonged to the grocery business.

My last great exploit in the army was a Thanksgiving Party which I was drafted to organize for our battalion. I was perfectly willing, but told the sergeant I would need a horse. 'I'll have to get around, you know, and it's a pretty big camp.' I got the horse, and having become quite attached to it decided to hang on to it for a few days after the party was over. For this little indiscretion I lost all the credit due me for the organization of the party. My sergeant called me in, and without a single word of appreciation for my brilliant social achievement, said, coldly: 'Private Weisgal, I understand you are fond of horses.' 'Yes, sir,' was my reply. 'You will go down to the corral and clean horses for the next three days.'

This was terrible punishment. I was totally unsuited for any kind of animal husbandry, and one day in the corral was enough to provide the nauseous proof. I called Rabbi Leon Spitz of the local Jewish Welfare Board that evening, and between contractions of my stomach muscles, explained my situation. 'Rabbi Spitz,' I moaned, 'they are persecuting Jews here. I am dying a thousand deaths.'

The good Rabbi came over the next morning and I was reassigned for special duty with the Welfare Board. While I was thus engaged the order came for the whole company to move north for demobilization. My company officer, who hadn't liked it at all when I had been relieved of my corral duty, saw an opportunity to pay me back. He called me in and informed me: 'Private Weisgal, since you are on special duty, your name has not been included with the rest of the company.'

I thought this was an outrage, and I carried my complaint through the length and breadth of the camp, with gratifying results. My protest was recognized as legitimate, but the ways of the army are strange. My name hadn't been on the original list, and the original list could not be changed, an order being an order. My name was therefore put on a special list, all by itself. But again, an order is not always an action; the company list waited and waited, and my company remained in Camp Hancock for another three months. My own private, personal and exclusive list, was added to another list in the making, and within two weeks I was in Camp Dix. There I helped to demobilize others and was myself demobilized early in 1919.

On my first day in New York I was walking, in uniform, along 14th Street toward Fifth Avenue. I had just turned the corner from Sixth Avenue when I ran into Lipsky. His greeting was brief: 'What the hell are you walking around in that uniform for? Why don't you get back to the office and do some work?' Not exactly a hero's welcome.

5   Schism and Union

The years immediately following my return from service were filled for the Weisgal family with joys and sorrows, joys of reunion, sorrows of eternal separation. Though I was well on in my twenties, independent, ambitious, it never occurred to me to live elsewhere than at home until I was married. We were crowded, of course, but we lived close together in another, warmer sense. I was wanted at home, and I wanted to be at home. It would have hurt my father deeply if I had left before marrying, and I was bound to him by ties of deep respect and affection. I am sure, on looking back, that this relationship was deepened by his uncompromising and quite uninhibited authoritarian attitude toward his children. I remember being slapped by him when I was already in my majority—and it did not occur to me to resent it. It was on a Sabbath, and he was taking an afternoon nap in a room near the kitchen. The tea kettle was boiling softly on an asbestos mat on the stove, which had remained lit since the previous day since it is not permitted to light a fire on the Sabbath. Passing the kitchen I noticed that the flame had gone out. Sure that he was fast asleep—Sabbath morning was his busiest working time—quick as a whip I struck a match and applied it to the burner. It was unthinkable that my father should not enjoy a glass of tea when he awoke from his Sabbath nap! But he heard, leapt to his feet and before I knew what had happened delivered three ringing slaps. I put up a defense—verbally, that is. I quoted verses from the Bible and Talmud. I spoke of honoring one's father, and of *pikuach nefesh*, danger to life, which permits the breaking of the Sabbath law. I was certainly stretching a point implying that his life would have been endangered by not having a glass of tea although his livelihood certainly depended on his voice. 'You *sheygets!*' But I could see that he was pleased by my defense and I could see his point of view. I had transgressed against one of his most precious sanctities.

All of us had the same feeling toward him. I can recall only one incident in which he was genuinely, though unintentionally, hurt by one of his children. The 'culprit' was Abba, my oldest brother, and the issue involved was one of professional pride.

Abba it will be remembered left Kikl as a young man and, after his stint in Nyesheve as choir leader, completed his musical education at the Conservatory in Breslau and later in Vienna. After World War I—when he served as an officer in the Austrian Army—he became a cantor in Eibeschitz, a town in Bohemia made famous in Jewish folklore by Reb Yonasin of Eibeschitz, a renowned scholar in the eighteenth century.

In 1921, Abba came to America with his wife Aranka and his two sons Hugo and Freddie. For all our years in America, we were still Kiklites at heart, but Abba (who now called himself Adolph but reverted to Abba with the advent of Hitler) had become thoroughly alienated from the ways of East European Jews, not to mention Kikl. He spoke no Yiddish, only German, and he looked, dressed and comported himself like Kaiser Wilhelm. Like father, he wrote music and had a magnificent voice.

In Vienna, he had done some work in opera and was anxious to continue it in the United States. It was Leo, who, without a moment's hesitation, gave him the money to continue his studies. In the meantime Abba took on odd assignments, and it so happened that one of them was for the High Holy Days in the synagogue of a prosperous German Jewish community in Baltimore. To clinch that important assignment I got my friend, Jacob Fishman, the managing editor of *The Jewish Morning Journal*, to give Abba a flowery write up. With his superb singing and his imposing Teutonic style, Abba landed a life job as cantor to Baltimore's largest synagogue and after almost sixty years is still going strong there. I think he is the only cantor in America who was able to upstage the Rabbi by the sheer beauty of his *chazones*. Well, one day, not long after our family reunion, my father, eager for appreciation from his son the accomplished musician, took out two huge tomes of his compositions and presented them to Abba. Alas! He did not get it. Before committing himself I presume Abba wanted to acquaint himself with the material in his meticulous German style. I was as wounded as my father and in private asked Abba why he hadn't said anything in appreciation of the gift he had received. His reply was, 'Don't you think I should have looked at the music first?' Typical German. Intended or not, it was thoughtless. He realized it only later, when the deep influences of Kikl reasserted themselves and his Germanisms began to wear off.

My father died before he reached the age of sixty. He didn't live to see the many ways in which Abba gradually began to modernize his works. In the course of time he published two volumes of father's compositions.

Abba's cantorial style, unlike that of the cantors of Eastern Europe, was greatly influenced by Salomon Sulzer and Louis Lowandowski. He rarely allowed himself the pleasure of using the style of let us say a Savel Kwartin, a Rosenblatt or a Mordecai Hershman so beloved by all the Kikls of the world. His German Jewish clientele of Baltimore was happy with what they euphemistically called chorale music.

On the occasions when I spent a weekend in Baltimore, I would refuse to go to his *shul* unless Abba promised to sing one piece of my father's music in its original rendition. I was especially fond of his *Kadushah*. It brought me back to Kikl, and the memory of my father. For the sake of the record and my own pleasure, I reproduce this piece of music.

ECHOD HU ELOHENU
for cantor and mixed chorus (SATB) a cappella

Choral setting by ARNOLD CHAITMAN   ABBA YOSEF WEISGAL

The mills of God grind slowly, but they grind exceeding small and sure. Many, many years later, when Abba's own son, Hugo Weisgall (spelled with two l's), had already made a name for himself as a serious American composer and conductor, I was spending a weekend in Baltimore. It was and still is my custom to attend Abba's *shul* during one or two of the festivals. It was a Saturday night, after the *havdole* ceremony, the leave-taking of the Sabbath, and Abba said to me: 'Meyer, I've just written the most fantastic *Kiddush*. You've got to listen to it.' We all trooped down to the basement, where Hugo had his studio and Abba gave him the music to play while he sang. When he had finished he turned to me: '*Nu*, how do you like it?' I demurred, deliberately, and said: 'Why don't we ask a professional musician. What's your opinion, Hugo?' Hugo shrugged: 'Not bad, but I've heard better.'

It must not for a moment be imagined that Abba's single act of thoughtlessness toward my father clouded their relationship. My father was deeply affected by the reunion—they had not seen each other for nearly twenty years, and the returning son brought with him not only a fine record of achievement but, what was more important, my father's first two grandchildren. These were at least some consolation for the two tragedies which had struck our family in rapid succession.

Helen, my twin sister, the fiery Zionist, a gay and restless spirit, went out one Sunday in the pouring rain to collect money for the Jewish National Fund. She was in bed for the rest of the week with a cold. On Friday I went with my father for a visit to Leo in Larchmont, where he had his business. That evening Lodzia called to tell us that Helen had suddenly worsened and been taken to the Lebanon Hospital. On Saturday afternoon we got the news in Larchmont that she had died. We did not tell father; we only told him that we were all going back to New York that night. When Lena, Leo's wife, left a note for the milkman, 'no milk,' my father knew at once what had happened. '*Chaya iz geshtorben,*' he began to sob. We tried all the way to comfort him, but in vain.

Within a year my younger brother Emanuel drowned. He was only eighteen or nineteen years old, a handsome and brilliant boy. One Sunday he organized a picnic for his YPSL branch and they hired a boat to go up the Hudson. At some point they anchored the boat and went swimming. Two of the youngsters got into trouble in the water and Emanuel dived in after them. The two boys managed to get back into the boat but Emanuel's body was recovered only three days later. His head had hit a rock when he dived. Father got the news immediately, and took to his bed. He died shortly after of a broken heart. The two deaths, following so closely on each other, were too much for him. That was 1921, two years before I married.

There were two curious incidents which preceded my father's death and reflected the complexity of this pious, authoritarian and strangely wonderful man.

Abba arrived with his family just at the time we were sitting *shiva*, in mourning for Emanuel. Leo and I went to the boat to receive them with explicit instructions from father not to mention Emanuel's death. He didn't want the moment of reunion to be clouded by the tragedy. As we entered the house there was no sign of mourning. My sister Rose, at father's instruction, was sitting at the piano, gaily playing and singing a welcome.

The atmosphere was maintained until all the embraces and initial exchanges were over. Only then did father break down and tell Abba about Emanuel.

Not long after, when he was near death, father called all his children together and made one of the strangest pronouncements ever to come from the lips of a devoutly religious Jew. He absolved us from the duty of saying *Kaddish* for him.

Anyone familiar with Jewish life and tradition must realize the enormity of this waiver. *Kaddish*—the prayer for the dead—is one of the most sacred prayers of all. Jewish fathers often refer to their sons as 'my *Kaddish*,' the one who will recite the blessing '*Yisgadal v'yiskadash shemai rabo*,' every day, three times a day, during the first year and thereafter on every holiday and Sabbath when the memorial prayer is intoned. This act of my father's can only be compared to that of a devout Catholic voluntarily foregoing the Last Sacrament.

But he didn't leave it at that. 'I know how "observant" all of you are. My soul will not be redeemed (or, as he put it, *aliyas neshomo*,) by your *Kaddish*, but if you want to remember your father, come together once a year and sing *meine sachen*, my songs.'

For almost thirty years, for as long as Leo was alive, we observed father's memorial day in the manner he proposed. From Baltimore, Boston, New Jersey—wherever we children happened to be living—we came together, usually at our house, with husbands and wives, and later with our own children, to sing his *sachen*. Abba always showed up late at those gatherings. He was ready to sing to his father's memory but he could never reconcile himself to not saying the *Kaddish*. Before coming up to the apartment he would slip into a nearby *shul* and recite it.

When I look back at the period that followed my return from the army, I see that it falls journalistically into three sections: 1919–21, 1921–30, and 1930–2. I edited a series of Zionist periodicals in close conjunction with Lipsky; they were, in that order, *The Maccabean*, *The New Maccabean* and *The New Palestine*. I first met Weizmann in 1921. I was one of his several 'secretaries.' There was intermittent correspondence between New York and London but our personal relationship did not develop until 1931, when I was in Toronto editing *The Jewish Standard*. In that interval my three children, Emanuel, Helen, and David, were also born.

The two years 1919–21 were also the period of my apprenticeship in Zionist politics. Besides managing *The Maccabean*, without being officially designated as its editor, I was Lipsky's deputy in the Organization Department, Fromenson's deputy in Public Relations (or whatever it was called in those days), and Isaac Carmel's deputy in the Speaker's Bureau. In short, I was everybody's deputy.

This period in American Zionism constituted, we can now see, a holding movement organizationally, and *The Maccabean* reflected the state of suspended animation. The Balfour Declaration had brought about a critical division in world Zionism, not immediately perceived but becoming clearer from month to month. The European leadership, Weizmann, Ussishkin and the others, looked upon it as the springboard for an intensified political activity. The American leadership, Brandeis, Frankfurter, Mack, looked upon it as the successful termination of Zionist political action. Or as Shmaryahu Levin said of Brandeis' program: 'All that remained was to drive the mosquitoes out of Palestine and bring in the Jews.'

The crucial difference came drastically to the surface at the 1920 Zionist Conference in London. But the roots of the difference went deeper; they were nourished by two wholly disparate conceptions of the nature of Zionism.

For Brandeis, Zionism was a logical—and sociological—solution to the plight of European Jewry. With scientific planning, intelligent investment and the application of free, private enterprise, such and such a number of Jews could be transferred every year to Palestine into an increasingly absorptive economy. The *kibbutzim* (then called *kvutzot*) and the other cooperative agricultural settlements, which he himself had seen in Palestine, were not his idea of either profitable or wholesome development. Weizmann operated on an entirely different wavelength. He envisaged Zionism as the process of the creative rebirth of the Jewish people in which national forces would be harnessed to the upbuilding of the ancient homeland. The pioneering groups then in the homeland were the spearhead and the hope of Zionism as the expression of Jewish peoplehood.

Until the 1920 Conference Brandeis was unchallenged leader of the American Zionist movement. This was, to some extent, because the movement had not yet cut a wide swath in American Jewish life; it was small enough to be dominated by prominent personalities, and Brandeis' legal position was often likened to that of Justice Holmes. When he was nominated by President Wilson for the Supreme Court, there was a real struggle in Congress, fraught with not a little anti-Semitism. He was charged both with representing capitalism (rich Jews) and socialism (poor Jews). When asked whom he actually represented, he answered: 'I represent the situation.' In all events, with Brandeis' accession to the Supreme Court, his leadership weakened. His spokesmen had none of the personal authority that he enjoyed. Moreover, the movement was evolving into a mass movement and 'the silent leader' could no longer hold sway, although his philosophy of Zionism had its important advocates.

Brandeis' attitude was not related to the local scene alone; it also governed his general approach to world Zionism, and more specifically to the work of the upbuilding of Palestine. For Brandeis and his followers the political destiny of the Zionist movement—hence its structure and program—had been fulfilled and completed by the Balfour Declaration. According to this view the framework was there for the practical work which was to create a bona fide Jewish State. Each Zionist organization of a given country would carry on independently, and as it saw fit, in the practical private-initiative program.

Whatever the merit of such an approach to the creation of a new country, it is plain that it would have meant the end of the World Zionist Organization and, in a larger sense, of the world Zionist movement; also the disintegration of the central leadership and ultimately the fragmentation of world Jewry on the very eve of its unification and redemption. It was Brandeis' plan to retain the supervision of the funds contributed by America, whereas Weizmann insisted that all funds, from all countries, were to come under the direct control of the World Zionist Organization. Furthermore, on the vital question of funds Weizmann looked to American Zionism for unprecedented contributions, whereas Brandeis was a decided minimalist. He doubted the ability of the movement to raise more than a half a million dollars for national funds—in which he was proved wrong not long after.

The two points of view were essentially irreconcilable. In London an open schism was formally averted, but the lines were drawn: America versus Europe as contestants for Zionist leadership. American Zionism could not, of course, be easily dismissed; it was young, still uncrystallized, unsure of itself; but it had a great matrix for future growth, a Jewish community that was large and growing, prosperous, free and buoyant. It was, after the destruction wrought in Europe by the First World War, the most promising source of funds. And therein lay the most obvious claim to leadership as viewed by the official American Zionist leaders.

They came home to prepare for the coming Zionist convention to be held in Cleveland in June, 1921. It was here that they expected to consolidate their position and to carry through their program. But if ever a leadership misjudged the temper of its rank and file, it was the American Zionist leadership *sans* Brandeis in 1921.

The simple truth was that American Jewry was still largely European in its sentiments; it was predominantly Yiddish-speaking, and of the folk.

Shmaryahu Levin spoke to its emotions, Lipsky gave formal expression to its attitude. The Weizmann-Brandeis conflict went deep into the body of the American movement. There were no areas of indifference, and the lines formed clearly: for American Zionism it was either Brandeis, or to be exact, his representatives, or Lipsky, and Lipsky meant Weizmannism in America.

The storm broke at a full meeting of the American Zionist Executive which was the interim authority between conventions. I was not a member of that body, but I had enough credentials to warrant my attendance. (If my memory is correct, I was responsible for renting the room at the Pennsylvania Hotel where the session was held.)

As mentioned above Brandeis had already for some time been the 'silent leader'; Jacob de Haas was his spokesman. At crucial moments de Haas would ask for the floor, and say, 'I have in my pocket a document which proves . . .' But the document, presumably from Brandeis, was never produced. De Haas was something less than an adequate substitute for Brandeis, but there were others, men of larger stature, on the side of the 'invisible leader,' men like Stephen Wise, Felix Frankfurter, Judge Julian W. Mack. They were a formidable group.

Lipsky had just spent several weeks in hospital, following an operation. He came to the meeting looking pale and drained. When he rose to speak there was a deathly silence, compounded of suspense and of sympathy. He held on to the back of a chair to support himself, and, with every eye in the room on him, made a simple statement: 'Justice Brandeis has ceased to be my leader. I will no longer follow him'—and therewith he tendered his resignation as head of the Organization Department. The meeting dissolved into chaos.

Suddenly I became a much-sought-after man. De Haas called me in the next morning and said 'Weisie'—this was the name he always used—'Weisie, this is your big chance. You can become head of Organization. We're going to give those guys the biggest shellacking of their lives.' All doors seemed to be opening for me; everybody whose assistant I had been was resigning. I answered: 'All right. I'll give you my answer tomorrow.' There was no doubt in my mind or in anyone else's as to where my loyalties lay, but none of my friends urged me to do anything because I was too unimportant. I figured the first step to importance was resigning—which I did, as editor of *The Maccabean*, and as assistant to the various departments.

The rebels, or the Lipskyites, as we were called, set up an office at 50 Union Square. The convention, at which the decisive battle would be joined, was some months away. We decided that we had to have a weapon of our own, a paper to rival the monthly *Maccabean*, and what better name could we give it than *The New Maccabean?* We expected to run it against the old *Maccabean*, but to our complete bewilderment the old *Maccabean* simply did not appear, and its death remains till this day a complete mystery. A smaller official weekly called *The New Palestine* did appear but it was nothing but an announcement sheet. The Brandeis group had all the money, plenty of brains and ability; they also had the established facilities. Whether they suffered from overconfidence, or whether they thought it beneath their dignity to dispute the field with us, what happened was that the old *Maccabean* folded up, and *The New Maccabean* had the field to itself. Many years later Lipsky wrote: 'When destiny led us to the Cleveland Convention in which the controversy between the Brandeis group and the Weizmann group was fought out in democratic fashion, it was inevitable that in our campaign we should use the publication called *The New Maccabean*, with Meyer as manager of the temporary enterprise. That was his grand opportunity. *The New Maccabean* appeared weekly until the day of the convention. It had a circulation of over 30,000 . . . To a large extent, the victory at Cleveland was due to the propaganda of *The New Maccabean*.'

The manner in which we issued it, penniless as we were, is a lesson in cheek. I betook myself to *The Brooklyn Eagle*, where we had published *The Maccabean* till then and went to see the head man, Mr. Aberly. I gave him an honest picture of the situation. 'The worst that can happen, that is, if we lose, is you'll be out about $30,000. But we'll win, and we'll be your customers for the next fifteen years.' My enthusiasm infected him and he gave us credit. We paid back every cent, and we were his customers for more than fifteen years.

We produced a lively paper in which no subject of Zionist interest was taboo. We reduced organizational verbiage to the indispensable minimum and concentrated on the issues. We avoided personal abuse, distortion and vulgarity. It was during this time that my editorial wings sprouted. We turned the monthly into a weekly, and during the convention it was issued daily. We worked feverishly, often twenty out of twenty-four hours, and it never occurred to us to become tired. There have been more critical moments in Zionism; there have been more visibly dramatic issues; but even at this distance I believe that the 1921 American Zionist Convention was of decisive importance in the history of Zionism.

The convention, as we have noted, was set for June. In April Chaim Weizmann came to the United States for the first time, heading a delegation that included Albert Einstein, already known to all the world, Menachem Mendel Ussishkin, the long-time leader of Russian Zionism and director of the Jewish National Fund for the purchase of land in Palestine, and Dr. Ben Zion Mossinsohn, director of the Herzliah Gymnasium, or High School, in Tel Aviv. Shmaryahu Levin was added to the delegation. The official purpose of Weizmann's visit was the launching of the Keren Hayesod in America, the fund for colonization work in Palestine; he had a secondary objective very dear to his heart, and that was the erection of the Hebrew University, the cornerstone of which he had laid toward the end of the First World War. But since the American Zionist leadership was opposed to the raising of public funds for colonization work, and was determined to encourage only private enterprise, and since again, the American Zionist leadership was determined to have exclusive control of any funds raised in America, the coming of Weizmann to America at this juncture was an assertion of the authority of the World Zionist Organization over the local authority of the American leadership. Weizmann was the elected President of the World Zionist Organization, but that title does not describe the reverence in which his name was held. In the eyes of the Zionists—and this included, as was soon proved, a large section of American Jewry too—he was almost a Messianic figure. Only he would have both the official and personal authority to challenge what may properly be called the secessionist spirit of the American Zionist leadership.

We, the loyalists of the world movement, but rebels against the local Zionist leadership, decided to organize a rousing reception for Weizmann, and I was asked to take charge of the arrangements. This was done in a frankly partisan spirit, for we were no longer part of the official American organization. I think it is fair to say that the American Zionist leadership would have liked Weizmann's arrival to pass completely unnoticed; we, however, were determined that it should be marked by the kind of popular reaction that corresponded to the magic of Weizmann's name. We advertized the event as one of classic importance. I had friends in the Yiddish papers, and I urged them to write up the coming event in the appropriate manner. We created a magnificent mood of anticipation, and the realization more than lived up to it.

It was a Saturday, *shabbos,* when the boat arrived, but the passengers did not disembark until after sunset. During the day tens of thousands of Jews walked down to the docks from Manhattan, from the Bronx and from every section of Brooklyn. Toward evening they were joined by thousands more in wagons, trucks, carts and private cars. Nothing like it had ever happened in the history of New York Jewry. The procession stretched all the way from the Battery to the Commodore Hotel, where the delegation was to stay. Weizmann recalls this reception in his autobiography: 'We intended, of course, to proceed straight to our hotel, settle down, and begin planning our work. We had reckoned—literally—without our host, which was, or seemed to be, the whole of New York Jewry.'

This was my first meeting with Weizmann, though I am prepared to believe that he remained quite unaware of my existence.

Prior to the confrontation in Cleveland there were endless negotiations between Weizmann and the Brandeis group, with all kinds of intermediaries including Samuel Untermeyer, considered one of the greatest lawyers in America. They came to nothing; but they were not without value, for they served to make clear how irreconcilable were the two views of the Zionist movement and of the function of the World Zionist Organization. When we met in Cleveland we knew that there was no possibility of compromise; but, though we, on our side, were optimistic as to the outcome, we did not know how decisive the victory would be—and a marginal victory would have been a disaster.

The first issue to be raised was ostensibly technical—but it was actually a decisive test of strength. This was the election of a chairman of the Convention. Judge Julian Mack, a highly respected figure, was nominated by the Brandeis group; the Lipsky group countered with another Federal Judge, Henry J. Dannenbaum of Texas. Dannenbaum was elected by an overwhelming majority. On the last evening—I should say night, for the session lasted until two in the morning—the 'rebels' took all but 76 of the 400 votes. It was an almost total repudiation of the Brandeis' leadership, or followship, and it was immediately followed by mass resignations on the part of the defeated leaders. Many people thought that this was the end of the Zionist Organization of America. That same night de Haas had the great presence of mind—in the midst of all the turmoil—to dispatch someone to New York to remove all the files from the office. We, the victors, came back to an empty office.

Gradually the secessionists all returned to the bosom of the mother organization and The League for Palestine, which they had founded as a substitute for the Zionist Organization, dwindled away into an economic enterprise for Palestine. Stephen Wise was the first to come back; but the basic differences between the two conceptions of Zionism were to crop up from time to time with varying degrees of violence.

When the smoke of the 'great war' receded there remained another private battle to be fought in the rather prolonged war of attrition being waged between me and my wife-to-be. It took another two years, till the spring of 1923, before I could safely wire Moish Samuel who was out of town: 'The Bastille has fallen.'

I have mentioned my wife in passing as the secretary to the objectionable Mr. Mervin Isaacs. She was Shirley Hirshfeld, of the Boro Park Hirshfelds, one generation removed from Galicia. I never let this blight on her genealogy come between us. She was dark, beautiful, bright and not easily impressed. I cannot say that my wooing of her moved smoothly toward victory. Indeed, my suit almost foundered in the political struggle. We had, in spite of Mr. Isaacs' contemptuous predictions, reached the talking stage; we were in fact friendly. But when the Lipsky group broke away from the American Organization, and we set up shop with *The New Maccabean*, I committed the tactical error of asking Miss Hirshfeld for a copy of the membership list. She not only refused, but broke off all relations, refused to talk to me, or come near me. She held out for about three months.

I had not had much experience with women and had been fleetingly in love only twice before, once with another girl in the office; and a second time, after the war, with a girl I met in Parksville, New York, where I was recuperating from pleurisy. She was about nineteen or twenty, short, blonde, well-shaped, rather pretty and intelligent. Her greatest attraction for me was, I imagine, that, like Everest, she was there. When we parted she tearfully pledged me to a meeting with her in her home in Bensonhurst, Brooklyn. Bensonhurst was in those days a sort of garden city, a notch or two higher than Boro Park. And so to Bensonhurst I made my way one Sabbath afternoon on an official visit. The street, the house, the garden all looked good to me; so did the preparations that had been made for my reception. The girl looked good, too. And then her matronly mother appeared. I say matronly by way of introduction. She was friendly, she seemed to approve of me—but she was, to put it quite bluntly, a barrel of a woman. I saw my future wife thirty years hence, and though I kept my thoughts to myself, while sipping the coffee and nibbling the cake, I made my decision.

Shirley's mother stood the test. My friendly relations with Shirley were reestablished when the new Administration took over. This was the beginning of the serious campaign, which, as I said, lasted two years. I do not know what role Shirley's parents played in that period, but I know that I had formidable rivals, among them a successful shoe salesman who must, to thoughtful parents, have offered far brighter prospects than a Zionist journalist. When I finally passed the 'talking' stage, I made a pilgrimage to

Boro Park. Despite the '*sheytl*' and the apron, I recognized in Mrs. Hirsh-feld certain durable qualities which I know now her daughter inherited, and I was right. This is what we call in Yiddish a *veiten kuk*, a far-seeing eye.

In the excitement of this discovery I saw in the stucco house in which they lived a palatial home of infinite grandeur. Their *mikveh* across the street, elegantly called the Turkish Bath, was transfigured in my imagina-tion into a Roman bath. It wasn't long before I discovered that the stucco house was not theirs: they could hardly pay the rent. The baths were mort-gaged to the hilt. Whatever the baths produced was half stolen by the non-Jew who 'bought the bath' on Friday afternoon and 'sold it back' on Saturday evening. These twenty-four hours were the busiest in this Terme de Boro Park, but no religious Jew operated his business on the Sabbath. And my father-in-law was extremely devout. As a matter of fact, the only question he asked me when I requested his daughter's hand was: 'Do you lay *tefillin*?' The one serious objection they had to me, one which persisted over the years, was that I was not religious enough, I, Meir, son of Shloyme Chaim, *der chazan von Kikl!* What a thought! My piety merely expressed itself in unorthodox ways.

When the day of days arrived I had to find the money for Shirley's wedding dress, and my last remaining dollars went to the taxi driver who carried me and as many of my family as could be squeezed in from Lenox Avenue in Harlem to Boro Park. I, too, was fittingly decked out, and to take the subway was of course out of the question.

My brother Abba came up from Baltimore to conduct the ceremony. My family was there *en masse*, and Lodzia was perhaps the proudest of all to see her favorite married off. I have been told by many friends who were present at the ceremony that I was pale with excitement and that I was led to the *chuppah* (bridal canopy) looking more like a lamb being led to the slaughter than a bridegroom in the hour of his glory. Shirley says that my shoulders were hunched so high under my hat that my face was barely visible. When Abba, after tying the knot, intoned the memorial prayer for my father, *El Mole Rachamim*, 'God full of mercy,' I was shaken by sobs. When it came to that part of the ceremony in which the bridegroom must stamp on a wrapped up glass and smash it in one blow, I missed: a frightful omen foreboding impotence. What a beginning! But the funereal atmosphere disappeared as soon as I kissed my bride.

Among the guests were of course all my friends from the American Zionist Organization, lead by Mr. and Mrs. Louis Lipsky. Most notable among them was Shmaryahu Levin, who, in my father's place, brought me under the *chuppah*. We were close friends and would meet almost daily either in the office or at the Richelieu Restaurant at the corner. But for my in-laws, the Hirshfelds, the presence of such a celebrity was world-shaking. Our friendship was regarded by them as the outstanding achievement of my life, so far my only one.

The speeches that evening were, as might have been expected, interminable; the hall was thickly sown with Zionist orators, and with a captive audience they ran wild. Of what was said, the praises, the wishes, the warnings, the hopes, I remember nothing. But Shmaryahu Levin's speech I remember vividly. He ignored me completely—I was merely the groom. He addressed Shirley by the name he always used for her and by which she came to be known by most of the Zionist world: *Sheyne Leah*, Beautiful Leah. He spoke with eloquence and charm, and with the hypnotic hold on his audience which was his special characteristic. He described the sad lot of a woman married to a dedicated Zionist—and he spoke not only from observation, but from experience: the long nights she would spend alone, her husband sometimes thousands of miles away. With each word I felt my heart sinking, and my hard-won conquest slipping as it were from between my fingers. But it was done with such grace, and ended on such an optimistic note, that I forgave him.

When the festivities ended at midnight three-quarters of the wedding party, myself and Shirley included, adjourned to Atlantic City for a Zionist convention. Thus began our married life.

6   The Editorial Desk

In 1921 when we returned victorious from Cleveland to our ransacked offices, I inherited the official publication of the movement, *The New Palestine*, successor to the defunct *Maccabean* and the now suspended *New Maccabean*. It was an inoffensive little offering of eight and sometimes sixteen pages. In theory, a subscription cost $2 a year. In fact, it was a reward to every dues-paying Zionist whose $6 reached the central office. He had merely to indicate whether he wanted *The New Palestine* or *Dos Yiddishe Folk*. In theory, again, $2 out of every $6 was set aside to cover the costs of printing and mailing. We had no budget for writers' fees because we had no writers. In fact, the $2 went the way of the other $4 into the general administrative pool and every time a bill from *The Brooklyn Eagle*, our printers, came in, I was accused of creating a deficit in the budget.

About once a year a small item in six-point type at the bottom of the last page announced to an incurious world, in accordance with postal regulations, that I had taken an oath before a Notary Public to the effect that I, Meyer W. Weisgal, was, to the best of my knowledge, the managing editor of the publication, that Louis L. Lipsky was the editor, and I, Meyer W. Weisgal, was the 'business manager.' I never pressed for a slug with my name on the masthead. I insisted on anonymity, not God knows, out of modesty, but as a matter of expediency, principle and self-defense. I had already learned my lesson on *The Maccabean*. Non-writing writers, budding leaders, aspiring politicians and literary aspirants stood as it were in line before the editor's desk, bearing bulky manuscripts or bursting with invaluable journalistic expertise. I was able to point out to them that I was *not* the editor, and the higher authority was Mr. Lipsky (whom they did not dare to pester). For a while the dodge worked; later the changed character of the paper offered me some defense.

I decided very early that *The New Palestine* did not have to and was not going to remain a timid and insipid house organ or a publicity sheet for Zionist chairmen. I believed that with some effort, imagination and money it might become not only interesting to members, but to the general reader. The going was hard at first; paying for professional writers when there were so many willing amateurs around was something unheard of in the Zionist world; but I insisted on a writers' budget. If I was going to be charged anyway with deficits, I wanted the right to create them. I gradually assembled about the paper a group of talented writers with reputations. Furthermore, I demanded independence from the administrative machinery and the pressures of department heads and vice-presidents. Fortunately, I was always the last one at the printer's and my policy was, 'print first, ask questions later.' Once a hundred thousand copies were off the press no one was going to demand a rerun. As a result of all this, *The New Palestine* soon took on the character I wanted it to have—of a serious publication.

I had an unofficial inner editorial board consisting of Louis Lipsky and Maurice Samuel and a periphery of known writers. Some were at the beginning of their careers, others were already established. *The New Palestine* became a magnet which drew into the Zionist orbit so-called alienated Jews—the term was not so widespread then, but the reality was a recognized phenomenon. In most cases I awakened their interest with the 'bribe' of a visit to Palestine—to see for themselves, no obligation attached. Sometimes it worked, sometimes it failed. Ludwig Lewisohn and Vincent Sheean were two good cases in point. I got to know, and like, both men.

At that time, the early twenties, Lewisohn was at the height of his career. He was the literary editor of *The Nation* and famous for a number of books, particularly *Upstream*. He was, however, remote from the Zionist ideology. I sent him to Palestine for a series of impressionistic articles, and he returned with a song of Zion on his lips. Like all converts he burned with a bright new flame which outshone all the older lights, and as a writer he brought to us not only his distinguished name but as felicitous a style as was known in America. He was also a superb translator from the German, the language of his boyhood. In appearance he closely resembled the portraits of Goethe, and the older he grew the more remarkable the resemblance became. My association with Lewisohn lasted well beyond *The New Palestine* period and through an assortment of wives—his, not mine. I mention them because they obtruded themselves into his literary life. As a writer Lewisohn belonged entirely to the moderns but as a lover he was thoroughly old-fashioned; every time he smiled at a woman he thought he had to marry her. He had a succession of four wives and became so bogged down in marital complications that for a long time my personal contacts with him were restricted to Sundays, the one day he could come to New York without fear of being served a summons. One such Sunday he delivered himself of a long dissertation on the survival of the Jewish people; it was learned, illuminating and well constructed, and it ended with a flourish: 'Herr Redakteur'—he liked to address me in German—'in my great devotion to the Jewish people, I am in danger of neglecting my own survival. You must help me.' The long and short of it was that henceforth he had to get $50 an article instead of $25, or he would be unable to meet his alimony payments. In this respect I was able to help, but not in another and more important one; as his devotion to Zionism grew, his popularity with the outside world declined. But this did not affect the brilliance of his style.

My experience with Vincent Sheean was very different. A young Irish newspapermen, Sheean had a wide audience. He was attracted by the idea of a visit to Palestine; the Zionist idea, too, interested him—I believe it was Dorothy Thompson, herself a convert at that time, who introduced him to it. Sheean understood that he would be free to write exactly as he felt, and I was perfectly certain that our Palestine would seduce him. And seduced he was, but not by the Jews. He was taken in hand by Mrs. Kitty Antonius, the wife of George Antonius, the leading Arab intellectual of the time, and became convinced that the Arabs, not the Jews, were the coming force in Palestine. I must record that he returned all the money we advanced him, because he refused to write a single word for us.

Another writer who came into my orbit at that time was a tall, handsome Dutchman, a minister of the gospel who had chosen not to occupy a pulpit. His name—as yet unknown—was Pierre van Paassen, and our rapport was instantaneous. He was brought to me by Isaac Carmel, a Zionist organizer from Leeds who now lives in Jerusalem and spends his time, in his own words, 'taking care of an old man.' Carmel had made van Paassen's acquaintance in Atlanta, where van Paassen was then working for The Atlanta Constitution. It was only during the Second World War, when he wrote Days of Our Years, a Book-of-the-Month Club selection and an immediate success, that he became a prominent figure. We appointed him our European reporter—as a side line, of course; he was foreign correspondent for The New York Evening World and The Toronto Star. Van Paassen was no 'convert'; he was a self-made Zionist and his Zionism sprang from his profound love of the Bible, his intimate familiarity with its promises and perhaps from a sense of Christian guilt toward the Jewish people. There may have been still another element in his Zionism—the frustrated national longings of the minority people to which he belonged, the Walloons, working itself out in a passionate espousal of the Jewish minority. In Europe he recruited a host of writers for *The New Palestine*, among them Charles Gide and Edmond Fleg. Van Paassen was an unusually imaginative journalist—a quality not always desirable in his profession; journalists are supposed to report 'facts.' He was sometimes in hot water as a result of 'on the spot' interviews in far off places which were created in his Paris office. He was nevertheless a great asset to Zionism and was made an honorary citizen of Tel Aviv after the war.

My close friend Gershon Agronsky, whom I last mentioned as a member of the Jewish Legion, left New York early in the nineteen-twenties to settle in Jerusalem, where he founded the English-language daily *The Palestine Post*, now *The Jerusalem Post*. I bestowed on him the title of 'Special Representative of *The New Palestine*,' and he too rounded up local talent for us, including Julian Meltzer, of whom I will have more to say later. We began to feature poems and short stories by young Palestinian writers and reproductions of the works of Palestinian artists. By 1924 we had risen, say, to the level of a solid widely respected journal. We had expanded to thirty-two pages; our subjects ranged over many fields not immediately within the Zionist purview—philosophy, economics, *belles-lettres*, book reviews, general political issues. We could even point to the beginnings of that ultimate symbol of success, a body of regular advertisers; they were not exactly General Motors, but they constituted pleasant little financial oases in the deserts of 'unproductive' literature.

At that time my opposite number in the Organization was Dr. Shimon Bernstein, a Hebrew scholar of some note, the editor of *Dos Yiddishe Folk*. He would come regularly into my office driven by a colleague's concern for my future. He would sit on the edge of my desk and point out that I was systematically digging my own grave; I was a fool to surround myself with such a galaxy of brilliant writers—Maurice Samuel, Pierre van Paassen, Ludwig Lewisohn, Robert Weltsch, Leonard Stein, Marvin Lowenthal, etc., everyone of them more talented than I. I answered tranquilly that I had never noticed any one of them panting for my job; they were head over heels in love with the writing craft and utterly intent on their journalistic careers—with Zionist writers' fees what they were, they had to be. I was, moreover, quite sure of one thing:

they were excellent writers, but I was an orchestrator, and not a bad one either.

Every newspaper—and in a sense we were also a newspaper—had on its staff what are euphemistically called 'rewrite men.' Actually they are ghost writers. Now I had managed to fight off most of the pressures of would-be exponents of Zionist theory and tactics, Zionist philosophy and action, eager seekers of a niche in the hall of fame or at least in the columns of *The New Palestine;* but there were times when leaders of genuine merit devoid of articulateness had to be given some space, as was the case when we produced one of our outsize issues for a gala occasion. This situation provided a permanent career for a fascinating character called James Fuchs, who wrote under the name of Jacques Renard. The literary helplessness of some of our Zionist leaders provided Fuchs with his bread and butter.

He took his job with a certain amount of seriousness. He was a prolific writer capable of imitating many styles, and of inventing a suitable one where it did not exist; in this he was helped by a discriminating insight into the character and equipment of the man he was writing for. He invested each article with the exact degree of sophistication, erudition and originality, and would charge us according to the intellectual capacity of the 'author.' For the boor, or ignoramus, he took only $5, for the half-baked intellectual $7.50, and for the man of quality $10. Sometimes he had no material at all to work on, there was no 'lead,' everything would have to be invented. This might happen at the last moment, when some sort of copy had been expected and had not turned up by the time we were going to press; it might not be just a 'leader' but a man of literary standing who *had* to be in that issue and had not kept his promise. Then I would shout over the noise of the presses (he was half-deaf), 'Fuchs, I need 250 words by so and so. How much?' He would stand frozen in thought, making a genuine effort to assess the degree of imitative ingenuity called for. Sometimes, after a great inner struggle he would hold up five fingers. These were his moments of truth.

On the whole, he was a man of integrity, but on one occasion he found himself in a jam, and out of panic, as I suppose, so overreached himself that were it not for the humor of the situation I would have got rid of him.

My attention had been drawn to a series of articles in *Die Zukunft,* a distinguished Yiddish monthly appearing in New York, by a man called Ya'ari Poleskin. He had written his reminiscences of a fascinating period in Palestine life, crammed with hitherto unpublished material. I sought him out and came to terms with him regarding republication in *The New*

Palestine. Casting about for a translator, I approached Fuchs, who of course took on the job.

I had read and reread the articles a number of times and when Fuchs produced his translation, on schedule, I was baffled by the extraordinary disparity between what I read there and what I remembered of the original articles. I reread them and compared them with the translation; any resemblance between the two was purely coincidental. I went to look for Fuchs at his rooms; he was not to be found. I ended up in the Café Royale, his favorite hangout, where I told my story to some of the *habitués*. There I learned that Fuchs did not know a word of Yiddish, that Herman the waiter had read the material out to him, while Fuchs had taken notes. Since Fuchs was half deaf and Herman almost illiterate the result was, to say the least, quaint. I had to do the translation myself. When Fuchs finally turned up and tried to collect, he argued that his—and Herman's—creation had special literary merits of its own. It reminded me of Boris Tomashevsky's famous Yiddish translation of Shakespeare: *iberzetst un farbessert*, 'translated with improvements.'

I cannot mention the Café Royale, which was to early American Zionists and Yiddish journalists what Sardi's became to New York's theatrical folk, without pausing in homage to one of its most famous frequenters, Chona. Indeed, no history of American and even international Zionism can pass over him in silence. He appeared at every Zionist Congress, every American Zionist Convention, every assembly, every public demonstration—and in between he was always to be found at the Café Royale. The most salient feature of Chona was his ubiquity. He never did anything, he never was anything; one could only say that he was always there.

He was a man of enormous bulk, outsized feet and unbelievable *chutzpe;* he had a shuffling, shambling walk with a built-in lurch, and he always carried a heavy cane as a brake. He had a shock of tousled hair, strong spectacles and deep dimples in his seldom shaven cheeks which we all believed were the marks of a bullet that had passed through them. His dress was always in the same state of unpresentability, giving rise to a famous riddle: 'Who wears Chona's clean collars?' His laugh was a combination of bellow and snort, but infectious. He was a kind of self-appointed, universally indulged court jester, shooting his darts—often they were sharply pointed, not to say poisoned—in all directions, but mostly at the enemies or rivals of those he happened to be sitting with. It was his boast—not an idle one—that he had never done a day's work in his life. Once he walked through a line of pickets striking against the Yiddish newspapers. They called after him: 'Scab!' Chona turned on them with the indignation of an impugned virgin: 'No one has ever dared to accuse me of working a single day in my whole life.'

What did he live on? The correct question would be: 'Whom did he live off?' and the answer: 'Whom didn't he live off?' Myself, Lipsky, Wise—anyone in public Jewish life; the list of contributors would be as impressive as that of the most distinguished philanthropic enterprise. He was the greatest *shnorrer* of all time not excluding Zangwill's fictional King of Shnorrers, and when he wasn't pocketing handouts he was 'joining' someone for a cup of coffee or a sandwich. His *chutzpe* developed a sort of sublimity that inspired genuine awe. When he applied for his naturalization papers he gave three personal references: Louis D. Brandeis, Julian W. Mack and Stephen S. Wise, with all of whom he was, of course, on a 'first name basis.' On one of his innumerable trips to Palestine—all of which were financed 'by popular subscription'—he accosted a group of school children and began examining them in Zionist history. 'Who is Herzl?' They told him. 'Who is Weizmann?' That they were also able to answer. 'And who is Chona?' They were stumped till one of them ventured an explanation: 'That we learn only in the higher grades.' Such is the story—as Chona told it.

When the State of Israel was established Chona decided that his place was with the pioneers and builders. His benefactors got together, tendered him a banquet on Second Avenue, set up a pension fund for him and shipped him off to the Holy Land. Everybody from David Dubinsky, the great labor leader, to Louis Lipsky was there, and great was the rejoicing at the prospect of seeing him permanently settled at a distance of six thousand miles. When I moved to Israel the predictable happened: Chona in all his slouching dishevelment presented himself at my doorstep in the middle of the Weizmann Institute. I told him briefly that I would do something for him on one condition—that he keep out of my sight; I didn't consider him an appealing addition to the campus. Some days later I was sitting at a café in Tel Aviv and perceived Chona at a nearby table, silent and brooding. The friend I was with turned to him and said 'hello.' Chona nodded coldly. 'Don't you know Meyer?' asked my friend, in astonishment. Chona answered: 'The Meyer I knew in America is dead. This is a new Meyer.' Nevertheless, my weekly emolument was never returned.

Another interesting personality, of quite a different caliber, who drifted in and out of the various publications I edited was Dr. Samuel Melamed, of *The Chicago Jewish Courier* and many other papers. He was scholarly, wrote in several languages and had a number of books to his credit. Unfortunately his intellectual integrity bore no relationship to his equipment and talents. He was constantly in and out of trouble with the Zionist leaders; they were geniuses or scoundrels—always in print, of course— according to what he was getting from them. At one time he was furiously at odds with Solomon Goldman and wrote a pamphlet *Contra Goldman* on the model of Josephus' classical *Contra Apion*. Not long after, Goldman published a book, *A Rabbi Takes Stock,* and Melamed appeared in my office and asked to be given the review of it for *The New Palestine*. I refused; I told Melamed bluntly I did not trust him and he would be wasting his time. But Melamed pleaded that he would rise above his personal feelings, he would be objectivity itself; and what between his anxiety to get the job and an engaging stammer, he won me over. When he brought me the review I glanced at the first lines and saw: 'A rabbi takes stock, bonds, cash, anything he can lay his hands on.' I opened up on Melamed in my best style, which has frequently been compared to the richer forms of Billingsgate. Melamed did not flinch. 'Meyer,' he said, 'I wrote the first line for my personal enjoyment only. Now sit down and read the rest.' I did, and I published the article.

One afternoon, toward the end of 1924, I was on my way home from the office when I stopped at the B.M.T. station in Union Square for the afternoon paper. Rocking comfortably Brooklynward, one arm hooked into the strap, the other holding the folded paper to my nose, I noticed a small item of some four or five lines to the effect that the Hebrew University would be opened in Jerusalem in April, 1925. A bright light exploded in me. I got off at Washington Square and went back to the office. From there I sent out a hundred telegrams and cables to people and institutions all over the world—everybody who was anybody was on the list.

I had not the slightest idea in what manner the opening was being organized in Jerusalem; I only knew that the reflection of that opening in the pages of *The New Palestine* had to be something equally memorable. It was not enough that the event itself was of the first magnitude; it had to be made to appear as such to the world at large.

Among the people I cabled for articles, messages and greetings for the special Hebrew University edition of *The New Palestine* (the actual conception of which was still rather vague in my mind) were Achad Ha-Am, Arthur James Balfour, Bialik, Max Brod, Albert Einstein, Millicent Fawcett, Charles Gide, Paul Painlevé, Henrietta Szold, Rabindranath Tagore, and Chaim Weizmann. When, within the next few days, the answers began to come in, my superiors began to suspect that I was up to something; what that something was they could not guess, but they smelt 'deficit.' I had, in fact, already expended a respectable sum in cables, and it suddenly dawned on them that I might even be offering some of my prospective contributors real remuneration for their articles. I was hauled before the Administrative Committee, made to explain myself, got myself rebuked and censured and, what was more important, told roundly that I would not get a single penny for the enterprise. Characteristically, however, they did not tell me to drop the idea.

Well, I *had* to get the money for the issue, and I did so by organizing a special Publication Committee for advance sales. We disposed of 150,000 copies before we went to print. I worked day and night for six months on the Hebrew University issue, while getting out the regular weekly as we went along. Working with me were Maurice Samuel, Joe Brainin, Henry Montor and Marie Syrkin. Henry Montor was a fugitive from the Hebrew Union College. Although he had a brilliant scholastic record he refused to be ordained and came to New York in search of literary fame. He married Martha Neumark, the sister of Joe Brainin's wife, and thus was drawn naturally into our circle. He was a man of extraordinary talent and of an even more extraordinary capacity for work; he eventually carved out a niche for himself in Zionist circles as one of the most ingenious and phenomenally successful fund raisers in the history of the movement. He was the brain behind the United Jewish Appeal and Bonds for Israel, as well as the organizer of Materials for Israel at the crucial period preceding independence. Montor, however, had a distaste for pious phrases, and this did not endear him to the Zionist regulars. When he first went to Lipsky for a job, Lipsky asked him: 'Do you want the job because you are a Zionist or because you need a job?' Montor's answer was: 'I don't give a damn about Zionism.' Lipsky took him on. For quite some time, without Harry's ever knowing it, I used to pay his dues to the Z.O.A. just to keep the wolves from howling. He picked up enemies on every hand by a sort of natural anti-affinity, but the friends he made in those early years still remain close to him though he has long since left the Zionist arena for a successful business career in, of all places, Rome. Marie Syrkin, who became a Professor of English literature at Brandeis University, was the daughter of Nachman Syrkin, one of the founders of the Zionist Socialist movement. She was in those days at the beginning of a distinguished career as Zionist writer and polemicist, and she took over from Chaim Greenberg the editorship of the Zionist Labor monthly, *The Jewish Frontier*, a position she still holds. She had had a short-lived marriage to Maurice Samuel, which was annulled by her father on the grounds of her youthfulness; Samuel was too bohemian for his tastes, a rather strange reaction from a fiery revolutionary socialist.

This regular staff of five was supported by a part-time but industrious auxiliary group of three pregnant women, Sally Brainin, Shirley Weisgal and Martha Neumark. Sally's and Shirley's pregnancies were advanced, Martha's was less obvious, and for some mysterious reason was treated as a secret. There was a vast amount of secretarial work and proofreading to be done—this special issue was twenty-five times the size of the regular edition; for convenience we established a special office in the apartment on University Heights where Joe and Montor were living under one roof. Toward the end Shirley and I moved in with them; it became for the time being a kind of kibbutz. Every morning Sally and Shirley went through a solemn ritual—the careful measurement of their respective girths, and bets were laid as to which would see the light of day first, the infants or the magazine. The magazine won by margins of three and four weeks respectively.

That Hebrew University issue came to be a classic in Zionist journalism and is today a collector's item and a reference source for the period. It contained, among other features, Maurice Samuel's translation of Bialik's immortal poem of *yeshivah* life, *Hamasmid*, which attracted so much attention that I prevailed on Moish to prepare a small volume of Bialik translations, which I edited.

Summing up the effect of the Hebrew University issue of *The New Palestine*, which appeared on March 27, 1925, a week before the inauguration ceremonies of the university, Lipsky wrote, *inter alia:* 'No issue of any periodical ever published by any Zionist Organization, or for that matter by any other Jewish publication agency, has been received with such deep satisfaction and such cordial approbation.' This I believe to be a simple statement of fact. He went on in a crescendo of praise and mentioned in passing that my name appeared 'as of right it should' as editor of the special issue. Actually it was Lipsky himself who put it there to surprise me. He had prepared a slug with my name on it, had sent it to the setter with instructions to insert it in the proper place after I had put the paper to bed and left the printer. The slug became permanent only in 1928. The Zionist Administration was so impressed that it ordered 75,000 more copies. It was just enough to turn our original profit—we had cleared $6,000—into a loss.

Some time after, when I had barely come out of the frenzy of that enterprise, the treasurer of the Organization, Herman Conheim, came to see me. Conheim was a German-Jewish aristocrat, a man of letters, and very rich. He was a brother-in-law of Shmaryahu Levin. He came, with friendly pomposity, to congratulate me personally on the success of the special issue and to inform me that the Administrative Committee had voted me $1,000 as a tribute. I refused it, with probably unnecessary heat, whereupon he said that my answer was offensive. In turn I explained that I was acting entirely on the defensive. In those days $1,000 was quite a sum—especially to me, with my $80-a-week salary. But I had my 'reputation' and my 'future' to consider. If I were to accept a $1,000 tribute, my friends of the opposition would turn it into $10,000 overnight, and there happened to be in existence a semi-underground opposition journal called *Al Hamishmar*, 'On Guard.' Nor would it stop at $10,000: it would portray me as siphoning off enormous public funds into my pocket, and might in the end convince some members of the Administrative Committee who had voted me the tribute in the first place. What was more important, I told him that the Hebrew University issue was only the first of a series of its kind; and I did not want to be accused of being on the lookout for bonuses. Conheim heard me out patiently, pondered the matter, and saw my point of view; nevertheless, he insisted that something had to be done, some mark of appreciation was called for. In the end it was agreed that the Organization would send me as one of its delegates to the forthcoming Zionist Congress.

7 Zionism and Zion

It would be difficult to imagine a more dramatic setting for a Zionist Congress than Vienna in the summer of 1925. This was the city from which Theodor Herzl had gone to Paris as the correspondent of the famous *Neue Freie Presse* to become, to his own astonishment and history's gain, the founder of the modern Zionist movement. Twenty-one years after his death the Fourteenth Congress was being held in Vienna against the background of a ferocious anti-Semitic demonstration by the *Haken-kreuzler*. We did not know, could not even dream, at that time, what horrors lay in wait for the Jews of Europe; even Hitler's name was little known then. The demonstration confined itself during the two weeks of our stay to threats and window smashing; but there was an ugliness in the atmosphere, a sense of foreboding, which brought home to the American delegates the somber realities of the Jewish problem. I wrote my wife: 'Last night was the first genuine feeling I had of what is meant by a pogrom although it was far removed from such. Jews running, hotels closing, streets darkened, police chasing and charging . . .' In another letter, written a day or two later, I wrote something which was probably the typical Zionist reaction in those days, a stupid reaction for which may God forgive us: 'These *Hakenkreuzler* will be making many Jews Zionists.'

Nevertheless, the proceedings of the Congress were little perturbed by the tumult in the streets. This was the international parliament of the Jewish people, convened for a two-week session every two years, and into those two weeks it had to cram both the business of the movement and the emotions accumulated and pent up since the last session. There was magnificent rhetoric, the conflict of divergent ideologies, political maneuvering in the plenum and in committees, and in it all a sense of fellowship overriding the divisions and the personal attacks. Little wonder that the sessions did not break up until the early hours of the morning. Had it not been for Avraham Harzfeld, one of the colorful pioneers of the Palestine colonization efforts, who would end a deadlock by getting everyone to join in Hebrew songs, the sessions might well have run into each other until the delegates dropped in mass exhaustion.

The climax of a Zionist Congress was always the General Debate which followed the reports and the formulation of various resolutions. It was here that the master orators dominated—and at the Fourteenth Zionist Congress the great clash came between Weizmann and Vladimir Jabotinsky. It was a case of high eloquence pitted against supreme debating skill. As I wrote in one of my reports to *The New Palestine:* 'American Zionists know Weizmann as an orator, but they have had little occasion to observe him as a debater. In debate he is unsurpassed, combining an extraordinarily quick wit with a deadly marksmanship which invariably finds the chink in his adversary's armor.'

Jabotinsky was then, and for many years continued to be, Weizmann's most consistent ideological adversary. Eventually he broke away from the Zionist Organization to found the Revisionist Zionist Organization, which fathered the terrorist groups in Palestine and later the right-wing Herut party. Bitter arguments are still being waged in Israel as to which of the two men had indicated the right path. For Jabotinsky the use of force was paramount; Weizmann found it degrading even when it was necessary. The essential philosophic difference between them can be summed up in two Hebrew words: *kagoyim,* 'like the nations,' and *bagoyim,* 'among the nations.' Jabotinsky saw Israel 'like the nations,' rising *b'charbi u–v'kashti,* 'by sword and bow'; Weizmann's motto was: *Zion b'mishpat tipadeh,* 'Zion shall be redeemed in righteousness.'

Jabotinsky was one of the most gifted and fascinating characters on the Jewish scene. Passionate Zionist that he was, he nevertheless made the impression of an un-Jewish Jew. He came to Zionism as an adult, when his education was completed and his character had crystallized. He was already accounted one of the most brilliant journalists of the Russian press, and was a dazzling orator in several languages—Russian, English, Hebrew, Yiddish, German, French, Italian and even Flemish. He was a prolific writer—a novelist and poet—and a master translator. In person he was small, quite ugly, military in his bearing and possessed of tremendous charm. Many compared him to the flamboyant D'Annunzio, of whom he was a great admirer.

During the twenties, when he spent a good deal of time in the United States, he often used my home—with my permission, of course—for

The three strongest influences of my life: Shmaryahu Levin (upper left), Chaim Weizmann (upper right) and Louis Lipsky (below), sitting next to my friend Nahum Goldmann (right), on the occasion of Lipsky's 80th birthday. I sent this picture to Lipsky inscribed: 'Now don't tell me this was not a good speech'

above With Maurice 'Moish' Samuel and Joe Brainin, a trio of more than 50 year's duration. *below* With Gershon Agron (Agronsky), Berl Locker of the Jewish Agency and a young Golda Meir in Jerusalem

Dorothy Thompson, 'the most striking woman whose path ever crossed mine' (see chapter 15), examining a bust of herself I commissioned from Jo Davidson
With Pierre Van Paassen   With Dr. Stephen S. Wise

At last: Editor-in-Chief

political meetings. He knew that I was thoroughly a Weizmannist, but he also knew that I enjoyed a good political set-to; my friends would come to these evenings—Lipsky and Abe Goldberg among them—as to some performance by a star orator, which is perhaps the best description of the occasions. Every gathering ended with poetry readings in several languages by Jabo, as we called him, the women starry-eyed, the men envious.

Jabo's oratory, though of the highest power, lacked the fire and spontaneity, as well as the Jewish content, of Shmaryahu Levin's. Every word and gesture was planned. The story is told that from time to time he would seem to be groping for a word, and would turn to the audience, waiting for someone to supply it. When that happened, Jabo let a quick smile of relief pass across his features. It so happened that one of his admirers followed him from one town to another, and when Jabo in the midst of the same oration began groping for the same word, the fellow rose from his seat and, quite bewildered, said: 'But Mr. Jabotinsky, I told you what it was last night!'

Jabotinsky's demand was for mass immigration into Palestine 'NOW,' whatever the conditions of the country. He accused the Weizmannists of narrowness of vision, pettiness of method, lack of a great program. He claimed to represent the Herzlian dream. Weizmann's rebuttal of Jabotinsky's thesis was merciless: it was, he said, nothing but a play to the gallery, a refusal to reckon with the facts. 'There is no royal road to the Jewish Homeland. There is only the road of slow and patient work.' The exchanges between the two men were stinging and bitter. I was greatly surprised, immediately after the debate in Vienna, to see Weizmann and Jabotinsky walking arm in arm toward a nearby café. I wanted a word with Weizmann, but the sight of this earnest intimacy made me change my mind. With Weizmann political differences did not spill over into personal vindictiveness, even in the case of this arch opponent; the two families remained friendly all their lives. A curious contrast was the relationship between Ben Gurion and Jabotinsky. Although poles apart in ideology, the two men had much in common in political practice; nevertheless—or perhaps consequently—they were at all times mortal enemies, and Ben Gurion carried this enmity even beyond the grave. After the establishment of the State of Israel, Jabotinsky's followers wanted to reinter his bones in Israel, on Mount Herzl, where the Zionist great lay buried. Ben Gurion, then Prime Minister, opposed the idea. It was not until Eshkol succeeded him as Prime Minister that Jabotinsky's remains were accorded a state funeral.

The Vienna Congress was the beginning of my education in world Zionism, and I owed not a little, as a novice, to the wisdom of the man I traveled with from America as a fellow-delegate, and with whom I shared the *Königliche Zimmern* in the Imperial Hotel (at $7.30 a day). Jacob Fishman, the managing editor of *The Jewish Morning Journal* was an almost unique specimen among Yiddish journalists; in style, in manner, he was remote from the verbosity and hyperbole of his colleagues, and belonged rather to the best in English journalism. His daily column was a model of lucidity, and as an editor he put great emphasis on world news and on straight reporting. Yiddish reporting was usually twenty percent fact and eighty percent commentary; until Fishman's time there was actually no such thing as a Yiddish reporter; everyone was a 'writer.' There used to be a quip about *The Chicago Jewish Courier*, a Yiddish daily edited by my friend Melamed: 'How does *The Chicago Tribune* know today what *The Chicago Jewish Courier* is going to write tomorrow?' The same could be said of all the other Yiddish papers, until Fishman became the editor of *The Jewish Morning Journal;* thereafter *The New York Times* could never be accused of anticipating *The Jewish Morning Journal* by twenty-four hours. Fishman's knowledge of the European scene was wide and detailed, and I learned much from him during those two exciting weeks in Vienna. He was a bachelor, a life-long devotee of my wife and her cooking, and a permanent fixture in our house on Friday nights and holidays.

My appetite whetted by the Congress and by the famous European personalities I met there for the first time, I planned to continue my Zionist education by fulfilling my long-cherished dream of getting to Palestine. But the time was not propitious, and for urgent reasons I returned from Vienna to my duties in America. I was, however, determined not to let another year pass without satisfying my hankering. I was by this time in a much stronger position than after the Cleveland break. Besides being the managing editor of *The New Palestine*, I was the National Secretary of the Zionist Organization of America. At the Congress I had been a member of the all-important *Permanenz Ausschuss* (there is no such institution in Anglo-Saxon countries; it is a sort of combination of clearing house for resolutions, nominations, etc. produced by other committees) which justified my presence at the meeting of the Actions Committee of the World Zionist Organization called for June 1926 in London. This time I was not going to stop short in Europe; I would go on to Palestine, and for good measure I would make a pilgrimage to Kikl, the place of my birth, and see Polish Jewry.

I was not in those days the experienced and slightly blasé traveler that I have since become; I was subject to high moods of elation and collapses into despondency. Traveling with Moish Samuel by boat and train to London was a lively experience, but when we arrived at 2 a.m. and Moish's relatives appeared at that unearthly hour and carted him off to the northern wilderness of Lancashire, I suddenly realized that I was absolutely alone in the world metropolis, with not a soul I could telephone or turn to. I felt so lonely and miserable that when I reached the hotel I wept. Most of the night I sat at the window, but by morning I must have been asleep. At nine o'clock the phone woke me, and there was Lipsky's voice, sounding magically strange in that place. He had just arrived in London. 'Hello Meyer! When are you coming to the office?' Lipsky did not usually call me by my first name, and the unexpected warmth of the greeting lifted me back into a friendly world.

When I arrived at the Zionist office Weizmann was already there with other members of the Executive. He embraced me as an old friend, and I remember Miss Lieberman, his secretary, telling me afterwards that this was a signal honor—as indeed I felt it to be. He then invited me into his office and asked me for my impressions of the effect Jabotinsky's visit had produced in American Zionism, and whether the Revisionist movement was making any headway. When I had ended he invited me to sit in on the sessions of the Executive.

There was a great difference between the Actions Committee, of which I was a deputy member, and the Zionist Executive, of which I was not a member. The former was the interim parliament between Congresses, the latter was the equivalent of the cabinet of a government; it was, in brief, the holy of holies of the movement, and it was rare for a non-member to be invited to its sessions. By his action, Weizmann indicated that he put special trust in me, and that he wanted to groom me for a place in the leadership. Looking back on the subsequent years when I worked in intimate association with Weizmann, but not as a Zionist leader, it puzzles me that he, with his subtle and intuitive insights, should have thought of me—if in fact he did—as political material. I had not, and I have not, the finesse demanded for such a career, and my ambitions did not lie in that direction. Certainly I was ambitious, but not for political stardom. To be quite truthful, after the few hectic years in the inner circles of American Zionism, politics had become a bore. I had no stomach for the personal maneuvering, the longwinded speeches, the combinations, the quarrels and reconciliations, and the pompous reports. I must confess that even the sessions of the Zionist Executive, on which I had entered with much awe, soon palled on me. I spent most of the time writing letters to my wife, stopping only when Weizmann or someone like Chaim Arlosoroff took the floor. Arlosoroff was the Secretary of the Palestine Labor Movement, a young man of extraordinary ability, close to Weizmann and obviously destined for great things. He was murdered in Palestine in 1933 in the middle of his career under mysterious circumstances that have not been cleared up to this day.

During that stay in London I had a chance meeting with Hans Herzl, the son of Theodor Herzl. I wrote about him to my wife: 'As you know [he] became a Christian. He is the most tragic figure imaginable. He is dressed shabbily and looks like a lost soul. When I was introduced to him I turned all the colors of the rainbow, and then I almost broke down. *This* the son of Herzl, the greatest Jew of our time. It is unthinkable.'

During the sessions both of the Actions Committee and the Executive the miserable plight of Polish Jewry had been the subject of much discussion. Those were years of frightful economic decline, of a continuous rise of Polish anti-Semitism, of a systematic attempt to destroy the Jewish community by boycott, discrimination and persecution. What I saw during my brief stay bore out the worst of the reports.

Kikl was my first stop. For a long time I had dreamed romantically of this return of the local boy who had made good in the great American world. The reality was a bleak disappointment. First of all, there was almost no one to return to; Kikl was a classical deserted village. The few remote relatives I found there clustered round me eagerly and expectantly—whatever else I was, I was the fabulously opulent American. Sick at heart, I distributed what I had with me—about $500—and left before nightfall. Hardly happier was my visit to Sherpce, the place of my father's birth, where his mother was still living. I had seen very little of her as a child, in spite of the proximity of Kikl to Sherpce. I had retained a kind of photograph in memory from my childhood—a fabulously old woman sitting on a tree stump and nodding her head while she read aloud from the *Tsenerene*, as we pronounced it, the Yiddish devotional book for women. And what was strange about her was the absence of glasses. Few indeed were the old women who could read, and all of them wore glasses with enormously thick lenses. But not my *bobe;* this was what made her different from all other *bobes.*

It was with a sense of the unreal that I found her exactly as my childhood memory had retained her; all the world had changed, but not my *bobe,* Rachel Abba's. There she was, still seated on a tree stump, still reading, without glasses, the tattered *Tsenerene*, and she must have been well on in her nineties. But now I understood the whole picture; the tree stump was at the entrance to her *galanteria*, a tiny dry goods store. The paucity of customers gave her ample time to indulge her pious practice. Of course I had to introduce myself, explain that I was the son of her son Shloyme Chaim, the *chazan*. She examined me and my outlandish apparel very carefully, and then asked me why her son never wrote to her any more; all she got was periodic regards through Lodzia. I don't remember what story I made up to conceal from her that her son had been dead these five years, but somehow I satisfied her.

Sherpce was not as disastrously forlorn as Kikl. My grandmother gathered together whatever family was available and I was honored at a chicken dinner which probably put the family into hock for a month. But the old lady was full of life and humor. When we sat down to dinner she gave me a shrewd smile and said: *shem zikh, ess nit*, turning upside down the traditional Yiddish invitation: 'Don't be shy, eat.' From Sherpce I had to wire to Warsaw for money.

Warsaw itself was an even greater shock. Never had I seen such mass poverty, such haggard and emaciated Jews, such utter squalor and filth. I was torn between pity and nausea. I walked the Nalevky and Szyka and other famous streets of the Warsaw ghetto in a kind of stupor, unable to understand how a people could let itself sink into such ruin and despair.

A few days later I was writing my wife gay letters from aboard the S.S. *Hesperia, en route* to Palestine. The sunshine of the Mediterranean overlaid the ghastly memory of the forlorn Jewry of Poland, and the prospect of the Homeland, with its infinite hope for Jewry, chased the phantoms of the exile out of my mind. I had a foretaste of the boundless optimism of Palestine in the high mood of my fellow-travelers. Among them stands out in my memory, both as person and symbol, Ittamar Ben Avi, the son of Eliezer Ben Yehuda, a legendary figure, who had died in 1922. He may be said to have been the Theodor Herzl of the Hebrew language; as the former had organized the hope of the Return in a modern organization, so the latter had put Hebrew into modern usage. For some four decades he had worked on his monumental lexicon while his wife Hemdah had scoured the western world collecting the funds for its publication. No word but modernized Hebrew had ever crossed the lips of anyone in Eliezer Ben Yehuda's household, and this iron insistence on Hebrew as the language of everyday use, when nearly everyone else regarded it as the language of ritual and scholarship, was an example for

the whole of the Jewish community. Most remarkable of all was his per-
sistence in the face of almost uniform discouragement, and his success—or
his wife's—in raising the means for this work. A mathematical Hebrew
lexicographer once calculated that every new Hebrew word invented by
Ben Yehuda had cost the Jewish people something like $980.

I was too late by four years to make the acquaintance of this remarkable
man; but my friend Joe Brainin, who, the reader will remember, served
with his brother Moe in the Jewish Legion, had met him, in a manner of
speaking, and was fond of recounting the circumstances. Joe and Moe were
quite innocent of Hebrew, but their father, Reuben Brainin, was, as I
have mentioned, among its great modernizers. As an act of piety, Joe
and Moe were to carry their father's greeting and homage to Eliezer Ben
Yehuda. They did not quite succeed. On the one leave of absence which
permitted them to visit the Ben Yehudas they were greeted at the door
by Hemdah, who, with finger on lip, whispered her request for silence,
and promised them the greatest experience of their lives—the sight of
Eliezer Ben Yehuda at work on his fabulous lexicon, on condition, of
course, that he was not to be interrupted. She would lead them by a back
path to the window of his study, and they would be permitted to look
in on one of the wonders of the age. They followed her and at the signal
peeped through the window; and they saw the miracle of Eliezer Ben
Yehuda fast asleep at his desk. That was the nearest they got to him, and
Joe's account of it was the nearest I myself got to the immortal Eliezer
Ben Yehuda.

But his son Ittamar, with whom I traveled on the *Hesperia*, I had already
known in New York, and there was something exactly right having
him as my companion on the ship: he was the first man I had ever heard
speak modern, Sephardic Hebrew, so different from the Hebrew I had
learned in the *cheder*, the singsong *loshn koydesh* of the prayer-book and
the *Torah*. This was a crisp, elegant tongue, with *ahs* and *ots* where we
had had *oos* and *oys*. I once heard him deliver a Hebrew lecture in New
York to an audience of Hebraists of the old school. It was like going to
the opera. The sounds were magnificent and no one understood a word.

Ittamar and I were inseparable on the boat. He was a handsome man
and his thick locks were always falling over his eyes. He was a fascinating
talker, and he began to initiate me into the Sephardic pronunciation of
Hebrew. When we docked in Alexandria overnight we found a crowd of
Jews awaiting us; this was the usual thing when boats arrived with pilgrims
or immigrants 'going up' to Palestine, and there was always the hope
that someone interesting or prominent could be captured for a Zionist

rally. Ittamar pointed to me, announcing in French that I was the National Secretary of the Zionist Organization of America. Under protest I was whisked away to a magnificent mansion filled with beautiful women and handsome men in tarboushes. I was utterly bewildered, and had not the haziest idea how I would speak to them, but Ittamar assured me that I could feel quite free; no one would know what I was talking about and he would be my translator. My speech, if it may be called that, was received with a polite ripple of applause. Then Ittamar got up to translate, first into French, for the majority of the audience, then into Hebrew for the rest. '*Monsieur Weisgal a dit,*' then '*Mar Weisgal amar . . .*' The audience applauded wildly at the end of each rendition, and I had a strong suspicion that any relation between what I had said and Ittamar had 'translated' was tenuous in the extreme. As we left there were loud shouts of '*Vive Weisgal! Vive Weisgal!*'

It is not my intention to give here a picture of the Jewish Homeland in the making as I first saw it more than four decades ago. There are many excellent accounts, to which I could add little. I can only report that the effect on me was stunning. It was infinitely more than I had expected, and infinitely better. I had of course tempered my anticipation by dwelling on all the deficiencies and difficulties I had read about and been told of, but my reaction was quite different from Weizmann's who wrote, con—cerning *his* first visit in 1907: 'I was so anxious to be detached and objective that I denied myself the advantage of my emotions.' *I* covered the land on the wings of an emotional binge. I envied the *chalutzim*, I marveled at Jewish Tel Aviv and I wept at the Wailing Wall.

As was befitting the arrival of the editor of a journal of international repute, I was deferentially welcomed by our Palestinian representative, Gershon Agronsky: 'You bastard, why don't you send us some money? We also have to make a living.' We hugged and kissed and he dragged me off to stay with him in Jerusalem. I must confess that I envied him; he had done what I could not bring myself to do; he had become part of the Palestine scene. All the same, he seemed to hanker a little for the land he had left. We sat up most of the night, and when we were not talking about Palestine I was filling him in on ZOA gossip and especially on the fortunes of 'The Friday Night Club.' This exclusive society had been born in the wake of the more or less simultaneous marriages of its charter members, Gershon, Joe, Harry Montor, Moish, Adam Rosen and myself. During our bachelor days we had been the mainstay of the old Café Royale, the Second Avenue Algonquin of the Yiddish journalistic world.

With all of us suddenly domesticated we had either to disband or reorganize. Every Friday night the six couples would get together at each other's homes, in rotation. Jacob Fishman, the bachelor and sage, both in years and content, was an honorary member; when his turn came round he would play host to us at the Rumanian restaurant on the East Side, Moskowitz and Lupowitz, famous for its cooking and Moskowitz's remarkable performances on the xylophone. Fishman would talk journalism and the history of the East Side, Gershon and I talked Zionism; Moish Samuel and Brainin talked literature in their three languages. Montor's subject, I must record in this truthful chronicle, was his fabulous collection of pornography. The wives carried on a marathon culinary competition, except for Sally Brainin, who could never distinguish between *gefilte* fish and a can of sardines; her specialty—of no use to us— was mathematics. Gershon Agronsky made the first breach in our numbers when he transferred himself and his family to Palestine, and the club breathed its last when I settled in Toronto in 1930. But there were fragmentary resuscitations in later years. Long after Fishman and Gershon had died and Montor had betaken himself to Rome, the remaining three— Moish, Joe, and I—would have Friday evenings as often as I was in town. They were not as lively as they used to be, and the talk had a tendency to drift toward ailments, blood pressure and the shape and size of pills. And now, with Joe recently gone, there survive of that goodly company only Moish and I, and one of our subjects of conversation, when we manage to get together, is the question of precedence. It is agreed between us that Moish would make the better funeral oration for me while I would excel in the funeral arrangements for him.

All that was in the unforeseeable future when I saw Gershon again in Palestine in 1926. He was a busy man; for *The New Palestine* was not the only foreign journal he represented in Jerusalem and on top of everything else he was the press officer of the Palestine Zionist Executive. It was through Gershon that I met his right hand man, Julian Meltzer, who was, many years later, to become *my* right hand man at the Weizmann Institute. In between he was the Jerusalem correspondent for *The New York Times*, a translator of merit and a frequent contributor to *The New Palestine*. When Gershon founded *The Palestine Post*, Julian joined the staff and remained on it as long as Gershon lived. Julian knew every street and alley of Jerusalem. I thought of Rabbi Shmuel who claimed that he knew the heavenly paths more intimately than the streets of Nahardia, and I learned more from Julian in a few days than I could have done from a dozen guide books.

The outstanding event of my first visit to Palestine was my first and last venture into the field of international relations. One day Gershon came up with the brilliant idea that I should head a delegation to the Emir Abdullah, King of Transjordan, in his capital of Amman, bringing him the greetings of American Jewry on the occasion of the Jewish New Year. Even I was slightly aghast at the suggestion. I asked him who could possibly authorize such a delegation and elect me as its spokesman? But these questions were tangential and of no interest to him; as a journalist he was fascinated by the idea as such. Sure enough, he opened negotiations with the palace in Amman, and meanwhile hunted up a few American Jews and invited them to join the delegation; it included Peter Berdishevsky, an authority on beet-sugar chemistry, Madeleine Levin-Epstein, wife of a prominent dentist in Jerusalem, and a few tourists. Somewhat to my dismay an audience was actually arranged.

Gershon had arranged everything in style; a black limousine and chauffeur delivered us at the palace where we were ushered into the Royal Presence. The Emir was dressed in a magnificent flowing *abaya*. I, in deference to my surroundings, sported a *kefiya*, the white Arab headdress with the golden circlet. I felt as if I had stepped into a scene from a second-rate Purim *spiel*. I bowed before His Majesty and delivered my message in English; His Majesty acknowledged it cordially in Arabic. Neither of us understood what the other said so no harm was done, and the following day *The Palestine Post* hailed the encounter as a significant development in Arab-Jewish relations. We spent the evening in an Arab night club as the guests of the Emir. We watched belly-dancers until midnight, when another delegation—a group of sheikhs—appeared on the scene and claimed the royal box. An altercation began between the ushers and the new claimants to the Emir's hospitality. When I saw the glint of jeweled daggers I thought it a high act of diplomacy, as well as the better part of valor, to beat a hasty retreat to the Philadelphia Hotel.

When I returned to New York I wrote a series of articles for *The New Palestine* and *The Brooklyn Eagle;* they were purely reportorial, and the diplomatic coup was given its due; but the deeper effects on me of that first visit to Palestine never appeared in print.

There was a kind of turmoil in me. A number of my friends had already settled in Palestine; their decision was the logical outcome of their Zionism; but I did not follow their example for another thirty years. Even then the decision was made for me, and though I accepted it with alacrity, it troubled me that I had not acted with their determination and consistency.

I could explain this irresolution ideologically. The fact is that I have never believed, as Ben Gurion does, that to be a Zionist one must settle in Israel. On the other hand I never believed, with the Brandeisists, that Israel was only for the poor and oppressed, while the Zionism of American Jews was best expressed in dollars. Finally, I did not (and do not) consider the achievement of national and political sovereignty the ultimate goal of Zionism. For me Zionism has always been the most comprehensive expression of the revitalization of Jewish life, drawing strength from the re-creation of a Jewish civilization in that ancient, derelict land on the shores of the Mediterranean. Settlement, investment and political independence were all instruments in the process; but the power of Zionism lay in its regeneration of Jewish life everywhere, in the elevation of its form and content. It is possible that in the light of the tragedy of European Jewry this concept will seem facile and even meaningless; for me it is the only concept of Zionism I can hold on to. The failure of Zionism to save the Jews of Europe is no more relevant to its meaning than the failure of Socialism or of Christianity to stay the hands of the murderers.

My Zionism found full expression in America; it would have found just as full expression in Israel. Why then did I not make the change earlier? The answer dawned on me in my later years, and it explained something that goes back to my early manhood years. When I contemplated joining the Jewish Legion in 1917, it was not only my prior induction into the American army that prevented me. There was also a certain hesitancy. I was quite conscious that everything I had achieved—not much, to be sure—I owed to America. A profound gratitude, which has grown with the years, held me in its coils. An equally profound attachment pulled me toward Israel. I was always haunted by that wonderful phrase of Yehuda Halevi's: *libi b'mizrach ve'anochi b'sof maarav*, 'my heart is in the East and I am in the West.' As the years passed, and my sojourns in Palestine and, afterwards, Israel, became longer and longer, the phrase reversed itself. When I was in Rehovot I wanted to be in New York, when I was in New York I wanted to be in Rehovot. Which was the wife and which the mistress, I found hard to say.

8   Last Days of Editorship

I have already described how, after the great 1921 split in American Zionism, the Brandeis-Mack-de Haas group, the secessionists, gradually
returned to the Zionist Organization of America. By 1927 they once again
occupied most of the high offices, though their opposition to the national
funds and their narrow emphasis on private capital had not diminished.
They had not forgiven their defeat in Cleveland; in particular they har-
bored a deep resentment against Louis Lipsky, who had emerged as the
unquestioned leader of American Zionism. For that matter, in spite of
their rising influence he was still the man beloved by the Zionist rank
and file, and they were determined to undermine his position on the home
front and strike through him at Weizmann. Because of their prominence
they already controlled the purse strings of the movement in America
and their devotion to the cause of Palestine was equalled, paradoxically,
by their hostility to the World Zionist Organization. Weizmann was
of course thoroughly aware of the situation. He wrote at the time to
Lipsky: 'They seem to wish to drive the Zionist Organization into bank-
ruptcy. They have not buried the hatchet at all. America is starving
Palestine and destroying a great many forces which will never again come
into the movement.'

From 1922 on, when the League of Nations ratified the Balfour Declaration in the San Remo Decision, Weizmann had been working toward
the extension of the Jewish Agency for Palestine, as stipulated in that
decision. The plan was to bring into the work those large Jewish bodies
which were interested in the development of Jewish settlement in Palestine
while disowning identification with the Zionist movement and its philosophy. During several visits to America Weizmann had succeeded in
gaining the support of men like Louis Marshall, who like Brandeis was
a great jurist and was widely respected for his Jewish community work,

and Felix Warburg, a senior member of the banking firm of Kuhn, Loeb and Company and a prominent philanthropist. Both men, unjustly called assimilationists by some, were non-Zionists. In the oddest way, Weizmann needed these men not only for their financial power, but in order to offset through their influence among non-Zionist organizations the efforts of the Brandeisists to win control of the Zionist movement. It should be noted again that Justice Brandeis himself maintained no public connection with the group to which his name was attached.

All these developments naturally affected me, both as editor of *The New Palestine* and Secretary of the Zionist Organization. *The New Palestine* was under constant attack on three fronts. The anti-Weizmann Zionists attacked it for being pro-Weizmann, the pro-Weizmann non-Zionists for being too Zionist, the pro-Weizmann Zionists within the Organization for being too imaginative. In short, I was in a state of perpetual conflict. I even resigned four or five times, but never—until the sixth time or so— emphatically enough. It was always Lipsky who dissuaded me from taking the fateful step, but the atmosphere became more and more suffocating.

At the risk of sounding more than usually immodest I must record that I was actually the chief cook and bottle washer in the American Zionist Organization. Lipsky was the leader; I was his Chief of Staff, reconnaissance man and trouble-shooter. Although primarily editor of *The New Palestine* I was, as National Secretary, a formally elected officer. Just as the Brandeisists were aiming at Weizmann through Lipsky, they were aiming at Lipsky through me. At the 1928 Convention they came up with a not-too-ingenious but effective bit of strategy. I was to remain the National Secretary but as an appointed employee, not as an elected officer. It is obviously easier to give the boot to an appointee than to get rid of a nationally elected officer. I balked, of course, but again Lipsky argued me out of my stand; he softened the blow by pointing out sagely that power resides within. In the long run he was right, but involved in daily battles as I was, I could not see it philosophically. A year later Lipsky himself was voted out of power, and he proceeded to prove his point by remaining, for many years, the untitular leader of American Zionism. The fact is that, like Weizmann, he never had a successor, only replacements.

At the beginning of 1929, on the twenty-fifth anniversary of Herzl's death, I began work on the Herzl Memorial Issue of *The New Palestine*, modeled on the successful Hebrew University special issue of 1925. I had every right to expect wide and enthusiastic support, but I should have known better. This time I had to contend not only with the objections of the Administrative Committee as a body and the indifference of its members as individuals, but with a new peril in the form of an efficiency expert, Dr. I. M. Rubinow, who had been the first head of the Hadassah Medical Unit in Palestine. His main function was to watch my every move like a hawk and raise objections the moment I moved a foot. The theory behind Rubinow's appointment was that imagination is the antithesis of efficiency. It was not easy to edit the weekly, gather additional material for the special issue, and run all over the country raising money, for of course I again had to do all my own advance financing. But this last chapter had a surprise happy ending. I was invited to St. Louis to address the local community on behalf of my special project, and Dr. Rubinow was despatched to keep tabs on me. I addressed the meeting in the basement of the Statler Hotel, and the audience was so impressed that it promised me $3,000. But Rubinow seemed to be even more impressed than the audience, for when I had finished he made a big supporting speech and on his return to New York told the Administrative Committee that they were crazy, that I was doing a wonderful job and that he intended to help me to the best of his ability.

The Herzl Memorial Edition of *The New Palestine* was, I believe, something unique in Zionist journalism for scope and thoroughness; it remains to this day a valuable reference work for the whole Herzl period of Zionist history. I ransacked the entire surviving Herzlian world for material, appointing representatives in all the European capitals for research into little known facts about the father of political Zionism. Among the contributors to the issue were Martin Buber, who had worked with Herzl, Georges Clemenceau (whose speeches in the Chambre Herzl had often reported), Stefan Zweig, Max Brod, Edmond Fleg, André Spiro, and my own private battery of writers. Maurice Samuel produced the first English translation (condensed) of the Herzl diaries, one of the highlights of the issue. I also got a tribute—I can no longer remember how this came about—from Ferdinand, King of Bulgaria. I dedicated the issue to Louis Lipsky, 'Leader, Teacher and Friend.'

At about that time there were rumors—I have no idea who started them—that I was leaving *The New Palestine* to bestow my talents on the Jewish Telegraphic Agency, recently founded and headed by Jacob Landau and Meir Grossman. Felix Warburg approved of the idea, it seems, for he wrote a letter to Weizmann saying: 'The vaporings of *The New Palestine* are just hot air with a good deal of poison gas in it. Unfortunately some of the papers read this stuff and take it for granted that it represents your and your colleagues' minds. I don't know if there is any truth in it, but I hear that Weisgal is leaving this noble sheet and going over to the Jewish Telegraphic Agency. I am sorry for Landau but I am not crying any tears for his leaving *The New Palestine*, for after all the tone in which he speaks . . . is impertinent, schoolboylike, and I am damned if this sort of rabble can put me on the defensive for statements which our official mouthpiece (for it is regarded as such) makes. It is for that reason that I suggest that, under the pretext of the $100,000 which we can use for better purposes, this sheet be discontinued for the time being.'

Weizmann never said a word to me about this letter, which came to my attention many years later; I insert it here as an example of the hostility which surrounded me. Warburg was, I think, misguided by his advisers; in time I was to become personally acquainted with him and to appreciate his great qualities.

When the Herzl issue was off my hands I went to the Zionist Congress in Zurich (1929), which was followed by the establishment of the enlarged Jewish Agency. Weizmann had managed to make of it a great representative body of the outstanding Jews of that time, Albert Einstein, Léon Blum, Lord Melchett, Felix Warburg, Louis Marshall, the leaders of the Yishuv (the Jewish settlement in Palestine), representatives of every Jewish community in Europe, Sholem Asch, Chaim Nachman Bialik—in short, artists, writers, scientists, left-wing socialists, right-wing industrialists and philanthropists, Jews of every variety of outlook (some of them, like Léon Blum, almost at the assimilationist end of the spectrum) united on one simple principle: the practical upbuilding of the Jewish National Home. It was a personal triumph for Weizmann, and, more important, for Jewish unity. But it was also a prelude to one of our bitterest experiences.

Many of the delegates and journalists at the Congress (I was there in both capacities) retired to Carlsbad and Marienbad for a rest after two weeks of strenuous and exciting deliberations. It was there that we heard of the Grand Mufti's reaction to the establishment of the Jewish Agency: riots had broken out over nearly all of Palestine, over one hundred and fifty Jews were murdered, and an immense amount of property was destroyed. The news came in successive waves, bringing, day after day, new casualty lists. The Carlsbad contingent moved to Marienbad, where we received from Avinoam Yellin, newly arrived from Palestine, a detailed report of the events (Yellin himself was killed in the riots of 1937). In Marienbad we constituted ourselves as a kind of rump Congress and formulated a memorandum containing ten demands on the British Government, whose vacillations and spurious 'even-handedness' was very close to complicity in the riots. For some reason which now escapes me I was chosen to deliver this document to Weizmann for transmission to the British Government. The Committee were in a hurry, and I was ordered to fly. (It occurs to me that I was perhaps considered the most expendable delegate. Flying was by no means as common in 1929 as it is now, and I remember that I boarded the plane frightened to death.)

Back in New York the week following, I cast about for means to bring home to our readers the full significance of what had happened in Zurich and in Palestine. I badly needed an affirmation, an encouraging statement. I learned that Winston Churchill, a friend of the Zionist cause, was lecturing in California, and I wired him for an article. I learned from his agent that I could get one—at a dollar a word. Without consulting anyone I asked for a thousand words. Churchill wrote, *inter alia:* 'Anyone who has seen, as I have, the beautiful garden township of Tel Aviv, or the fruitful groves of Rishon le-Tsion, will need no further convincing. Here, out of the blistering desert, patience, industry and civilized intelligence have created green smiling fields and vineyards and delicious shady groves, the home of happy, thriving, simple communities who even if there had been no Balfour Declaration would deserve the strong protection and the sympathies of free and enlightened people in every quarter of the globe.'

My first step on receiving the article was to hand it over to *The New York Times*, where it was prominently featured—a great coup for Zionism in those days, when a paragraph on the tenth page was usually what we got for a pro-Zionist statement. But when the bill came in the Administrative Committee went into convulsions. Who was this Winston Churchill? Just a former British Chancellor of the Exchequer, a former Secretary of the Colonies and one of the most brilliant journalists and lecturers of his day. Why, asked a member of the Administrative Committee passionately, should he be paid a dollar a word when for five dollars the thousand any Zionist hack could produce the same words, more or less? This was the atmosphere in the Zionist Organization of America in 1929, and this is what it remained for the next thirty years.

I had been up to my neck in it for fifteen years, and after my experiences in Palestine and Europe I felt that the ZOA reeked of provincialism. There was no *Schwung*, no *élan*, no incentive to the imagination, no intellectual challenge. There was Warburg's letter to Weizmann: I did not learn about it till much later, I only felt its effects in an obscure, frustrating way. There were the Brandeisists, who had never forgiven me for *The New Maccabean*, to mention only one of my misdemeanors.

Louis Marshall, the hope of the new pro-Palestine forces in America, died suddenly. Lipsky was no longer in command. I had to get out.

Toward the end of 1929 I sat one day in my office meditating on the next step when a lady walked in and introduced herself as Rose Dunkelman. She was a very large and very pleasant lady; she at once made the impression—which an ensuing friendship confirmed—of strength, decisiveness, determination, and, at the same time, of warmth, generosity, and idealism. I had never seen her before; I only knew that the Dunkelmans were Canadian Zionists and one of Canada's largest textile manufacturers.

'Mr. Weisgal,' she said, 'forgive me for bothering you like this, but we need an editor,' and she went on to explain. Toronto had acquired a new rabbi by the name of Maurice Eisendrath, a furious anti-Zionist who was poisoning the air of Toronto with his articles in *The Jewish Review*. At stake, said Rose Dunkelman, was nothing less than the soul of Toronto and perhaps of all Canadian Jewry. She wanted to found a paper which should be the antidote to *The Jewish Review*, and to that end she had purchased a moribund weekly which she proposed to rename *The Jewish Standard*. 'We need an editor,' she repeated, 'and we are willing to finance him. Can you get me someone like you?' With my usual restraint and modesty, I said: 'Mrs. Dunkelman, there is no one like me; you can have the original if you like.' She was nonplussed, but she seemed to like the idea. The enormity of my impulse dawned on me only after she had left.

On the strength of this verbal offer and immediate acceptance I at last resigned in earnest, as National Secretary, Editor of *The New Palestine* and member of half a dozen committees. I must admit that the funeral arrangements were all that could have been asked. A dinner was given me at the Astor Hotel, complete with half a dozen professional eulogists, and, I permit myself to say, a few genuine mourners. Among these last were Lipsky and Fishman; Weizmann cabled a warm message.

During the interim, while I was winding up my connection with *The New Palestine*, contributing my first articles to *The Jewish Standard*, and arranging for the transfer of my family, which now included Mendy, age five, and Helen, age three, I talked myself into the happy belief that just as the provincial town of Manchester could have its famous *Guardian* so the provincial town of Toronto could have its famous *Standard*. I will not claim that *The Jewish Standard* quite equaled *The Manchester Guardian* at its best, but it was a good paper while it lasted. The trouble was that it did not last very long. Nor did my illusion that I would no longer have to flounder in the swamp of Zionist politics; I merely found myself in a somewhat colder annex. Toronto was a wonderful city, the most cheerful I have ever lived in, with some of the friendliest and warmest Jews and Zionists. But Canadian Zionism had begun to veer toward Revisionism, and toward the support of Jabotinsky against Weizmann. I thought then, I think now, that Revisionism was a dangerous deviation from the basic principles of the Zionist movement, and I threw myself into the fight with all my energies. Unfortunately this kind of preoccupation was not conducive to the production of an independent Jewish journal of high literary merit; I was constantly involved in the kind of political infighting which was bound to have its repercussions in the paper; it was, after all, a Zionist publication. On one flank I battled with the Revisionists, who declared themselves to be the super-Zionists, on the other I was holding off the anti-Zionists led by Rabbi Eisendrath.

During my two years in Toronto I conducted a weekly debate with Rabbi Eisendrath, who was the pastor of the Holy Blossom Synagogue, the home of the rich assimilated Jews and the citadel of anti-Zionism. Debate is perhaps not the right word; it was a verbal donnybrook with no holds barred. I can still feel a stirring of the blood remembering some of my attacks on him. About thirty years later I was in Washington with Myer Feldman, President Kennedy's (and later Johnson's) adviser on Jewish affairs. It was a Sunday afternoon, and Feldman insisted that I accompany him to some important affair, which turned out to be a private reception attended by about a hundred people. The honoree (to use the 'inspiring' word now current) was Rabbi Eisendrath, now President of the Union of American Hebrew Congregations. Within a few minutes, at Eisendrath's request, I was making a little speech. The Toronto days were far away, almost over the horizon, but I described with some candor the sulphurous spirit of our former relationship, admitting that since then I had become mellower and he had become wiser—by becoming a Zionist.

The depression hit Canada somewhat later than the United States, and perhaps with less force, but soon there was no money for such luxuries as an educational publication. One day Mrs. Dunkelman and her friends came to me and offered me $50,000 to take the paper over. I answered with Dr. Weizmann's observation when he received a gift of some Arabian horses from the Emir Feisal: 'I don't like gifts that eat.' All I could promise was to help until I found a new position.

My two-year stint with *The Jewish Standard* of Toronto was made memorable for me by my deeper involvement, toward the close, with

European and world Zionism. I attended the Seventeenth Zionist Congress, at Basle, as delegate and correspondent. It was there that I met Dr. Nahum Goldmann, later President of the World Zionist Organization and of the World Jewish Congress. When I saw him for the first time he was surrounded by a bevy of beauties, his natural decor for many years. I was captivated by his bonhomie and his conversational charm. In 1931 he was probably the youngest of the rising stars on the Zionist firmament; almost of the same age was Chaim Arlosoroff, the Palestine labor leader, equally brilliant and promising, but cast in an entirely different mold. During his many years in the movement Goldmann was alternately pro- and anti-Weizmann. At the 1931 Congress he was in one of his anti-phases, and I, taking the matter much to heart, disagreed with him violently. Nevertheless it was impossible not to enjoy his company, and our political differences did not cut across our developing friendship.

I remember sitting next to Shmarya Levin during Nahum's speech at that Congress. Shmarya listened with the appreciative but critical attention of a connoisseur. When the applause had died down he made the penetrating observation: '*Der umglik mit Nochumke iz, es kumt im on azoy leicht. A rede muz men oysveytikn.* The trouble with Nahum is that he does it so easily. A speech must be sweated out.' Whatever its general truth, the observation applied excellently to Nahum. Despite his outstanding gifts and his dedication, he was incapable of agonizing over anything, whether it was an address, or a beautiful woman, an article, or a political action. Everything came to him easily. He has for that reason been unjustly accused of lightmindedness. One can be quite serious while expressing oneself with urbanity and wit. Nahum, aware of the accusation, dismisses it with a smile. Once, in New York, he was introduced by Lipsky as 'the great moderator.' He repudiated the characterization with a smile: 'Mr. Lipsky has called me a moderator. What is a moderator? A man who has no passions. That certainly does not apply to me. I am like Vesuvius, boiling within, covered with lava; only rarely do I erupt.'

A charming and capable man whom I met again at that Congress was Dr. Arthur Ruppin, a German Jew and the foremost colonizing expert in Palestine at that time. Aside from his great contribution to practical Zionist work he was an outstanding sociologist. With him I had developed a friendship during his visits to America. Our conversations were carried on in German; at least his end was German, mine was something called *Kongressdeutsch*, a variety of the language which was neither German nor Yiddish but a rather interesting conflict between the two.

Some years earlier, while I was still with *The New Palestine*, Ruppin had come into my office and asked me for a photograph of myself. I was rather astonished, and asked him, 'What for?' 'A remembrance,' he said. I was flattered enough to betake myself to an expensive photographer. A few weeks later Ruppin was back in my office. He had been to Baltimore and made the acquaintance of my brother Abba. '*Ja*, a charming man. He speaks a better German than you. Could I have a picture of him too?' I was baffled by this weakness for the Weisgal type of beauty, but made arrangements to have him receive Abba's picture.

It was not until 1931 that the mystery was solved, not exactly to my satisfaction. At the Congress Ruppin presented me with the two heavy volumes of his classic work, *Die Soziologie der Juden*, in which, in a sort of rogues' gallery of Jewish faces, Abba and I appeared side by side. Under us was a notation that though we came of the same parents, one of us—myself—was of a Mediterranean type, the other Aryan. I might have forgiven him his subterfuge if he had not labeled us *Galizianer*, that ultimate insult in Yiddish folklore.

But the 1931 Congress was otherwise a memorable event for me because I was drawn there into closer contact with Weizmann, who had already become a dominating influence in my life, and with whom I was to work for the best part of two decades. That closer intimacy came about in the midst of a great political turmoil.

For the world at large, not less than for the Jewish people, the name of Chaim Weizmann had by that time become synonymous with Zionism. It was, with justice, indissolubly linked with the promulgation of the Balfour Declaration and with the granting of the Mandate over Palestine, with the redemption of the soil of the country and with the creation of its new cities, with the founding of the university and with the emergence of the new Hebraic culture. It was difficult to think of any important aspect of the national renaissance which did not bear the stamp, or at least carry some unforgettable trace of his creative participation. Yet 1931 was the year in which the movement rejected his leadership. The 17th Congress was a turbulent and passionate affair. It marked the end of many old friendships; it threatened to split the movement as it had been split once before, when it turned down the offer Herzl had received from the British Government for a substitute territory—albeit as a temporary one—in East Africa; it left behind the rankling memory of what looked like an act of national ingratitude.

The deep crisis through which the movement was passing could not be blamed on the leadership. The British government in London was revealing an ever-growing reluctance to implement the promise of the

Balfour Declaration, and the administration in Palestine, taking its cue from its superiors, was unsympathetic and uncooperative. The riots of 1929, and all that they had revealed of the scarcely veiled hostility of some of the high colonial officials, were still fresh in our memories. The Zionist treasury reflected the worldwide economic depression. On top of this an acrimonious controversy was raging in the Zionist ranks on the question of what was called the *Endzil*, or ultimate goal of the movement, allied to the question of 'a Jewish majority.' On this issue Weizmann had been outrageously misrepresented, and his refusal to issue bombastic statements was held against him. The delegates met in a frustrated and angry mood, which vented itself at the crucial moment in a vote of no confidence in the leader.

The next day I sent off the following dispatch to my paper:

. . . A curious thing happened. The opposition which for weeks and months has been assiduously preparing for its day of triumph was not jubilant over its victory. It was, instead, depressed. Even the bitterest foe felt intuitively a sense of remorse. But what the opposition did not realize was that this attempt at political assassination would become the symbol of Weizmann's apotheosis. For the moment there was only confusion, uncertainty, and a general questioning: 'What will Weizmann do now. Will he return to the Congress? Will he sulk in this tent?'

The closing session was convened. Weizmann was no longer on the rostrum—that three-tiered, improvised platform dominated in the background by a huge likeness of Herzl which gave the Zionist Congress the dignity and solemnity of a great national assembly. Weizmann in his familiar posture, his left hand over his brow, staring seemingly into emptiness, was missing. A strange, almost guilty feeling pervaded the Congress hall. The delegates' seats were sparsely occupied. The left wing of the Congress hall was entirely empty. The presiding officer rapped the gavel and asked the ushers to gather in the delegates from the lobbies and from their various caucuses. Gradually the seats began to fill up. But the left wing was still largely empty. Suddenly two ushers opened a side door and the figure of Weizmann, tall, stately, his expression grave, emerged, followed by a hundred or more delegates of the Labour Zionist wing. Slowly, and in measured step, as was his wont, he walked at the head of this group to the section reserved for the labour delegation. The atmosphere became electric. An ovation began, spreading in waves from the galleries to the hall, and thence to the platform. The whole Congress was engulfed in it. Weizmann remained seated. The applause gathered volume and continued till he was compelled to rise from his seat. It was the signal for a renewed acclamation. The delegates wept and in effusive continental fashion embraced and kissed each other. At that Congress, in the moment of his defeat, Weizmann was anointed the leader of his people.

The opening line of the dispatch read: 'Leaders are sometimes elected, sometimes not. Weizmann belongs to the elect.' As I walked on my way to the telegraph office, myself still deeply moved, I saw Weizmann slumped in a big chair in an extreme corner in the lobby of the 'Drei Koenige'

Hotel. He wore an old pullover and was sunk deep in thought. I approached him, the telegraph form in my hand, and he looked up. 'What particular piece of bilge are you sending off now?' he asked. 'Hadn't you better reserve judgment until you've seen it in the paper?' I answered. 'You're very optimistic,' was his retort. He motioned me to draw up a chair and as I did he said: 'Remember, no interviews.' 'Now that you're no longer President,' I answered, 'why should I want to interview you?' We both laughed, and Weizmann said, in Yiddish, '*Zei nisht kein sheygets*— don't be impudent.' We talked for some time of the Congress, of personal matters. He told me that now he supposed he would have plenty of time to write his memoirs, something he had wanted to do for a long time. On this we parted. But it must be remembered that Weizmann was then only in his fifty-seventh year, and his greatest labors and triumphs still lay before him: his memoirs were a long way off.

From that day on there was a different coloration in my relations with Weizmann. Inexplicably the ex-American Zionist functionary, about to become an ex-Canadian Jewish journalist and editor, who had sworn 'no return to the Zionist jungle,' began to address himself to the disavowed leader of the world Zionist movement as 'My dear Chief.'

9 'My Dear Chief'

And so it began—my long and close association with Chaim Weizmann. It started with a letter to 'My dear Chief,' the first of many hundreds written in 1931, shortly after my return from the Congress, the last in 1952, a few weeks before his death. The form of address never changed. He was 'My dear Chief' in and out of Zionist office; he remained 'My dear Chief' when he became the first President of the State of Israel.

Over the years many theories have been spun, friendly and otherwise, concerning my relationship to Weizmann. Those who knew us both and had no axe to grind, men like Isaiah Berlin, Louis Lipsky, Maurice Samuel, took the view that the relationship was founded on spiritual rapport as well as profound community of interest. On the other hand there was Lewis Namier, one of the important historians of the twentieth century, and an early collaborator of Weizmann's, who long regarded the relationship as a symptom of Weizmann's intellectual decline. He referred to me, in less somber moments, as Dr. Weizmann's court jester. Between these two extremes there was a whole range of reactions among Zionist functionaries and Zionists at large; at best I was a useful if pretentious understrapper, but the majority considered me an intruder into the private sanctuary of their Chief, as did, in passing, Mrs. Weizmann, who resented my intimacy with her husband. I had latched on to Weizmann, unneeded, unwanted, undetachable, in order to shine in his reflected glory. These derogatory opinions became particularly acerbic when I was officially appointed his personal representative in the United States in 1941.

By then I had known him for twenty years. It will be recalled that I met him for the first time on his first visit to New York in 1921, when I arranged the mass reception for him. I have already recorded that I was one of a dozen secretaries moving in and out of the hotel where he was staying and that I wasn't aware that I made any particular impression on him. I knew a great deal about him, of course, and had long admired him from afar. I was a Weizmannist ideologically, for I had imbibed my Zionism from Lipsky and Shmarya Levin. My admiration for the man increased sevenfold when I met him in person. He was then in the prime of his manhood, of majestic bearing, gracious, slightly aloof in public, but in private possessed of a personal warmth rare among leaders. What was most remarkable about him was the hypnotic charm he radiated. To use a much-abused word, he was charismatic to an extraordinary degree.

I can hardly speak of any relationship between us during the first ten years, yet it was during the very first visit that a communicating spark passed between us. It was in New York, after the famous Cleveland Convention. Weizmann addressed a rally, appealing to the Brandeis group to 'lay down their arms' and not attempt to destroy the Zionist Organization after their defeat. It was held in a hall on Second Avenue and Sixteenth Street, and I had been assigned to conduct him there and bring him back to his hotel. I was waiting in the wings when he walked off the stage. '*Nu, vi iz dos geven?* How was it?' he asked me. I answered: '*A gevald!* Tremendous!' He was pleased. It was, I think, exactly the word he wanted. I am not speaking of the commonplace compliment, or of the Yiddish language as such, except in so far as it was Kikl Yiddish, for Weizmann too came from Kikl, though his Kikl was called Motol. That particular word, in that particular place, with its note of admiration but not without its touch of humor, was of the *shtetl*. It might almost have been a password between us.

When I was admitted to his friendship in years to come, Weizmann always lapsed into Yiddish in our private conversations. There are Yiddish phrases freighted with associations that cannot be attached to English, and when Weizmann used them he knew that I needed no explanations or comments. But the rapport between us was not only linguistic; it had a basis in my intuition, and I am convinced this was a major factor in the shaping of our relationship. Weizmann's Yiddish was richer than mine; his intellect was immeasurably superior; his bearing and outlook were aristocratic; he was a scientist of the first rank and as a political figure had been in contact with the leading statesmen of his time. But there was one important, basic similarity: we were both offshoots of the *shtetl*, transplanted into the Western world, embracing it, yet never for a moment estranged from our beginnings.

Actually I did not remember that anything more than this reciprocal susceptibility existed between us at the time until recently when I came across the following letter from Weizmann written soon after his departure from America in 1921:

My dear Weisgal,   *Confidential S.S. Celtic,* 2/VII/21

    I have read through the scenario which Miss Loeb gave me and I find it rather atrocious. You must use all your influence to dissuade her from publishing it. It would only sound as a very cheap advertisement for all of us, melodramatic perversions of the truth, and would do infinite harm. I am writing to her directly too, but of course I cannot offend her by telling her what I really think of this creation. How are you all? I hope you are taking a little rest. I had a splendid rest on the voyage, which was ideal. Please give my kindest regards and *Shaloms* to everybody.

Yours ever,
Ch. Weizmann

It appears that my existence did impress itself upon him. First of all, he was convinced that I could exert influence in some quarters; more important, he trusted me.

It goes without saying that whatever side activities we pursued, he in the field of science, I in journalism and—as will be recounted shortly— the theatre, we were always immersed in the movement; there was always for both of us, a connection between Zionism and our other activities. The harmony of our origins and of our commitments balanced the differences between us in character, temperament, position and fields of endeavor. There is a German expression: '*Mit diesen Unterschied, möchte ich Klavierspielen.*' I could charge ahead with my bluster and *chutzpe* and accomplish things which I sensed to be necessary to the Weizmann conception of things. Weizmann never gave me orders or instructions, never told me 'do this' or 'do that.' It would have been foreign to our relationship. We were both going in the same direction, he on the high road, I on the low road, and we did not have to call the signals. My trust in him was implicit, as was his trust in me. He could not have done the things I did just as I could not have done the things he did. In the final reckoning, which I permit myself to make soberly after some fifty years, I was as necessary to Weizmann as he was to me.

Trotsky writes in his autobiography that 'writing one's life was the most difficult of all literary tasks. One is compelled to write about oneself.' I must confess that I found it extremely difficult especially when dealing with Weizmann. It would be absurd to parallel myself in any way with Weizmann. He was the greatest Jew of the twentieth century. Chance or destiny or whatever one wants to call it catapulted me into his orbit, and there I revolved for many, many years, close to him at his moments of triumph and his moments of bitter defeat. I was overawed, sometimes dazzled by his personality, but I was not altogether blind to his weaknesses. Like all great men he was generously endowed with these too. His trajectory was enormous. From the heights of euphoria or exuberance he could sink in a few minutes to the depths of depression. In these moments he was unreasonable, unapproachable, and his prejudices became self-defeating. It often required a jest or an irreverent remark to bring him back into high gear and I like to believe that this was one of my functions. Weizmann's close friend, Isaiah Berlin, evaluated this relationship better than anything I can offer; moreover he had the advantage of being objective as he was never personally involved. He wrote:

> He [Meyer Weisgal] was fortunate to have found in Dr. Weizmann the incarnation of his own ideal of what a man and (what he cared about more) a Jew could be. But Dr. Weizmann was fortunate, too, in having found in him a man whose combination of utter (if not uncritical) devotion and warm vitality responded to his own highly imaginative and many-sided sense of life.
>
> Men with such fiery, impatient, and large demands upon life as those that Meyer Weisgal has always made—above all, men as contemptuous of what is dry or small—inevitably attract a certain amount of criticism. I can vouch for the fact that Dr. Weizmann, whatever may have passed between him and Weisgal when they were alone, used to rise like a lion to his defense whenever the mildest reservation about him was expressed. He understood and valued the central characteristics of his friend and disciple—his fearlessness, his dedication, and his enthusiasm: Meyer was prepared to risk everything in a cause in which he believed, never retreated, never temporized, and openly scorned those who did. These honorable and gallant characteristics appealed to Dr. Weizmann deeply—he disliked craveness, self-protectiveness, and meanness more than most other vices.

I do not take wholly amiss Namier's characterization of me as Weizmann's court jester although he meant it derogatorily. I *could* make Weizmann laugh. I would often take the sting out of a nasty situation with a Yiddishism or anecdote. Weizmann never allowed himself the luxury of easy-going conviviality in public, but in his inmost nature he was a warm-hearted Jew, and it was hard on him that he should so seldom be able to act like one. For thirty years he was so to speak the royal emissary of the Jewish people. As the acknowledged leader he had, in and out of office, to maintain a certain distance, even with his Zionist colleagues. At the risk of being indiscreet I would add that despite the deep affection between him and Mrs. Weizmann, the atmosphere at home was charged with decorum. Mrs. Weizmann, it should be remembered, was a Russian-Jewish aristocrat. She did not speak Yiddish and was a stranger to the humor of the *shtetl;* and it was in a sense to the *shtetl* in me that Weizmann turned for relief. He would tell me some *chochme*, and I would reply in kind; but even in moments of the most friendly intimacy there were lines I never crossed.

These turns in our conversation, these anecdotes, intimate homely expressions, consecrated pleasantries, folklore references, helped him through many difficulties and frustrations. But they could only do so because he knew that I took my work—though not myself—very seriously. He also knew that though I was always ready to see the humorous side of things, I was dead serious about my Zionism. I had exchanged a number of letters with him before I began the 'My dear Chief' series, and though he was not exactly a religious reader of *The New Palestine*, he saw enough of it to get some measure of my straightforwardness in expressing my views, which were wholly in accordance with his. He had come to trust my opinions not out of any high regard for my ideological profundity, or my political astuteness, but out of a sense of rapport. I do not regard it as a virtue that I have no skill as a politician; I merely record it, and I believe that this struck a sympathetic chord in Weizmann. He himself was not a political operator. He was superbly skillful at the diplomatic chess game, and in political bargaining adept at detecting an adversary's weakness. A calm, unshakeable self-assurance helped him to ride out a political storm without revealing the vulnerable points of his own position; but he had no taste, no aptitude for that infighting which is the essence of political combat. His self-assurance was based on his faith in the ultimate triumph of morality and justice.

It could not be otherwise, for he was never able to deal from positions of strength either in the Zionist movement or in his negotiations with the British. He used to say that whenever he went to an interview with a British cabinet minister or another highly placed person he kept his fists clenched. 'If I ever opened them they would see that I've got nothing.' He never even developed what might be called a Weizmann party within the movement. Though his sympathies were always left of center, with Labor and the kibbutzim, he was never officially identified with any party of the left or right. He took his stand on principles which cut across political divisions and opposed political expediency with prophetic morality. He refused to strike bargains with his opponents and as a result was forced out of office twice, in 1931, and in 1946. But his defeats never affected his role as the undisputed leader of the movement, within or without.

Writing as I do today, some twenty years after the establishment of the state and close to twenty years since Dr. Weizmann's death, I cannot help but reflect on how Weizmann has influenced the character and development of the State of Israel.

In his excellent monograph on Weizmann, Isaiah Berlin writes: 'Dr. Chaim Weizmann was the first totally free Jew of the modern world, and the State of Israel was constructed, whether or not it knows it, in his image. No man has ever had a comparable monument built to him in his own lifetime.'

Without question, the life of modern Israel is the real expression of Dr. Weizmann's astonishing gift for creation. Perhaps more than any other statesman of our time, he succeeded in effecting an organic fusion between the abstractions of the mind and the practical activities demanded by man's physical existence. This fusion is reflected in the very core of life in Israel today. It is part of the flavor of Israel's politics, part of the cacophony of its unflagging discussions, its intellectual posture, its argumentativeness, of its addiction to theoretical formulae and its adoration of dedication. In all these, one recognizes easily two major and familiar chords—the spiritual turbulence of pre-revolutionary Russia and, parallel with it, the basic values of Anglo-Saxon democracy.

Just as these were the twin paths along which Weizmann's political concept developed, with no disharmony or clash ever interrupting their growth—so Israel is a coalescence of both types of social organization.

I would not like to be misunderstood. There is much about contemporary Israel that Weizmann would certainly have disapproved of, or that in any case would have distressed him. He would have been affronted by the overwhelming preponderance of sectarian and partisan influence, the ascendency of the military, the unending compromises with the clerical. He himself represented a Jewish nationalism that was always global. To him world Jewry and the State of Israel were an integral entity. The Jewish people and not Israel's citizens alone constituted the generating power that would make his vision a reality.

Weizmann always envisaged a coalescence of the best minds and hearts of Israel and the Diaspora in the joint striving of the Jewish people as a whole for self-realization. He never believed in the existence of any profound or insurmountable dividing line between Israel and the diaspora. To him, both were expressions of the Jewish personality. Israel had, after all, been established to redress the imbalance of the Jewish community as a whole. Once established it was to enable the Jews, as a group, to live in inner harmony. Fundamentally Zionism represented a synthesis of the creative energies of the entire Jewish people, inevitably linked by bonds of the deepest emotional and intellectual identification.

Weizmann would have heartily disliked everything in the State of Israel that is parochial, and everything that is most tolerant of expediency.

But the basic tenet of Weizmann's political and moral beliefs was his conviction that the character of a human being or, for that matter, of a nation, mattered more than anything else. In all his important statements, this theme reappears, implicitly or explicitly: 'What a man *is* means more in the long run than what he *does*. The same is true of nations.' And I am sure that the essential character of the Jewish State towards which he contributed so much, consciously or unconsciously, would have been not only acceptable but cherished by him.

To return to 1931. It was a crucial year for the world Zionist leader who was repudiated, and for the small man forced out of the inner sanctum of American Zionism. We were both, on our two very disparate levels, officially out. And it was then that there began the development of a personal affinity which, as it matured, had a profound effect on my life and, as I shall show, a not inconsiderable effect on the Weizmann heritage.

10 The Romance of a People'

My departure from Toronto was a long drawn-out affair. I could not continue with *The Standard* on the conditions offered me. To return to New York was out of the question. I only knew that whatever I would turn to, it would have to be related to the cause. For some time I considered the idea of settling in Palestine. Chaim Arlosoroff wanted me to edit a combined edition of *The Palestine Weekly* and of *Davar*, the Labor daily, in English. The offer was tempting, but I did not feel that I was ready for Palestine or Palestine for me. In the midst of this indecision there came an urgent letter followed by an urgent telephone call, from Solomon Goldman in Chicago.

The three leading American rabbis of that time were Stephen S. Wise, Abba Hillel Silver and Solomon Goldman, in that order. Goldman was a scholar and had written a number of serious books. He was a liberal in outlook and an eloquent speaker; he became in time the President of the ZOA. What he asked of me now, in his urgent letter and his more urgent telephone call was not, I felt, particularly friendly. He wanted me to come out to Chicago and become Executive Director of Zionist Activities for the Midwest.

'Sol,' I protested, 'official Zionist activities are exactly what I want to keep away from. I've had a bellyful.'

'That was in New York,' he said. 'It will be different here.'

'What do you mean, different?' I asked, derisively.

He explained: the movement in Chicago was dying on its feet, there was no initiative, no sense of direction, no program worth speaking of, nothing but plodding and deadening routine. Someone was needed who would give it a jolt, put some life into it, set it in motion again; and he insisted that that someone was I.

It was all very flattering, and I listened with pleasure, but remained skeptical. 'What about the central organization in New York?' I asked. He had anticipated the question. It was not going to be like New York. The Midwest was largely autonomous; I would have an absolutely free hand, I would be backed to the hilt by the Chicago group. I listened, I knew that Goldman was quite sincere, I suspected that he wanted to bring me back out of my northern exile, and I yielded against my better judgment—always remembering, however, that this was not a lifelong commitment.

For the next six months I commuted between Chicago and Toronto, editing *The Standard* one half of the time and getting a first hand view of the Zionist desert in Chicago the other half. My youngest son, David, had just been born, and Shirley was in no condition to move the entire household. David was my *ben zekunim*, child of my old age. I was thirty-eight when he was born. That was thirty-eight years ago. I look at him now, weighed down by an elegant beard and executive responsibility, bolstered by his wife Ruth and his own two sons, Benjy and Jonathan, and I am reminded of the 'feud' I had over him with Rose Dunkelman. Whenever I would return to Toronto for a few days from Chicago and refer to the baby by my pet name for him, 'Shtunkie,' she would rage. One day she threatened sanctions: if I persisted in calling him 'Shtunkie' she would call me henceforth 'Mr. Shtunk Senior.' So we settled on 'Bubbles' and the 'war' was over. To this day, my daughter, Helen, affectionately calls him Bubbles and he doesn't seem to mind it in the least.

When at last I moved the whole family to Chicago, I missed Rose most of all, not only as a loyal, dependable colleague, not only as a person, but as a sort of institution. Her home was known as 'the Zionist Embassy'—there was of course no Jewish State yet— and she was host to all Palestine visitors and the spirit of every Jewish and Zionist enterprise. We disagreed on one point; she objected strenuously to my sometimes lurid language, but when I was gone she wrote me: 'You picked us (as replacement) a young, and in your estimation, a good-looking man. Would you please find us someone old and *mies* (ugly), and if possible, someone who swears. Golly, how we miss you.'

The Zionist field in Chicago was strewn with dry bones and a thousand speeches were not going to revive them. The leadership was confined to two or three men, and they were powerless against the inertia of the community. I realized at once that in these circumstances pedestrian Zionist propaganda and routine education, however well intentioned, would produce no effect. There had to be, first, a reawakening, and I turned to the performing arts—music, drama, spectacle.

Here the reader must recall that I was the son of a *chazan*, and I had known from my childhood that the music of the *shul* was a far greater attraction than the long sermon designed to elevate the souls of the worshipers. To be sure, the *shul* was not allowed drama and spectacle, but if music alone could stir the soul, what would it not do allied with drama and spectacle? This inspiration did not come to me out of the blue: a few days after my arrival in Chicago I attended a performance of *Aida* at the Chicago Opera House, and a train of thought was set in motion leading into the heart of my problem. If ridiculous stories and childish plots like *Aida* and *Carmen* could be turned into meaningful and moving experiences by music, color and action, what could not one do with a heroic theme like that of Chanukah? The holiday of the Maccabees was not far off, and I decided to arrange a great spectacle telling the story of that ancient struggle. The highlight of the evening was to be: *no speeches!* The spectacle would deliver its own message. This was an unheard of proposal: a great Zionist affair at which the local Zionist orators would keep their mouths shut? Sol Goldman and Harry Fisher were aghast! They were quite willing to forego their own privileges, but there was X, there was Y, there was Z. How could it be managed? But I reminded them that I had been promised a free hand. If they wanted speeches, they would get no spectacle, if they wanted a spectacle, there would be no speeches.

All of the machinery and property of the Chicago Opera House, including that of the last performance, was placed at my disposal (how far is Egypt from Palestine?). Like Ecclesiastes I gat me men singers and women singers, and unlike him I gat me hundreds of Jewish schoolchildren, knowing that every kid who took part would fill ten seats with parents and relatives.

In Chicago the success of any enterprise was measured by the degree to which it interested the racketeers. By that criterion we were among the great events of the year. The racketeers printed some thousands of their own tickets, but on the advice of the 'cognoscenti' we put the police on their track, and most of them were caught and jailed. Since this was a Jewish affair, most of the racketeers were also Jewish. Among them were some youths learning the trade. They were brought before Judge Harry M. Fisher, a man of infinite wisdom and tact. He gave them first a tongue lashing and then a moving lecture on how they were defiling Jewish tradition. He dismissed them with a warning that should they ever appear before him on similar charges, he would put them away. He ended:

'Now go back home and learn how to be a good American and a good Jew.'

As for the real tickets, 27,000 people paid for them and came.

Now I had promised our public 'no speeches.' I wanted them to come, be entertained, laugh, weep and be edified. And I believed I had it all arranged. But I reckoned without the President of Chicago's Zionists— I will not rescue his name from oblivion—quite a decent fellow but altogether humorless, as one may still verify by consulting the two gigantic volumes he had compiled on Jewish wit and humor. When a Zionist leader sees an audience of 27,000, he loses control; he is an old fire-horse put out to pasture; the gong excites him and he has to run. This particular leader was a prime specimen of the species. As the performance was about to begin he told me that he was going to make a speech. I told him that a speech was superfluous, and moreover I had promised that no one was going to make one; I told it to him in one-syllable but no four-letter words. Thereupon he informed me, superfluously, that he was the President, and I was only a hired clerk; then he rushed out on the platform and spoke. He was happy, he declared, to see so vast an audience; he hoped that everyone would become a member of the Zionist organization; he—. But he got no further, for a chant rose from the audience: 'We want Weisgal, we want Weisgal.' The shout continued crescendo, and the President's words were drowned out. But we had to start the show; the actors, the singers, the dancers were waiting in the wings, and everything had been timed to the second. I jumped from my box on to the platform and the clamor died down: I said, 'Ladies and gentlemen, thank you. You are my reward.' I gave the signal for the start of the performance, and it was a tremendous success.

At six o'clock the next morning—we hadn't gone to bed until three— the President called me. He too had seen the morning papers, which had singled me out not only as a great showman but as a man of great restraint. Half sobbing, half raging, he kept repeating, 'You stole my publicity! You deliberately stole my publicity!' I said, simply: 'Mr.—, I'm through; you'll never see me in your lousy office again,' and I hung up. A few hours later I went to the office, packed my papers, and left for good.

That Chanukah festival was one of the turning points of my life. What I had regarded as an experiment became the beginning of a ten-year involvement in show business. Such are the dangers of a success. I was suddenly aware of a strong pull toward the world of the theatre; I was excited by the combination of artistic creativity and promotional ingenuity, and the element of risk and gamble suited my temperament. I was not lured by visions of the fabulous riches that await succesful producers; neither did I expect to ruin my family and impoverish my friends—as I subsequently did. Behind everything, I suppose, there was the memory of my childhood, the heady atmosphere of our home when it was filled with minstrels vying with one another for acclaim, the High Holidays when my father held the congregation enthralled, and I was part of the choir, or its soloist.

Whatever the causes, I was hooked.

I wrote to the National President of the Zionist Organization, Morris Rothenberg: 'Nothing I can say here will convey to you the extraordinary triumph of our Chanukah Festival. I am sending you herewith several of the clippings from the local papers. All of these stories were featured on the first pages of the Metropolitan newspapers—a feat never achieved by the Zionist Organization. The Zionist Organization is today on the lips of every Jew and every non-Jew in the city of Chicago.'

There is sometimes—fortunately—an interplay between opportunity and ambition: while I was making my preparations for the Chanukah Festival, preparations were also on foot for a vastly more important enterprise—the Chicago World's Fair of 1933, to be named 'A Century of Progress.' The Jews of Chicago had been asked to participate, and negotiations and confused discussion went on for months as to whether the Jews were a race, a religion or a nation, and, whichever they were, could they be appropriately represented by a building, and if so, what kind of a building, etc., etc. At one point Harry Fisher and Sol Goldman came to me for advice, but I was too busy to think about it. Then came the success of the festival, my resignation from the organization and, simultaneously the idea. I called up both of my friends and submitted it to them: not a building, not an exhibit, but a spectacle portraying four thousand years of Jewish history; it would have everything, religion, history, the longing for Zion, the return to Zion, and it would be called *The Romance of a People*. It would have something for everybody, Zionists, non-Zionists, the religious, the nationalists, everybody.

Goldman and Fisher consulted their friends. The response was enough to make a horse weep. It didn't have enough Zionism for the Zionists, or enough religion for the religious. Besides, they all asked, like a Greek chorus, where was the money to come from? I went to New York, to see Rothenberg, who, I was sure, had been impressed by the reports I had sent him. He would not even consider the merits of the idea. 'We've got no money.' In the end one man, Harry Fisher, was won over, and he gave me $6,000 for a show that eventually cost $150,000.

I was in business and opened an office. I went to see General Dawes, former Vice-President of the United States, now President of the Fair. He was conservative, deeply religious, and loved the Bible. I stated my case to him as follows: 'This is to be a Century of Progress, portraying all the scientific and technological achievements of mankind. In these achievements the Jews, leading participants, do not occupy a special place as Jews; they are a part of every country in which they reside. But we have four thousand years of history, from Abraham down to the present; *that* no one else has.' Then I told him what I had in mind. He listened, caught fire, and said, 'I will help you all I can.' And he did. He was a shrewd man; he was not only interested in giving us a chance; he was also interested in attracting Jews to the Fair.

The Romance of a People followed in general the pattern of the Chanukah Festival, but was on a much larger scale. The Chanukah Festival centered on a single episode. *The Romance* took in everything from the Creation to the Return. There are many claimants to the authorship of *The Romance*: Solomon Goldman, Maurice Samuel, Meyer Weisgal. The truth is that not a trace of our contributions remained in the final result. The retinue I had acquired during the Chanukah Festival was the real creator of *The Romance*. Isaac van Grove, an energetic Dutchman of Jewish descent and the former director of the Chicago Civic Opera, wrote the score and directed the production. He was assisted by Leo Kopf. Harry Beatty of the Chicago Opera who had given me the sets of *Aida* for the Festival and was by now a good friend, undertook the technical direction. Lazar Galpern, a gifted Russian Jewish choreographer, did the choreography and trained the dancers, of whom there were several hundred. I again got the Hebrew schools to participate, and three thousand Jewish children made up the chorus. With the professional singers, actors and dancers the cast reached six thousand. The production was scheduled for Jewish Day at the World's Fair, July 3, 1933, in Soldier's Field, with a seating capacity of 100,000. We worked furiously, we generated immense excitement among ourselves, but somehow there wasn't a corresponding momentum outside our ranks. Something was lacking, some special touch; and the specter of tens of thousands of empty seats haunted my waking and sleeping moments.

One day in the spring, three months before the fateful day, I was sitting in my office, more than usually perplexed, looking for the magic key to the problem, and seeing nothing. Then suddenly it came to me out of the blue, and I turned to my secretary: 'Get me Dr. Weizmann, in London!'

The startled young lady asked, 'London where?'

'England,' I said. 'Where in hell do you think London is?'

Transatlantic calls were not yet the commonplace things they have since become. My secretary looked as if she did not believe me, but after long hours of waiting the trans-Atlantic operator came through: 'I have Dr. Weizmann for you.'

The conversation ran somewhat as follows:

M.W.: Hello, Dr. Weizmann, this is Meyer, in Chicago.

Ch.W.: *Vos, bist meshugge gevorn?* Have you gone out of your mind? Is Chicago on fire again?

M.W.: No, but it will be when you come here. I want you to come to Chicago for 'Jewish Day.'

Ch.W.: What's that?

I explained as fast as I could.

Ch.W.: What's in it for the movement?

M.W. (with impressive emphasis and a prayer in my heart): If you will come to Chicago for one day, and make only one speech, even if for only five minutes, I will give you $100,000 for any Zionist fund you designate.

Ch.W.: Put it in writing.

M.W.: Goodbye, Chief. I'll see you on July 3.

I put it in writing, with the 'warning' that he was to make *one* speech. If two, the fee would go down to $50,000; if three, to $25,000.

In 1933 $100,000 was a considerable sum, and at the moment we had barely enough in the till to meet our bills, but I felt that if Jewish Day was to become something more than a run of the mill demonstration, if it was to be lifted to a memorable height and make a handsome profit too, only one man could do it: Weizmann. He was still out of office, but his name was still magic. In our ensuing correspondence he told me that he wanted the money for the Central Refugee Fund he was launching— Hitler was in power and the flight from Germany was in full swing; Weizmann was particularly occupied with the Jewish scientists, driven from their universities. In his autobiography he refers to my offer in these words: 'I was very much tempted, both for the sake of the funds and out of regard for the man.'

The mere announcement that Weizmann was coming to Chicago for Jewish Day electrified the country: Jewish Day at Chicago, till then of purely local concern, assumed the proportions of a national event. From towns and cities in every part of the United States and Canada came requests to be allowed to participate; every Jewish organization suddenly felt that it had to be one of the sponsors of Jewish Day and assure itself of hundreds, sometimes thousands of seats. The Zionist Organization of America shifted its convention from Atlantic City to Chicago, the B'nai B'rith did the same from Omaha. National youth organizations scheduled a rally in Chicago for July 3. Jewish life in America was suddenly concentrated round our affair.

For days preceding, trainloads of Jews, singly and in delegation, converged on Chicago. The newspapers were full of it. For once the Jews of America seemed to be acting in unison and harmony.

On the evening of the performance 131,000 people were jammed into Soldier's Field, and thousands were turned away. To accomodate the extra 31,000, we covered part of the playing field with seats. It is recorded in the official report of the Fair that it was the most impressive event of the Chicago World's Fair and broke all attendance records. Weizmann spoke—for ten minutes—and it was the climax of the evening. I do not ever remember press notices as ecstatic—that is the only word—and merited as those we received. For three hours dancers, chorus, soloists and narrators unfolded the drama of Jewish history from the time of Abraham to the rebuilding of Zion. *The Chicago Tribune*, not a particularly pro-Jewish paper, took the show under its wing for a second night, when it was attended by 75,000, mostly non-Jews.

Newspapers with live managers are always on the alert for special events which can be used to boost circulation. The fourteen columns of description in *The Chicago Tribune* apparently registered on the thirty-fourth floor of *The Daily News* building in New York. The papers were blood brothers, and Philip Maxwell, Special Events chairman of *The Tribune*, called Mr. Joseph Medill Patterson of *The Daily News* to tell him that they had a bonanza on their hands. I was despatched forthwith to the formidable Colonel Patterson, as he was usually called, bearing a letter recommending that the *News* sponsor *The Romance* in New York.

I had barely shaken hands with the Colonel when he announced, 'I'm going to Chicago this afternoon, come with us.' He was accompanied by his general manager, Max Annenberg, an uncle of Walter Annenberg, now U.S. Ambassador to the Court of St. James's. To Annenberg I said: 'What the hell did I have to come to New York for if I have to go back with you to Chicago?' But I went.

I was not accustomed to their ways of doing business. From the minute we got on the train until one o'clock in the morning, when we went to sleep, we sat talking and drinking. We talked about everything—except *The Romance*. One would have thought that they had suddenly been smitten with amnesia on the subject; or that there never had been such a thing as *The Romance*, and I was suffering from hallucinations. The longer we talked the more nervous I became. Moreover, with every second word a drink was ordered—or so at least it seemed to me. As we alighted from the train at ten in the morning Patterson said to me: 'Take this telegram for New York: WEISGAL OKAY GO AHEAD WITH PROJECT.'

My exile was over. I took the next train back to New York, and a few days later Shirley packed the children into a car and followed. We set up temporary housekeeping in the Peter Stuyvesant Hotel, on 86th Street and Central Park West. The 'Friday Night Club' opened its 'premises' again. Joe Brainin, who was running a literary agency called The Seven Arts Feature Syndicate, found time to take over the public relations of *The Romance*. Louis Lipsky sent me his wife's nephew, Dan Schacht, to act as stage manager and production assistant; van Grove came in from Chicago. It was old home week. And now that I was no longer in the employ of the ZOA, I could work together with it, making it one of the beneficiaries of the enterprise along with other organizations after Weizmann had received his $100,000. My own salary was $80 a week plus the promise of a bonus of $5,000 from *The Daily News*, payable on completion of my services. There were moments during the ensuing weeks when that bonus took on a spectral aspect.

We arranged to produce the show in the Polo Grounds, which had a seating capacity of 54,000. But the summer was drawing to an end, and we worried about the weather. We had been lucky in Chicago; would we have the same luck on September 14, the day we finally settled on, after long and anxious scrutiny of the meteorological records since the beginning of time? This time, though I had to build entirely new props, I at least had no money worries. We took in $150,000 on advance tickets within two weeks of the announcement. Of course we could not touch that money, but I found it good to look at; so did *The Daily News*.

The night of September 13 we had a dress rehearsal, and in my admittedly biased judgment it was even more marvellous than Chicago. We had professional actors and singers and again, three thousand Hebrew school children. There was a contagion of bliss in the air, and the world was transfigured as if a great magician had waved a wand over it. Then, as we were dispersing, a few wet drops descended on my face, and I felt a deadly chill. We assured each other with feverish eagerness that it was nothing, just some dew in an unusual form. Well, within half an hour there was a deluge which would have impressed even Father Noah. It did not last forty days and forty nights, only four; but even the Fire Department could not save our newly built props. The Polo Grounds were turned into a veritable lake on which we could see all of our precious scenery floating about.

We took refuge on the thirty-fourth floor of *The News* building, waiting for God to remember us, and hoping we would not wait as long as Noah. Then the telephone calls began to come in, from ticket-holders and others: 'What's going to be with *The Romance of a People?*' I went down to the switchboard and told the girls to say that an announcement would be made shortly. 'Meanwhile,' I said, 'I want you to keep a record of the number of in-coming calls, so we can keep track of public opinion.

In three days there were 42,000 calls. I estimated that even if half of them were from ticket-holders who wanted their money back, the interest shown by the others indicated a tremendous potential audience; Annenberg agreed with me. On the fourth day, while the rain was still pelting down, we held a full meeting of the Committee, with Mr. Nathan Strauss, Jr., in the chair. He had been chosen for that role because of his reputation for financial astuteness, and he now rose and delivered his considered opinion that the enterprise would have to be given up and the money returned to the ticket-holders. Thereupon Annenberg rose in his turn—he was a big man with terrific drive—banged on the table and said: 'Mr. Strauss' (he pronounced it *Shtrowss*, which infuriated the chairman, who wanted it pronounced *Straws*), 'I don't know you. I haven't met you before. But I have a contract with this guy (pointing to me) to put on a show. *The New York Daily News* never goes back on its word to its readers. The show will go on.' Then, pointing to me again: 'Remember, you're under contract.' Strauss made no answer; he—my symbol of respectability—stalked out of the room, slamming the door. Nobody accompanied him.

We did not announce Strauss's resignation; we just ignored it, and nobody was any the worse. Now we began to look for an indoor place. I went to Albany to see Governor Lehman and I asked him for the biggest armory in New York City. It happened to be in the farthest reaches of the Bronx, 197th Street to be exact; it was, moreover, a Federal armory. But Lehman was wonderful; he called Washington on the spot and got us the armory for three weeks.

This was my first encounter with Herbert Lehman who was elected and reelected several times as Governor and was, with the possible exception of Al Smith, the greatest Governor New York ever had. He was also a great human being and in the course of time we became good friends.

He and his wife Edith visited us in Rehovot and our families were intimate for thirty years.

As for *The Romance*, two minor problems remained. One, the armory had no seats; two, every word you uttered at any point came back in a resounding echo five minutes later. We got the American Felt Company to insulate the whole place and got Sears Roebuck to build 21,000 seats. It was not 54,000; it meant three nights for every one that we had originally planned, but this was the most they could get in and leave room for the show; and now we feared neither wind nor weather. The only thing that could stop us was an earthquake. After ten days of suspense we announced to the public that the show would go on, and tickets could be exchanged at Leblangs & Co., on the basis of first come, first served. The evening before the tickets went on sale thousands of people gathered on Broadway waiting in line throughout the entire night for Leblangs & Co. to open.

Nearly a million people came, by subway, by bus, by car and on foot to the remote corner of the Bronx to see *The Romance*. We played for six weeks. On the first night everybody was there, from the Governor, the Mayor and Jim Farley on down. Even Nathan Strauss was there, slightly sheepish but not displeased; only a few insiders knew that he had abandoned the ship when he believed it to be sinking—or rather, sunk. We could have gone on for months, but the army had other plans. When the show closed in New York I was called into the Colonel's office to receive my 'reward': a sealed envelope which I knew had to contain a check for $5,000. Gentleman and man of the world that I was, I did not open it in the presence of the Colonel. '*The Daily News* never goes back on its word.' But five seconds after leaving the building I examined it: the check was for $10,000.

With the cheers of Chicago and New York ringing in our ears, we went on the road, with Philadelphia as our first stop. By now we had developed what we thought was a foolproof formula for the production and its promotion. The local Zionist organizations took over the sale of the tickets and recruited the huge cast; for this they received fifty percent of the take. We had closed our books in New York, deducted the $100,000 for the Central Refugee Fund, and turned the surplus over to the ZOA and other Zionist organizations. For operating capital we depended on the local organizations. In Philadelphia we also received the most generous help from *The Philadelphia Ledger*, one of the Curtis publications. Our great additional drawing card in Philadelphia was Albert Einstein, who agreed to attend the opening night. We were going to start with a bang, and it looked as though Philadelphia, with a much smaller Jewish community than New York, would equal its record.

The bang came, right enough, but in the form of a blizzard—the worst in the 107 years for which Philadelphia had kept records. We promptly rented a dozen station wagons to round up the cast and all the V.I.P.'s who had reserved—but not yet paid for—the high priced loges. I despatched Joe Brainin to Princeton to bring the Einsteins and he finally delivered them after an Arctic trek across the snow-covered plains of New Jersey and Pennsylvania. I am sure it was only under the impact of Joe's impeccable Viennese German that Einstein succumbed and agreed to come.

The reviews were not less enthusiastic than those we had received in Chicago and New York, but the bad weather persisted with implacable malice and we ended up in Philadelphia with a deficit. I was certain that the ZOA would cover the deficit out of the earlier profits; I was mistaken. Without its help I went on to Detroit and Cleveland, but their niggardliness and shortsightedness had taken the heart out of me. What ate at me most was their blindness to the propaganda value of The Romance, the spirit of which was Zionist through and through. I think it fair to say that the approximately million-and-a-half people who saw The Romance of a People in the various cities we played derived more from its Jewish and Zionist spirit than from all the standard publications and speeches of the ZOA.

I almost regretted having reestablished contact with them. I vowed that whatever I would undertake of a character similar to The Romance of a People would be free from similar entanglements. And though I had become tired of The Romance I had ideas—I have never been short of these. Indeed, there was a particular one that had been germinating for nearly a year. While I was working in Chicago on The Romance I read an item in the paper that Max Reinhardt had to flee Germany. In one of my inspired moments I sent off a cable: To Max Reinhardt, Europe: IF HITLER DOESN'T WANT YOU I'LL TAKE YOU. The cable never reached him, but the idea stayed with me. Its purport, to put it simply, was to put together a Reinhardt-directed spectacle on a theme resembling The Romance, as a sort of answer to Hitler; but unlike The Romance it was to be the project of some of the greatest artists of our time.

Here I was, with the $10,000 bonus burning a hole in my pocket, The Romance over, in every sense, and the idea reviving and becoming more and more attractive. I decided to deliver the $100,000 to Weizmann in Europe, and go on to Paris and see Reinhardt.

The few friends I consulted in New York before leaving uttered the
direst warnings. 'You would need an Otto Kahn or a government subsidy
to cope with Reinhardt's personal expenses,' they told me. 'He lives on
champagne and caviar, smokes $3 cigars and travels with a personal
retinue rivaling that of a Turkish Pasha.' Even the theatre-intoxicated
Lipsky tried to discourage me. Only the Viennese Joe Brainin egged me
on. It goes without saying that what I found irresistible in the project was
the obstacles.

Reinhardt was doing *Die Fledermaus* at the Théâtre Pigalle. Finding the
theatre was easy enough, but getting at Reinhardt was a different story.
His retinue was indeed numerous, and its chief purpose was to guard him
from the intrusion of outsiders; of these there seemed to be thousands,
each one with a marvellous proposition for the supreme theatrical figure
of his time. I did not even attempt to break through. I went instead to
Pierre van Paassen, then the Paris correspondent of *The Toronto Star*.
Pierre, though an extremely shy person—I often wondered how he had
distinguished himself in a profession so unsuited to the shrinking violet
type—seemed to know everybody, and he arranged an interview for me.
He accompanied me to the Théâtre Pigalle, saw me through the barricades,
and left me with Reinhardt. Shirley, who had come with us, waited outside.

We were warned, before we were admitted, that I had exactly ten minutes in which to say my piece. I had come equipped with a mass of production photos of *The Romance*, and I spread them before the great man as
I explained what I had in mind. In my halting German—I have since mastered this distortion of Yiddish—I said: '*Dieses Schauspiel muss Hitler
unsere Antwort geben*, this spectacle must be our answer to Hitler' (we did
not dream then of the coming unbelievable horror, or I would not have
used such language, which in retrospect sounds almost flippant). Reinhardt
listened impassively, but he listened, he made no motion to dismiss me.
The ten minutes stretched into twenty, forty—I lost count; Shirley claimed
afterwards that I had kept her waiting for hours. Finally Reinhardt came
up with some questions: 'Who will write the book? Who will compose
the music?' I had no answers ready; I wanted first to establish the combination of Reinhardt's direction and Weisgal's enthusiasm. I told him that
he was free to choose his collaborators. He suggested Franz Werfel as
playwright, Kurt Weill as composer and Norman Bel Geddes as designer.
I swallowed hard, thinking of the remainder of my $10,000 kitty. But
when I left Reinhardt late that afternoon we had agreed on two things:

a) we, Reinhardt, Werfel, Weill and Weisgal were to meet in Salzburg during the summer of 1934 (it was now late November, 1933) and b) I would deposit $10,000 as an option on Reinhardt's services in an American bank.

I sent a cable to Joe Brainin and asked him to make the rounds of my family for the deposit. In three days I got the answer that the money was in the bank. Joe went first to Newark, where he spoke to Leo, by this time a successful businessman, and tried to sell him the idea that a Reinhardt production was a tremendous business opportunity. He should have known better than to try that ploy with Leo, who told him that as far as he knew Reinhardt only spent money, never made any for anybody. But, he added, if that was what Meyer wanted, he would do his best; and he did. He and Joe then went together to Josh, who in addition to running his profitable newsstand at Columbia University, had developed a golden touch at the race tracks. (He claimed that his Talmudic training and his study of the secrets of the Kaballah had given him the right mixture of reason and intuition.) He was as ready to back me as if I were the immortal Eclipse.

But of course Leo and Josh were only a beginning, and the option money represented a fleabite. A Reinhardt production was not a Zionist festival; I needed real money, and between the Théâtre Pigalle and Salzburg I knocked on many doors. On my way back to New York I stopped over in Carlsbad where Weizmann was vacationing and I told him of my new *mishugass*. He listened with warm sympathy, and told me to go and see Mrs. Rebecca Sieff, in London, who would surely help me.

She was the wife of Israel Sieff (now Lord Sieff of Brimpton), one of the three senior members of the great firm of Marks & Spencer, the other two being the late Simon Marks (later Lord Broughton) and Harry Sacher. All three were ardent Zionists; all three had begun their careers in Manchester where they had become admirers and close friends of Weizmann during the years when he taught chemistry at that university. All were men of great abilities, but Sacher, although not in business, was unquestionably the most gifted of them. He was a writer and lawyer.

He and I had already met in America a few years earlier, when I was still in the employ of the ZOA. I remember a curious fragment of conversation with him—I believe it took place in the Ambassador Hotel. When I entered the room he asked me, abruptly, 'Have you ever heard the words "unearned increment?" ' I confessed I had not. He explained them cryptically as follows: 'How would you like to go to bed a poor man and wake up a rich one?' I answered that I could hardly imagine a more pleasant catastrophe. 'That's just what's happened to me,' he said. I ultimately discovered that this was his way of telling me that Marks & Spencer had become a public company. In any case he was exaggerating—he certainly had not been a poor man when Marks & Spencer had been privately owned. He had been a success as one of the editorial writers on the *Manchester Guardian*, and he had been the highest-paid lawyer in Palestine in the early Mandate days. I had always thought, before I came to know him personally, that Sacher naturally belonged to the Brandeis group. His intellectual clarity, his apparent coolness, his legal training, his background—he was one of the early students of the London School of Economics—would seem to place him in that camp. But he was, like his wife Miriam, his brother-in-law Simon Marks and his sister-in-law Rebecca Sieff, a Weizmannist. Of this remarkable family, more later; at the present point in my narrative I was about to enter the orbit of Rebecca Sieff, universally known as 'Becky.'

She received me in her Mayfair apartment. Standing on a raised area of her reception room, beautiful, statuesque, elegant, she looked like a duchess—or at any rate like my idea of a duchess. I was suitably impressed—but I was not taken in, I knew that she was a warm-hearted Jewess and a fervent Zionist. She was the founder of the WIZO, the Women's International Zionist Organization, and she spoke my language, or let me say that she understood it perfectly, for when she had heard me out she asked, bluntly: 'How much is it you want?' My rejoinder was, 'How much have you got?' We settled in the end for £15,000, a fortune in those days. But what pleased me more than the giving was the manner of it. We had become friends and we remained friends for thirty years.

When I got back to New York I incorporated myself as the M.W.W. Productions. It was primarily, like Du Pont, Rockefeller and Ford, a family business. Josh had put in $5,000, Leo $17,000, my three brothers-in-law $5,000 each; my share was the $7,000 remaining from *The News* bonus. Joe raised $7,000 and came in as promotion manager.

When I finally arrived in Salzburg in August, 1934, as a corporation, I had the beginnings of a reasonable financial backing. I also had Louis Lipsky with me as adviser. We met at Reinhardt's Leopoldskronschloss, and I had never set foot in anything so magnificent. Reinhardt lived as he directed, on a spectacular scale. The establishment swarmed with servants catering to the wishes of the master and his guests. Aside from the principals, there was Rudolph Kommer, Reinhardt's representative and factotum, known as Kaetchen—an extraordinary character. He was a Galician Jew and wanted everyone to know it because he was always

announcing that he was 'Aus Czernovitz.' He moved in international
society with an ease to the manner born and knew everybody and everybody's friend, Otto Kahn, Bernard Baruch, Claire Booth Luce, all the
Astors—he lived with one of them in New York. One of his specialities
was arranging international *shidduchim*, matches, between impecunious
artists and rich ladies. Alexander Woollcott devoted a whole chapter to
Kommer in his *While Rome Burns*. Sam Behrman, the American playwright, made Kommer the principal character in his novel, *The Burning
Glass*.

Reinhardt's day never began before four in the afternoon and seldom
ended before five in the morning. Our discussions revolved round the
play and music, and from the beginning there was a dispute between
Werfel and Weill as to whether it was going to be a musical drama or a
drama with music.

Franz Werfel was then in his early forties. He was fat, clumsy, jelly-like,
a gluttonous eater contemptuous of table manners. It was difficult to
identify his person with the sensitive lyric poet he was known to be. He
had just established himself with the publication of *The Forty Days of Musa
Dagh*. In this book Werfel expressed through the Armenians his awareness
of the Jewish tragedy (he told me the Armenians '*waren meine Ersatz-
juden*'), but he never consciously came to terms with his Jewishness. The
mystic strain in him which might have identified with Chassidism he
transferred to the Catholic Church, but the advent of Hitler kept him from
formalizing his conversion. I spent a whole night walking with Werfel
in the garden and explaining to him, as well as I could, that this was a *Jewish*
play—that and nothing else. It was our history, the history of his and
my people, that had to be portrayed—not some alien or abstract concept.
Remote as he was from Judaism, there was enough of the poet in Werfel
to grasp at the idea even through my barbarous German.

Kurt Weill was a quite different kettle of fish. Like myself he was the
son of a *chazan*, the descendant of a long line of rabbis; but unlike me he had
shaken himself free of Jewish life. His most famous work was *Die Drei-
groschen Oper*, an 'opera' of unconventional music around Berthold
Brecht's reworking of Gay's *The Beggar's Opera*. He did not appear to
me the most suitable choice of composer for the score of a Biblical pageant;
but I had given Reinhardt a free hand, and his instinct turned out to be
right. Weill's score settled once and for all—at least as far as I was concerned—the much debated question: this was a musical drama.

There was no lawyer handy, so it was Kaetchen who drew up the contract. It read, in part:'The party of the second part [that meant Reinhardt

and his associates] undertake to devise, write and compose a musical biblical morality play to express the spiritual origin, the earliest mythical history and the eternal destiny of the Jewish people to whom they belong.' It was a strange document drawn up in a strange and ominous setting: three of the best-known un-Jewish Jewish artists, gathered in the former residence of the Archbishop of Salzburg, in actual physical view of Berchtesgarden, Hitler's mountain chalet across the border in Bavaria, pledged themselves to give high dramatic expression to the significance of the people they had forgotten about till Hitler came to power.

Thus was born *The Eternal Road*, for me a Via Dolorosa which I trod as a mendicant for three long years. It was a brilliant theatrical achievement and one of the greatest money-losers in the history of the theatre till then. When it was over the fortunes of my family lay in ruins, and those of some of my friends were dented and badly bruised. But nobody regretted it. Big losers and little losers were united in one sentiment: it was worth every penny.

11 'The Eternal Road'

The Eternal Road, originally *Der Weg der Verheissung* (*The Road of Promise*), was scheduled to open not later than March, 1935. After ten postponements it opened in January 1937. It was to cost between $150,000 and $200,000; it cost more than half a million. In all other respects it was faithful to the original terms of the contract, as well as to the conception. It was a musical biblical morality on a grand scale. It was artistically and Jewishly the greatest theatrical production of all time. Burns Mantle, the then high priest of New York theatrical criticism, called it 'staggering,' Reinhardt's greatest, and gave it the four-star rating. A few weeks before it opened one perceptive commentator wrote that he did not know whether *The Eternal Road* was the title of the play or the name of the route it was taking to reach Broadway. It was both, and short of appearing on stage, I walked every inch of it.

Professor Reinhardt and Helene Thimig, the Viennese actress, not yet his wife, legally that is, arrived in New York a month or so after the contract was signed. Reinhardt had just turned sixty and was at the height of his creative powers, the universally acknowledged supreme master of his trade. He radiated a charm irresistible to men and women alike. Restrained and low-keyed in conversation, he had an electrifying effect on his listeners, almost as powerful as Weizmann's. They said of him that he was *ein einmaliges Exemplar*—or in our phrase, they broke the mold after producing him. He was so self-confident that he never had to be in a hurry, hence was always late and behind schedule.

Those who called him extravagant were too sweeping. He was an uncompromising perfectionist, and material resources existed only for the expression of spiritual values—for which the theatre was incomparably the most effective medium. It goes without saying that I was completely under his spell.

Helene Thimig made at first an impression of coldness and haughtiness. On closer acquaintance she proved to be sensitive, undemonstrative, and in spite of her gifts as an actress, shy. At the pinnacle of her career she broke her contract with Vienna's famous Burgtheater, attached herself to Reinhardt, and followed him round the world. She was the most striking person in his entourage.

Next to her was Rudolph Kommer, whom we have already met in Salzburg as Kaetchen. Kommer was Reinhardt's conscience, his chief negotiator, business manager and liaison officer for all contracts. His, too, was the responsibility for keeping Reinhardt's theatrical empire if not always solvent, at least afloat.

Another important member of the staff, involved in *The Eternal Road* from the moment of its conception, was Heinz Herald, the Professor's *Dramaturg*. There is no English equivalent for this term; even the most opulent English or American theatrical organization does not permit itself the luxury of a permanent *Dramaturg* on its staff. He must be a scholar thoroughly familiar with world literature and history; as the final reader of scripts he is the court of last resort on the acceptability of a play or the adaptability of a novel to the stage; he does all the research and accepts the responsibility for the authenticity of scenery and costumes; he may also offer suggestions on the casting.

Herald was a small man, deceptively meek in appearance. He kept in the background, and in Reinhardt's company rarely voiced an opinion if others were about. Alone with the Professor, he was articulate, persuasive, and on occasion adamant. His apparent humility notwithstanding, he could be hard as nails with the playwrights swarming about with dreams of achieving that supreme distinction—a Reinhardt production.

Reinhardt had also brought along his private secretary, Livia Castiglioni, a girl still in her teens. Her job, as far as I could make it out, was to follow him about and preserve for posterity his every remark. To her Reinhardt also dictated long letters filled with sardonic wit. Livia was the daughter of an actress, the widow of the Austrian financier Camillo Castiglioni, who in his palmy days had 'angeled' several Reinhardt productions. When his multi-million-dollar enterprises collapsed and he vanished from the scene, Reinhardt showed his gratitude to the mother by employing her daughter. This, I ought to say, was in keeping with his character; self-centered as he was—an artist's weakness and prerogative—he remembered favors and was generous to those in trouble.

Also in the Reinhardt entourage, but not strictly of it, was Eleanora von Mendelssohn, a sister of Francesco, one of Reinhardt's assistants.

Tall, languid, cultivating an exotic appearance, Eleanora fancied herself
as an actress. Nor was she lacking in talent; what she did lack was the
perseverance needed for an exacting profession. Intellectually a dilettante,
emotionally a hedonist, she epitomized a certain section of the German-
Jewish *Hocharistocratie*, supercilious, indolent and doomed. She was madly
in love with Reinhardt—he had tried to encourage her as an actress but
had given up. She followed him into exile, finding some happiness in
being able to see him now and again. She spent much of her time day-
dreaming on a couch while a professional entertainer, who perhaps was
in love with her, sang sentimental Slavic songs, accompanying himself
on the guitar. Eventually she committed suicide, but not before she had
laid on me the full burden of her tormented heart; she was one of the
peripheral problems of *The Eternal Road*.

Reinhardt arrived in New York during the Ten Penitential Days between Rosh Hashanah and Yom Kippur. One of his first requests to me
was: '*Ich möchte Versöhnungstag in die Synagoge gehen.*' *Versöhnungstag* was
not yet in my German vocabulary, but since Rosh Hashanah was over I
figured out that it meant Yom Kippur. Accordingly I took him to Stephen
Wise's Free Synagogue in Carnegie Hall. Wise put on a magnificent
performance—music, oratory and even some prayers. He was perhaps
the most dramatic American orator of his time, and at his best overwhelming. As we left the synagogue Reinhardt turned to me and said:
'*Herr Weisgal* (whenever he called me this I knew something was wrong),
*ich wollte in eine Synagoge gehen; Theaterspielen kann ich besser als dieser
Rabbiner*—I wanted to go to a Synagogue, when it comes to theatre I
can do better than this Rabbi.' For Simchas Torah, the rejoicing of the law,
I took him to a chassidic *shul* on the Lower East Side. It only occurred to
me later that Reinhardt had not suddenly succumbed to an impulse of
piety. He wanted to recapture the old-world atmosphere of the synagogue, an important element in the play.

Ludwig Lewisohn was commissioned to translate Werfel's text, which
he did in masterly fashion. There was some difficulty in adapting the
English words to the score Kurt Weill had produced for the original
German verse, so that high notes should not coincide with an *oo* sound
and low notes with an *ee* sound, but in the end it was satisfactorily worked
out. And finally, Norman Bel Geddes drew up a model of the sets.

Concerning the genius of Bel Geddes there could be no two opinions.
He had collaborated with Reinhardt in *The Miracle*, and he threw himself
with ardor into *The Eternal Road*. But even genius has its limitations, and
the truth was that the spiritual content of the play left him cold; he had as

little feeling for the great historic tragedy of Jewish life as for the contemporaneous tragedy that was developing visibly in Europe. Technically the *mise en scène* was superb; but the Jewish content of *The Eternal Road* was carried by the text and the music.

Anyone familiar with show business knows that the great problem is to find a theatre to house the play. I was *not* familiar with show business, and I did *not* know it. I thought the theatre owners would compete furiously for the privilege of putting on a Reinhardt production. Nor had anyone told me that nearly the whole of New York's theatrical real estate was owned or controlled either by the Shubert brothers or the Klaw and Erlanger heirs. In any case the Professor doubted from the very start whether New York had a theatre suitable for *The Eternal Road*.

There were two theatres outside the Shubert empire that came under consideration. He was entranced with the revolving stage of Radio City Music Hall, with its elevator-operated orchestra pit and its amphitheatric auditorium that afforded unobstructed sightlines from every seat. Time and again he had me take him to the Music Hall, where he would sit in the front row of the mezzanine all but shedding tears. 'How can they desecrate this wonderful theatrical instrument by using it for piffling amusements—a lone comedian standing in the middle of this magnificent stage, or a bevy of Rockettes tap-dancing across it?' But I knew there was no possibility of getting the Music Hall—it was controlled by the Rockefeller interests.

The other theatre was the Hippodrome, and, with no other prospect in sight, I put down a $5,000 option on it. Unfortunately that happened to be the moment when Billy Rose had the irresistible idea that the Hippodrome was the perfect place for the production of *Jumbo*. He enlisted the aid of Bernard Baruch, whose secretary he had been at one time, to get our option canceled, and succeeded. *Jumbo* also lost half a million but Jock Whitney could afford it. Billy Rose not only did not lose a penny, he drew $1,000 a week for his efforts, while my family lived on charity. My ultimate consolation, soured by the long wait, was that critics said *The Eternal Road* made *Jumbo* look like a pygmy.

We had no theatre, and no prospect of one. One day I was out walking with Reinhardt in Central Park when he stopped in front of a huge playing field. Reinhardt gazed at it, transfixed; slowly his face took on light and luster until at last it positively glowed. I watched him in fear and trembling. 'Here!' he exclaimed, 'Here!' and I shuddered. What he wanted was to build the sets on the field and then throw up a huge tent around them. His enthusiasm almost had me convinced.

That is where we might have ended up if Bel Geddes had not come with the announcement that our search was over. He had looked at the old Hammerstein Opera House on 34th Street, next to the Hotel New Yorker, and that was it. I went down immediately and I did not like the looks of the place; it was old, unused, shabby, and off the beaten track. But Bel Geddes swept aside my objections. 'Any theatre,' he said in a matter-of-fact way, 'will have to be structurally altered for my sets, and this one has possibilities.' I gave in because the only alternative was Reinhardt's tent; and Bel Geddes embarked on 'structural alterations' of the Manhattan Opera House akin to God's alteration of the universe during the six days of creation, except that God's was cheaper and faster. It soon became clear that no timetable could be set; there was just no way of knowing how long it would take to refurbish the theatre, construct the sets and install new seats. In his initial dig Bel Geddes hit rock, and then water, like Moses. Rehearsals were abandoned and the cast dispersed to the four winds.

And here I was, the putative producer of a mammoth theatrical enterprise the cost of which was becoming astronomical. I had neither money nor professional knowhow to handle the situation—I had only obstinate enthusiasm. Notwithstanding the dimensions, theatrical and financial, of *The Romance*, the Reinhardt project was new to me in the all-important sense that it was my first free enterprise—free, that is, of any organizational connection or sponsorship. I needed money, hard money, and in my naïveté I imagined that the ideological significance of the enterprise would open doors to me. I had already made a considerable list of prospects— men of substance who would be willing to contribute to the Jewish answer to Hitler. Besides, wasn't Reinhardt's name the greatest of all theatrical assets?

I miscalculated in two ways, as I discovered when I spoke to some potential angels of the common or garden variety. They were not sensitive to the call of Jewish pride; and when I proudly announced the name of my director, the reaction was: 'Okay—Reinhardt is all right, and Weisgal may be bearable, but who could stand a combination of the two?—not to mention Bel Geddes. Who's going to control this million-dollar baby?' My salvation—if I can call it that—came from very different types.

Among the first angels I landed was Morris Eisenman, who would have been a natural for a Yiddish Falstaff. He had been in America for some three decades and had never bothered to learn English. 'I don't need it,' he would say, '*mameloshn* meets all my needs.' A Russian Jew, he had

worked his way up from pushcart peddler to one of the principal part-
nerships in the Metropolitan News Service, a business which at one time
had a monopoly on the distribution to newsstands of all the New York
dailies and a number of other publications. Success had never gone to his
head. All his life he remained an intelligent, warm-hearted ignoramus with
a profound reverence for the scholarship he deemed beyond his reach.
I knew him from the Café Royale, where I had met him through Shmarya
Levin, to whom Eisenman looked up as to a god. Levin's Hebrew enterprises for the young Jewish Homeland—a new English-Hebrew, Hebrew-
English Dictionary, a new edition of the Hebrew classics—were among
the beneficiaries of Eisenman's generosity. Shmarya Levin withdrew to
Israel (he died there in 1935) and Eisenman looked on me as his alter ego.
When I told Eisenman what I was up to, this almost unlettered Jew
grasped at once the wider meaning of my enterprise. He took me down
to his bank and drew out four crisp new bonds, face value $10,000 each.
He did not suspect, nor did I, that this was going to be merely a down
payment. But Eisenman did something much more unforgettable: for
the duration of the production, which stretched over more than three
years, he sent Shirley a weekly bread-and-butter check for $100. I was
able to tell all other investors that I was not drawing any salary, and that
I would not ask for a penny for myself until the production showed a
profit which, as I have indicated, it never did.

Another of my generous backers was Maurice Levin, the owner of
Hearn's Department Store. I was introduced to him by Israel Goldstein,
the Rabbi of the B'nai Jeshurun Synagogue, prominent Zionist leader,
and good friend (at this writing he lives in Israel). Levin was one of Goldstein's parishioners. I told my story and asked him for $25,000. 'You
don't need $25,000,' he said. 'You need $50,000.' I didn't argue.

I had an interesting meeting at that time with the philanthropist Felix
Warburg, head of Kuhn, Loeb & Co., who had written such 'delectable'
things about me to Dr. Weizmann while I was at The New Palestine. He
said: 'I don't believe in the whole thing, but I don't want to hurt you.
I know that every Jew in New York is going to ask you if Warburg is
with you, and I don't want to give those people an excuse not to help you.
So to keep you honest I will give you a token $10,000 in my wife's name
and you will be able to say truthfully that Warburg is participating.'

There is one more man I must mention at this point: Alfred Strelsin.
He helped me greatly and, despite the fact that later he multiplied his
help tenfold in the telling, I did not begrudge his boasting. He was always
surrounded by a bevy of beauties; these I did begrudge him. Another

character was William Rosenblatt, the head of a brokerage firm, the brother of Judge Bernard Rosenblatt, a leading Zionist and one of the founders of Afula, which was planned as the Tel Aviv of the Valley of Jezreel but has remained, sad to say, nothing but an overgrown village. From William Rosenblatt, who had a reputation for closefistedness, I extracted $25,000. How I managed it seems to have been a mystery to him, for several days after giving me his check he asked me to see him in his office. I went down, feeling certain that he was going to ask for his money back. I found him in a state of bewilderment. He was certain that I had mesmerized him and/or that I was the greatest fund raiser on both sides of the Atlantic. He offered me a job with his firm—a contract for five years at $50,000 a year; and to impress me with the seriousness of the offer he took me to a champagne and caviar lunch in his penthouse. I told him I could never sell stocks and bonds; if he hired me and kept me he would go broke and I would go out of my mind. Years later I would meet him in Europe, or in Israel, and he would taunt me with: 'Idiot! You could have been a multi-millionaire.' I could only say, 'So what?' Dewey Stone, one of the gentlest souls in captivity, with whom I became deeply involved in later years, used to say: 'You don't want to be a millionaire; you just want to live like one.'

With the Manhattan Opera House undergoing its interminable facelift and the opening in the unforeseeable future, there was no point in my holding on to Reinhardt. More solvent producers were clamoring for him. I released him temporarily to direct *A Midsummer Night's Dream* in the Hollywood Bowl. When that had finished its successful run Reinhardt asked me to take it with him on the road, and with nothing better to do— more exactly nothing at all to do—I agreed. It was a pleasant interlude, a comparative calm before the storm which was to burst on me with the last phase of *The Eternal Road*.

When we brought the set of *A Midsummer Night's Dream* to Chicago it was only mid-November, but this was Chicago, and the temperature was below freezing. Two or three nights before the opening Reinhardt came into the theatre, took one look at the scenery and said: '*Herr Weisgal, das ist kein Sommernachtstraum, das ist ein Winternachtstraum.*' It was the foliage; either we resuscitated it, returned it to its blooming splendor or we called the show off. Being no horticulturist I did not know whether the wilted greenery should be watered and put in the sun—which was not shining—or packed in hot water bottles. I just sat in the theatre, after the Professor's departure, and pondered. Suddenly I came to myself and went to see my old friend of the Chicago Opera House, Harry Beatty.

Harry listened patiently, nodded, and began to make telephone calls. I looked and listened, not catching even a glimmer of an idea. 'Whom are you calling?' I asked. 'None of your business,' he answered. 'Have you got a couple of thousand dollars to spare?'

I hadn't the money with me, but my word was good. The next day truckloads of shiny green pine were unloaded at the theatre along with boxes of Christmas holly. It was not exactly Mediterranean, but it was green and alive; the show went on. I managed to worm the secret out of Harry. He knew everybody in Chicago—and that included a number of resourceful gentlemen whose names were less likely to appear in the social than the police register. For a few thousand they had made a midnight raid on the nearby forests of Wisconsin, denuding a not inconsiderable area for the benefit of our production.

As the producer of the road show I had under contract Mickey Rooney and Olivia de Haviland. Hollywood wanted them for the film version and they asked me to release them. That I did so without recompense will help to explain why I never became a theatre mogul.

In the midst of these adventures I became involved peripherally in Reinhardt's marital complications. He had been divorced several times from Elsa Hymes, at one time a distinguished actress and the mother of his sons Gottfried and Wolfgang. One divorce had been manipulated in Riga but was not recognized in Austria or Germany; another was contracted in some obscure town in Switzerland and also failed to qualify anywhere else. When Miss Thimig came to America with Reinhardt she was determined to legalize things once and for all, and not only for the sake of her aged father, a religious man. On one of the runs which was to take us back to New York from Hollywood, it suddenly occurred to every one that Reno was somewhere in between. When we crossed the border into Nevada Miss Thimig could no longer contain herself and insisted on cabling her father 'HEUTE WAR MEINE HOCHZEIT, Today was my wedding day,' though the *heute* was still several days off—she did not realize that Reinhardt had to establish residence in Reno as a preliminary.

The supporting cast in this marital comedy consisted of Gottfried, who despite a natural resentment helped smooth the way to his mother's acquiescence, Mr. Ronald Button, Reinhardt's American attorney, whose interest in the affair was purely financial, and my harrassed self, sitting in the wings as the chief witness. I wrote to my wife: 'Never did a man sit so innocently in Reno as I.' When the joyous moment arrived I affixed my signatures: to the divorce, and a few minutes later, in the same chamber, before the same judge, to the marriage. In the final scene of this international entanglement everyone was smiling. The Professor and his new wife were congratulating each other. Gottfried was telling funny stories, Miss Hymes had fallen into a pleasantly reminiscent mood, Mr. Button was getting signatures on checks and I was getting reservations on the next plane to New York.

There was only one woebegone person in New York and that was Eleanora Mendelssohn, who saw the last of her fantasies go glimmering over the horizon. A few weeks later we were arranging a banquet in honor of Reinhardt, with invitations sent out to New York's Four Hundred. Money was not mentioned, but the purpose was to raise funds for *The Eternal Road*. A half hour before we entered the banquet hall, Eleanora came to me and asked me to arrange one moment of gratification for her as recompense for all her misery: she wanted to enter on Reinhardt's arm. How this was to be managed she left to my ingenuity. I could not refuse her. I told the protocol man that I claimed the privilege of being Miss Thiming's escort; Reinhardt, standing alone, was snatched up by Eleanora, who enjoyed her sad little triumph with shining eyes. She was grateful to me till her dying day, which was not far off. My last encounter with her was a few months before her suicide, after *The Eternal Road* had run its course. She came to me desperate for money, which she probably needed for narcotics, or Christmas presents—I don't remember which. She wanted $300, and offered me in exchange a fine etching of her great-great-grandfather, the illustrious Moses Mendelssohn. I gave her cash and told her I wasn't interested in collateral; nevertheless she left the etching at the desk downstairs. I never saw her or heard from her again. The etching is my only memento.

Returning to the main thread of the story, Bel Geddes was merrily 'restructuring' the Opera House, and I took up again my Via Dolorosa, carrying not a cross but a collection box. My family had already contributed over $100,000, some at the very beginning and more as time went on and my problems mounted. They must not remain anonymous for their generosity was beyond the call of duty. None of them were rich; by today's standards they were actually quite poor and some even borrowed money from friends just to help me. Leo led the list with $30,000. He was by now a successful auctioneer but in his heart he remained a revolutionary. Next came my brother-in-law Gabriel Balkin, who was married to my youngest sister, Esther. Gabe was a super-salesman for I.

J. Fox and Company, the furriers, and he never tires of reminding me how I extracted $17,000 from him, a pleasure in the telling worth at least ten times the money to him. Then came the newspaper merchant and would-be rabbi from 116th St. and Broadway. All his piety went into the $10,000 he gave me. He claims that his being an 'angel' gave him new status with his professor friends from Columbia University, one of the most notable of whom was John Dewey. I doubt this. His rabbinical training and his race-track intuition certainly made him the most unusual newspaper dealer on Broadway. Last but not least my brother Sam, a tailor, gave me $5,000 and I am sure that though none of my family made 'easy' money, Sam's was the hardest earned.

The law firm of Philips, Nizer, Benjamin & Krim gave me a rent-free office in the Paramount Building and handled all legal matters. Not only did they never get a penny for their trouble—they paid for the privilege. It was probably the first and last time in the history of the legal profession that a prominent law firm subsidized an insolvent client; they gave us $25,000. During the entire period of preparation for *The Eternal Road*, Philips, Nizer, Benjamin & Krim were the most loyal and devoted friends. They were privy to all of my agonies, knew the most intimate detail of every financial transaction. They also knew how I suffered without a whimper. Theirs is one of the great legal concerns in America, but a legal concern with a heart and soul.

And still it wasn't enough, and of course the deeper I went the tougher the going became. Such hopes as I still had of enlisting 'regular' angels became dimmer when the opposition from the ranks of the theatre professionals crystallized. To them I was an outsider, an impudent intruder, a poacher on their golden preserves. From Billy Rose and other spectacle producers the word spread: 'Keep away!' A Reinhardt-Weisgal combine, given free access to the sacred checkbooks, might well introduce chaos into an orderly and finely conducted exploitive relationship.

But even if I could have found a Broadway producer willing to take over *The Eternal Road*, and endowed with character enough to say 'No' to Reinhardt's demands, there was still the question of the play itself and its original intent. *That* I would not compromise on, and at the same time I was firmly convinced that what I had in mind could not be reconciled with the outlook of the traditional commercial theatre. When all was said and done, it was a Zionist undertaking. And now it was too late in the day to prove that I was not a reckless spendthrift who did not know the meaning of such words as 'profit' and 'loss.'

Revolving these problems, I hit upon an idea. What I needed was a sort of straw man, an associate producer in good standing who would satisfy my box-office-minded angels that their investments would be protected from Reinhardt's creative urges; and I found the ideal man in Crosby Gaige, whose honesty and conventional record as a successful producer did not show the slightest trace of reckless abandon to the dramatic muse. Semi-retired, he was devoting most of his time to the culinary arts in the capacity of president of a society of gourmets.

I explained the situation to Gaige. I did not want him to help in the fund raising; I did not need him as an assistant Reinhardt-tamer. I wanted a Platonic union, a marriage in name only, as a reassurance to prospective sponsors. But as co-producer he would share in the glory; and if I remember correctly, I also offered him a modest financial compensation in the form of twenty seats a night which he could sell.

Gaige, a very sweet man, adhered to our understanding and never injected himself into the business of the production. I gained the impression that he had checked me off as a lunatic, and he fully expected me to break my neck long before any opening night. When the curtain went up— figuratively—for the première, he was the most surprised man in the world, and said as much at a dinner under the auspices of his gourmet society.

I have already paid tribute to the genius of Bel Geddes. What he did with that ancient, dilapidated Manhattan Opera House was beyond human imagination. He had begun by tearing out the proscenium to make room for a synagogue which was the bottom level of action; above that he had constructed a five-tier stage for the historical action and the mass scenes. Somewhere close to heaven, six stories above the ground level and in full view of the audience, was the choir. We had built elevators in a semicircle to the rear of the stages to transport the scenery. Miles and miles of electric cables had been installed to achieve the most visionary lighting effects.

But Bel Geddes was not yet through: he wanted me to build an annex on 35th Street for the various props and then build a moving ramp to bring them on stage. Here I drew the line and told him I was not in the warehouse business; he would have to find another solution. Then it was Reinhardt's turn. He decided that the synagogue was too small and not deep down enough. '*Der Kontrast zwischen Erde und Untererde muss unterstrichen werden*, the contrast between the world and the underworld must be emphasized,' he said. I had held out against Bel Geddes's last flash of

The Eternal Road. above Discussing plans with Max Reinhardt. *below, left* Franz Werfel, book. *below, right* Kurt Weill, score

The Romance of a People, Chicago World's Fair, 1933, broke all attendance records

Scenes from *The Eternal Road*. *above* Joseph being sold into slavery.
below The dance around the golden calf

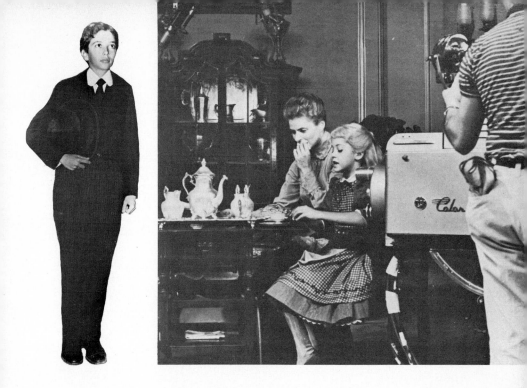

Theatre unto the third generation. *upper left* My son David in 'French Without Tears.' *upper right* My granddaughter Alexandra with Ingrid Bergman in a TV production. *below* My son Mendy (Michael Wager) with Siobhan McKenna in *St. Joan*

The Palestine Pavilion, N.Y. World's Fair, 1938. *above* Stephen Wise explains to the planning committee how it should be done. *Left to right* Israel Brodie, Louis Nizer, Dr. Wise, Gottlieb Hammer, Louis Lipsky,

Samuel Blitz, Harold Jacoby, George Backer, MWW, Israel Goldstein, Dr. Emanuel Liebman. *below, left* Entrance to Pavilion. *below, right* 'Weisgal's Private Army' (see page 158)

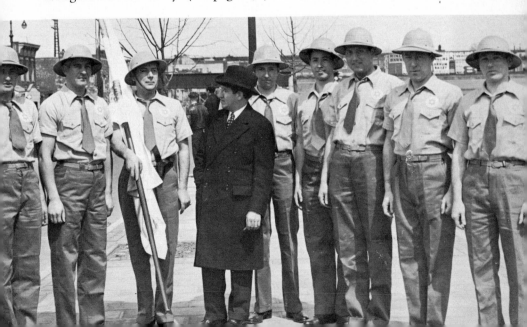

above Albert Einstein at the Opening of the Pavilion or 'The Great Betrayal' (see page 158). *below* Einstein and his sister; Miss Helen Dukas, his secretary (to the left); my son Mendy at the professor's feet

techno-megalomania; I succumbed to Reinhardt's latest explosion of theatrical insight. His expanded and deepened synagogue, added about $75,000 to production costs and reduced the income from each performance by several thousand dollars. It had been necessary to rip out the first three or four rows of the orchestra—my best seats—while the depth of the synagogue reduced to nil the visibility from certain seats in the balcony.

Several months before the opening I severed all connections with Bel Geddes. Had he remained he would have gone on improving the stage and delaying the opening till old age overtook both of us. Harry Horner, a young and brilliant designer and general factotum for Reinhardt, came from Salzburg to pave the last stretch of *The Road*. He did a splendid job.

I brought back Bel Geddes for the opening night; he was after all, the creator of the magificent sets. Of course he had criticisms; the lighting wasn't what it ought to be; more amber was needed, and so on. I told him it was too late. But he was gratified, all the same. I must add here a postscript on Bel Geddes. In 1939, when I was organizing the Palestine Pavilion at the World's Fair, George Backer, who headed the committee, suggested that we get Bel Geddes to do the designing. I was terrified, and said so. Backer wanted to know the reason for my agitation. 'First of all,' I told him, 'there isn't money enough in the Federal Reserve Bank and the Bank of England combined for the kind of pavilion he would dream up. Secondly, his *model* for the Pavilion would probably be larger than the whole of Palestine.' Later Geoffrey Hellman included this story in his profile of Bel Geddes for *The New Yorker*. When Bel Geddes saw the proofs he threatened to sue us for business libel—he had no sense of humor. At the Fair, he did the General Motors exhibition on a budget estimate of $2,000,000. The Futurama turned out to be the showpiece of the Fair, but its final cost was $10,000,000. Fortunately for Bel Geddes, General Motors could afford him.

In the original cast of *The Eternal Road*, Sidney Lumet, who eventually became a director, was to play the young Isaac who cries out in a piping voice 'Father!' when he sees Abraham lifting the sacrificial knife. Reinhardt had rehearsed him for days on that single word. During the interim his voice changed and he sprouted hair on his upper lip. We had to get someone else, Dickie van Patten. Lumet played instead the youth in the synagogue where the Jews had gathered fleeing a pogrom. The cast included Sam Jaffe, Rosamond Pinchot, Florence Meyer (the dancer and daughter of Eugene Meyer, Chairman of the Federal Reserve Bank and

Publisher of *The Washington Post*), Lotte Lenya, and hundreds of dancers, singers and extras.

Slowly but surely the place began to resemble a theatre. When I asked Reinhardt casually one day toward the end what we should cover the newly built seats with, he answered: '*Mit techeser*, with asses.'

Came the dawn of the opening night. Anyone who has ever been deeply involved in the opening of a production is familiar with the tense atmosphere, the nervous excitement, the uncontrollable flaring of tempers over last minute snags. One of Bel Geddes's magnificent elevators for moving the scenery stalled for a few hours, raising the possibility that Jewish history might be portrayed without the golden calf and the Tablets of the Law. But this was a trifle compared to the *coup de massu* which fell on us four or five hours before curtain time. In most dramas the great chase, the race against time, is saved for the last act. With us it was the prologue.

I was backstage supervising everything in general and nothing in particular when one of my boys informed me that a gentleman from the fire department wanted to see me. I thought he had chosen a strange time to come round selling tickets to the Firemen's Ball. I was nowhere near the mark; his message was of a quite different import. The place, he informed me, was a firetrap, and we could not open; there were too many lighted candles around. This was, as the British say, the pink limit! Every ticket had been sold. All of New York's nobility, Jewish and Gentile, was coming. And here was this brutal ukase. Nothing I said seemed to make the slightest impression on the man and I soon realized that if we were to be saved it could be only by intervention in the highest quarter. I called Dr. Stephen Wise, who was a friend of the Mayor's—La Guardia—and told him he must produce him, in person, immediately, no matter what. Wise found La Guardia somewhere, busy watching a fire—that was his hobby. In the meantime I also called the City Comptroller, who was in charge of the theatre, and discovered that he was quite friendly and not as unmanageable as the Fire Department. But it so happened—as I soon discovered—that La Guardia hated his guts because he was a Tammany Hall Democrat. Catching sight of him, he yelled, 'Get that shyster out of here!' When his nerves had settled, La Guardia surveyed the situation, and issued an order to station fifteen policemen and sixty firemen on the spot. I promised with tears in my eyes to fix everything the following day.

It was now an hour or two before curtain time and I could not go home to change. I sent for my clothes and took a room next door at the New Yorker. I was utterly exhausted, and on changing clothes discovered I had

forgotten to ask for a clean pair of shoes to go with my tuxedo. The ones
I was wearing were covered with the dust of twenty centuries of exile. I sent
the shoes to be shined; at fifteen or twenty minutes to opening time
they had not been returned. I called in a contingent of bell-boys and asked
them to take off their shoes; I found a pair that fitted more or less and
told their owner to wait in my room till mine came back; if they came
before curtain time he was to bring them to the theatre; if later, he could
keep them, and I assured him that he would not lose by the exchange.
Finally I asked him to make my tie. He asked me to stretch out on the bed.
'What do you mean, stretch out?' I asked. He informed me that until
recently he had worked in a funeral parlor, so I lay down, and he made my
tie with a dexterity that exonerated him.

I got to the theatre about ten minutes before the opening. The air was
vibrant with expectation, the more so as the packed audience had no idea
what to expect. We had no curtain; all the effects were based on lighting—
$60,000 worth of it. When the first lights went on dimly they revealed
only the small synagogue, and the Jews, men, women and children,
huddled together in fear—nothing more. Then the *chazan*—a marvellous singer, and a *goy* by the way, called Mathews, began to chant 'And
God said to Abraham . . .' Slowly the stage began to light up, revealing
the depth and height of five broad ascending tiers, and finally, at the top,
the choir—one hundred singers in the robes of angels, a heavenly host.
The audience caught its breath and one could hear a collective 'A-ah.' I
knew the play was made.

At four in the morning we got the reviews, and this time *we* caught
our breath. They were ecstatic. Dan Shacht, one of my assistants, jumped
up on a table and announced he was going home to make a baby. He was
convinced that he had a job for at least five years. Brooks Atkinson of
The New York Times wrote: 'After an eternity of postponements *The
Eternal Road* has finally arrived at the Manhattan Opera House, where it
opened last evening. Let it be said at once that the ten postponements
are understood and forgiven. Max Reinhardt and his many assistants
have evoked a glorious pageant of great power and beauty.' There was not
a dissenting voice and lines formed outside the box-office. Our troubles
should have been over—but that would have been too good. One newspaperman, writing of the long torment of getting and keeping the show
going dubbed his story *The Odyssey of an Optimist*. That was me—the
story of my life, and I wanted it to be the title of this autobiography, but
my friends thwarted that plan—they used it for a book of tributes presented to me on my seventieth birthday.

"he Eternal Road" Is Staggering

test of Reinhardt Spectacles in the
Greatest of Bel Geddes Settings

...h to convince me that we
have seen its like before, nor
...kely to see it again. At half
...llion dollars a spectacle, "The
...nal Road" is quite likely to be
...ectacle to end spectacles. Pro-
...ers of the Meyer Weisgal ca-
...ity arise not oftener than once
...ry generation or so. He is the
...ney-raising genius who has
...ven three years to this amazing
...erprise.

There is no time for detailed re
...ort. Reinhardt has never, so far
...s we have seen his work, han-
...led crowds with such clarity of
...novement and impressiveness of
grouping. Nor kept his central
theme moving more comprehend-
ingly.

World's Greatest.

It is, so far as we may believe
the record, an achievement beyond
comparison with any that has pre-
viously been realized in a world
that has rather gloried in the competition of sheer magnitude and
visual impressiveness.

I have no idea just how long
"The Eternal Road" will run, but
I should say at least a million Jews
and half a million Gentiles will
want to see it at least once.

It is impossible to describe
grandeur of Reinhardt's pro
tion, the pictorial beauty.
rhythmic movement of the pec
on his far-flung stage, the excit
colors, the overpowering splen
that scene in Egypt, for
mple, where the slaves work
the relentless whip of a sava
kmaster, the color of that, t
ding splendor of it. One e
merges into another, a
r emerges and recedes into th
shadows of the huddled figure
...ne temple.

...many unseen hands weave its magical scenes. In a town th
knows a spectacle when it sees one this is more inventive th
the "The Miracle," larger than "Jumbo," handsomer th
"White Horse Inn." I never realized until last night how lar
indoors could be and still stay indoors. When Prof. Reinhar
says size he means enormous.

THE AISLE

"The Eternal Road" Stag
By Reinhardt and Ge 'THE ETERNAL ROAD

Their Long Delayed but Visually Magnificent Sp One of the Notable Productions of
Finally Reaches the Manhattan Opera House Season Is a Religious Play

By JOHN MASON BROWN

...ises to moments of such visual
...eauty and magnificence as the
...odern theatre has never seen
...ualed or approached. So arrest-
... is Professor Reinhardt's deploy-
...nt of mobs on Mr. Geddes's five
...nic levels, and so glorious are
...e of Mr. Geddes's effects, due
...he sheer magic of his lighting,
...overpowering as the whole
..."The Eternal Road" is and tire-
...as are some of its interludes,
...impossible not to hail it as
...tage spectacle of all stage
...les

...ever. When the portals of heaven
open before Abraham, letting out
the rapturous light and sound of a
choir of angels, the goodness of
God becomes for an instant the
most overpowering force in the
Broadway theatre of 1937. And, ac-
...e to do justice to the
...omimes that course through
...nal Road" in one Inspired stream.
...s it possible to do justice to this
...ous miracle in a daily review. ...
...s Reinhardt has collected with
...Biblical pageant cast Franz
...ess. He excellent actors and
...of opera, spectacle this
...excellent actors and excellent
...Myron Taylor's chanting of
...es from the Holy Scrolls impre-
...t. Sam Jaffe, as the ad the dif-
...e various moods Biblical periods blend together
has conjured up 10d provide
...Biblical periods blend
phenomenal effect and

To Jews "The Eternal Ro
which is the eternal road of p
ise—must have a deeper signific
than it has for others. But its
terest is not limited to what
special to a race or a faith. In a
dition to its religious fervor, it als
has the merit of being an amazing
example of showmanship on
heroic scale.

By BROOKS ATKINSON

ALTHOUGH the theatre is a
godless institution, "the ves-
tibule to hell," as a New
York Jeremiah once called
it, one of the few notable productions of the season is a humbly
moving religious play. Franz Werfel's "The Eternal Road," which
Max Reinhardt has directed at the
Manhattan Opera House. From almost any point of view it is an
illustrious piece of work. Although
it has been mounted on the

ancient stories of the Pe
Franz Werfel has compose
of libretto that has scant
value and is also mysti
scure in its use of chara
stories, although it doe
a practicable structure f
cious, beautifully patter
Using that for their
Dr. Reinhardt and hi
assistants have built
spectacle that is no
stupefying in size
affecting. There is

'THE ETERNAL ROAD'

Immense Reinhardt Spectac
Played on 5 Stage Levels

panorama flung up acros
levels, drenched in color an
music and swept to glowing
hundreds of actors. As mere p
it is an extraordinary achievement, filled
with superb pictorial effects and set off
with all the celebrated stagecraft o
'ittle Wizard of Leopoldskron.
rief, a sight. A large, distinguished
much photographed audience gave
landsom almost took the roof off to let

If this sounds like the hosann
a worshipper, let us assure the
that it is only a modest tr
to a work of stage art that no
Yorker or visitor to our great met
olis should miss. And again th
with sweep and majesty. The
tre returns to its high estate
magnificence and to religion in
Reinhardt production. Enor
this soaring reality hit

Full houses from nine performances a week brought in $24,000. The weekly payroll came to $31,000. This meant raising another $7,000 a week just to keep the show going, without mentioning such a trifling matter as profit. It was the union bosses that killed us. We had spent $100,000 recording the music by means of a fantastic newly invented RCA method. Petrillo had agreed that we need employ only four 'stand-by' musicians but when the show opened he insisted on sixteen. We could have managed with a dozen or so stagehands because of the elevators and moving ramps; the union insisted on forty-eight. There was nothing to do but continue raising money if we wanted to keep the play running; it ran for six months and each pay-day was a minor miracle.

Meanwhile Werfel came over with his wife, Alma Maria Schindler Mahler Gropius Werfel. She was a large woman, and in her day had been one of the reigning beauties of Vienna. She was a demonstrative Catholic and wore a heavy gold cross on her rather formidable bosom. I installed them in a suite at the St. Regis—*noblesse oblige;* $100 a day more or less wasn't going to make any difference. Besides, Werfel wasn't at all happy with the production. 'Why all the scenery, why all the music?' he wanted to know. 'This play should be put on with black curtains—that's all.' Well, you can't please all the people all the time; at least I pleased his wife by sending her a bottle of crème de menthe every day. She had recently lost her daughter by Walter Gropius, the architect, her second and only non-Jewish husband, and was drowning her sorrow.

At one point William S. Paley, head of Columbia Broadcasting System, gave me $25,000 to be used only when I had received the balance of the money I needed. But life is stronger than agreements. I went to Paley's lawyer and asked his advice. 'Go ahead and use it,' he said. 'He really doesn't care. He made the condition only to prod you to get the rest.' Paley's version of the story is slightly different. Fortunately this didn't affect our friendship nor his generous participation in my later undertakings—notably the Weizmann Institute of Science. More than thirty years after *The Eternal Road,* at one of the annual Weizmann Dinners in New York when Paley was introducing the main speaker, Victor, Lord Rothschild, he allowed himself to make the following delightful quip (much quoted soon after in the papers): 'Anyone who has dealt with Meyer knows that it's both an enriching and impoverishing experience.' I shall leave it to others to agree or disagree with the first half of the accolade. But I am willing to assert without reservation that I have not yet succeeded in impoverishing Bill Paley, nor his family and certainly not his beautiful wife, Barbara. Apart from his great charm and natural wit his most important asset was his mother (is, I should say). A small charming old lady, filigree-like, much devoted to art, particularly Jewish art; she herself paints. I never fail to visit her when business or pleasure brings me to Palm Beach.

Some people claim that I went so far as to borrow money from a waitress at the New Yorker. I don't remember that. But I do remember the rape, or seduction, or whatever it should be called, of my brother-in-law Adam Rosen. Adam was married to Shirley's sister, Ricky. He was Palestine-born and had come to the new world to seek his fortune. He owned a moderately successful travel agency which specialized in trips to the Holy Land. Adam had one consuming passion—an impressive stamp collection; it represented the labor and hoarding of a lifetime, and he cherished it far beyond its worth on the market. But that it had some worth kept on recurring to me in those desperate days. Shirley threatened me with the direst consequences if I ever went 'that far.' Adam had already given me what money he had; but seeing my plight he one day 'volunteered'—I did nothing more than hint—to hock the collection for me. When we went to the bank he told me that he felt as if he was going to his own funeral. It fetched $10,000. (He got it back eventually; in the ensuing years I paid back nearly all—well, not all—of my debts to the family.)

The man who really got his money's worth out of *The Eternal Road* was Morris Eisenman. He went to see it almost every night and always paid for his ticket. He loved to walk around backstage pinching the young dancers. He loved even more watching Moses hurl down the Tablets of the Law before the golden calf. Sometimes he would come to the theatre just for this scene. One late afternoon he was with me at Nizer's office when we were having our regular weekly huddle on the next instalment. The conference stretched on and on, unrelieved by a single inspiration. Eisenman was getting nervous; it was past curtain time and he had an uneasy feeling that he was going to miss Moses. At the last moment, unable to contain himself, he burst out with, 'Take whatever you need, just let me go.'

Spring came, the dead season for the theatre because of Lent. It occurred to me that since this was a biblical show Cardinal Hayes might be persuaded to give Catholics a special dispensation for *The Eternal Road*. I put Harry Hornstein, from the promotion staff, on the job, and it appeared that the Cardinal was willing. To make the deal binding—and to get some additional publicity—I wanted a convent to sponsor the tickets for the first night of Lent. After long negotiations an agreement was reached with a convent in the Bronx. For some mysterious reason they wanted to sign a contract with me personally, so an appointment was made for a delegation of three nuns to visit me. They could hardly have picked a better time. They arrived together with the furniture removers, who were stripping the office because of arrears of rent. I was shouting at the top of my voice and must have been using language not exactly appropriate for a delegation from a convent. The nuns, terrified, walked out. Hornstein burst into a wail of fury and frustration: 'For three weeks I slave to get this thing going; and here's how you go and botch it up.' This is not a stenographic record of Hornstein's outburst—it was too lethal for repro-duction here. Standing among the ruins of the office I couldn't have cared less; I was fed to the teeth. An hour later the nuns reappeared, heralded by my secretary, who signaled me cautiously in Yiddish. Suddenly my indifference disappeared, and in an instant I was transformed into the greatest spiritual figure of all time. 'My dear friends, you walked in, you walked out. What happened?' 'Oh,' they answered, 'we just went around the corner to the Church and prayed for your soul.' Having thus done their futile but well-meant bit for my spiritual salvation, they did their equally well-meant but no less futile bit for my financial salvation.

There is one incident which towers above all others as a mirror of my desperation. One day a committee of well-meaning Jews came to see me at the office. It was one of those days on which everything had gone wrong. The committee announced that they had come to present me with a plaque for outstanding services to Jewish culture and art in America. A plaque was exactly what I needed and I told them so. They were offended and rose to leave. Suddenly an idea hit me with the force of a Brink's van. 'Gentlemen,' I said, calling them back, 'I'm sorry if I have offended you in any way. The fact is that your approach to the whole matter is wrong. I am not the guy who deserves that plaque. True, I produced the thing, but without the help of Mr. So-and-So (and I mentioned one of my most generous contributors), I can assure you that *The Eternal Road* would never have seen the light of day. It is to him that the plaque should be presented.' The committee were skeptical at first but after I detailed the extent of his generosity, they reluctantly saw my point of view. One problem remained: my name had already been etched into the bronze. My long association with the printing profession solved that problem. I proposed that they use raised letters, infinitely more elegant than etched. I also advised them to make it a public presentation at City Hall.

When Mr. So-and-So received word of his award he immediately called me. I congratulated him warmly (he really did deserve some kind of recognition for his efforts) but added that it was too bad the show would be closing down before the presentation was made. 'We'll keep it going for another few weeks,' was his rejoinder, 'How much will you need?'

The play ran until the summer; by then I was physically, emotionally and psychologically exhausted. It was only then that the unions came forward with some compromise proposals. But it was too late; I simply could not go on.

On the day the show closed the cast said they wanted to do something for me. They knew I was broke, literally without a penny to my name, as they also knew I had sworn not to take any salary until the production showed a profit. We had been evicted from our apartment and had moved into a fleabag hotel on Amsterdam Avenue. Only Eisenman's weekly check to Shirley kept us from the poorhouse. Thus the last performance of *The Eternal Road* was a 'benefit' for the producer. Everybody, including the union people, worked for nothing, something that had never happened before. That last show was a matinée, and everyone connected with the play came to it. It was like going to a funeral, only the weeping mourners were so to speak the corpses. I myself was in the wings, crying. When all was over, Sam Jaffe announced that I was the beneficiary of $4,800—income from the 'benefit'—and the cast and audience began to shout for me. Sam pulled me on to the stage and handed me a wire from Reinhardt in California, but just as I began to read it all the lights—all $60,000 worth of them—went out. The power company was not in a sentimental mood. One of the cast struck a match and relayed it to Sam, and by the light of a dozen matches I read:

MY DEAR FRIEND THE GREAT WORK THAT YOU AND I BROUGHT TO LIFE NOW LIES RIGIDLY MUTELY ON THE DARK STAGE YOU SUCCEEDED EVEN THOUGH TEMPORARILY IN INTERRUPTING THE DANCE AROUND THE GOLDEN CALF AND RAISING THE TABLETS ANEW BUT NOW WE MUST RESIGN OURSELVES THE LIGHT THAT WE LIT TOGETHER IN THE MANHATTAN OPERA HOUSE WILL SHINE UNDIMMED IN THE HISTORY OF THE THEATRE AND OF THE JEWISH PEOPLE IN FRIENDSHIP MAX REINHARDT.

12   A Jewish State in Flushing Meadows

My theatrical association with Reinhardt did not end with the closing of *The Eternal Road*. I went on to produce a few plays with him in Hollywood, among them Goldoni's *Servant of Two Masters*. Reinhardt also founded an experimental theatre in Hollywood and I helped him raise some money for it. His main support came from a great admirer, William S. Paley. Reinhardt wrote me fourteen pages of the dreams and hopes he attached to the enterprise. He wanted to establish 'the great American theatre' after the model of the Théâtre Français in Paris, the Burgtheater in Vienna, and the Moscow Art Theatre. He wanted to initiate a 'California Theatre on a scale much greater than Salzburg.' His mind was full of plans and fantasies. It was 1937 and he added: 'In Europe we went through war, revolution, depression, inflation, deflation and crises of every sort. In all this time the theatre did not suffer at all; on the contrary, the crowds were incomparably greater than in the well-fed period of peace. (Only the National Dictatorship has finally almost succeeded in killing the theatre; for art is intrinsically unable to flourish under dictatorship. How, indeed, can the theatre continue to exist if the artist is judged not by his talent but by his grandmother?).' He closes with: 'And you must at last be convinced, by the length of this *megillah*, how earnestly I am counting on your cooperation. Do not fail me. Dance tirelessly, and with my blessing, about all the golden calves you can find.' The German text of the above was ferociously impressive; it had biblical overtones. The last sentence is: '*Tanze unermüdlich und mit meinem Segen um alle die goldenen Kälber die Du finden kannst.*'

Reinhardt established his theatre, and his festival, and his dramatic school; but (to turn the phrase) his school of dramatics was on its way out. *The Eternal Road* was his last great piece, the grand climax of the Reinhardtesque; it was also his *nekome*, revenge, on Hitler!

In order to keep my Reinhardt threads together, I must jump ahead three or four years. I had by this time done with the theatre, or so I thought. I had finished the Palestine Pavilion at the World's Fair which was showmanship of another variety—more of this later—and was already working with Dr. Weizmann.

Reinhardt had returned to New York from Hollywood. He stayed first at the Ambassador Hotel and then, when the money ran short, at the less opulent Gladstone. He continued to hold court, however, regardless of the state of the bank account. Helene Thimig was with him, as was Gottfried. One day Gottfried called me: his father was giving a party that evening for some actors and actresses, among them the incomparable Stella Adler, directors, producers and playwrights, and my presence was a must.

Shirley and I arrived in the midst of a very gay assembly, We seemed to know everybody from one transmigration or another, and before long we were sitting in a circle reminiscing. 'Come on, Meyer, tell us some stories from *The Eternal Road,*' someone asked, innocently I thought. By then the tragedies had taken on a humorous coloration. Tragedy and humor are kindred souls; it is only a question of the passage of time.

It didn't take long to get me started and whenever some detail escaped me, I had half a dozen prompters to fall back upon. 'Tell the story about the way Bel Geddes hit water,' came from one side. 'Don't forget the one about the Jews with the plaque,' came from another. I began to have the feeling that everyone there had been given a cue sheet, designed to evoke from the vast store of my three years' eternal hardship the tragic, the hilarious, the scandalous, the divine. It wasn't until two or three o'clock in the morning that the party broke up.

A week later my suspicions were confirmed. I learned that the party was no party, that everyone had been rehearsed by Gottfried, everyone, that is, but me, aided and abetted by his father, and everything recorded in the next room. Gottfried had an idea for a play and I was his major source of material. It was to be called 'The Magnificent Mr. Maibaum' and Mr. Maibaum was merely a dramatic rendering of Mr. Meyer Weisgal during the days of *The Eternal Road.*

Gottfried's novel idea was that I would actually play the part of Mr. Maibaum, the producer, Reinhardt would play the part of the director and Bel Geddes would be the villain. He planned to create a composite angel out of Eisenman, Maurice Levin and Alfred Strelsin and some of the others, include a running debate throughout between the composer and the author on whether it was a musical play or a play with music, and spice it with some of the back-stage love affairs that had gone on during the run.

There was a further novel aspect to Gottfried's idea: we, the characters of the play, would be not only the actors in it but also the director, producer and angels. We would make a fortune and recoup all the losses we suffered from *The Eternal Road*. My family would get their money back; Adam would be able to unhock his stamp collection. We would have a hit the likes of which had not been seen since *Abie's Irish Rose*.

Every Saturday afternoon for weeks thereafter, as the writing progressed, I was called in by Gottfried to check on the authenticity of the script. The entire production would be mounted on a shoe-string budget not exceeding $75,000.

What's the old saying? 'Man proposes, God disposes.' Reinhardt suddenly died. We lost our enthusiasm. Pages of the unfinished play are now mouldering in Gottfried's Schlossingen near Salzburg, not far from Leopoldkronschloss, where *The Eternal Road* was conceived.

At the same time that Gottfried and his collaborator (whose name I have forgotten) were sweating over every line of 'The Magnificent Mr. Maibaum,' another sure-fire theatrical success was germinating in my mind. The reader may recall that my so-called literary career began with an essay on *The Merchant of Venice* during my last year of high school. The character of Shylock had always fascinated me. Some fifteen years after my first encounter with the worthy gentleman, I purchased the serial rights of *The Last Days of Shylock* by Ludwig Lewisohn, for my Toronto paper. In 1940, I came upon a play by St. John Ervine called *The Lady of Belmont*, meaning Portia, who was the undoing of Shylock in the *Merchant*. It wasn't exactly Shakespeare but it was a fascinating play. Portia and Shylock become intimate friends, visit with each other often and recount their experiences. They turn out to be the only authentic people in the story. All the others—Antonio, Bassanio, Lorenzo—are revealed as scoundrels, thieves, pansies and what not.

I went to Reinhardt with the idea of producing—after we were through with 'Mr. Maibaum,' of course—a 'double header.' With the same actors, the same theatre, the same sets we would produce on alternate nights *The Merchant of Venice* and *The Lady of Belmont*. People would buy one ticket for two evenings. Reinhardt reserved judgment until he had read the play, a copy of which I immediately produced for him. A week later we were deep into discussions as to how the play would be mounted. Reinhardt would direct it; I would produce it; our angels who would have regained their wings from 'Mr. Maibaum' would finance the double header. Alas! Reinhardt died and as with 'Mr. Maibaum,' I lost all interest in *The Lady of Belmont*.

A few months before he died I witnessed an unusual scene, unplotted in any of his *régisseur* books. It was 1942, in the thick of the war; Soviet-American friendship was in full bloom, and a delegation of Soviet artists came to the United States on a goodwill mission. Two of its members were Shlomo Michoels, the Yiddish actor and director of the Yiddish Art Theatre of Moscow, and Itzik Pfeffer the poet, both of whom were to be murdered by Stalin shortly after the war; but while they lived they were being used as Jewish symbols of anti-Fascism. At a tumultuous rally in Chicago which both men were to address, the platform collapsed and Michoels broke a leg; he was sent to a hospital in New York. It so happened that Reinhardt was in New York at the time. He had directed Michoels in Mendele's *Benjamin the Third*, and hearing of his arrival in town, was seized with a great longing to see him again. But he wanted to see him without Soviet companions—not an easy matter. Soviet delegations when sent abroad move about in 'protective alliances'; that is, they always contain one stooge, unidentified, of course, to keep an eye on the others.

Pfeffer, poor bastard, was Michoel's bodyguard. He came with him to New York and would not let him out of his sight. Joe Brainin was at that time chairman of the American Committee of Jewish Artists, Writers and Scientists which was the official host of the anti-Fascist delegation. Joe's passing flirtation with the Soviet motherland did not damage our friendship. One day I asked him to try and spirit Michoels—who was equally anxious to see Reinhardt again—out of the hospital and to my house. Providentially, Pfeffer was at the moment substituting for Michoels at an out-of-town meeting, under the conviction that his ward was safely and immovably strapped down in the New York Hospital. Strapped down he was, but not safely and immovably; for we got him out by a sort of James Bond operation. Somehow Michoels managed to convince the doctor that the destiny of Russia, and of the free world, depended on his secret disappearance from the hospital for a few hours; the escort of a nurse was firmly rejected, and he was released in Joe's keeping for one evening. Joe brought him to my house, in a cast and on crutches.

It was a highly emotional occasion, with many reminiscences and much drinking. As the evening wore on Michoels held forth eloquently on the glories of the Soviet motherland, the freedom she afforded her artists, the roseate future that was in store for all. He also tried to explain to Reinhardt why outside the theatre he did not think it necessary to associate himself with things Jewish. But as the night wore on, and the alcohol produced its effect, he lost his way, began to weep, and to lament the lot of the Jews of Russia. It was a pitiful and shocking sight and we were thoroughly uncomfortable. Then, having wept himself out, and perhaps sobered up a little, he changed tack once more, turned to Reinhardt and begged him to come to the Soviet Union. It was as if he had forgotten his own words. 'You will be received like a king,' he said. 'Flowers will be strewn in your path. I can even get Stalin, personally, to invite you.' Later he confided to Joe that he had only played the drunk, otherwise he could not have summoned up the courage to say what he said. An invitation did, as a matter of fact, come, but not from Stalin.

In 1943 Reinhardt died as the result of an accident while he was walking his dog in Fire Island. He was only seventy years old, and in remarkably good health. His family insisted on an orthodox Jewish funeral, and I undertook to arrange it and have it done in good taste. Wanting for my dead friend the best of both worlds, I went to Stephen Wise, who presided at a most dignified ceremony—possibly the only orthodox funeral in his career. Reinhardt was buried in a *tallis*.

After the war a clamor arose over the final disposition of his body, for which cities competed—Vienna, Salzburg, Berlin—as they did of old for Homer's birth. But Reinhardt had never wanted his remains returned to Europe; he wanted to be buried in Palestine, and for the time being his body rests in a vault in America. It is now proposed that he be reinterred in Israel on the hundredth anniversary of his birth, 1973, and that a theatre be established in his name, which will contain a library of his *régisseur* books, which are, of course, theatrical treasures. Each of them is about five times the size of the play. Every gesture, every move, every turn, twist, grimace, pause, stress is indicated. Reinhardt would go up on the stage and act every part, man, woman or child. He molded his actors as a sculptor molds his clay; it was a great experience to watch him.

Years after his death his son Gottfried called me from Hollywood, where he worked at M.G.M. as a producer and director, to say that forty *régisseur* books had been put up for auction and had been bought by Marilyn Monroe; Gottfried hadn't the money at the time to buy them himself. I bought them back for $1,000 from Miss Monroe and gave them to Gottfried, who later repaid me.

Gottfried was very close to his father and—considering the environment he came from—peculiarly Jewish. He showed great understanding for our problems with *The Eternal Road* and helped us innumerable times in solving some of them. His brother Wolfgang, also in films, was another kettle of fish. He was rather remote and cold and reserved. He rarely took an interest in what was going on at the Hammerstein Opera House. Strangely he once confided in me that he fasted on Yom Kippur—whether in the interests of his girth or his soul I never was able to discover. To me he seemed a complete *goy*.

One day in September, 1967, I was sitting in the house in Rehovot dictating these memoirs. Israel had recently emerged from the Six-Day War and the inundation of Jews for the Holidays and the fiftieth anniversary of the Balfour Declaration was about to set in. Rehovot and the Institute were still tranquil; all one heard was the clatter of workmen behind the house constructing a small mansion for Isaac Wolfson— background music. I had just begun to draft the chapter on Reinhardt, and I had fallen into a nostalgic mood.

The doorbell rang and Yaki Sheibe, my major domo, private nurse, chief tactician and sometimes cook—in short a 'sabra' jewel—informed me that a young man wanted to see me. I made a lightning trip back through thirty years and went to greet my visitor. Very young he was, eighteen or nineteen, and extremely handsome. 'My name,' he said, 'is Tom Reinhardt.' He was the son of Wolfgang, Max's grandson; he had come from Munich to settle in Israel, and planned to study biology in Haifa. Thus did Max Reinhardt reach the Promised Land.

But having mentioned Reinhardt's sins, I am reminded of my own— or at least those of them in which Reinhardt had some share. When my first-born, Mendy, was at Harvard, he made his debut as an actor in a Russian play called *Mashenka*, and I invited Reinhardt to come up with me to see it. Mendel was sixteen or seventeen and was cast in the part of a septuagenarian. Reinhardt sat and watched, and when it was over he pronounced judgment: '*Er ist fabelhaft.*' Had I not been besotted enough to repeat it, Mendy might have turned his back on the theatre and become a professor of English literature at Harvard.

But now I must take up the narrative again. When *The Eternal Road* collapsed—and I with it—and I had ended all my other commitments to Reinhardt, there came a pause, I still had some irons in the fire, but essentially I was a free agent, with some of the $4,800 'benefit' still in my pocket. I toyed with the idea of going back to edit a Zionist journal—I was not exactly fascinated by it—and dropped it when Henry Montor called me. He was chief fund raiser for the United Palestine Appeal; he wanted to know if I was interested in the project of Jewish participation in the

approaching New York's fair of 1939. It was Chicago and 1932 all over
again. The Jews had been invited to participate, and there was already a
committee of notables which had not decided what form the participation should take. It was headed by George Backer, who was being
groomed by Felix Warburg for the place of leadership in American
Jewry, and one of its members was my old comrade-in-arms Nathan
Strauss Jr. Neither Backer nor Strauss nor Montor knew what they
wanted, and the best Montor could do was to offer me to them.

I went to see George Backer, whom I had never met before, and we
talked for a long time. I was immediately captivated by the man. He was
handsome, articulate, full of charm, endowed with fine tastes, a student
of history and a writer. After long years of friendship with George it is
my considered opinion that he would have been one of the great forces
in American Jewry but for one deficiency in his life: he had never had to
earn his living. Somewhat to my surprise he was ready to agree to a
Palestine Pavilion. It must be remembered that the sentiment in favor of
the Jewish Homeland was not, in 1938, the universal and solid thing it is
today. For that matter Backer himself was not a Zionist; I had expected
him to balk, and countersuggest something 'Jewish,' not 'Zionist.' Instead, he simply asked me to draw up a plan, which I did. According to
George's account, the genesis of the Pavilion and his first encounter with
me simply threw him off balance. Allowing for literary license and the
alleged serenity of what he called his 'pre-Weisgalian universe' his version
is on the whole true. He writes in his chapter of *The Odyssey of an
Optimist*:

Mr. Henry Montor rescued the meeting. 'I think you'd better send for Meyer Weisgal.'
    I didn't know Mr. Weisgal, but any suggestion would have seemed a happy one at
that moment. 'How do I get hold of him?'
    'I'll talk to him tonight,' said Montor, 'and he'll be here by eleven tomorrow morning.'
    I went to bed that night without the slightest notion that it was my last night in my
own world.
    The next morning at eleven Mr. Weisgal arrived accompanied by energy, determi-
nation, and an immediate question: 'Well, what's the trouble?'
    And with that almost obvious question I lost hold of the pavilion. A little frightened,
I answered: 'Well, some people think there ought to be a Palestine Pavilion.'
    'That,' said Weisgal, 'is a very good idea.' He stopped and yesterday's silence was
renewed. But only for a moment. Then he said: 'Well, why don't you do something
about it?'
    With a certain horror I realized that Mr. Weisgal was an ignorant man, that he didn't
know of the great physical law prohibiting the creation of something out of nothing.
    Nevertheless, his ignorance proved to be terribly important because it led him to say,
'You don't seem to know what to do. Shall I do it?'

To this day I do not know why I said, 'Oh, yes—that would be fine! Just go right ahead.'

He was younger then by almost thirty years and had a little more patience than he has now. He allowed me a few questions. For almost ten minutes I was allowed to ask what he expected to do and how. But after that he said, 'Now look, if we're going to get this done, you're going to have to stop asking all those questions.'

Since I had lost command with his first sentence, there was no use in further pretense, so I retired—rather gracefully, I thought—to the small chair beside my desk.

My plan included not only the grand idea as such, but the method of raising the necessary funds. Somewhere in the small print I included a salary for myself—$250 a week—which I did not think excessive in view of the fact that I would be raising most of the money for that and for everything else too.

A few weeks after my appointment I was less than delighted to read in *The Chicago Jewish Chronicle* the following editorial:

From present indications, and judging from newspaper reports, Meyer Weisgal is on the way toward again inveigling the Jews of New York into an enterprise which is doomed before it is started. The Jews of New York were hopeful of proper representation at the coming World's Fair to be held next year—a representation which would be a credit and an honor to the Jews of America and the world over. The plan as it stands now is not a 'Jewish Pavilion' but a 'Palestine Pavilion,' which may or may not be the right thing. But to have Weisgal the generalissimo of this great enterprise is certainly not showing good judgment. While Weisgal has vision, ability and enterprise, he has no understanding of the value of money—especially somebody else's money. At present it is figured that it will be necessary to raise $250,000 to finance the Palestine Pavilion, but before Weisgal gets through with it it will be more likely to take twice that amount [etc., etc.].

Actually the Pavilion did cost almost twice as much, but it ran for nearly two years, instead of one, as originally planned, and the income covered the expenditure. I don't know whether the *Jewish Chronicle* ever ate its words, and whether it ever saw the real point, namely, that the Palestine Pavilion was a great event in the life of American Jewry. Its opening attracted the largest single day's attendance in the history of the Fair, and the total number of visitors to it was over two million. That article had been brought to my attention by my secretary, Nell Ziff, whom I had hired for the Pavilion not only because she was a highly intelligent college graduate who knew shorthand-typing, but because she had a rich Jewish and Hebrew background and I knew I wouldn't have to spell things out for her. On top of it all she was the President of Junior Hadassah. The match was so perfect that Nell stayed with me for years into a variety of other enterprises. When she finally abandoned me to marry, she eased my crisis by sending me her younger sister, Reva. Reva, too, married eventually and left, but after raising a family, returned and is with me still in my New York office.

About eight years ago I got a letter from Nell, who was living in Chicago. In the letter she enclosed some yellowing typewritten pages. It was the draft of an article I had dictated to her under the influence of our joint indignation at reading the *Jewish Chronicle* article. It was called 'In Defense of MWW by MWW or the Odyssey of a Lunatic in the Zionist Vineyard.' The article was never published—in fact, it was never finished: it was filed away. I lost interest in the whole business; it served only to let off steam. Somehow Nell preserved it for over twenty years. But I am way ahead.

The story begins with Grover Whalen, the President of the Fair. If we were going to have a Palestine Pavilion the first thing to be negotiated was a site at Flushing Meadows. From Backer's office—having none of my own yet—I called Whalen and he sent a limousine to bring me out to him. We walked around for a while and he gave me a general idea of the layout. One section had been set aside for the national pavilions, and that is where I wanted us to be. There was of course no Jewish State as yet, but I believed in its impending arrival on the scene of history, and I wanted the idea of Jewish sovereignty to be anticipated there, in Flushing Meadows. It was essential to my conception of our participation. The management of the Fair did not see it my way, but Whalen did. He was an Irishman; he knew something of the British efforts to abort the Jewish Homeland; and there was no love lost between him and the British. So one day we were in the area of the national pavilions, the next day we were out; the upshot was a compromise on the borderline, and the contract was signed.

Concurrently with these negotiations we explored the financial possibilities. First in line were the Zionist Organization, Hadassah and the other Zionist groups. The Keren Hayesod—at that time the central fund for the upbuilding of Palestine—and the Jewish National Fund, the land-buying agency, lent us, after a great deal of haggling, $150,000. We had, on our Board of Directors or on the Advisory Board, every Jew of prominence who was willing to be associated with the enterprise. Stephen Wise was Honorary President; George Backer, President; Israel Goldstein, Chairman of the Board; Louis Lipsky, Louis Nizer, Harry Fisher of Chicago, Julian Mack, Robert Szold and a host of others were among our supporters. One particularly valuable adjunct was Harold Jacobi of

Schenley Whiskey; he was our Treasurer and gave us an office on the twenty-eighth floor of the Empire State Building.

Having rejected George Backer's suggestion that Bel Geddes design the Pavilion, I came up with the name of a Palestinian architect, Aryeh el-Hanani. He was unknown here, and I had heard of him only as the designer of the Levant Fair of Tel Aviv; but what I wanted was something authentically Palestinian. I reached him and he started work. We would meet soon in Palestine.

But first we laid the cornerstone as an earnest of our intentions. It was a somber and moving ceremony, with none of the high spirits usually attending such occasions. I must recall the year again—1938. Hitler had been in power five years. The ultimate infamy of his designs against the Jewish people was still concealed, but enough had been revealed to cast a pall over our future. In Palestine the Grand Mufti had enlisted the Axis powers in *his* special effort to liquidate the Jewish Homeland in the making. Since 1936 the Yishuv, our Jewish Palestine, had been in a state of siege: colonies were attacked, orchards and grain fields set on fire, roads mined; senseless assassinations by roving bands were frequent. In those days, ignorant of severer trials still to come, we quoted from the Song of Deborah: 'The highways were unoccupied, the travelers walked through byways.' The description was not exact for our time, but it was true that traveling between Tel Aviv and Jerusalem was for a time done in convoys and under military guard. And meanwhile the pressure to get out of Germany was becoming frantic. Thus the atmosphere in which we performed the ceremony was heavily clouded—as it happened, literally not less than figuratively. Mayor La Guardia signed the dedication scroll, which read: 'In an hour of darkness for the Jewish people, a ray of light, pointing to a future of hope and security, radiates from the ancient Jewish Homeland in Palestine. . .' And Thomas Mann was the main speaker.

The underlying idea of the Palestine Pavilion was to depict in simple and impressive form Jewish achievement in that country. We were not seeking to make a political point, either in respect of the Arabs or even of the British; we wanted to make a statement of fact: that in 1938 Jewish Palestine was a reality; its towns, villages, schools, hospitals and cultural institutions had risen in a land that until our coming had been derelict and waste. It was certainly not our intention to turn the Pavilion into a bazaar for the sale of Palestinian products, as certain groups shortsightedly urged. That attempt had been made more than once, elsewhere, with unhappy results; the effort to sell goods instead of the idea of the Jewish rebirth and the rebirth of the land had ruined several exhibits.

I wanted a miniature Palestine in Flushing Meadows. I did not want a miniature American extravaganza—I was not going to compete with General Motors, or with the Soviet colossus that looked down on all the other national exhibits. Palestine was small but dynamic and graceful; its people were hard working and idealistic; the architecture of the Pavilion, the setting and the interior displays had to reflect just that. And, to anticipate a little, they did it; the modest Palestine Pavilion won the second prize at the Fair for aesthetics and beauty of design.

There was much to be done before we achieved that result. It had become obvious to me that I could not give orders to el-Hanani, the architect and designer, and his associates, from a distance of six thousand miles, and rely on them to bring over completed plans. I had to go over, absorb some of the atmosphere, get the feel of that Jewish homeland in the making, pick up ideas on the spot. And I judged that the best time would be around Rosh Hashanah-Yom Kippur, as the High Holidays practically paralyzed New York Jewry.

Twelve years had passed since my first visit to Palestine, and I planned to spend ten days there and catch the spirit of the country—that was as much as I could manage. Even so the ten days dwindled to nine; for I was marooned in Alexandria for one day, waiting for a plane. With a guide I spent the evening walking around. I was filled with horror by the juxtaposition of squalor and oriental splendor, tortuous alleys choking with the accumulated filth of a thousand years squeezed in between frontages of wide, elegant boulevards. I wrote in my notes at the time that if these people should ever rise in revolt, their access to their overlords, in whose backyards they lived, would be very easy.

From Port Said to Palestine the air route lies over the sea. I was, on this, my second visit, approaching the country by air, and I must record that the sight of Tel Aviv from the air was not inspiring; it looked tiny and helpless. Nor were my spirits lifted by my reception at the airport. No one was there but a Tommy with a fixed bayonet. I waited half an hour for some other sign of life, and finally a call came through from Haifa, advising me that a plane was on its way for me. Would I kindly wait another hour? I said no, and hung up. Finally I managed to find a taxi, and after an uneventful ride was dumped in front of the Tel Aviv office of Misr Air, the Egyptian airlines, to be greeted at last by Emanuel Rosen, my brother-in-law Adam's brother, the Palestine half of their travel agency. His first question was: 'Are you really here?' I was still annoyed and angry. 'Where do you think I am?' 'You should *bensh gomel*,' he said, recite the prayer for delivery from danger. 'Yesterday two Jews were killed by marauders on the road from Lydda to Tel Aviv. You should have waited for the plane.'

With Emanuel at my side, still mumbling about '*gomel*,' we drove to the Gat Rimon, Tel Aviv's Waldorf Astoria. There was a great to-do on my arrival, with the owner and the clerks extending themselves, apparently anxious to make my stay as comfortable as possible. I was immediately dubbed 'Doctor.' I protested but to no avail. I remained 'Doctor' until I departed. In quick succession there arrived Aryeh el-Hanani, Avraham Idelson and Alexander Yevzeroff of the Levant Fair, Elias Newmann, the artist, and the inevitable Chona, at this juncture a resident of Palestine. The mix-up of the plane and the car had become an '*affaire célèbre*' with explanations and counter-explanations flying back and forth until I was exhausted by the interminable apologies. I pleaded that we should let the case rest for further discussion at a later date, but I was nonetheless comforted by the solicitude in the oft-repeated refrain: 'But you might have been killed.'

It was Friday afternoon, and for the next nine days I crammed something like seventy-two hours into each day. Actually, I doubt if I slept an average of four hours a night.

The first object of my attention was the Fair Grounds north of Tel Aviv, beyond the Yarkon River. I was delighted by the fine work being done there in olive wood and copper. I met other assistants of el-Hanani, artists, artisans and laborers. In my usual debonair fashion I put them all at ease, which, I was later told, was not exactly the thing to do. I must maintain the aloofness of an 'American entrepreneur.' How to speak Yiddish, and remain aloof at the same time was, for me at any rate, impossible.

El-Hanani presented me with the schedule that had been worked out for me. It included receptions, public addresses, courtesy calls, meetings— enough to keep a man busy for a month. I laid down the law: no ceremonies. I would travel by day, meet my co-workers by night, and that was it. I was compelled to make one exception—I had to receive my colleagues of the press, or they would be mortally offended. At least, that was how Gershon Agronsky had put it.

At midnight, after dinner at el-Hanani's home, I let myself be inveigled, half asleep as I was, into going for a late coffee to Ginati, Tel Aviv's Café du Dôme, the gathering place of its intellectuals. It was famous also for its expulsion of Chona, who like Moses could 'behold it but not enter.' There we were met again by Idelson and Yevzeroff, and continued our talks of the afternoon. But before long I was drawn into the crowd.

Zionists I had imagined long passed into the great beyond were there sipping tea or coffee, putting the world in order and arranging the Jewish future. Ginati was the newsmart of the Jewish metropolis, where you heard every evening what would appear in the papers the next morning. A murder on the highways, a clash between Arabs and our settlers, a statement by the British, the last utterance of Hitler—all were heard first in Ginati. So were the latest witticisms. 'Weizmann has just sent a cable to Benes!' 'What did it say?' 'Do not despair, Benes, England will take care of you as it does of me.' I listened fascinated. The liveliness, the humor, the satire and the grimness of the talk around me filled me with a sense of the indestructible spirit of my people. As I was to learn in later years, and under even darker circumstances, it is always the Jews outside of Israel who easily lose heart. In Israel, or Palestine as it then was, they carried on with undiminished vigor and faith.

Three Jews who had each lost a son recently in attacks on northern settlements were discreetly pointed out to me. I glanced at them furtively. They sat there, sipping their coffees, participating in the conversations. How could they conceal from those that did not know of it the anguish gnawing at their hearts? When I took leave of my friends I asked to be permitted to walk back to my hotel alone. I wanted to take in what I had just seen and heard. Death hovered over the country—and here Jews laughed, jested, argued, as if they were surrounded by a tranquil world. Unable to sleep that night, in spite of, or perhaps because of my exhaustion, I sat for some hours on the balcony of my room, facing the sea. I was beginning to understand what the phrase we had so often and so easily bandied about, 'a normal people,' meant in reality: a people that took danger and death in its stride, not cowering in the cellars of Kishinev, as Bialik describes them in his famous pogrom poem, not fleeing from the threat of the killer, but facing him; unshaken, unpanicked, as part of life's business.

I was to return to Ginati almost every night of my brief stay. It was a fascinating aspect of the life of the country, or perhaps I should say mirror. I learned there almost as much as in my feverish travels.

These I began the next morning. Almost everything I saw was new to me. Those who have been recent visitors to Israel for the first time may be enormously impressed; their experience is enviable in its way; but it cannot compare with the impressions of one who had been there almost at the beginning of the work, returned there twelve years later, and was stunned by the transformation. There were new settlements everywhere, graceful little towns and villages dotting the countryside, roads where there had been bridle paths, orchards where there had been sand dunes, grain fields where there had been swamps. Tel Aviv was a city of 150,000 inhabitants—what had looked so tiny and fragile from the air revealed itself, on closer inspection, as a world city in the making, bursting with vitality. And such was the impression all over the country, in spite of the murderous attacks on the colonies.

Sometimes I get the impression, as I look back, that it was easier in those days of the fierce beginnings, to get the spirit of the rebirth than it is today, with so much already completed. This much I can say, at any rate: it was on my second visit to Palestine that I knew with an inward knowing why I was a Zionist.

My first stop on that first day was the town of Ramat Gan, north of Tel Aviv. Abraham Krinitzi, its Mayor then and for the next thirty years— that's what you call progress—was a furniture manufacturer whom we had entrusted with the making of the eucalyptus doors for our Pavilion. I found him far more interested in trees for landscape than for timber. Ramat Gan was a real garden city in those days; it has since been 'damaged by improvement,' as O. Henry wrote years ago about New York. Krinitzi took me to see the synagogue, set in a lovely little park, where elderly Jews sat on benches whiling away the hours. Krinitzi paused there, to explain what it all meant to him. 'In the town I came from,' he said, 'there was a garden. Any Jew who tried to sit down on one of its benches was immediately chased away. I was always dreaming of a park where Jews could go after their prayers and sit on the benches under the trees.' Krinitzi died at the age of eighty-one or eighty-two in an automobile accident, while still Mayor of Ramat Gan.

From Ramat Gan we went on to Givat Hashlosha, the first kibbutz I really saw. I walked that Sabbath afternoon about its fields and buildings, I watched the children with their parents, and I remembered the unbelievably stupid tales that had been set going about these experiments in communal living, tales of promiscuity, of children not knowing their own parents, of husbands and wives in group marriages. I remembered the passionate debates in Zionist circles, and wondered what it had all been about. This quiet, respectable almost bourgeois setting, the peacefulness, the homeliness . . . And the pride they took in their new community center which was in process of construction, in their cowsheds, their hen roosts. . . The spokesman for the kibbutz was a comrade Milstein. And he stuttered—symbolically enough. The kibbutz was no place for talk. As we walked around he kept watching me closely. He caught me in a moment of perplexity—of moral perplexity, but not of the kind he seemed to suspect. 'You don't like it, eh?' 'Oh, that isn't it at all. I've just been thinking that I would like to be part of it, should have been part of it—but I didn't have the courage. And I don't have it now. America has spoiled me.'

The day drew on, I had to tear myself away. We went on to Ramat Hashavim, a small-holders' settlement made up entirely of German Jews, former professors, lawyers, engineers. In my notes on that visit I see the words 'victims of Hitler's brutality.' Had I then known what awaited those who had not left betimes! Here these former academicians had built a new life, and it was not a cruel one at all. This chicken and egg-producing farm, popularly known as Kfar Kukuriku, smelt of *gemütlichkeit* and efficiency. It was a semi-cooperative based on intensive cultivation. David Trietsch, 'the dreamer of Kurfürstendam,' was the father of the idea. I remembered how he had once come to me in the Am Zo Hotel in Berlin—this was during my first visit to Europe—and had expounded his fantastic notion of settling sixteen million Jews in Palestine—with facts, figures, charts, graphs to prove its feasibility. I asked Dr. Powitzer, the leading spirit of Ramat Hashavim, if Trietsch's principles were working out. 'Not quite,' he answered, 'but if he were only fifty percent right it would suffice.'

Our next stop was Natanya, perched on the sea. It was a thriving, unfinished city, reminiscent of an American boom town. I was told that it was the summer retreat of Palestine's Jewish 'millionaires,' those who had at least $10,000, or £10,000. Diminutive Oved Ben Ami, who years before had come to me to print an item in *The New Palestine* was enthroned as Mayor. (Like Krinitzi in Ramat Gan, he made it a lifetime job.) There were stories circulated about his immense wealth and his palatial home, and I was asked if I would like to see his home. My answer was an emphatic 'no.'! It was enough that he had conceived of Natanya and built it—with less idealism to be sure than the members of the kib-butzim. But Natanya was a fact, and in Palestine facts counted infinitely more than British colonial policy.

After Natanya we returned to Tel Aviv where el-Hanani was waiting to take me on a tour of the city. He considered it necessary that a proper artistic interpretation be put on what I was about to see. I tried to recall the Tel Aviv of twelve years before, but I failed. It was a different city, better and more beautiful. The houses were graceful, the balconies studded with flowers, the streets wide and clean, the public buildings imposing. In 1909 it was a sand dune. In 1938 a modern city of more than 150,000 people. In my notes I wrote: 'A people possessing this reservoir of strength will not be swerved from its historical course by political setbacks or physical violence. The constructive power of the Jewish people which has been released in Palestine is not pitted against a counter-force similarly constructive; it is pitted against forces of destruction and decay, British colonial intrigue and ineptitude, buttressed and supported by a world that is morally bankrupt and politically insane. Our work may be retarded for a while, but the facts, the immovable facts of Palestine, will write the last chapter here.'

On the third day my itinerary lay southward, through Rishon Lezion and Givat Brenner and Rehovot. On my way to Palestine I had stopped over in London to see Dr. Weizmann, and he had made me promise to pay special attention to his own special project, the Daniel Sieff Research Institute, later the Weizmann Institute. Dr. Benjamin Bloch, the Director, had been advised of my coming, and he had been instructed to give me a thorough briefing. To say that my interest in science was peripheral would be claiming an unwarranted degree of intimacy; I knew nothing whatsoever about it. I was interested in the Institute only to the degree that it might furnish me with material for the Pavilion. No revelation came to me as I wandered through the small compound. No voice from within or from above called out to me, 'Meyer, son of Shloyme Chaim Weisgal, of Kikl, for thee is reserved the destiny of turning this modest research center into a mighty institute.' If, some day, a Hollywood scenarist finds nothing better to do than make a Cecil B. DeMille spectacle of my life, he will have me stop at this moment, on a hillock overlooking the Daniel Sieff Institute, and cry out: 'Dear God, if I only had a hundred million dollars, I would show the world what a scientific institute in Palestine ought to be.' This hypothetical scenarist would be drawing entirely on his imagination. My notes for that day betray not the slightest premonition of what was to be my life's work. Indeed, they read a little drily: 'We arrive at the Institute, which is on the outskirts of Rehovot, an inspiring array of beautiful buildings, fine landscaping, with an incipient garden, shaded with trees. Weizmann, I am told, strolls here whenever he has to make a chemical analysis of the Zionist political situation. For other analyses he uses the laboratory. Dr. Bloch is away but he has assigned Dr. Frieda Goldschmidt (a former professor of the University of Berlin) to take us around—a charming elderly lady, herself a distinguished scientist. I listen to the descriptions of the scientific experiments and understand as little as the other visitors... My interest is not in pure science but in its relation to the building process of the Jewish National

Home.' My notes end up with: 'Weizmann also asked me to make a point of visiting his home. The watchman, a Connecticut Jewish Yankee, wanted a document from Weizmann to that effect, so I had to content myself with a view from the outside.'

That afternoon I met with my journalists and then with the directors of the Manufacturers' Association, managed to get to Habimah for a performance of *Shver tzu zein a Yid* by Sholem Aleichem, and brought my third day in the Holy Land to its conclusion . . . at Ginati.

The next morning I left for Jerusalem; it was the day before Yom Kippur eve. I had to clear up some political aspects of the Pavilion with the Zionist hierarchy, arrange for certain publications, see the Hadassah Hospital and the Hebrew University on Mount Scopus, meet a dozen people and get back to Tel Aviv before sundown the next day.

At the offices of the Jewish Agency I bumped into Dr. Arthur Ruppin. We almost kissed. '*Ach, Herr Weisgal, immer noch der selbe. Was macht Ihre schöne Frau und Kinder? Mit so einem Ponim solche schöne Kinder.*' He never forgot, nor did I, that he included me as a Jewish curio in his *Soziologie der Juden*, and made a Galitzianer out of me. I took the opportunity to tell him that if all his sociological facts were as correct as his information about me, his whole book was not worth a tinker's dam. He protested and tried to prove to me that I really was a Galitzianer, whether by birth or some previous transmigration. Ruppin's research department on colonization in Palestine was ready to cooperate one hundred percent with us. He was convinced that the Pavilion would be of great significance in showing the American people what was being accomplished in Palestine.

I went from Ruppin to a meeting with Eliezer Kaplan, the Treasurer of the Jewish Agency. I was glad to have his support of my long range view of the Pavilion. The Manufacturers' Association had been at him as at me the day before—they wanted to turn the Palestine Pavilion into a bazaar. 'We don't want *Zukunftsmusik*,' was the way they put it. 'We want results now.' But Kaplan wanted me to meet with the Manufacturers' Association again. 'I haven't the time,' I said. That sent him into a fury: 'You travel 6,000 miles to be here for ten days—and at such a time, the High Holidays.' I had forgotten that the holy days paralyzed Palestine as much as New York. 'You know,' said Kaplan, sarcastically, 'your Holy Days are imported from here.'

I had to return to the Agency in an hour for a meeting with Moshe Shertok and Bernard Joseph; in between I dashed up to the University to see Professor Efraim Hareubeni, the creator of The Garden of the

Prophets—a marvellous collection of the flora mentioned in the Bible
and the Talmud—I wanted some of them for the Pavilion. One had to
know Hareubeni to appreciate the agony of meeting him when one was
in a hurry. He was a diminutive Jew with dreamy eyes and a roundly
trimmed greying beard. He saw nothing but flowers. He took me by the
hand as if afraid I would escape. Every flower had a history, every leaf a
genealogy. For years, he and his wife studied and collected the flora of
the Holy Land, assembling them in glass cages. He explained everything
to me in the minutest detail. I was desperate. My time was running out.
Hareubeni never heard my plea. He kept on talking. I soon realized he
wasn't talking to me; he was talking to his flowers. Every flower was
three thousand years old. He himself had lived with them for three thousand years. For Hareubeni time was as eternal as his flowers. When we
finally extricated ourselves, I turned to Yevzeroff who was with me and
said: 'Your problem now is how to get the flowers to New York and
leave Hareubeni in Jerusalem.' He smiled as if to say: 'You'll take
Hareubeni with the flowers or you won't get any flowers. They are
inseparable.' He was right.

My discussion with Shertok, who later changed his name to Sharett,
and became Israel's Foreign Minister and Prime Minister in turn, revolved round the question of our political position in Palestine vis-à-vis
the Arabs. He felt that if we took up a political stand at all, we should
be frank, and make it clear that we had *not* come to Palestine for the
purpose of improving the lot of the Arabs; that happened to be the
byproduct. Our purpose was to find national self-expression for the
Jewish people: the Arabs had ample opportunities for *their* national self-
expression in the vast territories of Iraq, the Hedjaz, Saudi Arabia and
Transjordan. Palestine never was—and I add that it is not today—a
'national center' of the Arabs. I agreed with Shertok that our primary
message should be our own achievements and aspirations, and as for the
political question, we ought to steer away from that as far as the Pavilion
was concerned. And again, before we parted, I was glad to hear from
Shertok: 'For heaven's sake, keep it on a national scale, even if not a
piastre's worth of Palestine products is sold. Let's not make the same
old mistake.' I assured him that we wouldn't.

The next day, a few minutes before I left Jerusalem I ran into Joshua
Gordon, a famous character working at the Jewish Agency. I needed him
badly. I was set on going north, to Hanita, a kibbutz which had recently
been set up overnight, and I knew that if anyone could arrange it for me
it was he. The first thing he asked me, *sotto voce*, was, 'Are you very re-

ligious?' '*Comme çi, comme ça*,' I answered. Then he told me that the next day, Yom Kippur, Eliyahu Golomb, head of the Haganah, the Jewish Defense organization, was leaving from Tel Aviv at six in the morning for the military camp at Ein Harod, where 150 Jewish soldiers were being graduated. I would meet the famous Captain Orde Wingate, and then I could proceed to Hanita. Well, between being religious *comme ci, comme ça* and desecrating Yom Kippur there was a bridge I had never crossed. Joshua noticed my hesitation. 'This is war time. In a time of emergency, everything is permissible.' That evening, the eve of Yom Kippur, I salved my conscience with a double portion of piety: I went to services at the Great Synagogue on Allenby Road, presided over by the Sephardic Chief Rabbi Uziel, and then to a little Yemenite synagogue in the direction of Jaffa.

Six o'clock the next morning found me waiting in front of the hotel with a dreadful feeling that a thousand eyes were focused on me in my sins. It is not easy to break the habit of a lifetime. Eliyahu Golomb, apparently not as self-conscious as I, turned up promptly. He sat at the wheel of the car and next to him his bodyguard. The inside of the car looked like an armory. I only hoped that I would not be expected to give a display of my marksmanship on the trip. Golomb, a short, heavy-set man, was as unlike a generalissimo—that was his reputation—as one could possibly imagine; to me he looked like an old-style Russian revolutionary conspirator.

At Ein Harod there awaited us Orde Wingate, the British soldier who had fallen in love with the idea of the Jewish rebirth and was training our youth in guerilla tactics. He was already a living legend—the 'Lawrence of Judea.' That day there was to be a swearing in of his 'night-raiders'— but to my everlasting chagrin I was not allowed to witness the ceremony, which was said to be of the most awe-inspiring solemnity. Only Eliyahu Golomb was admitted—the driver and I waiting outside the barn till the young defenders of Israel emerged, Orde Wingate at their head. I had expected to see a tall, powerful figure of a man, clean shaven, the *beau idéal* of a British officer; instead, he was short, swarthy and bearded, and his uniform was something never seen at Sandhurst. I was introduced, and made an appointment to meet him that night in Haifa; *he* at least refused to travel on Yom Kippur. We met in a hotel room, and he came in with a kit bag which he immediately emptied on the table to check on the contents. All I saw was hand grenades and a Bible. I was immensely curious about this man and his fantastic role in our new history. I wanted to know what had moved him to imperil his standing with his superiors and with the British government, what it was that made a renascent Israel a primary interest in his life. He began to tell me of his deep—his fanatical—attachment to the land, his belief in Jewish survival, his profound distress at the duplicity of the British—and his conversation was like that of some seventeenth-century Cromwellian Puritan—filled with quotations from the Psalms and the Prophets. In midcourse the telephone rang, and he answered, staccato, 'Yes, *ken, ken*, yes.' Without another word he stood up, repacked grenades and Bible into the kit bag, nodded and left. The next morning I was informed that there had been an 'action' that night in Galilee, and that he had led some of his new inductees into battle. Wingate left a permanent imprint on the military tactics of the Haganah and of the Israel defense forces that grew out of it. To this day Israeli officers lead their men with 'Follow me!' rather than 'Advance' as the battlecry. After Wingate's death in Burma during the Second World War, his beautiful and brilliant wife, Lorna, whom I met often, devoted herself to the development of the Haganah. We became close friends.

There was one exotic corner of Jewish Palestine that, in spite of my insane schedule, I had to turn aside for, though it had little to do with our rebirth and nothing at all with the Pavilion. Gershon Agronsky had told me that Itzhak Ben-Zvi—the scholarly labor leader who later became second President of the State of Israel—had discovered in Galilee a village called Peki'in uninterruptedly inhabited by Jews since the most ancient times. Peki'in was in the nature of a suburb to the sacred city of Safed, itself not quite so ancient, dating only from the first century of our era. Whenever marauding bands threatened Safed, its Jews sought safety in the almost inaccessible mountain retreat of Peki'in which even in 1938 could not be reached by mechanical means of transportation. I had to hire four Arabs and two donkeys for the ascent; and our arrival created a sensation in the primitive village. It was, to be blunt, a miserable sight; it looked like the poorest of the Arab villages except in one respect: it had a *shul*—in a cowshed. The Jews, even on close inspection, were indistinguishable from the Arabs. When I returned to Tel Aviv I was haunted by the wretched alleys and squalid little houses—if they deserve that name. A friend of mine, hearing about the visit, asked me what it was like: I answered: 'We have a great God in heaven, Whose thought has always been for the preservation of His people. In His infinite wisdom He took us out of Eretz Israel for two thousand years and only then brought us back.'

I left Palestine in a profoundly perturbed mood. On the one hand my mission for the Pavilion had been successful; the work was proceeding on schedule, the standard of performance was high; a million loose ends had been tied together and I was convinced that the Palestine Pavilion was going to render a magnificent service to the movement. And on the other hand, deep down in me, there was a constant nagging. What was going to happen? War was palpably in the air, war, with all its cataclysmic possibilities. Returning on the *Queen Mary* I wrote: 'In the devastation to come will Palestine and our work be completely destroyed, or will there be left a saving remnant out of which a new people and a new hope will emerge? Are we perhaps the victims of a snare and a delusion? Out of the crucible of the First World War there came ideas and slogans. Today these ideas and slogans are dead, together with most of the men who conceived them. Shall we then say that it has all been a dream? I cannot believe it. What we have done cannot be meaningless. We are bound to the soil of Palestine by a thousand chains, chains that no storm can rend asunder. We are wedded to the soil of Palestine in an indissoluble union. We cannot escape from it even if we wished it.'

There was a special kind of unreality about Flushing Meadows in 1938 after my glimpse of Europe and Palestine. The flags of all the nations hung side by side, the fountains shot their waters into the air, the infinite inventiveness and ingenuity of man was visible in a thousand forms. But that which man could create he could, with the same *élan*, destroy. It took me some time to recover my balance, and to apply myself to construction of the Jewish State under the shadow of the Trylon and Perisphere, or, as the Jews were fond of calling it, the Lulav and Esrog.

Located as we were on the borderline of the National Pavilions, there was always some question as to whether or not we really 'belonged.' The decision was made and remade daily, and the outcome measured by the presence or absence of the Jewish flag on the bridge of flags in front of the Fair Administration building. It was like a game of musical chairs; one day we were in, the next day out. I had a man posted to keep me informed as to our daily status; if the flag was up, all was well; if it was not I would put in a call to Whalen and tell him I was closing the Pavilion. I sympathized with him; the State Department would say 'no,' claiming that they were under pressure from the British; Whalen, whose heart was with us, was glad to succumb to our threats and have the flag unfurled. This went on for months. The tone for this struggle was set on the day of the opening, when there was a march past of all the nations, and I of course insisted that it was our right to be in it. A confused and acrimonious struggle took place, but in the end the Fair authorities conceded that we belonged, and we rejoiced in our triumph. I had a contingent of Jewish soldiers, known as 'Weisgal's Private Army, ready for the occasion. At the last moment a detachment of the New York National Guard was inserted between our men and the last national contingent, to mark us off and to show that we were not exactly like the others. In reality, it made not the slighest difference—no one understood the distinction except for the Fair authorities and me. Later Grover Whalen would always recall with pride how he had protected the Jewish flag and the Jewish people.

On the day we opened the Pavilion 100,000 people attended the ceremony. The high point was an address by Albert Einstein. That week there was a full page picture of Professor Einstein in *Life* Magazine. He was shown standing before Mr. Krinitzi's eucalyptus doors under the inscription, 'If I forget thee, O Jerusalem . . . ' There is a story behind this coup. *Life* had made it a condition that Einstein alone appear on the picture, and that he be standing precisely on this spot; if anyone else intruded the deal was off. Joe Brainin and I planned the operation carefully. We knew that when Einstein toured the Pavilion he would be accompanied by a mob of our dignitaries not averse to seeing themselves in a national magazine. The essence of our coup was to isolate Professor Einstein from the crowd at the crucial moment, without giving him or anyone else an inkling of what we were up to. Thus isolated, he was to be shoved through the double door which was to be shut immediately on those inside. It worked! There Einstein stands, on his face a profoundly philosophic look which in reality reflects his complete bewilderment at the sudden disappearance of all his Jews. The deed having been done, Joe and I, together with Gottlieb Hammer (who kept our finances in order, and later became Executive Director of the Jewish Agency) and Itzik Hamlin (one of our most effective workers, the scion of a great Labor Zionist family) opened the doors. I should mention that the dignitaries escorting Einstein were as bewildered as he, and it was a week later, when they saw the picture in *Life* magazine that they finally understood the great betrayal.

I tried to get Weizmann to come to the opening day, but political commitments kept him in Europe and he addressed us by phone. Perhaps it was as well, for his presence added to Einstein's on top of the attraction exerted by the Pavilion might have been too much. When, immediately after the ceremony, the push to get in started I was afraid that the structure would collapse. I stood on one of the parapets and asked Solomon Goldman to stand on another, and we both pleaded with the crowd: 'Go to the Russian Pavilion,' I said, 'or somewhere else. Come back later. We'll

be here a long time.' One Jew in the throng called out: 'It's easy for you
to talk. You're already in Eretz Israel and we're still outside.'

They took it all in good humor and waited their turn; many of them
were not satisfied with that day's visit; they returned bringing friends,
and for its size the Palestine Pavilion broke all records for attendance
in that brilliant Fair. We could not charge admission to the Pavilion itself,
that would have been contrary to the rules of the Fair; but we were allowed
to charge admission to a special Hall of Dioramas of life in Palestine. We
sold quantities of tickets in advance to organizations all over the country,
splitting the proceeds with them and thus helping to finance the project.
We were so successful that, as I have mentioned, we remained open
through the better part of a second year.

Irving Lehman, the Governor's brother, and Presiding Judge of the
Appellate Division of New York, used to come Saturdays as if to an
orthodox service, to sit in a little court there. On one of those visits I
asked him why he came there so regularly, and his answer was the classic
'*Klein, aber mein*, small but mine.' He was not a Zionist. Henry Morgenthau Sr. came and spent many hours walking around, roaming in and
out. He reminded me that he had defended the interests of Jewish Palestine
when he was America's Ambassador to Turkey in 1914. It was true;
but I also remembered that in 1921 he had proclaimed: 'Zionism is the
most stupendous fallacy in Jewish history. I assert that it is wrong in
principle and impossible of realization; that it is unsound in its economics,
fantastical in its politics, and sterile in its spiritual ideals.' I had printed this
wisdom in *The New Palestine*. Morgenthau had a selective memory,
like most of us. But that was the effect of the Pavilion. The Jews had
something to be proud of.

13 Return to the Fray

To this day it saddens me to remember that I did not attend the Twenty-first Zionist Congress which met in Geneva in the summer of 1939. There were dozens of delegates from the countries of Eastern Europe, particularly Poland, old friends I had met in Europe and Palestine and America, of whom I might have caught a last glimpse before they were swallowed up in the holocaust of the Second World War. For this was the year of the Stalin-Hitler Pact, and the anticipated storm broke over mankind; hesitantly at first, during the period of 'the phony war,' later with a fury that had no parallel in history. Of all the peoples that were to suffer in the general disaster, none was to approach the Jewish people in the extent and depth of its afflictions. We did not guess, we did not dare to guess, what lay in wait for most of the Jews in Europe; but at the very outset the prospect was horrifying enough. Hitler had made Germany uninhabitable for the Jews; hundreds of thousands of refugees filled the cities of as yet unconquered Europe. And this was the summer that followed England's White Paper restricting Jewish immigration into Palestine, the one country that could have taken in a sizable number.

Dr. Weizmann had urged me to attend the Congress. I could not: I was in the very thick of my work for the Palestine Pavilion. My heavy schedule notwithstanding, I did find time to do a number of other things at Weizmann's urging. I received repeated messages from him asking me to perform certain chores pertaining to the Daniel Sieff Research Institute in Rehovot. Various people arrived in New York from Europe with letters from him, requesting my assistance in matters political and financial. I did whatever was possible.

Early in 1940 Dr. Weizmann came to the United States. He requested the Board of Directors of the Palestine Pavilion to release me temporarily to help him. I was genuinely happy to be of use to him. A few days before he left to return to London he wrote me the following letter:

My dear Meyer,

Now that my visit to the United States is drawing to a close, I am anxious that the many activities initiated here be continued without interruption after my departure for London. After so much energy has been poured out it would be a pity that all should go to waste by reason of a failure to follow up what has been begun.

I need hardly repeat what I have so often told you privately, how grateful I am to you for your invaluable work in arranging for me to meet with individuals and groups who have hitherto taken little or no interest in our work. Contact with these people must be maintained and special work, for which each group may be fitted, assigned; because only through such work can their interest be kept alive.

The purpose of this letter, therefore, is to ask you, before I become engulfed in a thousand other matters, to undertake this work on my behalf and to act as my personal representative in the matters indicated above.

I should also like to feel free to call upon you to do other services for the movement which may be needed from time to time and which may be done more effectively outside official channels.

Yours ever,
Chaim Weizmann

I told him that I had to return to my work at the Pavilion but that I would devote as much time as I could to his special tasks. What I was afraid of, to be frank, was the prospect of being drawn back into Zionist officialdom. I had been a free man for too long. In May, 1940, he wrote me again, from London:

I ought to have written you a long time since, but events here have been moving with such vertiginous rapidity that things which seemed important yesterday have become utterly insignificant today. Since the invasion of the Low Countries, the danger has increased swiftly, and, as no doubt you will have seen from the press, we are now passing through grave hours . . . I can only trust that you and our friends in America will take counsel together, bearing in mind the terrible and indisputable fact that European Jewry, with very few exceptions, has been practically blotted out, so that the whole responsibility henceforth falls on America. . . The foundations of everything in which we believe and for which we live and work, are rocking, and unless the onslaught of the German hordes is stopped in time, we shall all go under. I am confident that it *will* be stopped in the end; but when, and at what cost, no one can say. It is such thoughts as these that govern one's life at present, and everything else seems to have receded into the background. This is why I would again appeal to you, Lipsky, Wise, all our friends, to stand together in these hours of trial, to create a real *union sacrée*, and to do your utmost to save whatever remnant of our people may be rescuable from the wreckage.

A kind of *union sacrée* did for a while emerge in American Jewry in the form of the American Jewish Conference, where the vast majority of America's five million Jews were represented, calling for the creation of a Jewish Commonwealth in Palestine, but that was not until 1943. It was the result of Weizmann's untiring efforts to create the broadest possible base of action in the American Jewish community, the non-Zionist as well as the Zionist sections.

Meanwhile Weizmann came to the United States again, in 1941, this time at the request of the British Government, which he was serving as scientific adviser. His main concern, however, was to harness American opinion in government circles for both immediate and long term solutions to our problems. By now he was dissatisfied with the imperfect working arrangement he had set up with me. He needed all of my time, and began to insist that I come to work for him officially.

The World's Fair had closed by then and I had become involved in something called 'The Non-Sectarian Anti-Nazi League.' I began to work for the League at the invitation of Samuel Untermeyer, a great American jurist, and even more so at the repeated request of my friend Isidore Lipschutz. Lipschutz was a remarkable man, a refugee from Belgium and one of the world's great diamond dealers. His chief interests, however, were his Jewish and Zionist causes. The Anti-Nazi League was actually his own invention and he financed it almost single-handedly. He later initiated a movement for the prevention of World War Three. I would venture a guess that during the past twenty-five years or more he has spent millions of dollars of his own money for a variety of public causes—quite apart from his generous donations to Israel and the Weiz-mann Institute in association with his brother-in-law and partner Charles Gutwirth.

America was awakening slowly to the grim fact that the forces which were overwhelming Europe were no less a threat to her. The Anti-Nazi League was devoted to the task of hastening that awakening, lest it come too late; Pearl Harbor, which vindicated our efforts—and made them superfluous—was still in the future. However, my work for the League did not engross all of my energies, and I was strongly attracted to Weizmann's offer. I told him that I was ready to come over completely, relinquishing all other obligations—but that on one condition, namely, that I should be responsible to him alone. That granted, I would handle any assignment, large or small, in his name. I was not under any circum-stances to become a functionary of the Zionist Organization. Weizmann agreed, and asked only one question: 'What about *achtzen-dreitzen*'—a Yiddish expression I had not heard in years; its meaning, for reasons I have never discovered, was 'money.' Who would pay me? I answered that this was no problem; I would obtain as much as was needed at once, and something extra to meet a few of the commitments on his list. Within forty-eight hours I brought him $150,000, partly from Lipschutz himself. Lipschutz was sorry to see me leave the Anti-Nazi League but he understood that Weizmann had priority. All that he and Gutwirth wanted for their contribution was a personal meeting with Weizmann. In fact all they really wanted was to shake Weizmann's hand. Weizmann asked me to send some of the money to Ivor Linton, the Jewish Agency representative in London, and some to the Sieff Institute. With what was left, added to more that I succeeded in raising soon after, we bought an office building for the Jewish Agency, being reorganized in America because of the situation in Europe; we financed the Lowdermilk Plan, a kind of T.V.A. or rather J.V.A. (Jordan being the valley we were interested in); and finally, my salary was provided for.

A few days later I put the official seal on my position in a letter to Weizmann, in which I outlined my views on the reorganization of the Jewish Agency for Palestine in New York, and the preparatory steps toward uniting American Jewry in a non-controversial, non-ideological program for the upbuilding of Palestine and the transfer to it of the maximum number of Jews within the shortest possible time. I wrote: 'Once the terms 'Zionist' and 'non-Zionist' are completely eliminated from the composition of the reorganized Agency, we should not be fearful of presenting a wide-scope settlement program involving hundreds of millions of dollars and substantial government financing. The feeling of a great, unprecedented, supra-party action must be created.' Another clause read: 'While it will be my duty to carry out the policies of the reorganized Agency here, it should be understood that I am acting as your representative and that my ultimate responsibility is to you as the President of the Jewish Agency. I will expect an agreement, executed by all the parties concerned, to avoid any misunderstanding as to my permanent association with the executive work of the Jewish Agency.'

That was the agreement we came to in April, 1941. My association with Chaim Weizmann, which had been twenty years in the making, was thus formalized.

He told me that he would have to call in the Zionist leaders and advise them of the step he was taking. I answered that I had no objection, but added: 'Don't ask them; just tell them.'

Weizmann called a meeting at the St. Regis Hotel; it was attended by all the leaders of the various Zionist groups, Louis Lipsky, Stephen Wise, Morris Rothenberg, Robert Szold and Chaim Greenberg. Weizmann described the arrangement he had reached with me. Here and there one could sense a certain chafing under the saddle and sure enough, the following day, Weizmann received a letter from Robert Szold casting rather nasty aspersions on my character. Weizmann didn't take it seriously. 'I see you have a lot of friends,' he said, holding the letter but not showing it to me. Szold and I had been on opposite sides of the Zionist movement since the split in 1921 and, after some wrangling with Weizmann over the letter, I discovered that he had certain suspicions regarding the half a million dollars lost in *The Eternal Road*. I, of course, became livid with anger, threatening to sue him. Weizmann tried to laugh it off: 'What do you care? It doesn't affect me. Why should it affect you?'

The long and short of the story is that after a dramatic confrontation, Szold and I shook hands and he invited me to lunch. 'You know,' he said, 'you and I have been in the Zionist Organization all these years and we've never even had a cup of coffee together.' The slate was wiped clean that day; in the ensuing years we made two strange discoveries: I, that he wasn't as bad as I thought him; he, that I wasn't as bad as he thought me.

I have often wondered what it was that prompted Weizmann, a man of the most subtle tact, to mention that letter to me, and to precipitate what almost amounted—for the first and last time—to a break between him and me. I finally realized that, knowing both Szold and myself, he thought that this was the best way to bring the matter to a head and get rid of what must have been for him a vexatious problem.

After this, getting the cooperation of Robert Szold for the creation of Weizmann's *union sacrée* was easy enough; much more difficult was getting the cooperation of Abba Hillel Silver, who, it will be remembered, had also been one of the men to side with the Brandeis group, and who was to play a considerable role in the forging of American Jewish opinion during those crucial years. My relations with Silver were more complicated, and reached deeper, than those with Szold.

Dr. Abba Hillel Silver, one of the leading rabbis of America, made his first impact on world Zionism when, as a young man, he appeared at a mass demonstration in London's Albert Hall. He was instantly pronounced the new Demosthenes of the Zionist movement, the destined successor of Stephen S. Wise. So he might have been—had it depended on oratory alone. For there was no challenging that next to Wise he was the greatest orator to come out of American Jewry. But though when addressing the people *en masse* he had the voice of Jacob, in dealing with individuals he had the hands of Esau. He lacked Wise's broad sympathies and his natural liking for people. He was all wrapped up in himself.

My first collision with Silver came in 1929 in connection with the Herzl Memorial issue. Every rabbi in America has what is called a 'slush fund,' and when I asked Silver for a contribution to the project he responded with a generous grant of $2,000. Then he sent me a poem for inclusion in the issue. I might have used a poem on Herzl had it come from a Bialik or Tchernichovsky. But a rabbinical sermon disguised as a poem, however well meant, was not grist for my editorial mill. I returned it to him with a request for an article. Soon after I received a note from him: 'When you need money, you know where to come; when I send you a poem you can't even print it.' My answer, equally terse, was: 'Even a rabbi can sometimes afford to be gentleman.' This poetic exchange cast its shadow over our relations for a number of years.

In 1934 I brought *The Romance of a People* to Cleveland. It was difficult to break into that city without Silver's blessing—everything had to be 'cleared with the rabbi.' I asked a certain lady to take over the Women's Division of the sponsorship; she was also the chairman of the Ladies' Auxiliary of his temple, and she went to Silver. He advised her against the project, telling her that 'Weisgal is probably greasing his own palm generously.' The lady returned, somewhat crestfallen, and I explained to her that I was working on a salary of $80 a week. She courageously decided to defy the rabbi, and took on the assignment. At a luncheon before the opening I referred to Silver in a few well-chosen but highly uncomplimentary words. This added a further dimension to the dulcet tones of our love duet.

A few years later Silver came to see *The Eternal Road*. I met him in the lobby and greeted him: his answer was a frigid nod. Then I heard that he subsequently delivered a magnificent sermon on *The Eternal Road*, praising it to the skies as a biblical production in the grand style, with not one word about the man—me that is—who had suffered so much to bring it about. There was this difference between us: whenever he made a good speech I applauded him and sometimes even shed a tear. He could not reciprocate. I must confess I was always moved by his manner and impressed by his oratory and his stage presence. Once in Carnegie Hall he was speaking about the Messianic era in which the Jews were living. The audience (myself included)—and the speaker—were at a very high emotional pitch. Silver was about to reach his peroration when a man rushed down the aisle and shouted: 'Here I am, the Messiah.' That finished Silver and the peroration. He turned to the audience and said: 'I didn't expect the Messiah to arrive so soon.' The spell was broken but the meeting ended on a jovial note.

In 1940 Weizmann, anxious to gather up all Zionist forces into a single powerful instrument, asked me to get in touch with Silver. I told him I was not the man to help in this instance, and told him something about our relationship; but he insisted. I swallowed my pride and wrote Silver:

Dr. Weizmann has entrusted me with certain duties in connection with his visit here. I would like to have an opportunity to discuss this with you at the earliest possible moment. I shall be available at any time convenient for you. I am not unaware of the fact that you are not particularly fond of me. You may have your reasons. Personally I think I am not as bad as you think I am. I have said certain things under provocation which, if I had been as old then as I am now, I probably would not have said. I think all of us are more or less guilty of youthful indiscretions. I can do no more than offer my sincerest apologies [etc., etc.].

His reply was:

I am pretty well fed up with people who insult you in public and try to get out of it by apologizing to you in private. The matter is not at all as simple as all that. I suspect that the reason for your writing to me at this time is not altogether one of penitence. I wish therefore to inform you that I will in no way identify myself with any activity in which you have a finger. I have no confidence in you.

I couldn't let him have the last word—not that kind of word. I wrote back: 'I am sorry I made a mistake. I was foolish enough to think that I might have been wrong in 1929 and in 1934. It is good to have your personal confirmation in 1940.'

I took Silver's letter to Weizmann with the remark, 'You see, once a bastard, always a bastard.' Weizmann brushed the exchange aside and insisted that I accompany him to Chicago, where he was to meet Silver. I had Solomon Goldman arrange the meeting. Goldman had also had his feuds with Silver but after he moved from Cleveland to Chicago, the heat was taken off this rabbinical schism.

I went to Chicago, but refused to meet Silver. Then Weizmann insisted that I accompany him to Cleveland. When the appointed hour came I stayed in my room, which communicated with Weizmann's, and firmly closed the door. After about an hour there was a knock, and there, to my astonishment, was Silver's burly figure. He invited me to join them at his house for dinner. Behind him stood Weizmann, silently admonishing me not to be a fool. I went.

Weizmann would not speak about what passed between him and Silver during that hour. But later that day, when I was reviewing the incident, reflecting sardonically on the art of politicking, Weizmann remarked,

'*Az men darf dem ganev nemt men im arunter fun der tliyeh*, when you need the thief, you cut him down from the gallows.' If he's still breathing, that is.

Silver became the Chairman of the Zionist Council and rendered magnificent service to the movement. We managed to maintain a cordial relationship for a number of years. He even wrote me letters of praise. But this friendly interlude was followed by another clash—which in turn was followed by another reconciliation. He was a man who nourished resentments for a long time. Thus his opposition to Weizmann, first manifested in 1921, never really subsided. In 1946 he joined forces with Ben Gurion to depose Weizmann from the leadership of the world movement.

Since one is supposed to speak only good of the dead, I will end by saying that if one takes the sum of the man and his works, he probably wasn't as bad as I thought he was. He rendered great services to Zionism at a very difficult time. He was a great tribune and his failings were the failings of a great many human beings including the writer of these lines. But with one difference. I possess a saving grace: *Kasheh lichos v'noach lirtzot*, hard to anger, easy to placate. I never hold grudges for much more than twenty-four hours. Silver could nurse them for a lifetime.

The history of Zionist developments in America during the war years has been the subject of many analyses and interpretations; and in particular attention has been focussed on the famous Biltmore Resolution calling for the establishment of a Jewish Commonwealth in Palestine at the close of the war. The developments, of course, were more important than the interpretations.

The Biltmore Conference took place in 1942; in 1943 the American Jewish Conference united all of American Jewry, Zionist and non-Zionist, on a common platform in favor of opening the gates of Palestine to Jewish immigration and establishing a Jewish Commonwealth; in 1944 a Jewish brigade within the British army was set up, enabling the Jews of Palestine to pursue the war against Hitler under their own flag. Finally, three years after the war, the Jewish Commonwealth, otherwise known as the State of Israel, came into being.

As I said, these were the developments; these are the facts. Who did what, why and how—this is how historians make a living. But this is also why people write autobiographies.

I want to dwell in some detail on this phase of Zionist history, not because I was a witness and participant in the events (those are merely my credentials), but because a distorted version of the developments has gained wide credence and I should like to make my contribution to the record. I refer to the 'rift' which occurred during the war years between Chaim Weizmann and David Ben Gurion, and I use the inverted commas intentionally. It is my profound belief that there was no major difference in the aims and policies of the two during that period. There was of course a difference of method, a great difference. But the 'rift' was completely personal. To put it bluntly, Ben Gurion wanted to be in command or— to put it more elegantly, he was impatient for the crown of Zionist leadership. As a result he had to find fault with Weizmann, impute to him political shortcomings, and invent political differences. This he did with bravura and utter disregard for fact. At the time and for many years afterward, especially when he *was*, indisputably, Israel's leader, it was hard to challenge his categorical pronouncements. Only in recent years, when his consistent overplay, overkill, and overrighteousness became the order of the day, did it become possible to examine that period more soberly.

When Weizmann came to New York in 1940 he was well aware that the United States had become the most important center of political activity in the world. And it was in 1940 that he first put forth his demand for a *union sacrée*. Back in London he continued to press his influence with the British Government for the creation of a Palestinian fighting force, and Churchill actually consented to the program as early as September 1940. It is so recorded in his War Memoirs. But it wasn't until 1944 that the British military authorities gave the final OK for the formation of a Jewish Brigade. Meanwhile Palestinian Jews served under British colors. In 1941 Weizmann spent another three months in the United States and continued his efforts in two directions: trying to influence the American government to support postwar Zionist demands and trying to achieve Zionist and Jewish unity for the expression of these postwar aims.

In October, 1941 Weizmann wrote me from London:

There is no need for me here to go over the pros and cons of the (British) Government's policy with regard to Palestine; they are too familiar to you to merit wasting too much time on it. But one set of arguments cropped up which I would like to bring to your attention and to that of our friends—namely, America. Our opponents in the Cabinet maintain the following point of view: It is true that in the last war the Jews of the U.S.A. played an important part and contributed greatly towards the entry of America into the war. But things have changed. The Jews are deeply divided with regard to Zionism. The American Government did nothing when the White Paper was issued and is therefore indifferent to the question of Palestine. We need not take America into consideration, and can pursue our policy of placating the Arabs.

It is of course quite true that the White Paper produced no reaction on the part of the

American authorities, but of course it is a fallacy to generalize it. Apart from the attitude of the Government, Jewish and liberal public opinion dislike the Palestine policy and that is important enough. I shall, of course, tell it to Winant [American Ambassador in London], with whom I am on good terms, but it is vital that something should be done to indicate that this quasi-indifference to the American Government is only in appearance and not in fact. Please act on it. Of course Wise, Lipsky, Neumann and the others ought to go to Washington and see Welles and explain the situation. A word from the White House and we could get the Army.

In that same month of October, 1941, Weizmann sent me a copy of an article he had prepared for *Foreign Affairs*. It was published in the January, 1942 issue, and constituted the first clear and open declaration of a demand for a Jewish Commonwealth in Palestine. The timing of this incident is of the utmost importance, for it proves that Weizmann had been pressing steadily for the acceptance of this policy. It should be noted that this crucial statement in *Foreign Affairs* was prepared and issued a full five months before the convening of the Biltmore Conference in May, 1942.

The Biltmore Conference itself, which I undertook to organize at the behest of Dr. Weizmann, was the first step in the *union sacrée*—the unification of the Zionist forces in America. The second step was the unification of all of American Jewry on a common platform. This came a year later with the American Jewish Conference.

We now reach the crucial point in developments. With Weizmann's declaration of policy, the Jewish Commonwealth had become the cornerstone of the Zionist program. It was an irreversible reality, as the years were to show. The Biltmore Conference confirmed his position.

Here is where the rewriting of history begins. Somewhere along the road, Ben Gurion decided that it was important for history that the paternity of the Biltmore Resolution be attributed to him, and appear as a victory of his conception over Weizmann's. And this is more or less what happened. I know a number of otherwise sane and intelligent people who today insist that not only did Ben Gurion create the Biltmore Program but that Weizmann was opposed to it!

My own role at the Biltmore Conference was not insignificant: at Weizmann's behest I organized it. It was the first public expression of his *union sacrée*. For months preceding it I had worked with Louis Lipsky on the draft of the program which, *with stylistic changes*, was eventually adopted. The entire program was drawn up in consultation with Weizmann. At the Conference itself, I had the honor of opening the proceedings with a few well-chosen words after which I handed over the gavel to the Chairman, Stephen Wise. It was clear to everyone from the beginning that the Biltmore Conference was conceived by Weizmann as a platform to express his program. If it had been Ben Gurion's program why should I, of all people, have been given, or taken, the signal honor of opening it? It would have been inconceivable.

As late as 1962 the debate was still raging. Ben Gurion had published the part of his memoirs in which the subject of Biltmore was mentioned. Julian Meltzer, unbeknown to me, writing in the London *Jewish Observer and Middle East Review*, took exception to some of the 'facts.' I was in London at the time. He quoted an Israeli historian, Dr. Yehuda Bauer, whom I did not know at all. He had done research on the period and claimed authorship of the Biltmore Program for . . . Meyer W. Weisgal. Mr. Arthur Lourie, then Israel's Ambassador to the Court of St. James's, joined the controversy with the 'authentic' story: '. . . the committee could not itself prepare the basic draft and I [Lourie] was entrusted with this responsibility. The general line was agreed on by the committee and derived of course from Mr. Ben Gurion's major address to the Conference, an address which formed the main theme of its deliberations.' I subsequently disclaimed 'authorship' of the document even though my fingerprints were all over it. Dr. Bauer must have found dozens of drafts lying in the Zionist Archives signed with the mysterious initials M.W.W. The final draft, drawn up by Mr. Lourie, was approved by Weizmann and subsequently by Ben Gurion. I remember the words of Weizmann when I showed him the document before it went to committee for final ratification. 'Let it go,' he said, 'maybe the language has to be straightened out a bit but that isn't important.' I think the most accurate and concise statement of fact regarding the issue is this: the Biltmore Program was conceived by Weizmann, articulated by Louis Lipsky (with me looking over his shoulder), styled by Arthur Lourie and appropriated by Ben Gurion.

It was after the Biltmore Conference that Ben Gurion struck out at Weizmann. Ben Gurion had arrived in America at the end of 1941. Weizmann was to arrive early in 1942 but the death of his younger son Michael delayed his arrival until April. During the interim it became clear that Ben Gurion was opposed to Weizmann's coming at all. But the pressure of the Zionist leadership in America was too strong for him to block it. Weizmann was still the unchallenged leader of the movement, above party, universally respected and loved. Furthermore, all doors in Washington were open to him.

During the sessions of the Emergency Council preceding the Conference, Ben Gurion's behavior put a terrific strain on everyone. He was tempestuous, convulsive and threatening. He berated people and was intolerant of any point of view that seemed at variance with his own. He acted as if he alone were conscious of the war and the danger to Palestine.

After the Conference, after a basis of cooperation between all the Zionist groups had been established, Ben Gurion began his attack on Weizmann. He wrote him a letter which for downright discourtesy was unique in Zionist affairs: either Weizmann was to subordinate himself completely to the directives of Ben Gurion or Ben Gurion would demand his resignation. It was, in view of Weizmann's commanding position in the world Zionist movement, a piece of nonsense. Within a few days the leadership was called together in Wise's study; present were Weizmann, Wise, Ben Gurion, Lipsky, Chaim Greenberg, the head of the Labor Zionists, Nahum Goldmann, Louis Levinthal, Robert Szold and myself.

The substance of Ben Gurion's two-hour statement was that Weizmann was playing a lone hand, that he was making the most serious political mistakes, and that if there was as yet no Jewish army, Weizmann alone was to blame. Either Weizmann was to change completely his course of action or submit his resignation. His statement, inferentially, bordered on a charge of treason. (Incidentally, the night before I had visited B.G. at his hotel on Lexington Avenue to warn him of his folly and to try and convince him that he would find no support for his accusations against Weizmann—not even among his Labor Zionist colleagues.)

The scene was painful in the extreme to all those present. Chaim Greenberg, I remember, walked out of the room with tears running down his cheeks. He paused long enough to say: 'I never believed I would live to see the day when such an outrageous discourse would be delivered by a leader of the Palestine labor movement.'

Weizmann's reply to Ben Gurion was brief and devastating. To that kind of accusation there could be no reasoned reply. He told Ben Gurion that he was having hallucinations and that the entire procedure was nothing but an attempt at political assassination.

There were subsequent meetings at which the Labor Zionists, Ben Gurion's party, met with him privately in an attempt to get him to cease the attacks. But Ben Gurion would make no promises; he would only say that he would take the views of the Labor leaders into consideration when communicating with the Executive in Palestine. During the rest of his stay in America, he did not attend the meetings in Weizmann's office, despite Goldmann's repeated plea to him that his actions were foolish and unreasonable.

The course of events affected Weizmann deeply. He was under a terrible enough strain because of his son's death, and in general, he was the
kind of man who could work effectively only in a setting of congeniality;
the burden of responsibility lay heavily upon him, but he took little
pleasure in the exercise of office as such.

In July, 1942, in the midst of all the turmoil, I wrote to Gershon
Agronsky in Jerusalem:

You know Weizmann as well as I do. If the atmosphere is made murky, he becomes
irritated and his usefulness is impaired. It would be absurd for me to enter into a long
dissertation about the enormous importance of maintaining the American front.
Weizmann is the only person in the movement who is capable of maintaining that front. Because of his prestige, and because of his scientific contributions here, and because of a
thousand other reasons, all doors in Washington are open to him. If he should suddenly
leave, it will be a terrible blow to the movement. This is not only my opinion but the
opinion of all who are conversant, with the brew concocted by B. G. . . His trouble is
lack of a sense of humor and an infernal messianic complex.

These observations of mine in 1942 had some very unpleasant consequences. Moshe Sharett (then Shertok) came to America soon afterwards
and refused to talk to me. He said: '*Rabban dakru!*' I had stabbed his
rabbi in the back. Twenty-three years later, when Sharett was dying and
I came to visit him in Jerusalem, he turned to his wife, Zippora, and said:
'He knew before any of us about *that man*.' Ben Gurion had tried and
almost succeeded in destroying Sharett.

The letter to Agronsky was apparently intercepted in Jerusalem by the
postal authorities, but fortunately I had been careful to leave many things
unsaid. Some time later I came to see Dr. Weizmann, and a gentleman
from Palestine whom I had never met was with him. 'I want you to meet
my friend Meyer Weisgal,' Dr. Weizmann said. The gentleman said: 'Oh
yes, I know him.' Then, looking into a small black notebook, he continued:
'He is number 1,885 in my file at the Post Office. He writes letters to a chap
called Gershon Agronsky. We intercept them, photostat them and send
them on to Gershon.' By the way he referred to Agronsky's first name, I
immediately suspected he was a member of the Haganah.

When Ben Gurion returned to Palestine a few months later, the
Biltmore Program was a fact; the Zionist movement had gone on record
calling for the creation of a Jewish Commonwealth, and the Zionist
General Council in Jerusalem confirmed this program. But a strange
thing happened en route. The Biltmore Resolution embodying the historic
act became Ben Gurion's personal property. In short, although he left
America rebuffed by the Zionist leadership, he entered Jerusalem astride

a white donkey. With no one around to contradict him, he brought the Messianic tidings. It is my humble opinion that Ben Gurion's attacks on Weizmann and his demand for his resignation in Dr. Wise's study came precisely because they were essentially in agreement. If on policy Weizmann agrees with Ben Gurion and Ben Gurion agrees with Weizmann, it is no good. There exists no *real* reason for displacing Weizmann. Therefore one must invent reasons. And so Ben Gurion invented reasons. Weizmann was responsible for the fact that there was no Jewish army. Weizmann acted alone. Weizmann did not appreciate the importance of America. The reasons were not accepted in America. So Ben Gurion went off to Palestine and presented the Biltmore Program as a victory of his conception over Weizmann's.

This is how history is made.

14 Mainstream and Sidelines: The War Years

From 1941 until 1946, when Weizmann was deposed, I served as Director of the Jewish Agency for Palestine in New York. It was a time- and energy-consuming office, especially during the early years of the war. There was the Emergency Council for Zionist Affairs, a roof organization of American Zionist groups, of which I was Secretary. I was Chairman of the Committee for Special Affairs, a kind of public relations department of the Council. After the Biltmore Conference in 1942, I began to organize the American Jewish Conference, which created a representative body for all of American Jewry. I coordinated our work with the Agency Office in Washington, promoted peace and goodwill within organized Zionist bodies and staved off the attacks of the anti-establishment Zionists, the Revisionists, who at this juncture in history appeared on the scene as the 'Jewish Army Committee.'

But no eight-hour job, even if it took sixteen hours, was enough to consume all my energies. My activities soon spread beyond the confines of the Jewish Agency and I became entangled in a variety of other enterprises. One of them was Dorothy Thompson's 'Ring of Freedom,' from which eventually Freedom House emerged. (About Dorothy Thompson, I shall write in a chapter devoted to her.) Another was the fortunes of *The Nation;* still another the editing of a book on Weizmann, a sort of '*Festschrift*' for his seventieth birthday. In my free time, I did some fund raising for the Daniel Sieff Institute. There were no organizational contradictions, separate secretaries, divided desks. Mine was an all-inclusive empire based on a simple premise: what is good for the world is good for the Jews (and vice versa) and by extension good for the Jewish Agency too. Since I raised my own salary anyway, I was my own boss.

One of the more peculiar projects which I took under my wing in 1941 was an experiment in medical science. One day Dr. Kurt Blumenfeld and

Martin Rosenbluth came to see me. Blumenfeld was one of the leading intellectual forces of German Zionism before Hitler, and a friend and follower of Weizmann and also, by the way, the actual converter of Einstein to Zionism. He had settled in Palestine during the thirties. Rosenbluth was one of the sweetest and kindest men in the Zionist movement. He had been interned by the British as an 'enemy alien' but released at Weizmann's behest. His brother, Pinchas Rosen, was later Israel's Minister of Justice. They had a mission. Numerous German Jewish refugees had reached the United States and among them was a Dr. Jacob who, according to my visitors, had 'invented' a cure for cancer. Many people swore that they had been cured by him. The long and short of our conversation was that Dr. Jacob required $75,000 to finish his research. When completed, he was prepared to give the results to Dr. Weizmann, who would in turn give it to the world, who would in turn give us Palestine in gratitude. It was exceptionally naive and exceptionally fantastic. But I was used to being caught up in fantastic propositions. I immediately cabled Weizmann for advice both as a scientist and the leader of the Zionist movement. Within a few days I received a cautious reply: 'Consult Professor Nachmansohn at Yale and if he thinks there is anything in it, go ahead.' I did. Nachmansohn thought that it might be worth something.

I met with Dr. Jacob, who spoke to me in mysterious terms about the pancreas and various other animal innards and how he was on the verge of wiping out this human scourge. He was also a first-class bridge player, which helped our discussions immeasurably. But the real problem for me now was how to raise the $75,000.

At that time I was very close to Dorothy Thompson. Weizmann to her was God and I was his representative on earth. She began by helping me get a place for the laboratory—to be exact, in the basement of her own home before it was renovated and became one of Manhattan's great meeting places for the intellectual élite. She also put me on the scent of money. 'Why don't you go see Dolly? [Dorothy Schiff, then Mrs. George Backer, was the owner of *The New York Post*.] Her mother died of cancer. She is likely to give you the money and when the cure is finally achieved, the first announcement will be made in the *Post* and the scoop will be worth a fortune to them.' I accepted her advice and went to see Dolly. Dolly listened and was greatly interested, only she had no ready cash. Here was the collapse of the Jewish State and a blow to suffering humanity—all because there was no money in the till.

Dolly, seeing the anguish on my face, suddenly jumped up. 'I've got an idea, Meyer, wait a minute,' and off she ran to return a few minutes later with a jewel box under her arm. I had never seen so many precious stones. The first thing she took out was a diamond-and-ruby-studded tiara. 'This is what my father bought for my mother for the coronation of King Edward VIII.' Then followed rings, brooches, necklaces, and bracelets. 'Take it all,' she said. 'You can get the $75,000 and whatever is left over keep for yourself.' I was profoundly touched, but said, 'Dolly, you don't really expect me to go into the jewelry business?' But inspiration followed inspiration. I picked up the phone and called Isidore Lipschutz. 'Isidore,' I said, 'I need you. It's a matter of life and death.' He demurred, he was busy, he was in the midst of some great transactions. But he came over. After listening to the story he took out his eyeglass to examine the jewelry. I sat there, my heart pounding through my vest. Finally he turned to Dolly and said: 'My dear Mrs. Backer. I would advise you not to sell these things. They are far too valuable and the market now is low. But if you are short of cash I will advance you the money. Put your jewels back into the safe. Never mind notes or collateral. Your word will do. I will advance the money to Mr. Weisgal for this sacred purpose.' That was typical of Lipschutz; he was ready to do everything for public purposes.

When Dolly recovered, she blurted out, 'Well, now, Mr. Lipschutz, I really couldn't ask you to do that. I suppose I can somehow find the money,' and turning to me: 'Would it be all right if I gave it to you in three monthly installments of $25,000?' What a question! I said 'Yes' and Dr. Jacob was in business. In Dorothy Thompson's basement the equipment and the mice came to life, ready for the kill.

While Dr. Jacob was busy curing the world of cancer George and Dorothy Backer and I spent endless evenings planning how the announcement would be made to the world through the good offices of *The New York Post*. This revolution in science would be a tremendous scoop; circulation would rise and this great humanitarian act would bring the world's gratitude to the Jewish people. These staggering possibilities came to an abrupt end. A few months later, a frustrated Dr. Jacob vanished; some say he committed suicide.

Here the story breaks off. Early in 1942 Dr. and Mrs. Weizmann were crushed by young Michael's death in the RAF. They had been on the point of setting out again for the United States when they got the news in Bristol. For a month they clung to the vain hope that the boy would be picked up at sea, but the hope faded and they set out again on their American mission, their lives visibly darkened.

I met them at the airport, took them to the St. Regis Hotel and arranged to come over later that afternoon. The conversation was stilted and trying. The agony was written on their faces. Then Weizmann casually asked me what had happened with Dr. Jacob and his cure for cancer. I could have told them the sad story briefly and without details. Instead, I launched into an embellished version, more embroidered even than what I have written above. The tragedy of the suicide receded under the ridiculous and bizarre and soon they were both laughing heartily enough. When I finished I said I had to get home to my wife and children, and left.

Early the next morning I received an urgent call from Dr. Weizmann. 'Meyer, I have to see you.' I rushed to the hotel, and as I walked into their room Weizmann, still in his pyjamas and robe, embraced me and kissed me. With a trace of tears in his eyes, he said: 'Meyer, I shall be grateful to you for the rest of my life for what you did for Vera and me last night. This was the first time since the disappearance of Michael that we have had a good laugh. I shall never forget it.'

When I told this to Dolly and George, they agreed that it was worth much more than the $75,000 they had lost.

In 1943 my son Mendy went off to the war and my daughter Helen joined a Zionist movement and announced her intention of going to live on a kibbutz in Palestine. Both events were harrowing—Mendy's for obvious reasons, Helen's because of the absolute certainty with which she denounced her bourgeois 'past' (which included her parents), and adopted the proletarian ideology of Hashomer Hatzair: dirty clothes, hitch-hiking to God-knows-where with attractive (or so she thought) young men of similar persuasion, and a contempt for formal education. At that time Moshe Furmansky of Kibbutz Mishmar Ha-Emek was in the United States as an emissary for the Hashomer Hatzair youth movement. His wife Elisheva worked for me, and he was forever complaining that I overworked his wife. One day I said to him: 'You give me back my daughter and I'll give you back your wife.' Helen's conversion to Zionism came as a relief to me at first: in her violent enthusiasm for causes (inherited, I suppose), she had been flirting with the Young Communist League. It didn't take long to discover what a mixed blessing her conversion was.

I cannot tell which was the stronger element in her tempestuous make-up, the Zionism or the Communism, but it is certain that she had devoted herself completely to the ideal of *chalutziut*. I found it a little ironical that Weizmann should chide me on the subject. 'What about the question of *chalutzim* from the U. S. A. about which I wrote you in my last letter? I am rather disappointed that you did not touch upon it in yours to me.' I never mentioned to him that I had already made the supreme sacrifice on that battlefield.

The year 1943 was one of the turning points in the struggle for the crystallization of the Jewish will to Zionism. There were many stages to be passed, but the one that we were now embarked on consisted, in effect, in the democratic expression of the character of American Jewry. What we called the American Jewish Conference was to be in effect a Congress of all American Jewry. As in the case of the Biltmore Conference, the lead was taken by Dr. Weizmann. There was a grouping of four forces, each represented by its secretary. They were, respectively, Lillie Shultz, of the American Jewish Congress; Maurice Bisgeyer, of the powerful B'nai B'rith, whose real head was Henry Monsky (although outside the Zionist camp he was won over completely by Weizmann); Miss Jane Evans, of the National Council of Jewish Women; and myself, the coordinator and, in a way, the *primus inter pares*, representing the Zionists.

This was the officially designated secretariat; in addition there was a large working staff, of which the most important member was Meir Grossman, a great journalist, the head of our public information bureau. His was a case of split personality. He was President of the Jewish State Party, a splinter of the Revisionists, but in his duties as a member of the Secretariat he was irreproachably correct. His unorthodoxy began with his off hours, when he was free to constitute himself almost a minority of one. I had known Grossman from the days of *The New Palestine*, when he himself was editing another journal. I remember a peculiar incident from the later days—that is, 1943. Grossman sent his daughter Rinna to see me; she informed me that she was ready to offer her services to the Jewish People, where they were needed. I thanked her and told her to come back in twenty years. She did, and twenty years later she became the editor of the *Rehovot* magazine of the Weizmann Institute. During that interval she gained her literary experience on *The New York Times*, at *Time* magazine, and when she was through there helped set up the Information Service of the Israel Consulate in New York.

It is difficult to convey the sense of expectation and of burgeoning hopes attending the struggles of that time. Much was being done at cross purposes, there was no unity of command, and yet there emerged dim feelings of destiny and of purpose. We had to establish an organizational instrument before an organization, as such, had come into existence; we were aiming simultaneously at the making of a people and the definition of a program. Two and a half million Jews took part in the polling of delegates—which made it the first democratic Assembly in the world's largest Jewish com-

munity. The elections were held locally and everybody had the opportunity of putting up candidates, Zionist, non-Zionist, anti-Zionist (every
Jew was some kind of a Zionist!) That the elections were fair and democratic was beyond dispute: numerous defeated candidates said so. I myself
voted for and was elected as a delegate representing the Poale Zion, the
Labor Zionists. When I 'congratulated' the Poale Zion on the wisdom of
their choosing me as a candidate, David Wertheim, their Secretary,
replied: 'Had you been with the Poale Zion for twenty-five years as you
have been with the ZOA, we would have let them have you.'

As things moved toward their climax I wrote to Weizmann: 'I shall
keep you informed as things develop . . . After all, it's your baby. I hope
it will not turn out to be a *mamzer* and that you will have some *nachas*
from it.'

Toward the end of August, 1943, the American Jewish Conference
opened in one of the large halls of the Waldorf Astoria. A 'Committee of
Five,' of which I was a member, organized it; Lipsky was its Chairman.
The most important subcommittee, the very core of the Conference, was
the Palestine Committee, with Abba Hillel Silver as Chairman and me as
Secretary. Its membership comprised the leading spirits of the voting
blocs. Judge Proskauer, of the non-Zionist American Jewish Committee,
the representatives of the Reform laity and the Rabbinate, whether
Zionist, non-Zionist or un-Zionist, were the principal factions.

There were wheels within wheels; all sorts of cross currents were at play.
The Zionists had a clear line—a demand for a Jewish Commonwealth.
What we can only call the 'partial' Zionists were more or less agreed on a
similar platform. We—that is, the hundred-percent Zionists—aimed at
bringing into the plenum one united resolution, avoiding a minority
report. What that minority report meant was wearisomely trite—
something had to be said about 'one hundred percent loyal Americans,'
as though that were a genuine issue. Yet as the shadow of an issue it proved
quite recalcitrant. No one challenged the undivided loyalty of American
Jewry to the United States; but somehow the spurious issue had to be
established, and the Committee split 62 to 2—the two negative votes
being those of Judge Proskauer and Jacob Blaustein, an oil magnate. The
oddity was that Proskauer really had a struggle with himself; something
was bothering him and he couldn't make out what it was. I was quite
concerned for him though I could not for the life of me make out why.
Describing this part of the Conference to Weizmann, I wrote: 'I must say
here that the behavior of Proskauer was not bad. He was visibly affected by
the arguments, notably by a personal appeal made to him by Herman

Shulman to take on a new client, the Jewish people. Believe it or not, a tear rolled down his cheek. But he was bound by the decision of the American Jewish Committee.' Shulman was a lawyer, too. He had become rich entirely by accident when he took on free of charge the case for Pepsi-Cola in the suit against it by Coca-Cola. He won and Pepsi-Cola showed its gratitude by giving him stocks in lieu of money. He was a devoted Zionist and his wife Rebecca was one of Hadassah's outstanding leaders, at one time its President.

There was only one real issue at the Conference—the Palestine resolution. All incidental debates were attended with impatience; one had the feeling that American Jewry was gathering up its forces in order to break through the hesitancies, fears and digressions of years of debate—and, if one liked, of centuries of accumulating momentum. And at the very last moment, as if to provide the decisive thrust, there came, from the fatuous 'American Council for Judaism, Inc.,' a full-page ad in *The New York Times*, denouncing the entire Conference as un-American and un-Jewish. The timing was perfect—but not in the intended direction. Seeking to confuse the assembly, the Council succeeded in swinging it almost completely in the direction of the resolution.

The great moment came; the plenum was opened and the air was electrically charged. Every delegate's seat was taken and the ballroom of the Waldorf Astoria was jammed to capacity. The session began with the reading of a message from Dr. Weizmann which, by a lucky chance, arrived two hours before the opening of the session. Weizmann was to have been the climactic figure of the Conference, but London was under the 'blitz,' and he elected to remain there; even so, his transmitted words sent an electric thrill through the audience. A burst of spontaneous cheering was followed by the impassioned singing of *Hatikvah*.

I do not remember having witnessed such an intensity of feeling at a public gathering. When Rabbi Silver sonorously read forth the resolution and came to the words 'Jewish Commonwealth,' there was a gasp, followed by an explosion of joy; pandemonium broke loose, as if all the pent up hopes of the past had converged on this moment and this place. People wept for joy. When the vote was called for all one could see at first was the forest of cards being waved in the air. There was a roar of affirmation—and after it, a long way after it—four opposing votes, against four hundred and ninety six. They were Joseph Proskauer (who had by this time dried his tears of the night before), Jacob Blaustein, Rabbi Louis Mann and Rabbi Louis Wolsey.

Afterwards Stephen Wise said to me: 'Can you imagine what would have happened to this Conference if by some magic Weizmann had walked into this hall at the climax of the proceedings?' I was deeply struck by the insight and generosity of the observation—it illuminated the entire meaning of Weizmann's role. Stephen Wise, a contemporary of Weizmann, had always been associated with the Brandeis group, and to the end there had remained a cleavage between these two powerful figures. But a deep mutual respect, touched with an increasing affection, had given each of them a special insight; and at this instant the two men came together.

Recalling things late that night, I thought a lot about the natural expression Wise had given to his admiration for Weizmann. There had been a long evolution in the history of Stephen Wise, and I had followed closely, and with admiration, the course of his career. I first heard him speak in Philadelphia when I was only twenty-one years old. He had taken the leadership in the creation of the American Jewish Congress, the first attempt to set up a democratic Jewish body politic in opposition to the then dictatorial or at least hand-picked group known as the American Jewish Committee. It was a struggle between an emerging democracy and a plutocratic group. I then considered Stephen Wise—and considered him till the end—a great man. There was a physical greatness about him, something leonine in his appearance, as well as in his voice, a commanding force and presence which needed no attestation. He was, through and through, a man of principle; he had rejected the foremost rabbinical post in New York, that is to say, in the entire country, rather than submit to the censorship of that august body, Temple Emmanuel. He had espoused the Zionist cause at a time when very few promising young rabbis were prepared to risk their reputations and careers. And yet—this was my painful and inexplicable dilemma—I had to disagree with him utterly. He was a Brandeisist to the hilt, I was a Lipskyite. I wanted him very much to be a Lipskyite too—I would have been glad to exchange many a Lipskyite for this particular Brandeisist; I think the more I liked him personally, the more unreasonable I found his Brandeisism. He knew me in a dual capacity, as the 'editor' of *The Maccabean* and as the operator of the newsstand at the entrance to Columbia University on 116th St. Every morning he passed by the stand with his two children, James and Justine, and a huge dog, and bought a paper. In the afternoons we would meet at the offices of the ZOA. I think he had an exasperated kind of admiration for me, working as I was a double shift as newsboy and editor. He was a warm and expansive person, and our relationship, with its ups and downs, was warm and generous. I remember an amusing incident dating back to Weizmann's fall from office in 1931. Wise and Mack were again the leaders of the ZOA, but among the Zionist masses the sentiment for Weizmann was very strong. At the ZOA convention a resolution was introduced expressing 'affectionate' regard for Weizmann. Somehow Wise could not yet go quite so far, and he struggled with the committee to modify its sentiments. I do not believe he was being small; he only wanted to register a minor degree of dissent. He settled for 'hearty.' I wrote to Weizmann that now he had technical grounds to sue Wise for 'alienation of affections.' I did not take Wise's verbal maneuvers amiss, either then or at any other time. I would come to him often, even in the days of his feud with Weizmann, to consult on some matter of policy, or, when I was involved in my theatrical enterprises, to use his friendly offices. Here he never failed me; I think it gave him a special kind of pleasure to help me when I had no political axe to grind. His last public act was to officiate at the marriage of my son Mendy, whose first wife, Mary-Jo Van Ingen, became a convert to Judaism. Wise spoke movingly of the great responsibility Mendy had assumed for the spiritual welfare of the new Ruth. Everybody cried— Jews and Gentiles. Wise died about two weeks later. Seven years later Rabbi Charles Shulman officiated similarly at Mendy's second marriage, to Susan Hammerstein.

The American Jewish Conference passed into history. American Jewry had risen to the height of proclaiming that a Jewish Commonwealth must arise in Palestine. Then came the big let-down; the thunder and the shouting died, a period of multifarious inactivity ensued, of which the chief feature was the infighting between Silver and Wise. The scene shifted to Washington, and the position of the American government was clarified as the complete absence of any position; two and a half million Jews on one side, and on the other the richest oil reserves in the world. There were contradictory statements, flurries in corridors, promises made to Jews, promises made to Arabs, secret documents and election speeches. The Jewish Agency office in Washington under Dr. Nahum Goldmann worked one side of the street, the Emergency Council in New York worked the other; occasionally they bumped into each other in the dark.

On November 9, 1943, I wrote to Weizmann: 'If I were asked to sum up the progress of our work in Washington for the past few months, I would say that it has changed from placid indifference or inactive benevolence to a state of mental disturbance, coupled with irritation and a plaguing of the conscience. This, I think, can be said to apply both to the Executive and Legislative branches of the government.'

In February, 1944, Wise and Silver rallied the Zionist ranks to intro-

duce a resolution into both Houses 'calling on Congress to take appropriate measures . . . that the doors of Palestine shall be opened for a free entry
of Jews into that country . . . so that the Jewish people may ultimately
reconstitute Palestine as a free and democratic Jewish Commonwealth.'
The Majority and Minority leaders of both Houses of Congress undertook
to support and pilot the Resolution. A canvas of membership of both
Houses indicated that the overwhelming majority was in favor of the
Resolution.

No real attempt was made to ascertain the opinion of the President himself, or to sound out the military, though wisdom and prudence should
have indicated such a course. It was taken for granted that the friendliness of
President Roosevelt was such as to welcome the 'pressure' from Congress.

In March I went to Washington for the Committee hearings, was present
at all the sessions and helped in the preparation of some of the material.
There was a preponderance of gentlemen of the cloth, which did little to
enliven the proceedings; there was also a superfluity of theological
material. When one rabbi, in answer to a question, remarked, 'It is no accident that in the United States the movement is headed by rabbis,' I could
not resist the comment, *sotto voce:* 'No, it is no accident; it is a misfortune.'
Rabbi Abba Hillel Silver, however, was magnificent. During the rest of
the proceedings we put a ceiling on rabbinical pronunciamentos. The
record of the laymen was, on the whole, superior, with Louis Lipsky and
Emanuel Neumann achieving special distinction.

During the hearings I discussed the situation with Congresswoman
Clare Booth Luce. This was how she summed the matter up: 'You are
assured of an almost unanimous vote. The vast majority is genuinely
interested to help the Jews get their home; some will do it for political
reasons, others because they think the British will not like it, still others
because they are anti-Semites and hope to get rid of the Jews. The categories constitute among them about 100 percent of the Congress.' So much
for the highly intelligent Clare Booth. But with the briefest of warnings—
and these at first extremely vague—General Marshall exploded a bomb-
shell at an executive session of the Foreign Relations Committee. He was
completely negative. Staunch friends in both Houses began to waver; in
the face of such drastic opposition from the military, they preferred to
suspend action; and rather than risk a showdown, with all its consequences,
the Executive of the Emergency Council agreed to follow suit.

The bitter pill was somewhat sweetened by a soothing statement
without any genuine substance on the part of Roosevelt. He granted an
interview to Wise and Silver assuring them that 'full justice will be done to

those who seek a Jewish National Home.' I wrote to Weizmann: 'The tragic part of the whole business is that Silver honestly thinks we had a great political victory, and he cannot understand why everybody is not shouting "Hurrah." He doesn't see that while it may be necessary to shout "Hurrah" in public, at least in meetings of the Executive we can afford the luxury of saying what the *yiddene* said about Czar Nicholas, "*er zol azoy koyech hobn tsu lebn vi ich hob koyech tsu shrayen Hurrah!*" [He should only have as much strength to live as I have strength to shout Hurrah!].'

Divided councils and empty rhetoric confused American Jewry at this juncture. The authorized leadership, at a standstill for the moment, was being pushed to the wall by the Jewish Army Committee, with which we had been having trouble for some time. It was a blood and thunder minority group without a genuine program; its sole purpose was to discredit the Emergency Council and the World Zionist leadership, portraying it as impotent if not downright treacherous. Its great cry was 'Action!' Its second cry, a note lower, was 'Money!' 'You give us money, we will give you action!' The 'action' consisted of giant advertisements in the newspapers calling for more action and more money. The words dripped blood as it were. It was the long-tested, long discredited demagogy of the Revisionists—and it was not without its futile results. Quite a large number of well-meaning people were drawn into the dervish dance, and a certain unrest was stirred up in Zionist circles. 'Something' was being done; 'something' was happening; but what that something was eluded definition.

As the Chairman of a Committee called 'Special Services'—a kind of public relations department of the Emergency Council—I was under constant fire to explain why 'they,' the Jewish Army Committee, were so successful. But what the success consisted of beyond the shouting I could not make clear. I can understand that shouting in the right place can be used to back up an action; I resort to such a device from time to time, as certain of my contemporaries can testify. But public shouting as policy has only short-term advantages. Trying to compete for advertising space in *The New York Times* with the Jewish Army Committee was becoming a bit farcical. The 'public relations' of the Emergency Council had other and more sophisticated plans, which called for effective, long-range pressures on public opinion.

For example, *Life* carried an article on Saudi Arabia which was considerably damaging to us. Without going into all the details except to say that it was a long and arduous project, a nine-page pictorial display on Jewish achievements in Palestine appeared in that publication not long after. Had the Army Committee been responsible for this, they would no doubt have printed a full-page ad in the *Times* heralding its appearance, claiming credit for it and declaring it the solution to the Jewish problem. We not only made no such claims; we did everything in our power to cover up our tracks. Had it come to light that we were in any way involved, I am sure that *Life* would never have used the material. In my report, which carried no names or credits, I said: 'It is understandable that in the present tragic position of our people there should be impatience, even despair, at what is euphemistically being called "Zionism in Action." It is precisely at such a time, when men's souls are being tried, that we must not mistake strident voices for political action . . . we must not exploit the mood of helplessness for motives which we shall one day be called on to expose.'

A pleasant and complicated enterprise to which I devoted a good deal of time was the Weizmann '*Festschrift*' referred to earlier. It was launched in 1943 and timed for the next year on Weizmann's seventieth birthday. Weizmann had left off writing his own memoirs under the pressure of the times and while I in no way considered my book as a substitute for his memoirs, I felt that the time and the occasion warranted public acknowledgment.

It was my intention to produce the book without consulting Weizmann because I knew that his reaction would be negative. He would have advised me to devote my energies to 'some more direct purpose.' His dislike of personal publicity was common knowledge. He never permitted himself to make what in the newspaper world is called 'good copy.' He was, as a matter of fact, so reticent in front of reporters that more often than not what appeared in the press after an 'interview' with Weizmann was something akin to science fiction. More than once Weizmann wished he had told something to the 'boys' and not compelled them to draw on their own imaginations. The technical details which confronted me were considerable. The subject called for collaboration from many sources, in many parts of the world, notably in England and Palestine. And there we were, in the midst of a world war, with a censorship which read into a simple request for an article a coded message for the comfort of the enemy. (It reminded me of the story Weizmann used to tell when, at the outbreak of the First World War, he advised someone in a cable that he was sending 'Gold to Berlin.' What Scotland Yard didn't know was that both Gold and Berlin were Zionist rabbis.) In addition to disrupted communications, the Zionist Archives—because they were indispensable source-material—had been securely sealed away for the 'duration' somewhere in the wilds of

Canada. Another obstacle as far as I personally was concerned was that Weizmann's activities as a chemist had been peculiarly interrelated with his Zionism. My ignorance of the subject was frightening, but it was clear that a comprehensive portrait of Weizmann had to contain a scientific aspect.

I left such matters to Dr. Ernst Bergmann, Weizmann's chief assistant, and the job proved to have been well done. I myself felt more at home with men like Thomas Mann, Norman Angell, Pierre van Paassen, S. N. Behrman, Dorothy Thompson, Sholom Asch, Maurice Samuel and their like. The introduction to the book was written by Supreme Court Justice Felix Frankfurter. I cannot tell precisely when the 'secret' ceased to be one, but on July 4, 1944, I wrote to Weizmann: 'I undertook this task without prior permission and without your knowledge, for which I hope you will forgive me. It was my intention to keep it from you until the job was done. But the attempt along the same line in England, about which I learned later, made that impossible and also considerably complicated the undertaking. I ask both for your blessing and for your forgiveness in advance for any shortcomings. I have nothing more to recommend me for the job than sincerity, abiding love, a certain degree of good taste and some little talent. I will need them all.'

On August 14 Weizmann wrote me from London: 'Nothing is more appropriate than that you should edit it, and I am genuinely happy about it. But you know my nature. I feel rather shy and humble and I abhor overstatement and praise. Please make molehills out of mountains, which I prefer to the other way.' In a letter to Weizmann which prefaces the book, I wrote: 'If in our zeal we sometimes permitted mountains to look like mountains, we ask for your forgiveness.' I added an epilogue to the book on the assumption that nobody reads introductions but that the momentum of the galaxy of writers who preceded me would carry readers through to the last page.

I had much joy of my tribute to the 'Chief,' not a little trouble, and some amusement. For some reason I became obsessed with the idea of opening the book with a sonnet by a Hebrew poet. Long before I had contemplated the *Festschrift*, I had wanted the greatest of our contemporary Hebrew poets, Chaim Nachman Bialik, to write something on Weizmann; now Bialik was dead, and Saul Tchernichovsky, who ranked near him, was also gone. There was only one living Hebrew poet left in that rank—Zalman Shneur; he happened to be in New York at the time, and became very excited when I approached him with the idea. To lead off a book on Weizmann with a sonnet was a magnificent idea. Of course he could not produce anything like that to order. He needed time. He needed leisure —a pause in the country, to begin with. It would also be helpful if I could see my way to advancing him the sum of $500. This I produced, hoping that it would be sufficient and immediate stimulation to his muse. At the same time I ruefully recalled that in 1917, on the occasion of the Balfour Declaration, Gershon Agronsky had paid the distinguished Yiddish poet Zalman Raizin exactly $5 for a similar laurel wreath. I wondered if the dollar had so sharply devalued in the intervening years. But I preferred not to bargain, and only set a time limit of two months. Shneur returned from the country with an epic, in Yiddish, of one hundred forty lines, ten times as many as I had bargained for. I ran with it to my court poet, Maurice Samuel, whose reaction was not merely negative, but unprintable. Being a Yiddishist myself I suspected that this had been my own reaction, but had not dared to be forthright about it.

Now began a merry dance. I did not want to give up the idea of the poem, it had already cost too much. I took it to Ludwig Lewisohn, himself a poet, and asked him what he could do with it. Unfortunately he could not read Yiddish. I therefore read it out to him, with all the dramatic fervor I could muster. Lewisohn laboriously transliterated what he could catch of the German, and freely translated what I explained of the Hebrew terminology. He wanted three weeks in which to complete the task, but at the appointed time called up and said, simply: '*Ich kann nicht, es ist über meine Kräfte*, I can't, it's beyond my strength.' I was appalled, I begged, I pleaded, I cajoled. The book was in print, I had left only the first form open for the poem. Finally I said: 'For God's sake, then write something of your own.' No, that would not quite do; there *was* something of Shneur's to be salvaged, and what Lewisohn finally produced was a fantasy of what might have been Shneur if Shneur had had any of Lewisohn's ideas on the subject. I woke up Samuel in the middle of the night. He used a good deal of improper language, but I made him listen to the end. 'A work of genius!' he exclaimed, 'now let me go to bed.' 'Listen,' I shouted, 'I've had more heartache over this lousy piece of work than over all the rest of the book. I don't want any of your sarcasm.' 'As a matter of fact,' said Samuel, 'it isn't at all bad.' 'That's enough,' I said, and rang up Lewisohn to congratulate him.

The next morning I went down to the printer and had the piece set up. To tell the truth I was so heartily sick of this minor nightmare that I had no idea of the merits of the poem. But suddenly a nagging thought intruded on my alert mind. Wasn't it possible that the great Shneur might have some notions of his own about his magnificent opus? Poets are notoriously sensitive souls; they are often quarrelsome, even litigious. With a sinking feeling I sent off a proof of the poem to Shneur and prayed for the best. That same evening there was a curt, savage call from Shneur. 'That's not my poem.' 'What do you want,' I said with sinister smoothness. He said he wanted a new translation. My reply was, 'either this, or nothing.' 'Then it's nothing,' said Shneur, and slammed the receiver down. I stared at empty space; to be exact, at *the* empty space. I thought of the possibilities. To reject was within my rights; to pass off something that Shneur hadn't written was to invite infinite trouble. I decided to reject. Fortunately there was a good deal of material which had overflowed our needs. I substituted one of the articles and cut it down to size. For weeks after I was plagued by letters, phone calls, and telegrams from indignant women all over the United States protesting my treatment of the great Zalman Shneur.

The book, *Chaim Weizmann, Statesman, Scientist, Builder of the Jewish Commonwealth*, was published in the fall of 1944. During those months I had, with all my incidental worries, rediscovered myself; I smelt printer's ink again, I was like a fish back in water.

Weizmann wrote a great deal to me at that time, and his letters are intimate and full of personal sentiment. He missed me, he wanted to see me; he hoped I could come to London. In September he wrote that he was planning to go to Palestine in November and he urged me to join him there.

It was my supreme desire to be with him on his seventieth birthday, even with the war rising to its frightful denouement. Weizmann took it upon himself to make arrangements with the British Government for my trip, and I arrived in time, bearing two birthday gifts. The first was the book. The second I could not carry with me; nor was it mine alone. It was The Weizmann Institute of Science.

15 Dorothy Thompson: Fact and Fiction

I pause here for an interlude in which I want to gather up the strands of one special story—or, to be more precise, one special person, alluded to in passing in previous chapters: Dorothy Thompson.

Our friendship began in 1940 and spanned, during its most active period, something more than a decade, running parallel with all my other activities—the theatre, Weizmann, my work as director of the Non-Sectarian Anti-Nazi League, the Ring of Freedom, etc. The chronological details of our contacts, our friendship and our failure of friendship are less important than the phenomenon of a person.

Dorothy Thompson was the most striking woman whose path ever crossed mine. In a memorial tribute to Sara Delano Roosevelt, mother of the President, Dorothy Thompson delivered, however unintentionally, her own eulogy. Speaking of F. D. R. she said: 'Fame and happiness are seldom twins, and of all forms of fame, that achieved through public life is usually most dearly paid for in personal happiness. A public career invites enemies, and the most bitter and vindictive enemies. It attracts sycophants, and exploiters whose friendship is feigned; it entails huge responsibilities, with little gratitude to those who assume them successfully, and immense blame for those who fail, after however heroic an effort.'

Dorothy Thompson, one of the truly great women of our century, spent her final years in an atmosphere of scorn, derision and personal vilification through circumstances in which misjudgment, rashness, and generosity of spirit were the principal ingredients. She was also the victim of her own greatness. Her mixture of impetuosity, drive, and obsessiveness carried her to extremes, and sometimes involved her in obstinacies which she clung to after she had lost sight of her objectives. There was a story in the thirties that Sinclair Lewis once came home and found his wife talking to someone. He stood on the threshold listening, and then left. After twenty-four hours he returned. Dorothy was still talking. He left and never came back. The story is revealing, if not wholly true. It was not that she was an uncontrollable talker. She was a *great* talker. She was also—and this is even rarer—a great speaker. She was a great and astute journalist, a remarkable writer and a volcano of temperament and excitability. She was easily convinced and easily changed her mind; but she was always carrying a banner. Not a conventionally beautiful woman, she was extremely handsome, and filled with life, verve and ideas.

I first met her in 1940 at her home at 88 Central Park West. She was giving a dinner for Weizmann, of whom she was already a devoted disciple, and I was slipped in among the dinner guests. Whether it was the occasional attentions Weizmann paid to me, or the obvious fascination with which I followed Dorothy's conversation and its interplay with Weizmann's, some sort of rapport between us was born.

Dorothy was at that time the most fiery anti-Nazi in America, and much of her anti-Nazism was rooted in her love of Germany and of the German people among whom she had lived and loved for a number of years. She was also a Zionist, and this even before she had known Weizmann; her devotion to the Zionist vision went back to the early nineteen-twenties. She was a friend of Barbara de Porte, subsequently the wife of Meir Grossman, herself a columnist. The two were schoolmates at Cornell and traveled together to London in the early twenties, where Barbara was going to attend a Zionist Conference, and where Dorothy Thompson, the aspiring young journalist, became involved. Nor was Dorothy's anti-Nazism merely a theoretical declaration of principle. She was the address for every German-Jewish refugee whose name was suggested to her; she found work for dozens of them, places to live, comfort, encouragement. Her farm in Vermont, Twin Farms, at which I was a frequent visitor, was surrounded by a real colony of German-Jewish—and other assorted—exiles.

The strongest bond between us linked us mutually to Zionism and Weizmann; yet it so happened that another bond, connected with the theatre, constituted a sort of accompaniment. I had Reinhardt, she had Fritz Kortner, also a prominent German-Jewish actor and director. Together Dorothy and I were going to organize a repertory theatre for the United States. This was one of the flash-in-the-pan enterprises; it began with tremendous *Schwung*—everybody who was anybody in the theatre brimmed over with enthusiasm—and then suddenly collapsed. She wrote to me in March, 1940:

One experience in the Broadway theatre, whatever it may have revealed to me as a playwright [her play flopped miserably], revealed a great deal to me as a journalist. The Broadway theatre is a combination of crap-game—in the field of finance—and of trade union dictatorship. I have no real quarrel with the trade unions. Their practice grew out of the wholly insecure and financially preposterous set-up of Broadway productions. Financially, Broadway is on the level with horse-racing or lotteries, only the chances in these are somewhat better than in the theatre. In such a game, everybody grabs what he can. You and I are interested in two individuals, Max Reinhardt and Fritz Kortner. Our idea was to found a theatre with these two and at least one other American director, and a corps of actors, on contract . . . The plan would be to produce classic and modern drama, plays that have been produced before, and such new ones as we can find, but only plays of definite literary and artistic merit . . . But in order to accomplish something, actions, not merely words, are needed. We must *start* the theatre. I mean we must start *one* theatre. If we succeed, others will follow.

We actually did reach a point when we seemed to be launched on the *one* great production; at least we were examining plays for it. Thornton Wilder wrote me with approval about the project, but tried to cool Dorothy down through me: 'She will get a lot of vague enthusiastic letters from people in the theatre—don't let her count on them for plays or promises to act in the theatre. These days everybody lends his name to letterheads and then disappears into a cloud of excuses. How well you and I know that from the Reinhardt-School history.' And how right he was!

We nearly had in hand a play by Wilder himself which had been commissioned by Jed Harris—an outstanding prototype of the Broadway producer so dear to Dorothy. After seeing Harris together with Kortner, I wrote a report to Wilder:

'The first conference resulted in the following "clarification":

1. that he [Harris] *is* the owner of the play;
2. that, in fact, the play does not exist;
3. if the play existed, he did not know if he liked it;
4. that he is prepared to make a contract with us, but—
5. that he must reserve for himself absolute freedom of action (including the right to void the contract);
6. that he expects to make enormous sums of money out of the play;
7. that he has no faith in the play.

'All of which reminded me of Heine's story about the two old women who were arguing about a kettle. One of them complained that the kettle she had lent to the other woman was returned in bad condition. In defense, the first woman said: "In the first place I never borrowed the kettle from you; in the second place, I returned it; and in the third place, it was broken when I borrowed it."'

A copy of this letter and copies of three or four dozen great but as yet unproduced American dramas are all that remain of that American dream except for the friendship Dorothy and I—a queer pair if ever there was one—built on it. While she was busy with these castles in the air she was also bestirring herself politically. Early in 1940 she helped to get Wendell Willkie nominated as the Republican candidate for President. Her column, 'On the Record,' in the *Herald Tribune* was one of the great forces of that movement, and it was devoured by everybody, supporters and opponents, with their morning coffee. A few weeks before the election she switched to Franklin D. Roosevelt and threw all her fervid spirit to his support. The shocked *Herald Tribune* fired her: an example of what is sometimes known as 'freedom of the press.' Through George Backer and Dorothy Schiff I helped to install her at *The New York Post*. It was at that time that she made her famous radio speech which began: 'I am tired, we are all tired'—against the nasty campaign depicting Roosevelt as an exhausted old man. When the election results were announced in the early morning I sent her a telegram: DEAR DOROTHY I SEND YOU MY HEARTIEST CONGRATULATIONS ON A GREAT AMERICAN VICTORY IN WHICH YOU HAD NO LITTLE SHARE.

When she began her campaign for the 'Ring of Freedom,' I ran it for her from my office at the Jewish Agency as a side show. Her aim was to forge masses of people into a big democratic movement upon which the New World would be founded. One day she took me down to the elegant Van Cleef and Arpels to show me the ring they had designed for her. Its theme was of two hands clasped over the Western hemisphere. Another firm massproduced the ring on a nonprofit basis, and like comrades in a youth movement—enthusiastic though a little selfconscious—we sported this badge along with thousands of kindred spirits. She spoke at hundreds of meetings and over the radio, urging all and sundry to unite in brother-hood and democracy and freedom. She was utterly indefatigable in her furious war on the indigenous and imported Nazis infesting America —a resounding voice calling for the American crusade on the side of the Allies.

Then one day a baffling thing happened. I received from her a letter concerning the 'Ring of Freedom' in which she dwelt on the insidious prejudice which the Nazis were building up in this country against the Jews; and she asked me if I could not get her a '*goyish*' name to head some committee or other. I was shocked; that she should have paltered even with the idea of a tactical consideration of this kind showed me that some-where in her environment she had encountered and let pass the anti-Semitic infection. I sent the letter back to her, saying that I did not want to keep it in my files, I did not want to remember it, I did not want ever to mention the episode in a moment of anger. She apologized contritely, and there the matter ended.

In 1943 Dorothy contributed the outstanding essay on Weizmann in the book I edited. At about that time, or a little before, Weizmann and Dorothy celebrated a *seder*—one of several—in our house. Dr. Mordecai Kaplan, the founder of the Reconstructionist movement, had published a new version of the Haggadah, and had sent us copies for the celebrants. One of the startling innovations in this revised version of the ancient document was the omission of the thunderous denunciation of the heathens who had destroyed Jacob throughout the ages: '*Shphoch chamoscho;* pour forth Thy wrath upon the heathens, who knew Thee not.' When Weizmann came to the spot where this should have been, he insisted on finding an authentic copy and reading it out. After a considerable to-do Shirley produced one from among her father's wine-stained 'hymnals,' and Weizmann as it were restored the passage—which he knew by heart anyway. Greatly puzzled by this procedure, Dorothy asked: 'Chaim, what is this all about?' Very carefully he translated it, saying: 'This is for you, my dear.' In the light of what was to happen to Dorothy later, his words were prophetic.

But at that time Dorothy Thompson was perhaps the leading non-Jewish protagonist of Zionism and the Jewish Homeland, the voice of Christendom ringing across the world in turmoil. Every Jewish organization wanted her, and I became willy-nilly her volunteer agent, or her intermediary. Then something else happened. Toward the end of the war Weizmann came out strongly against the Jewish terrorists in Palestine, and Dorothy mistook her cue. Weizmann was deeply and irrevocably committed against the Jewish terrorists; his was the warning and moral voice; and his was the moral authority. Dorothy was not Jewish, she could not speak with that all-commanding directness. She was bound to be misunderstood; the result was that her utterances against Jewish terrorism were violently resented by the leadership of the Zionist Organization of America.

Then, in the autumn of 1944, when I was in Palestine for Weizmann's seventieth birthday, I got a cable from New York asking me to intervene with Dorothy and get her to desist from her attacks on the terrorists. I answered that I could not pass judgment before I received a telegraphic summary of what she had written. I got it, and cabled back that I could not in all honesty repudiate her; she was sincere in what she wrote, no matter how noble the motives ascribed to some of the terrorists. The issue was an uncomfortable one; as a Jew I was permitted to share Weizmann's views on the terrorists; but Dorothy was not in the same position.

The campaign against her continued and rose to a climax. Hundreds and thousands of telegrams, letters and postcards poured into the offices of *The Post* and I have reason to believe that this 'spontaneous' expression was carefully organized. The editor of *The Post* at that time, Ted Thackeray, was a good friend of the Etzel, the major terrorist organization in Palestine. Dorothy compounded her difficulties by speaking out with great vehemence against the so-called 'Morgenthau Plan,' which sought to turn Germany after the war into an agricultural country denuded of its industrial potential. The coincidence was, from the point of view of the critics of Dorothy, a grim one. There were two strikes against her now. One day *The Post* people came into her home and dumped a sackful of letters and postcards on her doorstep. Within a few days she was fired from *The Post*. She was syndicated in hundreds of papers throughout the country, but she had lost her voice in New York. At that time she wrote to Arthur Lourie of the Zionist Emergency Council: 'I refuse to become an anti-Semite by designation.' Unfortunately that was more or less what had happened.

The attacks upon her became outrageous. She was accused, among other things, of having lined her pockets with the fees of Zionist organizations. This stung her deeply, and here I was able to support her protest. She had taken nothing for herself. Like most speakers in public demand she was under contract with an agent, and agents are perhaps the least generous of spirits—it is an occupational disease. All monies accruing to her from public lectures went into a trust fund, which I controlled, for the German-Jewish refugees who came into her orbit.

What followed is understandable. She had lost her position in the metropolis; her one-time friends had turned on her in a gathering tempest of resentment, and it was then that a tribe of new 'friends' gathered about her, as unsavory a lot as ever infested Judaism. Concerning Lessing Rosenwald himself, the leader of the anti-Zionist and anti-Semitic American Council for Judaism, I have nothing but good to say; but he was as innocent of the intentions of the Council as it was of elementary decency. But a certain Samuel Goldsmith, an overfed capitalist, moved in on Dorothy with cloying compassion, as on a soul rescued from hell fire, or from some unclean infection. This was Dorothy's 'conversion' to 'anti-Zionism.' All of my stupid Zionist friends, who had maneuvered Dorothy into this position, now came forward *en masse* chanting: 'We told you so.'

I would like to believe that if I had been in New York at that time I would have saved her from the extremity of her reaction, from being thrust out by the intolerant Zionists and drawn into the coterie of the utterly impossible Council. Dorothy could only function in an atmosphere of warmth, devotion and affection; and she could, and did, when denied authentic friendship, accept a spurious and calculating substitute. How excusable this was it is not for me to determine; I only know that my relationship to her remained unchanged. True, we chided each other when we met, and our meetings became less frequent; but there was no break.

After a number of years she went to Cairo and became a friend of Nasser. She even wrote an introduction to his book, and I wrote her off politically as a war casualty.

One particularly unfair legend which sprang up round her 'conversion' placed the blame for her change of heart on her new husband, Maxim Kopf, a Czech refugee. If anything, Kopf was embarrassed by the new climate in the household. He was an artist (a picture he gave me one Passover hangs in my home in Rehovot); he had been in a concentration camp; he not only had ideological reservations about his wife's new philosophy—he just did not like those rich American-Council-for-Judaism Jews who had become her bosom friends.

And then the great wave which had carried Dorothy on its anti-Zionist tide began to ebb. Her enthusiasm for the Arabs waned. Privately she resented more and more the ravings of her anti-Jewish Jewish friends. One day, in the early fifties, when Arab-Jewish hostility was in one of its periodic climaxes, she invited me to spend a weekend at Twin Farms. It was to be purely social but it inevitably turned into a long and soul-searching review of the whole lamentable turn of events. We talked far into the night, alone. I said to her: 'I have no intention of reconverting you. One doesn't jump back into one's former bed without a reasonable interval of reflection. You have been on both sides. You were an ardent Zionist from 1920 on, and your support was continuous until the break came. I think I can understand what happened, and I believe there is a great role you still have to play. You are a friend of the Arabs; you are certainly not an enemy of the Jews, though you still bear a deep grudge against some Zionists; for that matter, so do I. You have looked at each side in turn, and you know the best possibilities of each. You can become a catalyst for a peaceful solution of the problem. You are full of energy and vitality, and if you throw yourself into this task you could make a decisive contribution to the cause of both peoples.' This was one of the rare occasions in our friendship when she was absolutely silent for a long, long time.

When she spoke up at last it was to say, slowly: 'Meyer, what you have said has touched me very deeply. I want to think about it. I have felt very strange in this company; I know I have let my frustrations get the better of me. Ever since my youth my association has been with Jews—with

Zionist Jews. Weizmann was always my hero; and now I have to straighten myself out. What you have told me will not be forgotten. I think I can make a contribution, but I don't want to do it precipitately and impulsively. I am going to Spain to meet my son. When we come back let's meet and map out a rational program that will be helpful to the Jews and Arabs and the entire Middle East.'

These hopes and dreams came to nothing. She died in Spain after a brief visit to the State of Israel, where she was coldly and even rudely received. She harvested 'the immense blame for those who fail, after however heroic an effort.' Had she lived she might have helped to write a useful chapter in the history of Arab–Jewish relations, and her last years might have been happier ones.

16 Palestine: 1944

I have often meditated, in an amused and detached way, on the interplay between my deliberate plans and the unconscious workings out of my long-range actions. As I begin on this section of my life, I try to fix a point at which I can say: 'This is what decided the great issue for me; here, faintly perceived, are the inevitable beginnings of the most important of all my decisions.' I say it, I can even more or less document it, but I do not feel it. It is as though it began to happen without awareness on my part, as though it didn't have an identity, as though it only revealed itself years later.

I can arbitrarily set an approximate date and say, 'round about this time it dawned on me,' but I would be talking without conviction. Many things were happening, projects were afoot of more or less interest and importance, but none of them evolved in the massive way that *the* mature issue of my life evolved. My days were busy and exciting, there was movement, strife, improvization; I was in a vigorous and expectant mood, but what I was ultimately to expect dawned on me only after the proper interval.

Let me now take up the thread of my narrative. I had arranged to meet Dr. Weizmann in Palestine on the occasion of his seventieth birthday. This in itself was not exactly a run-of-the-mill arrangement. The war was on, Weizmann was in England, I was in America. With all due regard for Weizmann's personality and achievements, was this a time for me to travel some six thousand miles for a celebration? The answer was 'yes,' because it was so much more than a 'celebration.' Weizmann's coming to Palestine at this point in our history was part of the evolution of the Jewish position. We were past the decisive point of the Declaration for a Jewish Commonwealth. Dr. Weizmann's arrival in Palestine was in the nature of a confirmation of status. A Jewish Commonwealth was not yet in existence, but it was there, waiting for self-fulfillment.

Also waiting were other potentialities. The struggle was on not only between Jew and Arab; it was on between Jew and Jew, between the 'establishment' and the Jewish terrorists who sought to bring about England's creation of the Jewish Commonwealth by violence. And so it was that on November 6, 1944, four days before I set out for Palestine, Lord Moyne, the Under-Secretary for British Colonial Affairs in the Middle East, was assassinated by Jewish terrorists in Cairo. This was a shocking and hateful thing to Weizmann. I was advised by friends that under the circumstance Weizmann would not go to Palestine for some length of time, and there would of course be no point in my going either. Nevertheless, Weizmann's visit to Palestine took place as arranged, and with it mine. Each of us had his reasons, his more important, mine less so. It was Lord Moyne who had consented to the trip, and I felt I owed him this last courtesy. I went by military plane with Lord Moyne's retroactive permission, my visa stamped by Isaiah Berlin, then the First Secretary to the British Embassy in Washington; the accompanying letter advised all whom it might concern that I was traveling as a guest of His Majesty's Government, all of which had been arranged by Dr. Weizmann.

Cairo was still in an uproar over the assassination when we arrived, and every Jew traveling to Palestine was under suspicion. They were giving us a rough time of it. On the train from Cairo to Rehovot I made the acquaintance of a fellow-Jew. He had a big parcel of food with him, including a whole cooked chicken, and rations being short, and I a very much interested onlooker, he invited me to share the meal with him. Early the next morning we stopped at the border and my traveling companion was hauled out of bed and forced to undress. He was searched from head to toe, and the operation was carried out with a great wailing and commotion. I didn't like the behavior of the officials, and I said so. I was told to get the hell back into my own compartment and mind my own business. When they had finished with the outraged Jew, they turned on me. 'Take down your bags,' they ordered. 'If you want to examine the bags, take them down yourselves,' was the refined essence of what I said. The head British official was slightly nonplussed, but he called in a porter and ordered him to take down the bags. I was completely at my ease; I had nothing to conceal. The official, hoping for the worst—some weapon, or God knows, a hasheesh cache—was even more thorough than he had been with my companion, and threw everything on the floor and the seats. When he had finished and had notified me stiffly that 'this was all,' I handed him my letter, stamped by Lord Moyne, 'guest of His Majesty's Government . . . any courtesy, etc.' The man turned white. 'Why didn't you tell me, sir?' 'Why should I tell you?' I answered, and then added: 'Besides, as a newspaperman I came here to see what's going on. There are so many exaggerations about British behavior in these parts—of course I didn't believe them—that I asked the British Government to let me come and see for myself. I am very grateful to you for giving me my first story.' I certainly wasn't going to tell him that before I left Washington I had to sign a document swearing that I would not write a word about anything I saw or heard.

Sure enough, a day or two after my arrival I received a cordial invitation from the head of the British Public Information Office in Jerusalem to come up for tea. The tea was very good, the conversation cordial, and as I was about to leave the man turned to me, and in the best Oxford manner, throaty and courteous, suggested: 'Ah-er-um, by the way, are you-ah-going to write anything about the country?' I had no intention of taking it out on the officer from the train; besides, the speaker knew the rules as well as I did. 'No,' I said. 'I'm not here in that capacity. I'm just here to see for myself.'

And there was much to see, more than I could cram into the longest report, more than I could hope to learn, even in the most superficial way, in a year of observation. It was a new world, not only to the eye, but to the mind, new forces, new circumstances, a land bursting with vitality, but also a land girding itself for a great struggle. I wanted to take in everything at once, the political situation, the tremendous upsurge of productivity, the contest with the British that was sure to come—I measured my courteous Britishers with a careful eye—and above all, the people, the beginning of the ingathering.

On November 22 I wrote to Shirley: 'I've been here now for 72 hours, shuttling hectically to and from Jerusalem, Rehovot, and Tel Aviv. My permanent quarters are in Rehovot, with the Weizmanns.' And I wrote her about my meeting with 'the Chief'—a dramatic story that lost nothing in the telling. My train from Cairo was three hours late. By the time I arrived in Rehovot Weizmann was already in Jerusalem at a meeting of the Zionist Executive. I hired a car, rushed up through Bab-el-Ouad to Jerusalem, and arrived at one in the afternoon at the offices of the Jewish Agency. The place was jammed with people, beleaguered by soldiers and police. I had to identify myself three times in order to get through the line. Finally, flanked by two soldiers, I managed to break in. Just as I entered, Weizmann, followed by a tremendous throng, was coming down the broad staircase. He stopped short and the whole procession stopped with him. 'Meyer, here you are and I've been turning the place upside

down for you.' He embraced me heartily and took a good look at me, to
the general stupefaction of the assembled, who in turn looked at me and
at each other and inquired in whispers who the devil this stranger was for
whom the President was turning the place upside down. I felt a rush of
happiness to see him—also a not unpleasant embarrassment as Weizmann
told his aides that he would be returning shortly from the High Commis-
sioner and meanwhile I was to be taken care of 'as if it's myself.'

I had hoped to arrive in Palestine a week or so ahead of Weizmann; I had
a million things to attend to; at the same time I wanted to do nothing but
stare, drink my fill of people, get my bearings, taste the atmosphere. So,
what with these conflicting impulses, and Weizmann desiring to have me
continuously on call, I found each day crammed full to the hilt. On December 4 I again managed to dash off a few lines to my wife. 'It is now 6 a.m.
December 4—the day on which Palestine is celebrating Weizmann's
birthday. [The Hebrew calendar moves in mysterious cycles.] The last
ten days have been one damn thing after another. You must understand that
in addition to accompanying Weizmann, I have to be the recipient of
honors on my own account. And they are numerous. I don't know if
there have been reports of them in the United States, but appearances of
mine are reported here (in radio flashes and newspapers—don't laugh)
like the fall of Stalingrad. Believe it or not, darling, I delivered a half-hour
speech in Hebrew before an audience of 2,000 in a packed hall in Tel Aviv.'
I later learned that the hall held only about six hundred, but to me they
looked like a million, hanging as some were from the rafters. My figure is
therefore a compromise.

The reader must understand that it was extremely rare for someone to
travel to Palestine from America during the war, and so my advent created
quite a stir. I was swamped with invitations to address gatherings—it was
out of the question for me to accept all but a very few. But the particular
meeting I am speaking of, arranged by the city of Tel Aviv in honor of
Weizmann's seventieth birthday, could not be passed up. Israel Rokach, the
Mayor of Tel Aviv, Gershon Agronsky from Jerusalem, Herzl Berger of
the Journalists' Association were among the orators that evening in
Mugrabi Hall. I had intended to speak in English, but was informed that
it had to be Hebrew. I found a translator in no less a person than Dr. Harry
Davidovitz, an old friend from Cleveland, who had rendered Shakespeare
into brilliant Hebrew. With all his brilliance he had to do the job three
times; I hadn't enough Hebrew to do it myself, but I had enough to sense
that his first two attempts did not suit my style. With the third attempt we
got down to something I felt I could call my own, and I practiced it to

perfection. Davidovitz promised to sit front center for my protection. Mugrabi Hall was jampacked, and I, the headliner of the evening, was reserved for last. By the time my turn came I was all but paralyzed. Every speech had been delivered in an impeccable Hebrew—but the audience was dead, sitting on their hands. The atmosphere became more and more oppressive as the shadow of the speeches lengthened. The man who immediately preceded me, Herzl Berger, was nothing if not a Cicero. Suddenly it occurred to me that perhaps these hundreds of Jews were suffering from undue strain listening to all this Oxonian Hebrew. So I began my speech with an appeal in Yiddish: '*Yiden, hot rachmunes* —Jews, have mercy.' The effect was sensational; the audience broke into spontaneous cheers, and after that it was plain and easy sailing. Even my mistakes were applauded. In the middle of a sentence I came across a tricky bit of Hebrew conjugation; someone in the audience corrected me; a dozen others rose like one man to my defense, shouting that my form was good enough, and I wound up to a sustained ovation. When it was all over, Herzl Berger came up to me and said: 'If I had your ignorance of the Hebrew language, I too would be a great success here.'

I told Weizmann that after the birthday celebration I planned to move around the country for about ten days. He winced a little but more or less resigned himself to the idea. He wanted me to go with him on his trip but I realized that aside from his moving slowly, there would be too many flags, flowers and receptions on this 'royal' tour. He had not been in the country for five years and every colony and township was awaiting his arrival with bated breath. I did, however, accompany him to certain places. One of these was the Athlit Reception Centre, near Haifa. It was one of the most moving, tragic and fearful experiences I have ever had.

There were nine hundred people in Athlit, crowded into a barbed wire encampment, nine hundred 'fortunate' souls who had found their way out of the devastated villages, the death camps. But in the closing months of 1944 we did not quite know the meaning and extent of those two words, 'death camps,' or of the death trains, doomed ghettos and encircled forests. But what we saw was horrible enough—a mass of human wreckage, children without parents, mothers without children, husbands without wives, wives without husbands—those who had somehow managed to reach the shores of Palestine. It was as if the vast tragedy that had overtaken the Jews of Europe were being presented to us like a horrible prologue, a miniature of what was to be unfolded soon to a horrified world. They told their stories, and we listened, shuddering: a child that had seen her parents slain before her very eyes; a young boy who had watched a Nazi tank crush his older brother . . . I asked a young girl, 'How old are you?' She answered, 'I don't know,' and that simple, appalling reply stayed with me for a long time. I went out of Athlit that day bewildered and broken.

In 1926 when I returned from my first visit to Palestine I said or wrote somewhere that for a proper evaluation of what Palestine means to the Jews who settle there, an American Jew coming from the richest land in the world must go first through the corridor of the Polish Jewish ghetto as I had done. Only then would he be able to grasp the full meaning of the Zionist phrase: the rebuilding of a land and the rebuilding of a people. It was necessary for an American Jew to breathe in the poverty, the squalor, the helplessness—notwithstanding the spiritual richness—of the ghetto in order to understand the transformation which takes place. In 1944 it was no longer possible. There were no more ghettos in Poland, only smoke-laden graveyards. Athlit was the new corridor as were, later, the detention camps in Cyprus, the D.P. camps in Europe, and the ramshackle, over-crowded, disease-infected immigrant boats. I don't think there was any Jew alive, or Christian for that matter, who saw these miserable corridors of life and had any doubts about the necessity of Zionism. For long, long years the Jewish Homeland had been the hope of national rebirth; in 1944 it was the only possibility for survival. But let there be no mistake. Without the core of 600,000 Jews in Palestine, the survival of these displaced, physically and mentally tortured people would have remained one of the great enigmas of history. Never in the history of mankind were the dis-possessed so ardently, generously and warmly received into the arms of the more fortunate as were the Jewish survivors of Nazism. Everywhere in Palestine people waited, literally with outstretched arms, to take in the newcomers. No sacrifice was too great, no effort too demanding but that these Jews should be able to live again. No place was so small or so crowded that more place couldn't be found. Every Palestinian Jew saw in these miserable refugees a member of his own family who had to be succoured, nurtured back to health.

We are a strange people, we Jews. Give us peace and prosperity and we will torture one another with our disputatiousness, insensible bickering, inexcusable pettiness and rivalries. We become fractious, intolerant, insensitive. We are the most miserably divisible people when the sun is shining. But there is a streak of stubbornness and selflessness which breaks out in moments of stress which is almost inscrutable. I won't claim this characteristic for the Jews alone. We are simply, in most things, 'more so.'

I had the opportunity of seeing these same refugees from Athlit a few weeks later when I visited the settlements around the country. I will not say that it was hard to recognize them but one could sense that life was being rekindled inside of them. It could not have been otherwise. The love and affection and understanding which flowed from the settlers was in no way affected. It was the emotion they could never lavish on their own murdered fathers and brothers.

But here I must take exception to some of the aspects of resettlement and absorption which began in Athlit. I refer to the processing of the refugees, especially the children, which was carried out according to a Zionist party key. I mention it because I think it is the curse of Israel. In Palestine then, though somewhat less so in Israel today, one is not simply born into a family. One is born into a political party and if there are factions in that party one is born into Group A or into the left or the right wing. If it were possible every Jew in Israel would be the General Secretary of his own party with his wife and children the rank and file—that is, if his wife agreed with him. This might be funny if it weren't so tragic. And it might be considered regrettable for the maturing State of Israel. But it was inexcusable in 1944 to operate a party key in dealing with refugee children.

There were about three or four hundred children among those at the Reception Camp. All of them passed through a room in which sat representatives of the ultra-religious Agudat Yisrael, the orthodox religious Mizrachi, the General Zionists, the Labor Zionists and, for good measure, another Labor representative representing Henrietta Szold and the Youth Aliya. After spending an hour in there, watching the processing, I called this room the Inquisitorial Chamber. Each child, regardless of age, was asked: 'What did your father do first thing in the morning? Did he lay *tfillin* (phylacteries)? Did he eat kosher food? Was he a member of the Socialist Party? What paper did he read?' The children were catechized. What is worse, they were terrified. They had gone through Hell. They had been in Palestine only a day or two. They could not know that this wasn't the Gestapo, that these people were merely trying to help them, trying to find out to which category of living Jews they belonged and to decide if they should be sent to a religious school or a secular kibbutz. If my Hebrew had been fluent I would have burst out at the interrogators. Instead I left, silently reflecting on the tribal civilization that was being created. Jews had managed to create five separate school systems. The children of the aristocratic laboring classes never mingled with the children of the disdained bourgeoisie.

It so happened that this sorry episode was the subject of my last meeting with Henrietta Szold, in the winter of 1944, when she was lying in hospital, only weeks away from death. It was a grievance against the Yishuv that she took with her to her grave. For years this magnificently selfless and wise woman, the founder of Hadassah, had devoted herself to the disposessed children of Israel. She was known as the Mother of Youth Aliya and even the most hardened politicians of present-day Israel who were brought to Palestine under her aegis remember her with inspired reverence, an emotion they usually reserve for themselves.

I knew—and revered—Miss Szold from my early days in the Zionist Office. I remember once at a meeting at the office I used some particularly 'flowery' language in making a point. One chivalrous gentleman rose, enraged: 'How dare you use such language in the presence of Miss Szold?' Miss Szold, sitting with her eyes closed, merely shook her head and without even opening her eyes as a courtesy to her would-be protector said: 'Meyer can use any language he pleases as long as he does what he does.'

Immediately upon my arrival I had sent a message to the Nurses' Home that I wanted to see her but was informed that she was much too ill to receive visitors. Towards the end of December she twice requested that I come and I was allowed in for five minutes. The five minutes lengthened into forty minutes, despite the protests of the doctors and nurses who pleaded with her not to strain herself.

I was amazed. Here was a woman of eighty-four lying on her death bed, suffering from asthma and all the complications one could think of; yet her mind was as clear as a bell and her voice as resonant. When I told her of my experience at Athlit, she nodded knowingly. It had been her daily bread for ten years, ever since she began her rescue work among the Jewish children of Europe. Her last words to me were: 'Meyer, when you go back to America, speak the truth about Palestine. The truth is the most important thing.'

She asked to see me again the following week because she wanted me to take back a message to her Hadassah Board, but she took a turn for the worse. I was in Haifa with Dr. Weizmann when there was a call from Dr. Judah Magnes asking him to hold himself in readiness for any emergency. It looked like a matter of hours. She rallied again and Weizmann spent her eighty-fourth birthday with her. When she came out of her last coma she said: 'What do you want from this old *shmatta*? Why don't you let her go?' I never saw her again: she died on February 13, 1945.

There was one unusual encounter that I had in Jerusalem during that time which I remember well. I was sitting in the offices of the Jewish Agency in Jerusalem when the telephone rang. My caller addressed me in Polish, one of the numerous languages in which I am less than fluent. All I understood was that his name was Dr. Leon Fuks. I timidly asked him in a broken Polish (more broken than Polish) if he spoke any other language. He began again, in German: '*Ich bin Dr. Fuchs aus Vlotzlavack.*' Now I knew two things about him. My next approach was, '*Efsher redt ihr Yiddish?*' In that most beautiful and intimate of languages he revealed himself: '*Ich bin dem Sompolnyer Rov's zuhn,* I am the son of the Sompolnyer Rabbi.'

A film fell away from my mind dragging with it forty years of accumulated experience. The Sompolnyer *Rov* was the Rabbi of Kikl when my father was *chazan* there. Usually the rabbi of a community and the *chazan* didn't get along. Their fields of action were too contiguous. But these two were bosom friends. The Rabbi never interfered with the *chazones* and my father never ventured into the Rabbi's province. The Sompolnyer Rabbi was silent on the Sabbath, leaving the field to my father. He was active during the week as a wise and trusted counsellor, a settler of disputes, the patron of a group of twelve young Talmudic scholars. As an aside let me note that in America the rabbis killed the *chazones* and drove the Jews from the synagogues. They substituted boring services for heart-rending music. Today *chazones* is dead in America. All the great *chazonim* or would-be *chazonim* like Jan Peerce, Richard Tucker and Robert Merrill went to the Metropolitan Opera. The rabbis are busy during the week with politics and become book reviewers on the Sabbath.

When the son of the Sompolnyer Rabbi identified himself, memories welled up inside of me and I remembered how scandalized Kikl was when the rabbi's son left Kikl to study medicine in Warsaw and how he returned some time later decked out in a student's uniform.

I asked, not Dr. Fuks, but the Sompolnyer *Rov's zuhn,* to come over to my office, and within less than half an hour he appeared. I like to believe that I would have recognized him had I passed him in the street. He looked exactly as he had forty years ago. We fell to reminiscing about the old days and when I asked him what he was doing in Palestine, he told me he had come as a colonel in General Anders' army. That a Jew should reach such high rank in the notoriously anti-Semitic Polish army was extraordinary enough, but Fuks—we must remember that the war was still on—wanted to get out and find a job with the Histadrut sick fund or Hadassah; and he wanted to find it quickly. I mused for a while, and an idea came to me. 'Go home,' I said, 'leave me your address, and let's see what I can do.'

A few minutes after he had left I rose, worked myself up into the right mood and went storming into the office of Shlomo Eisenberg, the Secretary-General of the Jewish Agency. 'What kind of goddam office is this?' I exploded, 'and what kind of management do you have here?' Eisenberg looked at me bewildered.

'Hold on, Meyer, what's going on, what's happened?' 'What's happened,' I shouted back. 'I nearly killed myself on the stairs just now, that's what. You have four hundred people working here, and no doctor or dispensary. These are wild times; riots every day. How can you leave the place without the most elementary medical facilities?' Eisenberg fell back before the assault. 'Listen,' he pleaded. 'It's not so simple to get a doctor. Most of them are in the army. The others are with the Kupat Cholim or the Hadassah.' 'That's no answer,' I said, and added, 'Look here. You fix up a dispensary, I'll get you a doctor.' His answer was: 'You get me a doctor, and have him fix up the dispensary.' 'Oh no, my boy,' I countered. 'You get a room, whitewash the walls, put in a bed, and get a nurse. I'll find the doctor.'

Said and done! Eisenberg was still under shock as we set out to look for a room. We found one by the simple expedient of ejecting two Jews into another room—they apparently had no other business than drinking tea. Within a few days Eisenberg had fixed the place up and called me in to impress me with his efficiency, and daily he taunted me with the demand, 'Where's your doctor?' 'You'll have him,' I said, 'you yourself told me how hard it is to get a doctor.' I was keeping Dr. Fuks under wraps for the denouement. And there was a denouement, but not one that we had expected. I finally brought the doctor in. As we entered the room Shlomo Eisenberg turned ashen pale, and then sobbing like a child ran to embrace Dr. Fuks and fainted. We did not know that he had a heart condition. When, helped by Dr. Fuks, he came to, I, unnerved by the painful scene, learned that Dr. Fuks had been the President of the Zionist Organization in Vlotzlavack when Eisenberg had been its Secretary and Fuks' friend. For years they had lost all contact with each other, and neither knew whether the other was alive. I need hardly say with what joy Eisenberg confirmed Fuks in his post.

The next time I came to Jerusalem I found Fuks established in his dispensary, fully supplied with a white overall and a nurse who was not the last word in looks but made up for it in devotion. Fuks also brought along a son, Dr. Alexander Fuks, who was a lecturer in classical languages, and later became a professor at the Hebrew University.

Of encounters like that between Dr. Fuks and Eisenberg innumerable stories were told in Palestine and Israel. They are sometimes shattering in their effect, even—or perhaps especially—when the occasion is one of unexpected joy. My friend and legal adviser Avraham Levin told me of an incident I will never forget. His stories are usually cheerful; he is a great raconteur in Hebrew, English and Yiddish. But this story brought tears to my eyes. A young relative of Levin's, a budding barrister from London, was visiting him and had gone up to Jerusalem for the day. When he returned he locked himself in his room and refused to eat or to speak to anyone. It was all very mysterious and worrisome. When he finally emerged he told Avraham what had caused his shock. On the way to Jerusalem the bus had stopped to pick up an old woman. She did not have the necessary change for fare. The driver shrugged it away saying he himself would make up the difference. Some of the passengers engaged the old woman in conversation, in Yiddish—she spoke no Hebrew. She told them that she had arrived in Palestine a few weeks before, absolutely certain that she would find at least one of her sons alive. She had an intuition and she was traveling from place to place with this hope in her heart. Everyone in the bus tried to be helpful, asked where she came from, what her sons' names were, and who she herself was. When the young driver heard her name he suddenly stopped the bus and turned to her. '*Mamme! Dos bin ich!*' The passengers began to weep, and one by one they got off where the bus was standing, saying to the driver: 'Never mind us. Take your mamma home.'

Wherever I went, and I traveled tirelessly during those six weeks, I became increasingly aware of the stubborn optimism of the Yishuv. Actually the situation could not have been worse and everybody knew it. Yet a single trainload of survivors or a single mother discovering a long lost child was enough to generate a general rejoicing. In view of what was later to be revealed about the extent of the European tragedy, this optimism was naive in the extreme. But, I wonder, could we have survived without it?

Very often, during those weeks, I found myself engaged in self-examination, or, as the Jews call it, '*cheshbon hanefesh.*' Here I was, a 'privileged' Jew through no merit of my own. Forty years before, a congregation of Gerer Chassidim in Mlava had put the seal on my fate by refusing my father a job. The gift of life was mine; what was I doing with it?

I was now fifty years old, and the years remaining to be counted were far fewer than those that had passed. There had been a certain continuity of purpose or outlook in my activity, or activities, but in a sense I had scattered myself in too many directions. There were many small and big ventures, and all had one end in view; that end can be summed up in Palestine and the Jewish Renaissance. But I was left in the end with no continuity and no sense of overall achievement. There they were, *The New Palestine, The Jewish Standard,* the World's Fair, Reinhardt—but where was I? I had become a *Mädchen für Alles.* Even now, my job at the Jewish Agency was a prolongation of my multifarious stop-gap activities. I was there primarily to act for Weizmann, and this gave me *carte blanche* to do anything I considered useful and worthwhile. I could have used the occasion as a springboard for a career in Zionist officialdom. Many of my colleagues went on from that time to become top-echelon civil servants of the State and of the Zionist movement, diplomats, ministers, directors. But this was not my cup of tea. My drive and energy were now at their highest point, and equal to almost any challenge, but there was no challenge which sparked my imagination, and of which I could say, 'This is it.'

In short, I was like an unharnessed waterfall, spilling over into a dozen small streams, and wondering, 'What next?' What new venture would come my way? What particular service would I be called on to render? I was not, during this period and for some time to come, aware that as a matter of fact my course had already been charted, and that I was embarking on my most extended and significant Zionist venture, the one that would lead to my settlement in Israel: The Weizmann Institute of Science. In view at the moment, among other enterprises, the Institute was another contribution to my Chief. That I would become the chief executive of a scientific institute would have been laughable. But in five years such was the accomplished reality.

The times were such that no one could predict what the morrow would bring. Weizmann's greatness lay in the fact that his pursuit of ends had in it a touch of the inexorable. He accepted it as an implicit fact that meaningful deeds, performed in a given setting, were of themselves the buttresses of history. No political declaration, however weighty, counted as much for him as the founding of a settlement, the planting of a grove, the building of a school. When he laid the cornerstone for the Hebrew University in Jerusalem in 1918 he was creating a fact far more stubborn than the Balfour Declaration which had preceded it by a year. When, in the midst of the Second World War with European Jewry in flames and the framework of civilization tottering, he insisted that the little scientific institute in Rehovot be enlarged, he was not creating at random, nor was he indulging his oft-neglected scientific interests. He was establishing a fact amidst the shifting sands of history.

When people speak of Weizmann as the founder of the Weizmann Institute they misread him. It would never have occurred to him to establish an institute in his own name, or even to seem to be doing so. He shied away from such conceptions; they embarrassed him. What took place in 1944 was a tribute to Weizmann on his seventieth birthday; the genesis of the Institute was entirely different.

In the beginning there was the Daniel Sieff Research Institute in Rehovot. This had been established by Rebecca and Israel Sieff in 1934 at the suggestion of Weizmann, with whom they were on the closest terms, as a memorial to their young son, who had been a promising young scientist. Weizmann had a study and laboratory there. It was his retreat from the Zionist hurly-burly. After Zionism it was his greatest love. During the early Hitler period he had done all he could to woo renowned Jewish scientists in Germany and bring them over to Palestine, or failing that, elsewhere, but he had met with little success. He lovingly nurtured the small, charming compound in Rehovot, and it was never far from his thoughts. Much of our correspondence from 1940 on deals with the Sieff Institute, and there were individuals and groups in the United States who had taken it on themselves to keep the Institute going; there were pledges and promises about which Weizmann was always asking me to do something. In 1941 he wrote:

Rehovot: I am somewhat worried about the Institute. Unless matters are followed up with great energy, we may find ourselves in difficulty in 1942. I would be extremely grateful to you if you would have a serious talk with Josef [Cohn] and work out a plan for gathering the fruits of my efforts, so that we may secure the Institute's full requirements for the coming year.

This motif was repeated in many letters, and occasionally I did some fund raising for the Institute—not much. As a statistical curiosity I must mention the fact that the entire annual budget for the Sieff Institute in those days was £58,000. At this writing the annual maintenance and development budget of the Weizmann Institute is about 50 million Israeli pounds. I must interpose here something about Josef Cohn and his role in the Weizmann Institute. He was a German Jew born in Berlin, a member of the Blau-Weiss Zionist Youth Organization, who began his career with Dr. Weizmann by carrying his suitcases whenever the latter came to the city. One day Weizmann said to him casually, 'If you ever come to London, look me up.' Hitler saw to it that Josef came to London. By that time he had a Ph.D. in political science, and like every young Ph.D. he had written a book. His subject was political science, and Weizmann gave him some research to do. Eventually, in 1938, Weizmann sent him to me, in the United States; and in the course of time, particularly in postwar Germany, Josef's contribution to the Institute was as its European representative. He had access to Konrad Adenauer and every Chancellor after him, and he did a splendid job. My final act of friendship to him was to see to it that he may retire, in the dignity and security he has earned, on the campus of the Institute.

And now I come to the actual beginning of the Weizmann Institute, not quite unnoted at the time but almost casual. In 1944 a Birthday Fund was established in the United States for the purpose of enlarging the Sieff Institute. Weizmann wrote me in March, 1944:

There is another matter which worries me greatly. I can see that the work for the Institute in Rehovot does not prosper. There was some talk about creating a fund on the occasion of my seventieth birthday, but so far all I gather is that the collections in Chicago and Philadelphia, and most certainly in New York, have been a dismal failure, and the position is gradually decaying. Nothing came from Canada. I really don't know what to do. The only men who seem to be doing a job of work are Dewey Stone and Harry Levine. It is important that not only Rehovot should exist, but that it should be reconstructed and enlarged after the war, and funds for that should be built up now. Please advise me what to do.

These friends of Weizmann also came to me for advice. The Committee for the Sieff Institute in America was headed by Lewis Ruskin of Chicago. I am afraid that he and his Committee were not particularly imaginative, though they were completely devoted to Weizmann. They were not very clear about their arithmetic, either. At one point they spoke of a fund of one million dollars, but somewhere in the discussions a zero was dropped. When they discussed their plans with me I said: 'Gentlemen, raising money to keep the Sieff Institute going isn't something to set the imagination on fire. Dr. Weizmann is the center of Jewish world attention today, and if you want to celebrate Weizmann's seventieth birthday you have to do something that reflects the Weizmann name. People will say: If you need money for the Sieff Institute, go to Mr. Sieff.'

We met again a few days later and this time I proposed the building of a larger Institute, not unconnected with the Sieff Institute, but bearing Weizmann's name. The instantaneous reaction of the Committee was: 'The Sieff family will be offended.' I called Israel Sieff; I can't remember whether it was in Washington or London, during the war he commuted between the two. 'Would the Family have any objections if we establish a big institute in the name of Dr. Weizmann incorporating the Sieff Research Institute?' He said: 'Not at all. How much are you out for?' 'A million dollars,' I answered. 'Why don't you make it five million?' was the rejoinder. That was the green light.

The destiny, not only of the Weizmann Institute, but of the entire Zionist movement in England might have taken a different turn but for the warm friendship which developed between Israel Sieff (later Lord Sieff of Brimpton), Simon Marks (later Lord Marks of Broughton), and Harry Sacher, on the one hand, and Dr. Weizmann on the other hand when the latter arrived in England in 1904. Here were three young men, brothers-in-law, of extraordinary brilliance. Harry Sacher had already established a reputation as an editorial writer on the famous *Manchester Guardian;* Simon and Israel were gifted businessmen with a flair for empire building and a deep commitment to the modernization of the business methods of England, parallel with an instinctive relationship to Zionist thought. Their attachment to Weizmann was immediate and enduring. But it was not a one-way exchange. Weizmann's Zionist political leadership aside, his contributions to the rise of Marks & Spencer, the great firm headed by Simon and Israel, and subsequently taken over by Edward and Marcus Sieff, are publicly attested in the firm's official history. It is without doubt the most prestigious business empire in the United Kingdom. It may be said that with the possible exception of the Rothschild family, the Marks, Sieffs and Sachers, known affectionately throughout the Jewish world as 'The Family,' have made the greatest joint contributions to the Zionist movement, and this from every point of view, political, social, financial, cultural and scientific. And practically every branch of the family, reaching into the fourth generation, is deeply involved in the affairs of Israel.

Israel Sieff, Sigmund Gestetner and, later, Isaac Wolfson, became the spokesmen of the Weizmann Institute in London. After the death of Sigmund Gestetner, Israel's son, Marcus, took over as the leading figure in our activities and was as effective in the Weizmann Institute as his parents had been in the original Sieff Institute, but on a much larger scale. Hyam Morrison took Sigmund's place as treasurer and his associate was John Barnett, Sigmund's nephew. Scotty (as everyone calls him) Morrison and I became great friends and his services to the Institute continue to this day, aided and abetted by his enterprising and beautiful wife, Doris, and their children.

And now, to go back to my story. I prepared for the Committee a memorandum proposing a public effort on an international scale; the upshot being, as I had anticipated, that I was asked to undertake the responsibility for carrying it through. On November 2, 1944, on the twenty-seventh anniversary of the Balfour Declaration, and one week before I left for Palestine for Weizmann's seventieth birthday, the first meeting of the Board of Directors of the American Committee of the Weizmann Scientific Institute, Inc.—that was the name then—was held in New

York. A million-dollar target was set; five officers were elected, among whom I was not one; I was merely to run the thing on a volunteer basis from my office at the Jewish Agency.

Had I been graced with the smallest measure of clairvoyance, I might have spared myself a great deal of subsequent self-searching. I was happy to have undertaken the creation of the Weizmann Scientific Institute. It was an immensely useful thing, and it brought the Chief much happiness. But I had no inkling that there would be the great follow-up that was to mean so much to Dr. Weizmann, the State of Israel—and myself.

As December, 1944 drew to a close, and with it the birthday celebrations and related events, Dr. Weizmann began throwing out broad hints that I should remain with him in Palestine during January, and every time I mentioned the subject of my return home he would dismiss it. The simple truth was that I missed Shirley. The excitement, the honors and above all the proximity to Weizmann were all gratifying, but I was determined to spend New Year's Eve together with Shirley. Accordingly, over Dr. Weizmann's objections, I arranged for passage out of Palestine on December 23 and cabled Shirley to meet me in Montreal on December 31.

In Cairo, I literally crawled—that was the only way in—into a military aircraft similar to the one on which I had come and spent a miserable trip imprisoned in an oxygen mask and freezing from the neck down. It seems I wasn't the only one anxious to reach Montreal for New Year's Eve. The crew were in such a hurry that they forgot to close the fuel tank when we refueled at Gander. This of course delayed us considerably, but their basic philosophy was 'better late than never,' and we approached the frontiers of Canada before the chimes of midnight had been sounded. But no— Montreal Airport was closed because of a blizzard and we had to return to Gander. We trudged out of the plane and made our way to a dismal pub, there to usher in the Happy New Year. In order to drown my sorrows and try to forget that my wife was cooling her heels in a Montreal hotel, I allowed myself to become engaged in a game of poker. I began to win. This in itself was not so bad but every time I wanted to quit, I was called a bad sport. I was dying to get some sleep but I had to go on playing. There was no way out but to try to lose back everything I had won, and to this end I devoted myself until seven in the morning when the captain broke up the game. I had no luck that night: when we boarded the plane I was $700 richer.

17　On the Threshold

The spring of 1945 had come and we knew the worst. I say 'we knew,' as if we were really able to grasp it. We have never been able to grasp it. What we 'knew' was the factual account of the deliberately planned slaughter, the bestiality, the systematic doing away with six million men, women and children. At the worst of times, we had never believed that the diabolic mind of Hitler would translate insane fantasy into those facts. We had read *Mein Kampf* with horror and disgust; we had known about *Krystalnacht*, concentration camps, expulsions, cruelty, mass murders, everything familiar in the world of human behavior: but this was in a monstrous class by itself. We could not even see the 'facts' at first.

Then the ice that blocked our vision began to thaw, and snatches of the truth became visible. The worst of our forebodings paled before even the partial revelation. When Weizmann had knocked on the doors of Whitehall and Stephen Wise on the doors of the State Department, their supplications had always met with the same answer: 'The central problem is to win the war. When we win the war, we will take care of your problem too.' In a way it reminded me of the old Jewish socialist slogans about the Jewish problem: 'When the evils of capitalism and tyranny will be removed, the Jewish problem will automatically be solved. Witness the Russian revolution.' Well, witness!

When the war ended, Europe was revealed as one vast Jewish cemetery haunted here and there by gaunt survivors. A thousand years of Jewish creativity, Jewish culture and civilization, the center of our spiritual and intellectual life, the substance of Jewish life in all its aspects, religious and secular, had been wiped out in one blow.

It can be said with justice that the whole world suffered, and that the Jewish problem was small in comparison to the vast struggle that convulsed humanity. But was it really? Fifty-two million people died in the Second

World War; only six million were Jews. But they made up one third of the entire Jewish people and almost two thirds of European Jewry. Moreover the holocaust established new and terrifying facts, it was *sui generis*. The word 'genocide' is used all too easily nowadays. There has been 'genocide' in the past, there have been brutal wars of extermination; but they have been as it were 'intelligible.' They were wars for ruthless seizure of territory; they were not wars for the sake of extermination *as a principle*. This is what has made the abomination.

But even accepted as fact, an observable phenomenon, one might have imagined that among the nations of the world, and among the Jews themselves, a fundamental change would have taken place. Nothing of the sort happened. The British, in a sickening example of *plus ça change, plus c'est la même chose*, tightened their immigration restrictions on Palestine and increased repressive measures against the Yishuv! The Americans continued in their traditional division of labor: the Executive phrased pious sentiments while the State Department kept things 'under control.' Within the Zionist movement the various camps became more argumentative, and the overwhelming catastrophe through which we had passed only intensified the differences. Those who called for an armed uprising in Palestine pointed to the holocaust as proof that only by violence could we achieve our ends. Those who deplored violence pleaded for restraint and warned the Jews not to resort to the methods of the enemy. Anti-Zionists declared that Zionism was incapable of saving the Jews and leftists proclaimed that the Jews would be saved only by world socialism.

I do not mean to imply that there was callousness or indifference to what had happened. People were shocked and stunned. There was a deep feeling of betrayal and a common commitment: This will never happen again! But there was no unity of purpose either within the Zionist movement or within the Jewish world as a whole. The assimilationists continued to assimilate (or at least tried to), the communists sang hymns of praise to the Soviet Motherland, and the Zionists fought with the world and with each other for the establishment of a Jewish State.

In the summer of 1945 I left New York for London to attend an *ad hoc* 'world' Zionist Conference. It was a pitifully reduced world that I saw there. The only comfort was that in Europe, at least, the war was over.

I was met at the Air Centre by Ivor Linton, Weizmann's Political Secretary, and he informed me by easy stages that there was not a room available in the Dorchester, or in any other decent hotel, for love or money. He took me to the magnificent lodgings he had booked for me—

overlooking Hyde Park—at the Park Court Hotel. It was a third-rate flophouse with the manners of a fifth-rate whorehouse. Lodging had to be paid in advance.

The next morning, after a sleepless night, unwashed, unshaven, with the smell of the Clipper still on my crumpled suit (to have a suit pressed in London at that time one would have needed the personal intervention of the Prime Minister and the First Lord of the Admiralty), I appeared before my Chief. The reception was warm and affectionate all around. A million questions were asked, but I was not in an expansive mood. I could not get that flop-house out of my system.

At midnight I returned to it. To describe a night in that place is not possible. The long and short of it is that I did not sleep, and got up in the morning determined to get out, even if I had to sleep in Hyde Park. When I got to Zionist Headquarters in Great Russell Street there was what might be called, in the language of the German theatre, '*allgemeine Bewegung*,' soon followed by great jubilation. The Chief had gone in person to the Manager of the Dorchester and was rewarded with a huge reception room (almost a ballroom) at Brown's Hotel for one night!

After a few more moves I finally got settled at the Cumberland Hotel. I ate every evening at the Weizmanns' and did it uneasily because of the food situation but he refused to hear of any other arrangement. I spent my days helping to get the Conference into order and one source of pure pleasure was reading cables from various American Zionist dignitaries announcing their imminent arrivals and commissioning me to find them accommodation.

I was rather impressed by the absence of general destruction. I had expected nothing but ruins from Croydon into London. I was told that I had to go and see 'The City,' to get some idea of what really happened. Here and there one saw scars, but by and large London was still London, a very charming city.

The opening of the Conference was postponed a number of days because a delegation of Polish Jews was expected, and it was touch and go whether the Russians would permit them to leave. The conflicting rumors kept the Conference buzzing from morning to night, and it was with mingled feelings of hope and fear that we awaited these pall bearers of East European Jewry. Of what value was the Conference without these representatives of 150,000 Jews who were all that was left of a community of three and a half million Jews? As for the three million Russian Jews locked in Stalin's Russia, there was not even a glimmer of hope.

The Polish delegation did finally arrive—six tattered emaciated Jews out of Gorki's *The Lower Depths;* such at least in appearance, but not in spirit. In the fateful session there were remarkable characters. Moshe Sneh, who had left Poland before the war and settled in Palestine, was the chairman for that session. There was an audible sobbing when the session opened: here staring us in the face was the living witness of a murdered people. When Weizmann spoke his voice barely rose above a whisper; he was like a father at the graveside of his children trying to probe the will of an inexorable God.

Among the delegation of six there was a young girl of twenty-three, Chaya Grossman. She was a member of the Hashomer Hatzair and had been a partisan living in the forests and moving back and forth into the ghetto at the time of the uprisings. She survived, I believe, because there was nothing Jewish about her appearance; she looked Polish, with tawny hair, fair skin, light eyes and broad features. She was the last one to speak. Of her heroism, her leadership, her utter dedication, her iron will, much was known to us from the other members of the delegation. Her speech was a recital of endurance, fortitude and endless resourcefulness—no dramatics and histrionics, just a calm recital of what she had seen and what had happened to our people. They were the simplest and most impressive words I had ever heard. The Conference was transformed into one great partisan movement, and if she had uttered the simple words, 'Follow me, let us avenge the murderers of our people,' we would have got up and obeyed her. But she uttered no such words. She only described. When she had finished we rose to our feet in silent homage. Later I asked her in Yiddish, 'How could you maintain your calm when you spoke?' Her reply was terse, 'Had I been unable to maintain my calm I would not be here today.'

I returned to New York from that Conference sadder, wiser, subdued. I was also still in that mood of self-examination, of what I had called the *cheshbon hanefesh*, that had begun during my Palestine visit. I was fifty-one, and I did not know what lay ahead of me. I was still involved in the daily routine of the Jewish Agency, as its Director or Secretary-General. I knew that great and stormy times, days of decision, lay ahead of us. The Jewish situation had changed radically and catastrophically, while the urgency of rescue and survival pressed upon us more heavily from day to day. The doors of Palestine were still closed. Jewish patience wore thin, and people became irritated, inflamed. Hundreds of thousands of Jews who had never taken the slightest interest in the fate of their people began to ask insistent questions, to demand action. Some approached the questions constructively, others in a spirit of reckless impatience and demagogy. Jewish life became confused, its character sometimes deteriorated. There was no real leadership in America. Brandeis was dead; Louis Marshall was dead; Stephen Wise was old and spent. The new crop of leaders was pallid compared to the old.

In the summer of 1945 a Labor Government was voted in in the General Elections in Britain. For an instant there was a great uplift of hope and promise among the Jews of America. The party which had again and again recorded its enthusiastic support of the Jewish National Home was sure now to apply a wise and generous policy in Palestine. But in one short and brutal speech, Ernest Bevin, the new Foreign Secretary, extinguished our hopes. The White Paper policy of 1939, which had limited immigration into Palestine to a trickle, to be stopped altogether at the will of the Arabs, was reaffirmed in 1945 as if there had been no holocaust. When President Truman, after an exhaustive study had been made for him of conditions in Europe and Palestine, proposed to Prime Minister Clement Attlee the immediate admission of 100,000 Jews to Palestine, Bevin responded with—'another enquiry into the situation.' Thus was born the Anglo-American Commission of Enquiry on Palestine, which went to work early in 1946.

One night I was in the Essex House in New York with Weizmann. He was preoccupied with the work of the Anglo-American Commission which was then holding its hearings in Washington prior to its departure for Europe and Palestine. Into our *tête-à-tête* walked George Backer.

George was not then nor was he later a Zionist, but he had a profound attachment to Weizmann, and he brought an interesting piece of information concerning one of the men on the Commission, Mr. Richard Crossman. During the Second World War George had been part of a British-American intelligence team, something called Psychological Warfare. The team had been headed by William Paley, who now heads the CBS, and included, among others, Ritchie Calder and Richard Crossman. During this period George had got to know Crossman. He said to Weizmann: 'There's no one on the British side of the delegation that you have to fear except Dick Crossman. He's the brainiest of the lot, the most sophisticated, the most intelligent—and a real socialist, a leftist socialist at that. He is a man to be watched and feared. Moreover, he is Ernie Bevin's appointment.' I cannot say that this little bit of news exactly cheered Weizmann; his health had not been good, and his mood was pretty somber.

Weizmann turned to me. 'Meyer, you have to go to Washington.' And then to Backer: 'Give Meyer a letter of introduction to Crossman.' I was engaged at that time in trying to persuade Albert Einstein to testify before the Commission. It was not my idea. Zionist officialdom was convinced that Einstein would be our *pièce de résistance*, and I had gone out to Princeton to talk Einstein into giving evidence. I did not find him very responsive to the idea, and I remember walking up and down with him for hours—I still have a pain in my leg from that walk—getting him to agree. Finally I mobilized his secretary, Miss Helen Dukas, who had great influence over him, and together we pulled it off. He made one condition: I had to go with him on the train, I had to be with him at the sessions, I had to take care of him all the time. Thus I found myself going to Washington in any case. I looked over the note George Backer had scribbled for me to Crossman and saw that it would not do—it was not my style, it was too formal. I proposed that during the sessions I go over at some opportune moment and tell Crossman I had regards for him; if the response should prove friendly I would pursue the matter further.

I took Einstein to the Statler and went with him up to the hearings. I sat at the back of the room as inconspicuously as possible, observing the dozen men who had been chosen to solve a problem which, it seemed to me, God himself, let alone Churchill, Truman, and Bevin, had found impossible to solve. As the interrogation of the witnesses went on it became clear that the most penetrating questions were being thrown out by Mr. Crossman. Penetrating was hardly the word—devastating would be nearer the mark. I thought to myself: 'George is right. This *sheygetz* has more brains than the entire Commission put together.' When Einstein took the stand he started out very well, but under Crossman's interrogation he began to go off on a tangent, and his remarks ranged from the oppression of the Indians to anti-imperialism in general. Still, his presence on our behalf was not without effect.

When the first sessions ended I placed myself in a position where it was impossible for Crossman to avoid me. I was even ready to trip him if necessary. As he passed I said: 'Mr. Crossman, I have regards for you.' 'Really?' he said. He is generally very ebullient and responsive. 'From whom?' 'George,' I answered. 'George who?' 'George Backer.' 'Oh, George, how is the old boy?' 'Well, I just left him and came to see the proceedings.' 'But who are you?' he asked, and I sensed that the fish was hooked. I told him briefly. 'By the way,' he said, 'if you're so knowledgeable, you're just the chap I want to know. You surely know Mr. Dollek Horowitz in Jerusalem. That's one man I'd like to meet when I get there. Perhaps you can give me an introduction to him.' 'That's easy,' I said, 'but you don't have to wait till you get to Jerusalem. I can produce him this afternoon. He happens to be in Washington.' 'That's wonderful. Can you arrange it?' This was my first contact or collision with the man who had struck George Backer as being so formidable.

I immediately called up Dollek, told him of my encounter with Crossman and made an appointment. Dollek Horowitz was even then one of 'the' economic minds of the Jewish hierarchy in Jerusalem; he has since become, for three successive five-year terms, Governor of the Bank of Israel. Our meeting place in Crossman's room at the Mayflower lacked some of the dignity proper to the international issues we were to settle. The room was a somewhat oversized closet into which a bed and a single chair had been wedged. It barely accommodated one person with comfort. In my best expansive manner I said to Crossman: 'Is this all that the British Empire could afford for its representatives dealing with the fate of the world?' 'Remember,' said Crossman, 'we just came through a world war and we're still on rations. The allowance is very small, and I personally have no money to add to the allowance.' He stretched himself out on the bed, Dollek hunched himself up on the chair, while I sat on the edge of the bed with my feet dangling.

The discussion started off in earnest. Crossman had a fabulously retentive and inquisitive mind, and he wanted to know everything about Palestine, with particular attention to the kibbutzim, the Labor Federation and the economic structure of the country. All this fascinated him as a Labour Member of Parliament. Dollek, I must observe, was correspondingly brilliant and informative in his replies. The discussion went on for hours; we retired to the counter in the coffee shop for a break and returned to the room. By two o'clock in the morning I collapsed and left the field to the two unexhausted intellectuals. They were by then deep into Marxist philosophy, of which I knew nothing. Dollek walked me to the elevator; before I went down I said to him: 'Dollek, I'll make a prophecy concerning this man. If he's genuinely the socialist he seems to be, he'll be with us.' I repeated this to Weizmann when I returned to New York the following day.

Much to the annoyance of Ernie Bevin I was right. Bevin had been counting on Crossman to carry the ball for him, and Crossman did not play. He became a staunch advocate of our demands and has remained a staunch friend of Israel throughout, to the eternal disappointment of our prophets of doom and probably to the detriment of his own career. He and his late wife became close friends of Weizmann, and his friendship with me still lives. He has visited Rehovot often, and written and lectured on our problems.

Weizmann testified before the Anglo-American Commission when it held its hearings in Jerusalem. Crossman wrote of Weizmann's testimony: 'He spoke for two hours with a magnificent mixture of passion and scientific detachment . . . He is the first witness who has frankly admitted that the issue is not between right and wrong, but between the greater and the lesser injustice.'

Nobody was happy when the Anglo-American Commission issued its verdict, but the unhappiest man of all was Ernie Bevin. The Arabs were angry, the Jews disappointed. The Commission recommended the immediate admission of 100,000 Jews to Palestine, the abrogation of land restrictions in the country and the preparation of an international trusteeship. There was no mention of ultimate statehood for the Jews, or even partition. But it was a blow to the British White Paper policy, and that was one consolation. Or so we thought. We had reckoned again without Mr. Bevin. Having sworn to accept the recommendations of the Commission when it was launched, he wasted no time in rejecting them on behalf of the British Government as soon as they were announced. But the rejection of the report was not outright. Its implementation was made contingent on a variety of impossible conditions such as the complete disarmament of the Yishuv. This was May, 1946.

The laying of the cornerstone of the Weizmann Institute was set for June, 1946. That this particular act evoked no opposition from the Mandatory Government reflects the peculiar dichotomy in their policies. They did not seem to care how many cornerstones we laid, or to what purpose. They were pleased as punch every time an illegal cache of arms was unearthed under the floor of some kibbutz dining room, but completely indifferent to the fact that a scientific institute was being built under their noses. Whether this was naiveté or fatuous shortsightedness, that was the way Jewish States were built in those days and British Empires dismantled. But now, to bring the reader up to date on the fortunes of the Weizmann Institute I must go back to the middle of 1945.

I had taken upon myself to 'run' the affairs of the American Committee of the Weizmann Institute as a sort of side activity to my many duties at the Jewish Agency. My friend Ritchie Calder, the notable science writer who later became Lord Ritchie-Calder, wrote about me that 'science to him [at that point in my career] was a spectacular that he was prepared to stage as he had once done *The Eternal Road*.' I suppose he was right. My intuition, all I had to go by, told me that the enterprise had to be launched in high gear if we were to get anywhere beyond the usual Zionist appeal for worthy projects. This Institute had to enlist as its advisers a group of men high in the ranks of world science. Accordingly Herman F. Mark, of the Brooklyn Polytechnic Institute became the Chairman of our Scientific Planning Committee; an Advisory Committee for the Institute of Physics and Physical Chemistry was set up under James Franck of the University of Chicago; and an Advisory Committee for the Department of Applied Mathematics was established, headed by J. Robert Oppenheimer and including, among others, Albert Einstein. Ernst D. Bergmann, Dr. Weizmann's assistant, was of course the coordinator of all these committees.

Similarly, if we were going to raise money it could not be to the tune of 'Brother, can you spare a dime.' If you ask a man for $100,000 he may squirm out of it with a promise of $50,000. Ask him for $5,000 and you may expect $1,000. I set my sites on the higher registers and organized for 1945 the first of what was to become the Annual Weizmann Dinner at the Waldorf Astoria in New York. For the privilege of attending the Founders' Dinner we charged $2,500 a table. This gave our prospective clientele an inkling of what was in store, and only the hungriest came. Dr. Weizmann was the guest of honor. We raised $1,045,505.55 for a start.

It was an auspicious beginning, and I learned for all time that it is more efficient to extract $1,000,000 from a hundred people with large bank accounts than from a million people with small ones. (I pursued the principle by gradually contracting the number of people required to put up each successive million and eventually arrived at optimum efficiency: one for one.)

With this substantial sum in the kitty, it was possible to plan the laying of the cornerstone, and at this point, I must confess, my intuition failed me.

The actual ceremony was set for a day in June, 1946, and I conceived it as a great gathering of science and money with a big cast. But I was premature. It was too much and too soon, and the thing petered out. A cornerstone is only a promise, and the world—not to mention Palestine itself—was still too unsettled a place for such a grand performance. Instead, a more informal affair was arranged. A group of twenty-five American scientists was organized for the cornerstone ceremony, and in a reconverted boat, the S. S. *Vulcania*, twenty-five cabins were reserved to bring the guests in comfort to Haifa. At that time news had reached us of the ill treatment of Jews docking at Alexandria, and I thought it would be best to get permission from the State Department to have the boat go direct to Haifa. Eliahu Epstein (later Eliahu Elath) of the Jewish Agency in Washington was to make the arrangements.

Which is a little story in itself. When I first suggested it to Epstein he turned it down flatly. I said that if he would not do it himself he could at least arrange to have me meet Mr. Loy Henderson. Epstein, who was born to wear striped pants (he was Israel's Ambassador to Washington and later to the Court of St. James's) shuddered at the suggestion but realized I had made up my mind. In despair, he sat down to give me a thorough briefing as to how one ought to behave in the presence of great power. I was told to keep my voice at a low pitch, smile, be a model of decorum and in general convey an impression of sweetness and light. I listened with the gravest attention and promised to follow his instructions.

Epstein accompanied me to the State Department and we were shown into a large, musty, high-ceilinged room which looked like a museum vault. I was properly introduced and the discussion began. Everything went along quite affably until Mr. Henderson said something which provoked me into an outburst as violent in form as it was undiplomatic in language. Epstein's face took on a greenish tinge and he began to apologize profusely on my behalf. 'Mr. Weisgal is not familiar with diplomatic usage.' To which Mr. Henderson replied with great charm: 'Never mind, Mr. Epstein. This is the first breath of fresh air that has entered these rooms in years.' From then on everything went along smoothly. Henderson gave orders for the boat to proceed directly to Haifa, and I returned to New York a conquering hero, the founder of a new school of diplomacy.

While the boat was still on the high seas an order was received, and relayed to me in New York from the State Department, that the boat could not properly land in Haifa. The reasons given were too numerous to be convincing: the harbor was too narrow, the water too shallow, the docks too small. In short, it was the double-cross of the classic type, familiar to the chancelleries of Europe and America—and every other official center of policy. Fortunately nothing untoward happened in Egypt and the party made its way peacefully to Rehovot. My son Mendy, now a venerable twenty-one years, and a veteran of the war in the Far East, where he had been a Chinese interpreter, was with the scientists on this trip. I myself arrived by plane a few days later.

The cornerstone ceremony was a gracious and impressive affair, officiated over by Dr. Weizmann. Among the guest scientists were Louis F. Fieser of Harvard, David Rittenberg and Chaim Pekeris of Columbia University, Herman Mark, Kurt G. Stern and Peter Hohenstein of the Brooklyn Polytechnical Institute, and Yehudah Quastel, F.R.S., of University College, Cardiff. And of course we had our own representatives from the Sieff Institute, the Hebrew University, and the Haifa

Technion. The days were devoted to symposia on a variety of subjects which I assumed to be both illuminating and provocative because the scientists seemed to be enjoying themselves greatly. There is a Yiddish saying, '*az a shikse dreyt sich arum beim rebn in shtub ken sie oych paskenen a sheile,*' which in rough translation means that if a chambermaid hangs around long enough in the house of a sage, she will in time give off sparks of wisdom. This is what happened to me over twenty-five years of exposure to scientists. I began to catch on. In 1946 I had no idea what any of them were talking about, but I knew that the very fact that they were talking, and talking enthusiastically, was good for Rehovot.

When we returned to the States Fieser summed up his impressions with: 'I went over a scientist and returned a Zionist.' What really impressed most of the scientists was the spirit of the people and their tremendous eagerness to learn. Chaim Pekeris decided to return to the Institute in a permanent position and to bring others with him. So did Kurt Stern, but unfortunately he died prematurely. And young scientists from everywhere were beginning to put in applications.

Some time before the laying of the cornerstone I received a call from Ben Gurion and went to see him. He said: 'I hear that you are planning a Weizmann Institute in Rehovot. In my opinion it should be in Jerusalem, on Mount Scopus. Jerusalem is going to be the capital of the State. The Hebrew University is there and our scientific center should be there as well.' I was not unimpressed by the argument and I reported the conversation to Weizmann. His answer to me was: 'First of all, you don't put all your eggs in one basket. Two, you never can tell what may happen in this country. Jerusalem may be cut off one day. Three, we should have an institute of science nearer the coastal line. We have a university in Jerusalem and there are scientists there. But there should be no monopoly of education in this country; it should be distributed. We must have diversity. "*Kinat sofrim marbeh chochmah,*" is a wise old Talmudic saying, "the rivalry of scribes increases wisdom." Some day we will also have a university in Tel Aviv.' (A year later Weizmann broached the subject of a University in Tel Aviv to Dr. Werner Senator, administrative head of the Hebrew University.) But long before that became a reality, Weizmann's forebodings about the Hebrew University on Mount Scopus were fulfilled. Two years later Jerusalem was cut off and Mount Scopus became a useless military enclave for twenty years. All the scientists had to be flown to Rehovot under the most difficult and hazardous conditions. Rehovot became the birthplace and the center of 'Chemed,' the scientific arm of the Israel Army.

What Rehovot contributed to Israel's war effort is another story into which I will not enter here. But most of the hard-earned money we raised for the Institute went into that effort. I remember how, after the war, I went to Ben Gurion and said to him: 'Let's make an accounting. We want some of our money back for the Institute. After all, practically all of our money has been spent on this.' B. G. answered: 'When the story of the War of Liberation is written, the future historian will decide who saved whom: Rehovot Israel, or Israel Rehovot.' I answered: 'Mr. Ben Gurion, that's a wonderful epigram, but I can't build an Institute with epigrams.' I never saw a penny of our first million and we had to start all over again. But I am ahead of my story.

There are some observers of history who claim that in 1946 Weizmann considered himself politically played out and that he looked to the Weizmann Institute for a different source of inspiration and growth; the career of the statesman having been checked, he retreated into science. The observation is superficial if not malicious. For Weizmann science and the institutions of political sovereignty were twin phenomena. He could not 'retreat' into science; he had never left its precincts; and politically he had some enormous contributions to make in the next and last six years of his activities. The most pertinent summary of that period is implied in his memoirs, when he recalls the cornerstone laying. 'There was not a little in that ceremony of the summer of 1946 to remind us of that earlier ceremony, in the summer of 1918, when the cornerstone of the Hebrew University was laid. True we were no longer in the midst of a general war, and the Jewish National Home to which we were dedicating the new enterprise was substantially in existence. But it was a time of stress and difficulty, when men's minds were little occupied with this type of activity. It was the time of the 'terror,' and a time of bitter political disappointments and impending struggle. Like the laying of the cornerstone of the University on Mount Scopus, this was an act of faith, and it has been a continuous act of faith to carry the work forward.'

The terror which had gripped Palestine as the result of Britain's policy and the frustration and despair of the remnant of European Jewry rose to a climax in June, 1946. Theoretically there were three organizations and ideologies comprising the Jewish resistance in Palestine. The 'Haganah,' the largest of these and the official instrument of resistance was engaged in illegal immigration and thwarting British efforts to stop it by destroying radar stations and bridges. The 'Etzel,' (acronym of *Irgun Tzvai Leumi*, 'The National Army Organization') had adopted as its policy the terrorizing of the British out of Palestine. The 'Stern Group' was dedicated to

individual acts of terror and assassination. Theoretically, and in many instances in practice, there were fierce antagonisms among the three gtoups,
and fierce rivalries—including sometimes mutual betrayal to the British—
pitted them against each other. But there were times of covert cooperation
between the Haganah and the Etzel, and a blurring of differences in methods. The blowing up of the King David Hotel in Jerusalem, which housed
British military headquarters, was a case in point, although too many
versions of the story exist to enable one 'truth' to emerge.

My own feelings about the use of force were confused. From the stand-
point of Jewish morality I rejected it; but in the political context I was
beset by doubts. I expressed these in a batch of scribbled notes which I made
in 1946, and headed 'Random Thoughts of a Bewildered Zionist.' For
example:

The world seems to have a double standard as far as we are concerned. Millions of people
are being transferred in Europe from one place to another because it is either expedient
or just because a particular configuration demands the moving of masses of people from
one place to another. If the suggestion were made with reference to Palestine, it would
cause a violent upheaval in the chancelleries of the world: the Jews are the aggressors, etc.
Political violence in other parts of the world, and there is plenty of it, is given the name of
patriotism, resistance, revolt, partisan warfare, Marxism, de Gaullism, revolution. In
Palestine it becomes a very simple thing: terror.

Further on I wrote:

We owe nothing to the *goyim*. We owe them no apology. Nothing that we can do will
ever expiate their sins. But it has no relation to our acts. What is more important is the
question: What does it do to us? It eggs on evil as an end in itself. But there is
no compromise with evil. This is at the root of our mistaken policy. We thought that
by dealing with the Etzel or the Stern Gang we would influence them to a more rational
policy. But the reverse happened. We are smeared with the blood on their hands. What is
happening in Palestine is the greatest triumph of so-called Christian civilization. It has
succeeded in dragging us down to its own level. We were told, and a number of us
believed, that this is the only language the *goyim* understand. It may be so, but not when the
one who speaks it is a Jew.

And further:

We are afraid to speak up because it might give comfort to the enemy. But the enemy is
comforted and delighted by our misdeeds—not by instances of our exemplary behavior.
There was terrible disappointment on the part of the [British] government after their
attack on the Jewish Agency when there was no retaliation. They were looking for it as an
additional excuse to continue their work of destruction. One almost sensed an overtone of
satisfaction in all the clamor round the tragedy of the King David Hotel. What a good
thing! Perhaps if the [Mandatory] government had been less keen that the Jews should
besmirch their own record, and debase their own prestige, the tragedy might have been
averted. Even in this case the Haganah suffered defilement.

Twenty-two years have passed, nothing has really changed, either in the patterns of the world or in my own confused state. I still deplore violence even when exercised by the Israel Army. Yet I deplore even more the cynical double standard of a world which is 'upset' when Arab terrorists shell Jewish settlements and mine school buses but becomes hysterically vindictive about Israeli reprisals. The world is prepared to be with us when we Jews are the aggrieved party; dead Jews make excellent copy for moral Christian sermons. But woe to the victorious Jew! Such a reversal of historic Christian tradition is too much.

The issue of activism and Weizmann's attitude toward it was to become one of the major trump cards played against him at the Zionist Congress at Basle at the end of 1946 when he left the Presidency of the World Zionist Organization never to return.

Popular legend had it that Weizmann was opposed to any kind of activism. Even my good friend, Nahum Goldmann, reviewing in his autobiography the situation as it was in 1946—and we must remember that Goldmann was a Weizmannist for the better part of his political career—states: 'The former [Weizmann] firmly rejected all terrorist or activist resistance and continued to hope for an understanding with the British Government.' Since it is my good fortune to break into print after Nahum, I can refute him; an unforeseen advantage of literary procrastination.

Of Weizmann it was said that he was not only a pacifist; he was also an appeaser. Now what can truthfully be said is that Weizmann was a symbol of British-Jewish cooperation, and despite the fact that his trust in the British had broken down in those years, the symbol lived on. Weizmann had always hoped that the Jewish National Home would arise peacefully, through settlement and building, under an enlightened Mandate. He was right and wrong. He was right in that no amount of anti-British vilification would produce a Jewish state unless there were Jewish farms, schools and factories throughout the length and breadth of the country. He was wrong in hoping for a benevolent British interpretation of the Balfour Declaration. But he, as much as, if not more than many others was aware of the extent of British betrayal after the war. For him it was not only political betrayal; it was also a personal betrayal. That he remained a symbol of a policy which he himself finally rejected is an historical fact, not a personal choice. As to activism, I can state categorically that Weizmann was never opposed to Jewish resistance in Palestine. He was opposed to acts of terrorism, which he felt were foreign to the Jewish spirit. He could not condone indiscriminate killing. But he supported, and not only in words, illegal immigration and Jewish self-defense. He supported the

Haganah, he rejected their intermittent alliances with the Etzel. In this respect Weizmann stood on the same ground as the leaders of the Yishuv, Ben Gurion included.

Thus, for example, Ben Gurion had come to the United States after the London Conference of 1945, at a time when Weizmann was present. One day I had a call from Ben Gurion—an urgent call. He was staying at the Hotel 14, at 14 East 60th St. The hotel was owned by friends of mine, Reuben Barnett and his wife, Fanny, who had been my secretary years before and was later Weizmann's secretary in New York. We used to call it 'Kibbutz 14.' I found Ben Gurion lying stretched out on a big bed, pasha-like. The meeting, at which we two alone were present, lasted some three hours. He gave me a long account of what he wanted; the substance was: can you find me thirty Jews who will follow me blindly, who will do what I want without asking questions? And then he developed his view about the fight that was to ensue in Palestine after the war, the danger that would confront the Yishuv, the need to mobilize money, arms, machinery, science, professionals, etc. I sat and listened. When he had finished I said: 'B. G., I'll give you an answer within twenty-four hours.' He replied: 'I suppose you want to discuss it with your boss.' My answer was: 'Exactly.'

I came down to Weizmann the same day and unfolded the story to him. Weizmann listened carefully, without saying a word. As I got up to leave he said: '*Nu, loz sich arumdreyn an eydem in shtub.*' Literally this folk idiom means: 'O. K., let's have a young son-in-law hanging about the house.' The wider meaning of this idiom refers to a Jew who is looking for a son-in-law when he hasn't a daughter. A friend asks him, bewildered: 'What do you want with a son-in-law when you haven't a daughter?' The answer is: 'Who knows? Something good may come of it.' I didn't need another word from Weizmann. I went to Ben Gurion and said I would help.

Weizmann moved in the highest diplomatic circles as the representative of the Jewish people; his contacts were with Presidents, Prime Ministers and Secretaries of State. He could not afford—politically speaking, not personally—to be identified with the armed struggle. He had to keep his hands free. His policy was always that it was more important to do things than to talk about them.

I did Mr. Ben Gurion's bidding, that is, I contacted the man who I thought would be of most help to him in his area, my old friend Henry Montor, who had a genius for fund raising and knew everyone worth knowing. I have a suspicion that Ben Gurion actually talked to Montor first and Montor told B.G. that he should talk to me. At all events, Montor embarked on the project with tremendous zeal, discretion and, I might add, success. A 'club' of thirty Jews was organized outside of any official Zionist framework. These were people completely devoted to Palestine and prepared to do, silently and vigorously, whatever they were called upon to do. Essentially it was a plan to equip the incipient army in Palestine and provide the basis for a military industry. Harry Levine played an important role in this enterprise. These men, and others whom they recruited, scoured the country for old equipment which was shipped in pieces, and under various camouflages, to Palestine. They risked their reputations and even prison sentences to see to it that these materials eventually reached Palestine. Aside from this *sub rosa* activity, the 'club' also established a public channel, under the leadership of Mr. Rudolph Sonnenborn, a member of an old and distinguished Zionist family, called 'Materials for Palestine,' which forwarded medical supplies and hospital equipment. It was run by another friend of mine, Julius Jarcho, known to everyone as 'Rusty.' My involvement with these enterprises—which was quite considerable—is dealt with elsewhere; but it denoted—if only tacitly—Weizmann's approval.

I recall, in this connection, an interesting incident of the summer of 1946. A boatload of illegal immigrants had reached the shores of Palestine carrying thousands of refugees from the camps of Europe. The boat had been intercepted by the British. The tactics of the Haganah were to bring thousands of Palestinian Jews to the shore and into boats in the water, to mingle them with the refugees and exchange clothes with them so that the British would not be able to distinguish between the newcomers and the Palestinians. Nevertheless, hundreds of refugees were rounded up by the British and placed in a detention camp from which they were rerouted to camps in Cyprus. Weizmann went to visit the detainees in Athlit. My son Mendy and I were with him. We entered one of the barracks, a place that could hold about two hundred persons at most. In the few minutes after our arrival, hundreds upon hundreds of detainees had pushed through the barbed wire and cement barriers into that barrack. There must have been a thousand people jammed into that space, hanging from beams, crowded against the walls in human pyramids. Weizmann spoke to them and they responded, singing *Hatikvah*, the Jewish anthem of hope. I don't think any of us ever heard *Hatikvah* sung like that before, or since. It seemed to us that the whole assembly was weeping. Weizmann himself was shattered.

On our way back to Rehovot we passed a peculiar installation on a hill near Haifa. Weizmann, as was his custom, was sitting up front next to

Yossi Hamburger, his A.D.C., one of the high-ups in the Haganah. Weizmann turned to Yossi and asked him, 'What is that?' Yossi explained that it was a radar tower used by the British to spot approaching illegal immigrant boats. '*Farvos roymstu es nit arunter fun weg?*' asked Weizmann. 'Why don't you clear it out of the way?' 'Is that an order?' asked Yossi. Whereupon Weizmann replied: 'I don't give orders. I'm not a military strategist. I was just making an observation.' Whether Yossi took the observation seriously or not I cannot say; I cannot even say that he had anything to do with what happened later: the installation was leveled by the Haganah.

This was not terrorism. This was the resistance of a small people fighting against an imperial power trying to subvert, undermine, and frustrate its own solemn promises.

Weizmann used to say, 'Do more and talk less.' He could not bear the wanton destruction of human life; but he understood the necessity of Jewish defensive action.

18 Weizmann: Trials and Triumph

The year that led up to the United Nations Resolution on the Partition of Palestine in the fall of 1947 was one of the most feverish in my life, and my life has seldom been noted for its tranquility. The issues that converged in this interval of little more than a year led me through a dervish dance of activity. It began with the aftermath of Weizmann's demission as the President of the World Zionist Organization—as 'President,' not as 'leader' (which he remained throughout his life). His resignation from the Presidency coincided with a great leap forward in the fortunes of the Weizmann Institute. This was also the year that saw the completion of his memoirs. In all of these events I was intimately involved. I spent my time commuting from New York to Palestine, to Paris, to London —then London, New York, Palestine, Flushing Meadows, and in between I was doing odd jobs for the 'club' of thirty and its offshoot, 'Materials for Palestine.' During the early days of 'Materials,' I had a standing agreement with my friend Rudolph Sonnenborn that whenever I happened to be in New York on a Thursday, I would appear and say a few words. He never failed to introduce me as the father of the idea. When I got tired of the 'father' business I asked him to change it to grandfather. He complied and my new status thereafter carried with it less formal obligations.

My activities for 'Materials for Palestine' were less formal, livelier and more variegated. The 'materials' were machines and spare parts, surplus war goods, ramshackle airplanes and ships. They were come by circuitously, dispatched circuitously and then transformed miraculously into the tools of the army, navy and air force of an as yet unborn state. When this chapter in the history of Israel is fully chronicled it will make the adventures of James Bond look like the story of a Victorian nursemaid by comparison. The subject has been partially chronicled in a book called *The Pledge* by Leonard Slater. This effort is praiseworthy, but does not begin to tell the whole story.

One day, for example, we got hold of two airplanes, a real coup. We had volunteer pilots ready to take off at the agreed signal; but unfortunately the American authorities refused to give the signal. Official policy on arms shipments to Palestine was a flat 'no.'

At what seemed the last moment I was called in, and on the wildest chance, and with pure instinct, thought of Herbert Bayard Swope, who, besides his position as a distinguished journalist, editor and author, was a force to be reckoned with in the Democratic Party. He had never had anything to do with Zionism, or even Jews as such. In fact, we all thought he was a *goy*. There were rumors that, for unknown reasons, his sympathies were with Palestine, and that he had sometimes acted for us unofficially. I went to see him about the planes, and I told him that the situation was desperate, which indeed it was: these were the first planes we had laid our hands on, they were to be the nucleus of the Jewish air force; with them rested the destiny of Jewish air power. Herbert picked up the telephone and a brief conversation ensued. 'Hello, Jack [or perhaps it was Tom or Bill, or maybe Patrick—I do not know to this day to whom he was talking], this is Herbert. You remember when I was editor of *The World* and the Irish were fighting for their freedom, and you asked me to do something for you and I did?' Pause. 'Now I'm going to ask you to do something for my people. I want you to give orders for those two planes to leave this afternoon. That's the only payment I want from you for my services to the Irish Republic.' A few hours later the planes left.

There was a similar incident, having to do not with planes but with ships.

On one of my rare Sabbath days of rest I was interrupted by the intrusion of a young Jew, Danny Shind, who was one of the most remarkable people involved in this business and in all activities connected with illegal immigration into Palestine. It was to Danny Shind, in fact, that Weizmann had given over the first £500 after the war for the renewal of illegal immigration. He died, unfortunately, shortly after the establishment of the State.

Danny's irruption was curt and decisive: 'We're going to New Orleans.' The idea did not immediately appeal to me. 'When?' I asked. 'Right now,' he answered. As I reluctantly packed my toothbrush he explained the purpose of our mission. Three ships had been purchased in South and Central American countries and refitted in Philadelphia for illegal immigration. Under some kind of pressure from the Americans or British, or blackmail—no one knew exactly—they were not allowed to move out of Philadelphia. The man who could help us was a Jew from New Orleans by the name of Samuel Zemurray. I happened to know Zemurray—which was not his major asset, but happened to be mine at the moment. He had started out in life peddling bananas on a pushcart, and at this juncture in history was the President of the United Fruit Company, which practically owned half of Central America. He knew all the ins and outs of Central American shipping, including the 'bosses' at the docks and the government officials who could be persuaded for a consideration. It was clearly a matter which we could not conduct by telephone from New York, so off we went.

It was as miserable a trip as I ever made, sitting up all night in a plane trying to figure out how we could locate the man as it was Sunday. When we arrived in New Orleans we could not get a room at a hotel, so we conducted our negotiations from a phone booth. There was no answer from Zemurray's home; we tried several of his friends, but no one knew where he was spending the weekend. We stood for hours in a suffocating phone booth, pleading with operators and exchanges not to give up the search. Finally we learned that Mr. Zemurray was at his retreat, sixty miles from New Orleans, in a lodge with an unlisted number. At this stage I was informed by the head telephone supervisor that he was forbidden to reveal the number. I told him that it was a question of life and death for thousands of people. I said to him: 'Don't give me the number if it's against the rules. You can call him and tell him who is at the other end of the line. If he refuses the call, nothing is lost. If he agrees, let him call me here in the phone booth.' In about ten minutes the phone rang; it was Zemurray, and I experienced an ecstasy of deliverance. By this time Danny was so agitated that I had to support him physically into the car which I hired at Mr. Zemurray's insistence and expense. We were on our way. We finally arrived after surviving sixty miles of a suffocating humidity compounded by a deluge the likes of which I had experienced that September 1933 in New York in connection with *The Romance*. Zemurray heard us out, snorted a few times, and finally said: 'Give so-and-so $10,000, so-and-so $5,000,' and after a brief pause, 'and so-and-so $7,500.' He explained: 'It's less than $10,000 and more than $5,000. That's his place in the hierarchy.'

Within three or four days the ships left for Italy. One of them, I should mention in passing, was 'rechristened' *Yetziat Europa 1947*, or, as it came to be known, *Exodus*.

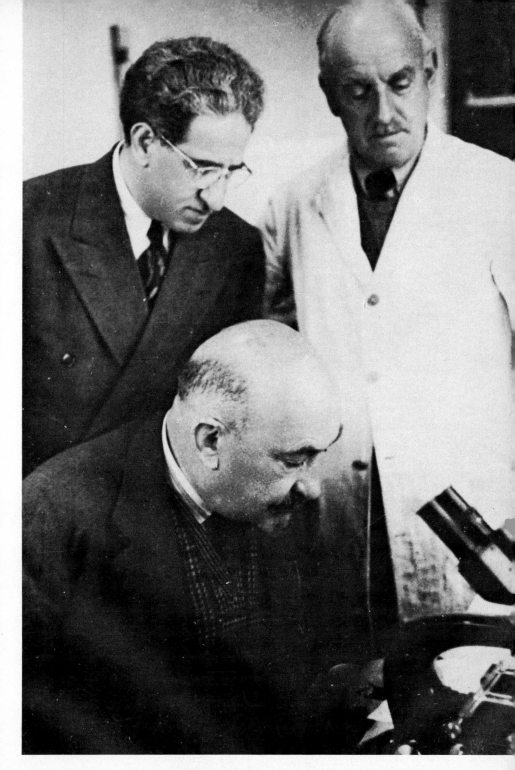

With Dr. Chaim Weizmann and Dr. Harold
Davies at Weizmann's laboratory in Rehovot

above Holding forth to Prof. Herman Mark after the cornerstone laying of the Weizmann Institute in 1946, while Dr. Weizmann and Dr. Ernst David Bergmann enjoy my scientific erudition. *below* The remnants of the holocaust: Athlit Detention Camp, 1946

above Shirley presents birthday cake to Dr. Weizmann at our home in Rehovot. *below* Shirley with Vera Weizmann

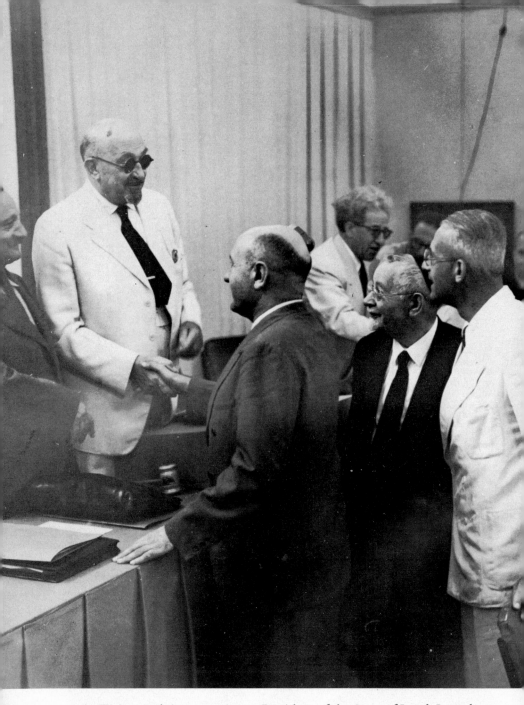

At Weizmann's inauguration as President of the State of Israel, Jerusalem, 1949, *left to right* Yoseph Sprinzak, Eliezer Kaplan, MWW, Rabbi Yehuda Leib Maimon, Fritz Şimon

Such activities belonged as it were to my 'spare time'; they fitted into the interstices of my official operations, which kept me, as I have said, in constant motion either at Weizmann's side or on his behalf in New York, London and Palestine.

And now, to turn back to 1946. Following the demise of the Anglo-American Commission, described in the last chapter, came the prolonged negotiations round 'the London talks.' The British designed them theoretically for the purpose of getting the representatives of the Jews, the Arabs and the British to agree to some formula; in reality it was nothing more than a holding operation. For the Zionist Executive it was a crisis of decision. Weizmann favored attending; Ben Gurion favored attending only on condition that partition of Palestine would be the basic premise of the discussion. Abba Hillel Silver was opposed on both counts; he opposed partition as a solution and favored a Jewish State in the whole of Palestine; the Hashomer Hatzair favored attending but opposed B.G.'s conditions because they wanted a bi-national state in the whole of Palestine. The World Zionist Congress, scheduled to meet in Basle in December, 1946, was to decide the question of the London Conference through its attitude on 'activism,' in other words: fighting vs. talking. The Executive met in Paris in the summer in preparation.

Weizmann had just had an eye operation and was recuperating in England. He was staying with Victor Rothschild at his country home in Tring; he was therefore unable to attend the meetings and appointed me his representative, and there was an unbelievable stream of delegations and individuals moving back and forth between Tring, London and Paris: they came and went, consulting with the Chief and carrying back their instructions and suggestions: Nahum Goldmann, Golda Meir (or Meyerson, as she then was), Eliezer Kaplan, the Treasurer of the Jewish Agency, Berl Locker and countless others. On my arrival at Tring I took a room at a little nearby inn, but Victor insisted that I come to stay with him. In Paris, though representing Weizmann, I was accorded the status of an observer, and whenever I rose to speak it was as if someone had waved a red flag in front of Ben Gurion. But I was not his only opponent; many members of his own party took up Weizmann's view, and they formed part of the back-and-forth ferrying of individuals and delegations across the Channel.

Nevertheless, at the Twenty-second Zionist Congress Ben Gurion and Abba Hillel Silver joined forces against Weizmann and ejected him from office. It was a master stroke, for it both ousted Weizmann and reaffirmed even if indirectly every policy he advocated. It was almost a repetition of 1931; a shabby maneuver, after which those who had accomplished it went into a state of shock over their performance. As before, he was not re-elected—but he remained the elect of his people.

There was a strange ambivalence in Ben Gurion's attitude toward Weizmann throughout the years. He admired him, even loved him, yet he saw in him the obstacle to his own ascendancy. Less than a month before the opening of this Congress, when the machinery for the ouster was well advanced, Ben Gurion wrote Weizmann:

Whatever your views are on all this, you remain for me the elect of Jewish history, representing beyond compare the suffering and the glory of the Jews. And wherever you go you will be attended by the love and the faithful esteem of me and my colleagues. We are the generation which comes after you and which has been tried, perhaps, by crueler and greater suffering and we sometimes, for this reason, see things differently—but fundamentally we draw from the same reservoir of inspiration—that of sorely tried Russian Jewry—the qualities of tenacity, faith, and persistent striving which yields to no adversary or foe.

That this outpouring of what I believe to be genuine affection was penned with one hand while with the other he was giving the signal of execution can only be attributed to that uncontrollable urge for power which I described to Gershon Agronsky in 1942: '[it was] as if a revelation had come to him urging him to take destiny by the forelock and make himself its master.'

I myself came to that Congress—strange as it must sound—as a delegate of the Mapai, the Labor Zionists. Some time before the elections, Baruch Zuckerman, the leader of the Poale Zion (Mapai) in America, and my old friend from the Grayzell Press in 1916, came to me in New York and said: 'Look, Meyer, you belong with us. You will buy a *shekel* [a token payment, in Zionist practice the form of registering a party vote] from us, and we'll send you as a delegate.' I don't know why I succumbed but I did. Since I left the Organization sixteen years before, I had sworn never to join a Zionist party; and here I was with a Mapai card in my wallet. I remained a full-fledged member for exactly three months. At the first meeting of the Mapai caucus in Basle I found the maneuverings so distasteful that I turned in my card and told them with my peculiar brand of eloquence what they could do with it.

And there I was, at the heart of this crucial Congress, a man without a vote. Nahum Goldmann came to my rescue with a complicated but valid device. He had in his pocket, as the residues of proportional representations, an eighth of a delegate from Argentine, a fourth from Brazil, a sixteenth from Chile, etc. Taken all together, seven South American countries contributed, unbeknownst to themselves, one complete delegate. I was a man restored to himself. But free to vote as I pleased.

Ben Gurion could not hope to carry the Congress on the strength of his own party, the Labor Zionists; they were too sharply divided on the two main issues: the attitude toward activism and participation in the London Conference. But he had a powerful ally in Abba Hillel Silver, who in return for the leadership of the American Zionist movement was prepared to deliver the votes of the ZOA. It was a marriage of convenience between labor and capital. The Hadassah Organization of America was strong enough, with its large women's organization, to withstand either seduction or rape. The religious Mizrachi delegation was prepared, as usual, to sell its favors to the highest bidder.

There was actually never any love lost between Weizmann and the Mizrachi; not that he was irreligious; on the contrary he had great respect for genuine piety, and if he himself did not adhere to every letter of the law he always adhered to its spirit. But he detested Jewish clericalism and in his autobiography, *Trial and Error*, he gives utterance to his fears that the future State of Israel will have to struggle against the attempts of religion to control the ministries of State. He writes on November 30, 1947—the date is important (the UN had voted for the Partition of Palestine into Jewish and Arab States the day before):

I have never feared really religious people. The genuine type has never been politically aggressive; on the contrary, he seeks no power, he is modest and retiring—and modesty was the great feature in the lives of our saintly Rabbis and sages in olden times. It is the new, secularized type of Rabbi, resembling somewhat a member of a clerical party in Germany, France or Belgium, who is the menace, and who will make a heavy bid for power by parading his religious convictions. It is useless to point out to such people that they transgress a fundamental principle which has been laid down by our sages: 'Thou shalt not make of the Torah a crown to glory in, or a spade to dig with.' There will be a great struggle. I foresee something which will perhaps be reminiscent of the *Kulturkampf* in Germany, but we must be firm if we are to survive; we must have a clear line of demarcation between legitimate religious aspirations and the duty of the State toward preserving such aspirations, on the one hand, and on the other hand the lust for power which is sometimes exhibited by pseudo-religious groups.

These were prophetic words. The State of Israel today suffers not a little from the fact that no government can be formed without the religious parties in it; and their price is high.

The Congress itself was a melancholy affair. For me personally it became even more melancholy—my old friend Jacob Fishman, with whom I had traveled to the Congress, suddenly died, and there were funeral arrangements for me to attend to.

Everybody seemed confused and bewildered. A strange unfamiliar atmosphere, altogether alien to the spirit of a Zionist Congress, hung over it. Instead of the lively, vigorous, even turbulent spirit which had always reigned over the *Mustermesse*, there was the heaviness of an impending bereavement and the shadow of the holocaust. It lurked in the corridors, it reigned over the plenum. And, as could have been predicted, the one achievement of the Congress was that no President was elected. This was what emerged from the mixture of demagogy, obfuscation and assorted unnatural alliances. It could hardly be otherwise.

I have pointed out that Weizmann had never sought support in political deals. If the movement accepted his position, he accepted the mantle of leadership. If it rejected his position, he withdrew. Had a vote been taken at that Congress on his presidency, there is no doubt that he would have been elected by an overwhelming majority. But Weizmann refused to stand for election as a separate issue. He measured his position by the vote on participation in the London Conference; it was 154 in favor, 171 against. The twenty-eight delegates of Hashomer Hatzair, passionately pro-Weizmann and pro-London, abstained because they would not bring themselves to violate their ideological virginity. They were in principle for a bi-national state, and 'delicacy' forbade the acceptance of a Jewish State or of partition. Ben Gurion, lacking a majority in his own party, found it by default in the foolishness of Hashomer Hatzair and the integrity of Weizmann. Having succeeded in deposing Weizmann, the Zionist Executive proceeded to attend the London Conference —through a back door. Fourteen of the nineteen members elected were on record for participation. It was 1931 all over again: Weizmannism without Weizmann. This was the net result of the Twenty-second Zionist Congress.

If I have created the impression that in all these developments Weizmann was a mutely acquiescent witness, unwilling or unable to let his views be known, I must correct it at once. He was silent in the lobbies and caucuses, but on the rostrum his was the most powerful and moving voice of the Congress. It was not a thunderous voice—he had never been that kind of orator, and now age, physical weakness, and the inhibiting effect of his half-blind condition, had told on his once magnificent presence. But what he said was in the authentic prophetic strain, counseling his people against despair, particularly when that clothed itself in heroic gestures and in desperate Samson-like acts of universal destruction. He said:

I warn you against bogus palliatives, against short cuts, against false prophets, against facile generalizations, against distortion of historic facts . . . If you think of bringing the redemption nearer by un-Jewish methods, if you have lost faith in hard work and better days, then you are committing idolatry and endangering what we have built. Would that I had a tongue of flame, the strength of prophets, to warn you against the paths of Babylon and Egypt. Zion shall be redeemed in righteousness, and not by any other means . . . Masada, for all its heroism, was a disaster in our history. It is not our purpose or our right to plunge to destruction in order to bequeath a legend of martyrdom to posterity. Zionism was to mark the end of our glorious deaths and the beginning of a new path, leading to life. Against the heroics of suicidal violence, I urge the courage of endurance, the heroism of human restraint.

When one American Zionist leader called upon Palestinian Jewry to rise in rebellion against the British, while American Jews would give 'full political and moral support,' Weizmann, enraged, cried back, 'Moral and political support is very little when you send other people to the barricades to face guns and tanks. The eleven new settlements in the Negev have, in my deepest conviction, a far greater weight than a hundred speeches about resistance—especially when the speeches are made in New York while the proposed resistance is to be made in Tel Aviv and Jerusalem.'

They listened with reverence, but reverence weighed light against partisanship and outright doctrinairism. That the Congress elected no president was a peculiar tribute to Weizmann. There was simply no other candidate. It reminded me of 1931. After deposing Weizmann then, the Zionist Executive sat locked in debate over the choice of a new president. The only candidate around was Nahum Sokolow, who had always been closely associated with Weizmann and Weizmann's policies. Sokolow was an old-guard intellectual, unquestionably the most erudite man in the Zionist movement, but lacking in fire. During an all-night session of the *Permanenz Ausschuss* some wit raised his hand: 'I want to nominate a man who has stature, vision.' There was dead silence in expectation. 'I propose Theodor Herzl.' Everybody shouted 'Blasphemy, Herzl is dead.' The man shrugged his shoulders: 'If a dead man, at least a great one.' After four years Weizmann was returned to the Presidency. In 1946 there wasn't even a Sokolow around. And true to their convictions and instincts, it was to Weizmann, the deposed President, that they turned in the turbulent months leading to the Partition Resolution and finally to the Declaration of the State of Israel; it was to him that they came again and again to speak before the Council of the United Nations and to the highest representatives of governments. And tired, infirm and half blind, he never failed them.

When I returned to New York from the Congress early in 1947, I was, personally, in a peculiar position. I was still the Secretary-General of the Jewish Agency in New York—or Director General, or whatever it was called. But Weizmann, my Chief, was out, and it was Abba Hillel Silver who ruled the roost, and about him I have said enough to indicate the tenor of our relationship. I came back to New York intending to quit, but friends, especially Maurice Boukstein and Gottlieb Hammer, urged me not to act precipitately. The peculiarity of my position lay in this: the offices of the Weizmann Institute occupied the largest suite in the Jewish Agency Building, and I was in the Agency Building whose purchase I had helped finance, both as Secretary-General of the Agency and of the Weizmann Institute. I had signed a three-year lease for offices in the Agency Building on behalf of the Weizmann Institute. I was not over anxious to stay on, but I wanted a certain decorum, if not courtesy, in the manner of my quitting. As we say in Yiddish, 'Nobody has to kick me out, I go of my own accord.' One day Silver came in, saw me, and called over Arthur Lourie, who had become Secretary-General of the Jewish Agency. 'What the hell is that man doing here?' he asked. Lourie answered: 'He's the owner of the building.' It was only a slight exaggeration, but the reverberations from Silver gave me the first good laugh of that miserable season. I wrote Weizmann my views on the utter disorientation of the Zionist leadership after the last Congress, and added that there seemed to be only one point on which the American leadership seemed to be unanimous—that I should get out of the building. 'Yesterday,' I wrote, 'they pressed rather hard on the subject and their final argument was: "Isn't it embarrassing for you to remain here?" I said: "Not at all. I never had any social relationship with my landlords. Why should it be different here?"' But I soon found new offices.

I spent that winter rounding up all the pledges that had been made to the Institute. The main building in Rehovot was taking shape. But willy-nilly I was still in the thick of political problems. After the failure of the London Conference, Mr. Bevin had turned the Palestine problem over to the United Nations. The new face of the Zionist leadership was not warmly welcomed by the American Government. Its leaders had little use either for Silver or for Ben Gurion, both of whom they considered intransigent. Nor was sentiment among American Jews by all means unanimous in its opinions of the new axis, and the Yiddish and Jewish press continued to fight the battles of the last Congress. Part of the Zionist press was virulently anti-Weizmann; he was made to take the blame for the impasse in the Zionist posture of affairs with unprecedented fury. Calm and dispassionate counsel was considered high treason. When some of us tried to put in a word of reason and caution, we were greeted with tirades which would have been offensive—to say the least—had they not been incoherent. I was 'warned off' by name in this piece of Anglo-American journalism:

The propaganda chief is not anonymous. Mr. Meyer W. Weisgal is not exactly unknown in many Zionist circles. The clamor will continue, and will be magnified by the press agent's usual techniques. Whether [Robert] Weltsch is a prearranged or an accidental collaborator in this new campaign, I do not know, but he fits in beautifully with his adulation of the great Weizmann who 'had steered the Zionist ship through the rough seas of political reality.' American Jews are fed up with appeasement and vacillation, and the continued deterioration of the Zionist position. Mr. Weisgal! Stop creating dissension, stop turning our friends into anti-Zionists, and go back to your boss. This is not 1921, and we shall not make the same mistake twice.

It was strange that they should hark back to 1921 for a parallel. The 'mistake' of Weizmann's leadership during those twenty-six years was merely to bring the incipient Jewish State into sovereignty exactly one year later. The slow and painful redemption of the land, the creation of national, economic and political institutions such as the Keren Hayesod and the Jewish Agency, the organic growth of a Jewish community in Palestine—all this counted for nothing on Rabbi Silver's balance sheet. Weizmann and Weizmannism had failed because as of March, 1947, the State of Israel had not yet been proclaimed. The fact that it existed was beside the point.

I wrote to Weizmann: 'Frankly, I wish I were not involved now in the affairs of the Institute. I would give these vermin the fight of their life.' His reply was characteristic Weizmann: 'I can see that the war-horse is speaking in you, but believe me what you are doing is a much more constructive piece of work than any fight with the windmills of Cleveland or any other place.'

On May 15, 1947, the United Nations established its Special Committee on Palestine, UNSCOP, which was to bring its recommendations to the General Assembly. In June I left for Palestine at Weizmann's request, in connection with the Institute and his appearance before the UNSCOP.

Weizmann, let me recall again, held no office in the movement. He had 'retired' to Rehovot to devote himself to the scientific center which was taking on flesh and blood. He had been succeeded in the political arena by men who had their fingers on the pulse of events. What had Weizmann to do with the UNSCOP? Only representatives of organized bodies were invited to speak their piece before this tribunal of the nations. But Weizmann was invited to speak because it was inconceivable that his voice should not be heard. The Executive of the Jewish Agency insisted that he appear. They insisted, moreover, that he meet informally with all the members of the UNSCOP. They knew only too well that, President or not, his was the voice of the Jewish people.

For days he was 'briefed' by a brain trust which included Gershon Agronsky, Abba Eban, Walter Eytan (later Ambassador to France), Mordecai Kidron (later an Israeli representative to the UN) and myself. Weizmann would throw out ideas, we would work them into paragraphs. Eban would attend to the style, the Chief would go over it, correcting, adding, subtracting. When the text was completed we were only half way through; what remained was to get the text set up in one inch type for Weizmann's failing sight. We had it done at the Jerusalem Post Press. In the last stages we were all ensconced in the Eden Hotel in Jerusalem, with a runner between us and the Post's printer. Kidron did most of the running.

At four o'clock in the morning, the day of the hearing, we got the last page. We checked it, took three hours sleep, then went to the hearings in the basement of the YMCA where they were being held. I wrote to my wife that Weizmann 'was as nervous as a cat.' So were we; we sat there trembling. When Weizmann sat down to give his testimony, he accidentally or deliberately shoved the prepared sheets off the table, and they scattered over the floor. He made no gesture to retrieve them, and began to talk extemporaneously.

'I speak,' he said, 'in my private capacity, but I believe I speak the mind of the overwhelming majority of the Jewish people everywhere.' And in a voice, which we strained ourselves to hear, he rehearsed before the members of the UNSCOP, who sat riveted to their places, the thesis which was to decide the fate of this last and most important of the councils. His language flowed magnificently. He spoke against terrorism as contrary to Jewish ethics; he advocated the partition of the country as the only way to Arab-Jewish cooperation. He seemed unaware of the masterly document over which we had poured our brains and sweat. (A year later at Lake Success he again abandoned his prepared speech and enthralled his audience.) I think he did this for two reasons: his sight was so impaired that he could not be sure of reading smoothly, and his views and feelings had become so much a part of him that he knew he could not go wrong speaking from the heart.

He used to tell a story about briefings. One day he had to appear before the Colonial Office in London. In the Zionist Executive every member knew exactly what he should say and how he should say it. The briefings were voluminous and vehement, and Weizmann listened attentively, then left, taking Berl Locker with him. When they returned, Locker reported with bewilderment: 'All our work went for nothing—all our deliberations and briefings. Weizmann spoke his own mind.' When the Executive voiced its disappointment and dismay, Weizmann replied with his story:

There was once a Jew who had a son he was anxious to marry off. But whenever prospective in-laws were interviewed, the young man would frighten them off by his wild exaggerations, and the *shidduch* [match] would fly out of the window. His father begged, cajoled, threatened, became vituperative: '*Idiot einer!* If *mechutonim* come to see you, let me sit next to you. The moment you begin to tell a story I will give you a kick, and you'll shut up.' The son swore to obey, and soon new candidates appeared. 'I went fishing yesterday,' he began, and received a kick from his father. It did not deter him. 'I caught a fish'—and there came a second kick from his father, equally ineffective. Now the father became frantic; something perfectly dreadful was about to happen, and as he kicked his son for the third time, the latter exclaimed, 'the fish weighed 10,000 pounds.' Well, the fat was in the fire; the prospective in-laws looked at each other significantly, and withdrew with all possible speed. The unhappy father wailed: 'Miserable creature! How can you possibly say such things? Ten thousand pounds! Didn't you feel the kicks under the table?' Tearfully the son replied: 'Yes, papa. If you hadn't kicked me, I was going to say 100,000 pounds.'

So, gentlemen, if you hadn't given me those briefings this morning I might really have gone overboard. It was only because of the briefing that I said what I did. Otherwise I might have bungled our whole case.

During the UNSCOP hearings Weizmann, at the prompting of the Zionist Executive, had invited the members of the Committee to two luncheons at his home in Rehovot; there were some eleven in the Committee, and a number of adjutants. I sat next to Ralph Bunche at one of these luncheons and I watched him as he followed attentively the conversation. When he heard Weizmann speak of oppressed peoples, he would nudge me slightly, as if to say: 'How well I understand this man, and how well he understands us Negroes.'

At these informal discussions Weizmann's force and personality profoundly influenced the members of UNSCOP. There is no doubt that when these men drew up their recommendations later in Geneva Weizmann's reasoned views and compassionate appeal had their influence.

On September 1, 1947, UNSCOP published those recommendations to the General Assembly of the United Nations: the termination of the British Mandate and the partition of Palestine into two states, Jewish and Arab. This was not yet the policy of the UN. It was only a recommendation which, to become valid, would have to obtain a two-thirds majority of the delegates in the General Assembly. But whatever the outcome, we knew that this was the final nail in the coffin of the British Mandate.

Here I must again pause to fill in on other matters relating to events in Palestine during that summer of 1947. Along with preparations for the UNSCOP and the guidance of the Weizmann Institute there was a third activity—to me a very important one—the long-delayed completion of Weizmann's autobiography. It had been simmering for sixteen years, and I had been responsible for making sure that the fire would not go out. In his acknowledgment to the book, *Trial and Error*, Weizmann makes mention of me, 'but for whose insistent prodding and continous help this task might still be awaiting completion.' Maurice Samuel, who worked with him on Volume Two and the revision of the whole book, was convinced that 'nagging' would have been a more accurate word. From that day in Basle, in 1931, when Weizmann first mentioned to me that he planned to write his memoirs, I never let up. Whenever and wherever we met, in Europe, or Palestine, or the United States, my first question to him was, 'How are the memoirs getting along?' To which he would as invariably reply: 'Tremendously.' And I in turn would say: 'Is that all?' Then in the hope of inducing him to make a real beginning I would coax him into a reminiscent mood on some period in the 'good old days.' An invisible listener should have been there to take down the narrative exactly as it issued from his lips. I said to him: 'Dr. Weizmann, all you have to do is just dictate this over again and you will have a best seller.' He winced.

Even in the hectic days of 1942, when Weizmann was shuttling between New York and Washington, absorbed in Zionist political affairs on the one hand, and in scientific conferences on hetones, high octane gas, and isoprene on the other, I would broach the subject. It had become an obsession with me. Once, when I came in to him in the presence of two of his collaborators, Ernst Bergmann and Josef Blumenfeld, he exclaimed: 'Aha! Here he is again with his memoirs. I think I will put you to work on some of these highly technical problems.' Then to them: 'His ignorance of chemistry is one of the wonders of the age.' His inhibition about finishing his memoirs, which were half completed by 1943, was neither inertia nor his preoccupation with affairs; it was primarily psychological. Memoirs suggest a breaking off, an awareness of fulfillment, a sense of withdrawal and retirement. But the tragedies of the Jewish people during those years made Weizmann a prisoner of destiny and kept him from the retirement he passionately desired. His encroaching blindness was another factor. It was difficult for him to read what he had dictated. After the war I mobilized Moish (Maurice Samuel) to work with him. It was a Herculean task to which Moish devoted not only his considerable talents but his love. Every sentence had to be read and reread. Weizmann was meticulous about every word; it had to be his own and no one else's. And until the summer of 1947, when I asked Moish to go to Rehovot to finish the job, the conditions of his collaboration were enough to strain even his devotion. During the periods when he was in New York Moish was at his beck and call. He had to drop whatever book he was engaged on—and during those years he was at work on a long historical novel—in order to respond to Weizmann's moods. He would go down with his portable typewriter to the Waldorf Astoria or the St. Regis, and settle down to an impromptu session. He fumed and fretted to me: 'I've got a deadline. I've just reached a wonderful streak, I can't break it off.' I would soothe him: 'Moish, when you're about to be raped, relax and enjoy it.' These irregularities of time and place were exacerbated by another circumstance: Mrs. Weizmann used to breathe down his neck. She had set herself up as an expert in Zionist history and a master of English style. To the Chief this was distressing, to Moish it was intolerable. Every time he came out of a session he would say to me: 'If that woman doesn't get out of my hair, I shall drop the whole thing.' I would say: 'You're doing this for the Jewish people, not for her. Take it easy.' After a few drinks the mood was restored. It was not till 1947 that we settled down to the job. With all his attention focused on the book. Moish was able, in spite of Mrs. Weizmann's interference, to complete the Chief's work in a few months. It was during this period of daily sessions in Rehovot that Mrs. Weizmann discovered in Moish his true mission in life: a gin-rummy partner for herself. She played the game as badly as she played bridge. Moish himself was no great genius at cards but, my sympathies for him notwithstanding, I was pleased: it let me off the hook. Her invitations to play had the tenor of royal commands. When the Chief would retire, punctually at 10 p.m., she would survey the battlefield for a victim. As long as Moish was around, I was safe. The sounds of his Oxonian English were more pleasing to her aristocratic ear than my American *cum* Yiddish. The only time I played with her that whole summer I remember vividly because the game was ended early on account of gunfire on the front lawn, or so it seemed.

The behavior of the British during that period can be characterized as the eighth wonder of the world in its shameless brutality. It reached its climax when the *Exodus*, which Mr. Zemurray had helped to leave the peaceful waters of Philadelphia, carrying 4,500 immigrants to Palestine, turned back, not to Cyprus, but to the death camps of Europe. The incident became infamous as historical fact, as well as the subject of Leon Uris's literary creation and Otto Preminger's cinematographic talents. That summer brought with it the prolonged vicious circle of repression, terrorism, reprisal and executions; one could never be sure whether what one heard was the rattle of someone pulling down the shutters or the rat-tat-tat of a machine gun.

On the occasion of the interrupted gin-rummy game there was no mistaking the nature of the sounds; for an hour we could hear the whine of bullets. When a quiet interval elapsed I decided to leave, but the driver suggested that we wait a few more minutes. Sure enough, it began all over again. (I have never doubted the thesis that all Israeli drivers have a secret line to Staff Headquarters and are really generals in disguise. I always thought that Yehoshua Harlap, the Chief's adjutant, guard and confidant, was one of them; he was so knowledgeable.) The shooting continued till one in the morning. The company that evening included, besides the Chief, Mrs. Weizmann, Moish and myself, Isaiah Berlin and Dr. Bergmann. We spent the evening chewing over the rights and wrongs of the situation, specifically what we ought to do if a wounded terrorist came to the door for refuge from the British. We finally decided to give him refuge and turn him over, not to the British but to the Haganah. By that time I made up my mind to brave the shooting for a good night's sleep in my own bed at the Institute's Club-House. I got as far as the main road from the village to the Institute when I was turned back by a Haganah man who said, politely but firmly: 'Lo kedai,' which meant in plain English: 'We would not advise you to go any further.' I returned to the Chief's house where I made my peace, literally, with a sleeping pill. In the morning we found out what all the shooting had been about. The Etzel had made extensive preparations for blowing up the military camp which lay between the village and the Weizmann house. The British were trying to frustrate that attempt.

Two days later Weizmann left Palestine for London. His memoirs had been completed, or rather, brought up to date. During all this period of preparation I had had to keep Mr. Cass Canfield, of Harper and Brothers, in happy suspense; now I was ready to advise him that in the next few days he would receive, at long last, the fruits of a decade and a half of labor. Cass Canfield saw in this book—as I did—a best seller.

The contract with Dr. Weizmann had been negotiated ten years earlier when I had been given power of attorney in all matters pertaining to it. The proceeds were to go to the Weizmann Foundation. At the beginning Cass Canfield and I had conducted ourselves with courtesy and formality; after we met all formality stopped, and our correspondence took on a certain warmth, tinged occasionally, in view of the protracted delays, with a note of levity, which is not to imply that he did not keep a wary eye on his publishing interests.

One day Canfield suddenly realized that despite our long correspondence an actual contract had never been signed, that is to say, simply was not in existence! 'All right,' I said, 'fix up a contract.' Some weeks later Canfield rang up saying the contract was ready. I came over, and as I took out my pen to sign it, he said, 'Aren't you going to read it over?' I looked at him and said: 'Mr. Canfield, would you really give me a document to sign that I couldn't sign sight unseen?'

Canfield groaned, took back the contract, and said: 'I'll just go over it again.' Later I was told that as he stumbled from the room he kept repeating: 'Jewish business methods! Jewish business methods!' But I don't think he made any changes in the contract.

By the autumn of 1947 the manuscript went the way of all manuscripts—to the printer; but it did not see the light of day until 1949. Events were moving faster than the presses. The UN voted for partition; some months later the State of Israel was declared, and Ben Gurion became Israel's first Prime Minister.

Unavoidably, the book contained reflections on the relations between him and Weizmann over the last twenty-five years or so. Rereading the page proofs I felt that the chapter dealing with Ben Gurion was an inappropriate introduction to the opening phase of Jewish statehood, Ben Gurion being not only Prime Minister and Minister of Defense, but also the man to whom the Jewish people owed so much during that period. I carefully suggested to Weizmann that the chapter about his relations with B.G. be eliminated. I gave him my reasons. He readily agreed, with this proviso: 'You can take out anything you like, but don't add anything.'

As a result, Weizmann's autobiography, *Trial and Error*, contains only four insignificant references to Ben Gurion, all of them in the last part of the book.

During the writing of his memoirs, Weizmann often met Mrs. Helen Reid, the publisher of *The Herald Tribune*. She became a warm admirer. One day, during lunch with her, he mentioned his weariness with the harrassments about 'the book.' Mrs. Reid reacted sympathetically, but, with the publisher's professional instinct, asked 'How about the serialization rights?' Dr. Weizmann answered with his customary: 'Talk to Meyer,' which she did. The serialization rights for *The Tribune* were sold for $25,000, a modest enough figure, as I was soon to realize. When the offer became known I received a call from someone at Simon and Schuster, telling me that *The New York Times* was interested in the serialization rights and was prepared to offer $50,000. I could only say, 'Sorry, you should have called sooner.' Competition among publishing houses is keen; what may sound today like a trifling sum was in those days quite considerable.

A few weeks before the beginning of the serialization one of Mrs. Reid's sons asked if I would appear before a meeting of the newspaper distributors and tell them about the book. I came. I knew some of them from my old days in the business. I made a Zionist speech, told them of the political importance of the book, and finished up with what I took to be a rousing sales talk. The results showed me that I had not needed to exert myself—they were out of all proportion to any effort of mine. When the serialization began there was a rise of some 60,000 in circulation; an unprecedented achievement. Mrs. Reid remarked ruefully some time later that she had achieved nothing like the same success with the Eisenhower memoirs, for which she had parted with $500,000.

To return now to the expurgated chapter on Ben Gurion: it has been for some twenty years in the archives of the Yad Weizmann. Many enterprising publishers in Israel have tried to lay hands on this 'gold mine,' and I must confess that there were times when I was particularly incensed by acts and utterances of Ben Gurion in connection with Pinchas Lavon, Moshe Sharett, Golda Meir, Levi Eshkol—the list is a long one—and was tempted to uncover the 'dangerous' treasure. But what Lipsky used to call 'the higher interests' of the State of Israel deterred me. It is still there, with other incendiary material—love letters and the like—which, perhaps after I and a few others are gone, will be available to scholars. *Trial and Error* was completed in August, 1948, and published only in 1949, so that the events of 1947 and 1948 could be included.

The recommendation of the UNSCOP for partition was scheduled to come to a vote in the United Nations Assembly in November, 1947.

The UNSCOP had proposed that the Negev be part of the Jewish State but in the jockeying that went on behind the scenes it became evident that the Arabs were to be appeased with a truncated Jewish State. A two-thirds majority was required for ratification, and every single vote counted. Weizmann was again called to action.

What the 'repudiated' leader of the Jewish people did then has been so often told that I will be brief. One week before the vote he went to President Truman and convinced him that the Negev must be part of the Jewish State. American objections were dropped. Weizmann then telephoned Léon Blum and got the French—who had been expected to abstain—to vote for partition. And Weizmann rocked the United Nations with his speech (again, as I have noted, not the one that Abba Eban had toiled over). He rose to speak after an Arab leader, Jamal el-Husseini, had explained that Palestine did not belong to the Jews, that the Jews of today were not really the same people as the ancient Jews, but were in fact Tartars, or some other obscure tribe unconnected with Palestine. Weizmann said: 'I heard my friend Husseini. I do not know whether I am a Tartar or a Khazar. All I know is that all my life I lived like a Jew, suffered like a Jew, and am still bearing the sufferings of my people.' The impression made by these words brought a thunder of approval from the audience. The chairman banged his gavel in vain. Not only the galleries, but the large majority of the Assembly joined in the applause. On November 29, 1947, by a vote of 33 to 13, with ten abstentions, the United Nations voted for the establishment of a Jewish State in part of Palestine.

That night there was a Labor Zionist rally called at the St. Nicholas Arena. When it had been planned, the outcome of the vote was unknown; it was not even certain that there would be any outcome. But there was, naturally, clamor that Weizmann should come to the meeting, and I took him. It seemed as if every Jew in New York wanted to be present at what turned out to be one of the supreme moments of triumph for the Jewish people, and when the car, escorted by police, finally reached the door of the Arena and Weizmann appeared at the entrance the cheering engulfed the building. He was lifted out of my protective grasp on to the shoulders of his people and carried into the hall. The Jews have only one way of expressing deep joy; they sing *Hatikvah*, and they sang it that night as it could never have been sung before. It reminded me of the *Hatikvah* in Athlit, albeit under vastly different circumstances. The Hope had been sanctioned by the nations of the world—'the Return to the Land of our Fathers, to the City built by David.'

There is the inevitable (and tiresome) question, before as well as after
the establishment of the State: 'Why Palestine?' Why could not the
Jews, a people of such enormous creative energy, have taken over empty
lands in Uganda or the Argentine and made them bloom? Why Palestine,
why Jerusalem? Think of all the problems you would have saved yourself with the Arabs if you had gone somewhere else? In March, 1968,
I was asked all these questions again by J. B. Priestley, when he spent
a few days in Rehovot. I began with a story. Following the Six-Day
War, after the City of Jerusalem had been reunited, there appeared a
cartoon in one of the Israeli papers. It showed 'Yisrolik,' the little fellow
with the fatigue cap whom the cartoonist Dosh has made into a symbol
of the young state, offering King Hussein advice as to how to get back
the city. 'Do what we did. Say over and over again for two thousand years,
'Next Year in Jerusalem.' That advice, something between an aphorism
and a witticism, is seen to be, on examination, a penetrating observation.

'Next Year in Jerusalem' has been the umbilical cord which has tied the
Jews of the world to the land of Israel for two thousand years. There is
not a prayer or a feast day or a fast day which does not conclude with
these words. All of Jewish expression, religious, liturgical, folkloristic
is permeated with a longing for Zion and, what is more, with an uncanny
self-identification with the conditions, agricultural and meteorological,
of the Holy Land. In the middle of January, in snowbound cities Jewish
school children plant saplings because in the Holy Land it is the New Year
of the Trees, the first blossoming of the almond. It may be a day of drench-
ing rain in New York in October, yet the Jews pray for rain, because
the harvest in Israel is over and the fields are thirsty. No other place in
the world could have evoked the affection, the illimitable sacrifice,
which the Jews made for a land which had been derelict for millenia.
Israel Zangwill once said, 'Give the land without a people to the people
without a land.' It was a neat epigram, but not wholly appropriate: there
were Arabs living in Palestine. But until the Jews began to settle there
at the end of the nineteenth century, it was one of the vast waste lands
of the Middle East. The Valley of Jezreel was known to the Arabs as
the Valley of Death; it was a malarial quagmire. Today it is Israel's bread-
basket. Hundreds of pioneers died in the redemption of the *Emek*, as
we call the Valley of Jezreel; nobody forced them in at gun point. Every
square inch was redeemed with love, as well as paid for exorbitantly
in hard cash. When Israeli paratroopers captured the Old City during
the Six-Day War, foreign correspondents stood open-mouthed watching
these young boys, most of them unsentimental kibbutz children, brought

up in the traditions of Marxism and atheism, lean against the Wailing Wall and sob unashamedly over the ancient stones. They were not weeping for the benefit of the Ministry for Religious Affairs, and not even in gratitude to God, in whom they did not believe. They were weeping over the old stones of Jerusalem which had filled every story and nursery song from earliest childhood on. They were weeping over the undying symbol of Jewish existence.

19 Weizmann: Triumph and Tribulation

On November 30, 1947, the day following the Partition Resolution, born of the European holocaust and the will of the Jewish people for national rebirth, Weizmann wrote the final chapter to his memoirs. The UN resolution was the climax of fifty years of Zionist struggle. Weizmann had had the rare privilege of bringing the impossible vision to fulfillment.

He had yet to add an epilogue to the memoirs; and though he faithfully traced in that epilogue his last acts as the political envoy of the Jewish people up to and including his election as the President of the new State by the Provisional Council of the Government, he refrained publicly from expressing the bitterness, frustration and deep hurts that had been inflicted on him at the very moment of victory. He desisted, as was his wont, from intruding his personal ordeals upon the record of history. But they were recorded in private letters he wrote to me *ad memoriam*.

There is a Hebrew proverb: 'Who is a wise man? He who can foresee events.' By that criterion, my political sagacity in the spring of 1948 hit a low mark. I was quite unable, in the whirlwind of action, to grasp the personal and political consequences for Weizmann of his presence in New York at the time of the Declaration of the State rather than in Israel.

There were two episodes in the unfolding of that policy: Weizmann's recall to New York from London in the winter of 1947–8, which was a necessity of prime historical importance, and Weizmann's prolonged presence there, which, while politically of enormous significance, did irreparable damage to his image in Israel itself. Weizmann remained in New York against his will, against his better instincts, at the behest of Ben Gurion and with the acquiescence of his friends. The ulnaterable fact is that while bombs were falling on Tel Aviv and David Ben Gurion was proclaiming the State of Israel, Chaim Weizmann was sitting in the Waldorf Astoria in New York. Weizmann's intervention with Truman against trusteeship, and his success in obtaining immediate recognition for the new state was eclipsed by the impact of the actual emergence of the State of Israel. There were two people who were acutely aware of this in its proper historical perspective, two wise men who *could* foresee events: Chaim Weizmann and Ben Gurion. But Weizmann, shackled by old age and his ever-present sense of responsibility, left the last act to Ben Gurion.

Weizmann had returned to London shortly after the UN resolution of November 1947, to spend a few weeks with his family before leaving for Palestine, for which he had booked passage on January 25. He was literally sitting on his bags when he was urgently requested to return to New York: the United States was having second thoughts about partition.

The leadership of the Jewish Agency in New York and Washington was virtually impotent. It had had no contact with the American Government since November, and was powerless to influence what seemed to be a serious movement to reverse the UN decision. In one of their rare moments of wisdom they came to me and asked me to get Weizmann back. Weizmann, they thought, could reestablish contact with President Truman.

I told them that if they wanted Weizmann to return to New York they had only to invite him on their own behalf. But there was the rub! They wanted Weizmann, but they did not want to invite him officially. He was 'out,' they were 'in'; *they* were running the show. If he could just be here, fine; but an official invitation might cast an odd light on the new leadership. Arthur Lourie, then Political Secretary of the Agency, asked me to use my influence with Weizmann. I told him: 'No, my dear boy. If you want Weizmann, you'll have to invite him. If you—I don't mean you personally, I mean the leadership of the Agency—haven't got the guts, I will tell him not to budge until an official invitation arrives.'

The situation became more desperate with talk of establishing a new Trusteeship for Palestine. The Agency finally had to overcome its scruples and Weizmann was invited: first, by an urgent personal cable from Eban; then officially, on the stationery, so to speak, of the Agency. Eban's presence too was resented by the American leadership. One must not forget that as an orator he surpassed the American variety, sin enough without considering his loyalty to Weizmann.

Weizmann came to America and had an interview with Truman, who promised to continue to press for the implementation of the Resolution. The State Department, however, was of a different opinion, and the crucial question remained: would President Truman accede to the pressures of the State Department or would he fulfill his pledge to the aging Jewish statesman? It is corroborated in Truman's memoirs that his promise to Weizmann swung the decision.

The question can be asked: had Weizmann left New York after his interview with Truman in March would the subsequent outcome— American recognition of the Jewish State—have been the same? Weizmann continued to apply pressure on people close to Truman; he continued to issue statements to the press on the absolute necessity of declaring statehood with the termination of the Mandate; he appealed to Truman in a letter on May 13 asking for recognition. I do not know. What I do know is that Weizmann himself was desperately anxious to get to Palestine, to be there. He was uneasy in New York and remained only because of the constant pressure on him from Palestine and from colleagues in the United States. He appreciated the importance of continuing to apply pressure at the political center of things, Washington and the UN, but he was obsessed by a suspicion that in certain circles he was not wanted in Palestine. His instincts told him that his place at that particular moment was where the bombs were falling—Tel Aviv.

Early in April Weizmann put the finger on me. I would go to Palestine to 'spy out the land' for him.

On April 17, 1948 I wrote him from Tel Aviv:

My dear Chief:
   It is now 3:30 a.m. I was awakened from my sleep about an hour ago by the noise of what seems to be a tremendous battle going on not far from here. Machine gun fire and the explosion of bombs fill the air. The earth is trembling and everything with it. Even as I write, the walls, the table, my pen and paper shake from the repercussions. Need I tell you, then, that I cannot sleep? And to what better use can I put these waking hours than to write you? I have been wanting to do so almost from the moment I arrived but I didn't know where to begin and what to say. A thousand questions well up in one's mind. But there is no answer, at least I have no answer.
   It would be impudent on my part to even try to evaluate the situation in Palestine. I have been here less than five days, yet it seems an eternity. So many impressions have been crowding in on me, each pushing out the other. If Palestine is a country where contrast is your next door neighbor, it is more so today than ever before. Joy and sorrow walk with each other cheek by jowl. Building and destruction go on almost at an even pace. The courage, the tenacity, the resoluteness of our youth, their reckless abandon of self in the struggle for survival, are sometimes contrasted with the ineptness of some of our leadership. To me, at least, this contrast is patent. But who am I to judge? I do not want to be unfair, for the leadership, too, lacks neither courage nor devotion—perhaps

it lacks judgment, sagacity, the necessary calm and imperturbability in the situation in which we find ourselves. Which may account, who knows, for certain tragic manifestations among some of our youth. But all in all, it can be said of our young people here what was once said of another youth: Never did so many (alas, not too many now) owe so much to so few. For in truth, my dear Chief, it can be said that our boys and girls, the flower of our people, are sacrificing their lives, often fighting with their bare hands and naked breasts, so that our people may live—not only here but everywhere in the world. I wonder if our people in America understand that?

We arrived Thursday evening about 11 p.m. after a rather boring and uneventful flight across the sea. It was a beautiful moonlit night, peace and tranquility reigned in Lydda. The rolling hills and undulating sands, the smell of orange blossoms gave us an unreal glimpse of what we were to find here. It was hard to believe that beneath this almost ominous stillness there was unrest, danger, strife and struggle; but there it was. This too is part of the realities or unrealities, depending upon your point of view, of Palestine. We went through the usual chores without too much difficulty. The officials, probably preconditioned, made a perfunctory attempt at looking at the baggage, but gave up in the end in listless fashion as if to say, 'go ahead, what the hell do we care.' Nothing was examined. Everything was nice and friendly. Arab and Jew mingled with affectionate greeting and back slapping, speaking Hebrew to each other! In Lydda, at that moment, it looked as if the Mandatory Government had already disappeared. Peace reigned supreme. Of course we could not leave that night. We remained till the following morning when a plane came to take us to Tel Aviv. 'Plane' is a slight exaggeration. It looked more like one of those toys seen in Macy's. It's part of our 'Royal' (or what they call here 'Yisroyal') Air Force. In about seven or eight minutes we were in Tel Aviv. After we alighted from the plane, our first greeting came from a tall, bearded young man who looked more like Robin Hood than a flyer. It was none other than Ezer Weizman, your Ezer.★ There was something symbolic in this meeting. Two days before I left his uncle in New York, and the first Jew I meet in Palestine is his valiant nephew. We embraced and kissed. I shed a quiet tear, but I doubt whether he did.

. . . Early Sunday morning, Shirley and I betook ourselves to Rehovot. With due pomp and ceremony an armored car (really a truck) called for us and we started on our journey. We went through winding roads, sand dunes, *pardessim* [orange groves], broken pavements, circuitously through Mikveh Yisrael and Holon and Moledet, reaching the main highway near Rishon. It was all exciting, uncomfortable, and yet pleasant. Why the armored car and all the appurtenances I didn't know, but the authorities so decided and we obeyed. The soldier with his rifle, in some curious fashion, had the gun pointed in my direction. I weakly protested against this position to which he replied: 'Mister, you don't have to be afraid. I cannot even commit suicide with this gun. It is just for *ma'arit ayin* [appearance's sake]. We passed innumerable road blocks, were duly searched, examined, all very friendly, all very genial. The girls and boys looked grimy, tired but sturdy and jovial. One beautiful young girl with burning eyes, wearing high riding boots, splendidly fitted uniform, rifle strapped around her shoulder, greeted us as we emerged from the *pardess* on to the main road. I suppose she, too, was for *ma'arit ayin*.

Our advent to Rehovot was a real homecoming. The joy, the excitement, were indescribable. It is so today with anyone coming from a far off land. It is hard to convey

★ Ezer Weizman, Weizmann's nephew, was the chief architect of the Israel Air Force.

the emotions that welled up in me when I came into the Institute grounds and saw what has been wrought here. It is something one has to experience personally to appreciate. In the midst of all this fury, anguish and sorrow, in the midst of death itself, our people are working, creating with a dedication rarely seen elsewhere, all in the hope of a better day to come.

My first task was, of course, to make the rounds of the new Institute, still unfurnished, though it looks almost completed. We went through every nook and corner, the laboratories, the new workshops—everything. Chana Itin remarked that for once I was rendered speechless. Indeed, I was. Perhaps one word expresses it—breathtaking.

It will probably take another two or three months to finish everything up, despite the fact that several hundred people are working on the premises. The long delays have been due to obvious reasons—abnormality of the situation, lack of material, held-up deliveries, etc., and all this added enormously to the costs. When I gave utterance to the thought or the possibility that perhaps we should quit temporarily and resume when times become more normal, there was on every face an unspoken expression of horror. I must confess, I felt rather ashamed of allowing such a thought to pass through my mind. Here nothing is halted. The words 'stop,' 'postpone for a better day' do not exist in our people's vocabulary . . .

The Institute is now working in three shifts, eight hours each, doing important scientific work with many more people than we ever imagined. What is being done here, Bergmann has described to you. It is all very important and essential. We in Rehovot are the only ones who can do it. What is the old Yiddish saying? *Got shikt die refuah far der makke* [God sends the remedy before the affliction].

All this, as I said, is being done under great difficulty and under the severest handicaps. It came home to me with striking poignancy Monday morning when rifle shots came flying from all directions. Our workers ran to cover and five minutes later it was all over and work continued as if nothing had happened. It was just a playful bit of sport on the part of some British soldiers who were passing through by train and making merry at our expense. Fortunately no one was hurt. Such are the conditions under which work here goes on everywhere. But it goes on.

This brings me to the question of your returning home. I know how your heart longs for Rehovot. I walked through your grounds yesterday and I prayed to God that you might be given some surcease to be able to return to that beautiful place and enjoy the comfort of home and the fragrance of your gardens. But I am afraid that it cannot be done. Every responsible person I spoke to—and I spoke to all of them—to Ben Gurion, Kaplan, Sprinzak, to the High Command, all of them are of the same opinion: They understand your desires, they appreciate your anxiety, they all know what it would mean to the Yishuv for you to be in their midst, and yet they think it unwise and imprudent for you to come back at this time. I know you will be hurt by this advice, but I cannot help it, I must tell you the truth. It is less dangerous for us poor mortals who count for little or nothing. You will therefore have to remain abroad *ad yaavor hazaam* [till the storm passes]. By then, I hope, the Institute will be completed, every department will be working, Neve Weizmann will be a blossoming garden and you will enjoy the work and the tranquility of your surroundings. Until then you will have to remain in the *Galuth* [exile].

To return to the general situation. As you know, for the last few weeks Jerusalem has been besieged, no one could get through there. The city was being starved out. It was the heroism, the courage, the self-sacrifice of our young people which opened the road between Tel Aviv and Jerusalem. Yesterday and the day before yesterday, as I returned from Rehovot to Tel Aviv, we passed convoys of hundreds of trucks of food and other essentials going up to Jerusalem. They converge from various parts at Rehovot. There they reorganize and go on their mission. It was heartening to see these hundreds of trucks laden with food going up to the City to bring succor and sustenance to their stricken people. I shall never forget that sight. The last few days we also had our great tragedies. The Hadassah doctors and nurses and poor Furmansky!* It is all so terrible; yet the grit, the determination, the will to live drives our people on to impossible tasks. People with such courage cannot help but win.

In the face of all this, my dear Chief, the voices that come from Lake Success mean so little—they are so unreal. There they do not know of what stuff our people are made. They know here that this is their *Masada*, but of a different kind. This time they don't mean to bequeath a glorious defeat, but a great triumph. There will, I am sure, be great suffering, we shall have many losses, we shall need ever greater exertions. If the world will not close in upon us we shall survive this ordeal and perhaps see a better day. And you, my dear Chief, will return to your land, conscious of the knowledge that the people among whom you will dwell are deserving of your presence.

With all my love to you and Mrs. Weizmann . . . in which Shirley joins me,

Affectionately yours,
Meyer

In light of the interpretations subsequently given to Weizmann's absence from the country, I think the above letter reveals a certain naiveté on my part. My devotion to him and my overwhelming concern for his physical well-being clouded my judgment. I also knew that Weizmann was the only one with sufficient influence to secure our interests in the United States. Weizmann's presence in America was of transcendent service to the Jewish State prior and subsequent to its proclamation; it was a disservice to Weizmann himself.

It is difficult to determine whether or not there was really, as Weizmann suspected, any premeditated design in the course that events followed. It was rather common knowledge that B.G.'s attitude towards Weizmann was highly ambivalent. Admiration, even affection, and envy walked hand in hand. Ben Gurion was, without doubt, the unchallenged leader of Jewish Palestine; but Weizmann was still the unchallenged leader of the Jewish people. He was the great elder statesman who had conducted his people to the threshold of statehood. Like Moses he took the people out of exile and brought it to the Promised Land. Like Moses, he was—figuratively speaking—not permitted to enter. Final victory was left to Joshua.

* On April 13, 1948, an armored convoy headed for the Hadassah Hospital and Hebrew University on Mt. Scopus was ambushed and seventy-seven people, including doctors, nurses and other professional personnel, were killed. Moshe Furmansky, a former emissary to the American Hashomer Hatzair, who converted my daughter, was killed in the battle for Mishmar Ha-Emek, the kibbutz in which he lived.

The question that bothers me as it bothered Weizmann is: did the modern-day Joshua assume the role of God by denying a blameless Moses entrance, or was the whole sequence merely the result of the force of circumstance?

Lest I be accused of exaggerating in retrospect—a pitfall for anyone writing of a period in which he was deeply involved—let me add a telling postscript to the events of those days.

On May 15, 1948, the State of Israel was proclaimed in Tel Aviv. On that same day Weizmann received a cable in New York from the Provisional Government of Israel. It read: 'ON THE OCCASION OF THE ESTABLISHMENT OF THE JEWISH STATE WE SEND OUR GREETINGS TO YOU, WHO HAVE DONE MORE THAN ANY OTHER LIVING MAN TOWARD ITS CREATION. YOUR STAND AND HELP HAVE STRENGTHENED ALL OF US. WE LOOK FORWARD TO THE DAY WHEN WE SHALL SEE YOU AT THE HEAD OF THE STATE ESTABLISHED IN PEACE.' It was signed by David Ben Gurion, Eliezer Kaplan, David Remez, Golda Meyerson, and Moshe Shertok, the five labor leaders of the new government. Two days later the Provisional Council of State elected Chaim Weizmann President, and the blue and white flag was raised over the Waldorf Astoria where he was staying. Yet—and here I come to the point of this postscript—when the Declaration of Independence was signed by the members of the Provisional Council, no room was left for Weizmann's signature.

An oversight? So it was later claimed by some. An unavoidable technicality? So others claimed: Weizmann was not a member of the Provisional Council, merely its president. He was not there when the document was signed. But the Declaration of Independence of the State of Israel was not a technical document, rushed through in the heat of battle. Every name affixed to it was an everlasting honor for the generations to come. Its text and signatories would be reproduced thousands of times over in history books and first-grade primers. Moreover, twelve, I repeat twelve, of the signatories of the Declaration of Independence were not in Tel Aviv when it was signed. Ten of them were in Jerusalem. Two of them were as far abroad as Weizmann—in New York. Yet place was left for their signatures. Could not the same consideration have been extended to Weizmann: 'You who have done more than any other living man toward its creation'? Apparently not. So the question remains: was there design? I have an opinion but not an answer. There was a long-range view of history behind this technical omission.

I have had occasion to deal with this matter many times, more often in anger than in sorrow. In 1957, I was being urged by the Government of Israel to take over the World Chairmanship of the Tenth Anniversary

Celebrations. I yielded with reluctance; it was a job no sane man would have undertaken. I asked Ben Gurion, who was then Prime Minister, to compensate me in advance by righting in some measure that historical 'oversight,' or 'technicality.' B.G. was busy writing all the time, as usual, while I was talking, and he dismissed the matter with a shrug. 'Weizmann doesn't need it.' I agreed. 'Weizmann doesn't need it, he's already dead. But,' I added, 'the Jews need it, Israel needs it, history needs it, the truth needs it.' But it was to no avail.

It was in 1967, fifty years after the Balfour Declaration and fifteen after Weizmann's death, that the injustice was partially rectified. The Eshkol Government issued a proclamation by the incumbent President of Israel, Zalman Shazar, at the Balfour Day Assembly in Rehovot. It was not the way I really wanted it, but this was how it had to be, for reasons which I have never been able to understand. It is a document of recognition which will lie, I was promised, side by side with the Declaration of Independence in the State Archives. At this writing, it is still buried somewhere.

The political slight wounded Weizmann deeply. But his reflections on the subject were sardonic. He compared himself with the *shadchan*, or marriage broker, of Pinsk, where he grew up, of whom stories were told concerning his struggles to make a meager living from his profession. In one particularly difficult case he ran himself ragged arranging a match between two young people who lived in different cities, where he had not only parents to contend with but relatives, partisans and all sorts of interfering 'well-wishers.' He did not even expect to collect a fee; all he wanted was the privilege of reciting one of the seven blessings under the wedding canopy. But in the end the young couple eloped, and when he arrived for the wedding he discovered that the ceremony had already taken place without him. 'I was, after all, the *shadchan*,' said Weizmann. 'They might have left one of the seven blessings for me.'

The fact of Weizmann's absence from Israel at the historic moment was subsequently given a variety of constructions by those directly responsible for it; somewhat craftier were those who put no construction whatsoever on it. This version simply places Weizmann in New York at the time of the Declaration of Independence—without rhyme or reason. There is no reference to the United Nations, no reference to Truman. One may assume, if one wishes, that he was vacationing.

One of the myths which was circulated at the time, and gained a certain credence, was that Weizmann in fact opposed the May 15 Declaration. The explanation? A sudden attack of timidity; fear of international disapproval. Rumors are of course more easily started than scotched; yet nobody knew better than Ben Gurion Weizmann's position on that issue; and nobody knows better than I that Ben Gurion knew.

During those weeks in Palestine, having made the rounds and reported to my Chief, I had little to do beyond dodging bullets. We were staying at the Gat Rimon Hotel which was not far from the Arab quarter of Manshieh. One night a bullet plonked into the wall just over my head. I thanked God that they could not shoot straight and began to contemplate the effect a hero's death would have on my public image. Also, how could I make Shirley a widow when I hadn't a penny to leave her? The next morning I betook myself to the 'Red House,' so called for physical and symbolic reasons: it was painted red and it was the headquarters of the Socialist leaders of Palestine. I reported to Ben Gurion that my wife and I were leaving Palestine. Ben Gurion exploded. 'In this historical hour, at this moment of crisis, *you* intend to leave? I won't hear of it. I won't allow it'—and so on, and so on. I pleaded a number of reasons, among them my lack of usefulness, the burden on the country of feeding us, and my poor marksmanship. Ben Gurion shouted me down. Tail between legs I walked out. Three days later there came an urgent call from the 'Red House.' B.G., his mood still explosive, but with reverse effect, said 'You must leave the country at once. Without a moment's delay. Immediately.' I asked him what new crisis had brought about this *volte face*, and he explained: 'Shertok [Sharett] is held up in New York. Communications have broken down. I must know *at once* what Weizmann thinks about declaring independence.'

The only transport available was a ramshackle Dakota, and it took some doing to get two seats, since I would not leave Shirley; but B.G. shouted them into availability. Arrangements were made for the plane to stop over in Nice just long enough for me to get word through to Weizmann in New York. Then I would cable back a coded message: 'Yes if yes, no if no.' Actually Reuven Zaslani, or Shiloach as he was later called, had given me a complicated cloak and dagger code to use. After some effort I convinced him that 'yes' and 'no' would do.

Before leaving I went to see one person, Yosef Sprinzak, one of the outstanding labor leaders and a close friend of Weizmann (he became Israel's First Speaker of the Knesset). I knew what Ben Gurion had in mind, I wanted to hear what Sprinzak had to say. I told him I was going to speak to the Chief, that I had to give him such and such a message and that I wanted his opinion. Sprinzak said: 'There's no question about it. I will tell you,' he replied. 'We're in a peculiar situation. We're like the young man who was pursuing a girl. After endless years of cajolery he succeeded in getting her into bed. In the morning she gets up a *virgo intacta*. What do you think people would say when they found out about it? That he behaved like a gentleman? That he showed consideration, wisdom, maturity? Not a bit of it. They would say he was impotent. And of us they will say that when we were on the brink of declaring a Jewish State we lost our nerve and collapsed.'

Sitting in the Dakota, I formulated and reformulated the little speech I would make to Weizmann when he asked what the opinions in the country were. The plane halted in Nice just long enough for me to transact my business. The prearranged call came through at once: 'Dr. Weizmann,' I said, 'I have a very important question to ask you. Can you hear me? It is urgent. B.G. wants your opinion now about an immediate declaration of independence.' His answer, in Yiddish, was clear and short. *'Vos warten zey, die idioten?* What are they waiting for, the idiots?' I said goodbye, hung up and sent back my 'coded' message.

A few days later the Declaration was issued and five Arab armies invaded the new state while the British Mandatory power retreated from the stage like some enraged vaudeville veteran hooted off by the audience, kicking over the lights, pushing through the props, spoiling things for the next performers. Weizmann was not able to return until four months later, in September, and during this further enforced absence he became more bitter and despondent than ever. His letters to me are of his deep frustrations at being powerless to influence developments either in the State of Israel or in the Institute. He was president of both and in a tortured moment expressed his wish to have done with the two offices. But let me return for a moment to my own story.

Our plane left Nice, headed for England, and I settled down to cope with a minor problem. We had no visas for the United Kingdom; our precipitate exit from Palestine left no time to go to Haifa where visas were granted. When we reached Passport Control at London Airport, we were shunted aside to let all the other passengers through. The man checked the passports a few times and then announced: 'You have no visas.' 'That's impossible,' I said, 'my secretary arranged everything before we left.' He looked again. 'There are *no* visas.' I was properly shocked at the inefficiency of my secretary. 'I'm sure there must be some mistake.' 'Well,' he said, as he stamped the passports, 'this is all highly irregular.' I breathed a sigh of relief and pushed Shirley through the lines. Just then a tall, muscular-looking Bobby motioned to me. I had momentary visions of the Old Bailey. Instead, he touched his helmet respectfully and said: 'You seem to be having a bit of trouble in the country you come from. Don't fret, sir, you will have your Jewish State. It is written in the Book and whatever is written in the Book will come true.'

This was the most touching reception ever given to me. The reader must bear in mind that we were at war! It could only have happened in what Herzl called: 'England, Free England, world-embracing England; you will understand us and our aspirations.' I took out a cigar and gave it to him. 'D'ya mind, sir,' he asked, 'if I smoke it later with m'tea?' I told him that not only did I not mind but that if he would meet me outside after I had gone through Customs, I would give him a whole box. I was quite a smoker in those days. But never have I parted so willingly with a whole box of Havanas!

We spent the 14th of May in England at the country estate of Henny and Sigmund Gestetner, two of the finest and most generous people who ever cultivated the Zionist vineyard. Their estate was called 'Four Winds,' and appropriately so because whichever way we turned we were practically blown over. They had established there a training farm for *chalutzim*, and the young people prepared a pageant to celebrate Israel's first Independence Day, in which we all took joyous part.

At the end of May 1948, Weizmann left the States, determined to make his way to Israel, but he was marooned in Switzerland. 'My great trouble,' he wrote me on June 27, 'is that I do not see any vehicle which could get me there. There are practically no boats going and if there is a boat, there is a risk of running into an Egyptian blockade. I can only travel in a pressurized plane. For the present they have stopped circulating between Paris and Israel. I hope they will begin again in September. You might make discreet enquiries whether we could not get a destroyer or a pressurized plane.'

Here, suspended in Switzerland, his sense of isolation was heavy. He was cut off not only from what was happening in the country at large but from information to which he was entitled as President. On July 9 he wrote:

I was very happy to receive your letter (from New York), which as usual is full of news. I read with a certain amount of skepticism your remark about Eban's intention to write a long political report. This has become a stereotyped formula which, a) is never carried out, and b) I detest. Usually it ends in a copy of a letter to Goldmann and I have to pick up the crumbs from his table.

His bitterness finds even sharper expression when he asks me about the possibility of arranging for an Israeli corvette to meet him in Marseilles:

I am troubling you with all these questions, which is really the business of either Aubrey [Eban] or Eliahu [Elath]. But I am sure that they are too highly placed for my liking and I prefer to deal with a common citizen.

Elath was Israel's Ambassador to Washington and Eban Israel's Permanent Representative to the United Nations.

In another letter he complains to me that all his communications with Dr. David Bergmann, the scientific director of the Weizmann Institute, have remained unanswered.

On July 30, he wrote me another letter, and then had a change of mind. He never sent it officially. But four days later he enclosed it in another in which he wrote:

I also enclose a draft of a letter which I have written on the 30.7.48. I did not send it off in the hope that some message would come from Palestine which might bring me some relief. And true enough, yesterday came a telegram from Moshe [Shertok] of which I enclose a copy. This renders the sending off of the letter less urgent. But I am doing it nevertheless *ad memoriam* because I am quite convinced that a similar occasion will arise again. The letter is meant entirely for yourself and you can destroy it after having read it.

I never destroy letters. I also never kept a diary. These apparently contradictory instincts about posterity are my compromise between modesty and a claim to immortality. I am printing the letter with the omission of some minor personal references. It shows the depths of his despondency:

Although I have not heard from you yet, I suppose one of these days there will be a letter. Since the establishment of the Jewish State, I have been trying to obtain some clear information both about policies and projects. I have been telegraphing and writing and so far have obtained no satisfaction. In fact, no reply has been forthcoming. Whether this is due to bad communications, as I am being told, or to some other causes, I cannot say. But I feel that it has reached the stage that I must take a definite decision.

From time to time I get glimpses of a Byzantine display of power and quasimilitary strength but nothing else. As you know, these are things which produce no echo in my soul. I realize that they are at war, but it seems to me that the moloch of militarism is having everything and everybody in his grip. As far as I am concerned, this cannot go on much longer, and as I do not see any hope of a change, I have decided to sever my connection with the Office which has been foisted on me. I am not in a position to cover with my name all that is going on at present in Palestine and to accept everything which the Government does without being able in any way either to influence it or to prevent it. It may be, that if I were on the spot, I might think differently or see things in another light. But I am not there and not likely to get there until the second half of September. Meanwhile facts are being created which one would have to face and I am not prepared to do it.

I really do not wish to create any trouble or difficulties for the new State which is already beset by a great many difficult problems but I cannot reconcile myself to being a sort of passive partner in an enterprise which is run on lines of which I cannot approve fully, anyway cannot acquiesce in them without knowing all the facts. And the facts are definitely withheld, whether intentionally or not, I cannot say.

I appreciate that the main actors in the new drama are very busy but that is neither a reason nor an argument for keeping me entirely in the dark.

You will, I beg of you, send a copy of this letter to Shertok [Sharett] that should serve as an announcement of my resignation. As soon as I know that this letter has reached them, I would announce it publicly.

Now about another matter, equally serious and equally unpleasant, and that is the Institute. Again I have no information of what is really going on there except some scanty communication to the effect that the whole Institute is switching over to what is called war work. This means that the entire scientific basis of the Institute has been changed. This has been done without any previous consultation or advice. Again, I understand the pressure under which our people are working, but as in the previous case, there was no reason why the information should not be forthcoming in time.

My hatred for all these military performances is so profound and ingrained in me since my childhood that it literally hurts me to feel that the Institute to which I have devoted so much energy and so many hours of endeavor, should be desecrated in a manner which I can neither explain or acquiesce in.

As you see, I am shaking off two oppressive burdens and I shall be looking forward with great joy to come to Palestine untrammeled by any ties of office . . .

Weizmann never threw off either the burden of Presidency of the State of Israel nor that of the Weizmann Institute of Science. But there is no doubt that the misgivings expressed in the above letter plagued him for the few remaining years of his life. What should have been a period of triumphal denouement was poisoned by his complete exclusion from the affairs of the new State. It can be argued that he was too old and infirm to play any effective part. Yet there was a good deal of life left in him and had the government or the unchallenged leader of Israel been blessed with a little more humanity and goodwill, Weizmann's declining years could have been spent in greater solace. Surely no longer a threat to Ben Gurion politically, he could have been accorded the courtesies of elder statesmanship—an ear open to his counsel. But even this was denied him. He was refused access to the Cabinet minutes; merely notified of their decisions. The Presidency was devoid of any but a symbolic importance, and Weizmann was not a man who could easily accept being turned into a symbol.

Weizmann spent his last years brooding and if he found relief it was in his tremendous store of folkloristic Yiddish philosophy, so richly laden with sardonic, self-deprecating humor. In a book I edited and published in 1961, Richard Crossman describes Weizmann during those final years in a term which Weizmann himself used: 'The Prisoner of Rehovot.'

But if Rehovot imprisoned Weizmann the leader and statesman, it gave wings not to Weizmann the scientist but to Weizmann's vision of science as one of the pillars upon which Jewish rebirth rested. He was given respite to see this domain of the spirit emerge.

20 Weizmann: The Last Days

In February, 1949, Israel held its first parliamentary elections to replace the provisional Council of Government which had come into being with the establishment of the State. On the evening that the First Knesset assembled to elect the President of the State, I was in Rehovot with Weizmann. We were waiting for the results to be telephoned through from Jerusalem. Not that there was any doubt as to the result; we were only waiting for the thrill of the moment. At precisely ten o'clock Weizmann rose and said: 'I am going to bed. You may sit and wait if you wish.' At midnight we were informed of his election.

Mrs. Weizmann gave him the news in the morning and a few hours later a delegation from the Knesset headed by Yosef Sprinzak, now the Speaker of the Knesset, came to announce it officially and to escort him up to Jerusalem for the inauguration ceremony. After he was sworn in Sprinzak ended the ceremony with 'Yechi Hanassi! Long live the President!' And then a small voice from the audience was heard: 'Yechi Hamelech! Long live the King!'

It was all done with brevity and simplicity within the Knesset, but the national response was one of boundless elation. The new state was entitled to flex its sovereignty with some fanfare. There were crowds outside the building waiting to cheer the President as he emerged with a guard of honor and those inside rushed to the roof to watch the procession from above. I wanted to get to the edge of the roof, too, but was stopped by Menachem Begin himself, head of the extreme right-wing Herut party, former leader of the Etzel and the most devoted of Vladimir Jabotinsky's followers. 'Don't push,' he said. 'He's not only your President. He's ours too.' I thought for a moment that the Messiah had come.

During that winter I prevailed upon a reluctant Weizmann to come to the States on behalf of the Institute, and I returned to New York to prepare for a dinner and campaign. My target was five million dollars. Illness delayed Weizmann and he did not come until April, by which time he was even more reluctant: he wanted to be in Israel for the first anniversary of Israel's independence. But pressure in the States and expectation were too much for him to deny.

In the midst of the excitement Henry Montor, of the United Jewish Appeal, and Henry Morgenthau, Jr., its Chairman, precipitated a crisis, saying, 'You want to bring the President of the State of Israel all the way to America for a little thing called the Weizmann Institute. You can't do it. We must use the visit for bigger things. Let's make a deal. We will take over the visit and give you the money you want. How much?' Five million dollars. We began to negotiate, and there were interminable phone calls between New York and Jerusalem with Eliezer Kaplan, then the Minister of Finance. In the end I settled for three million and honorable mention for the Institute as partner in the UJA Campaign.

The dinner was an unprecedented affair: Weizmann was sitting on a platform with a large basket in front of him. Jews from all over the United States had come to shake hands with the President of Israel and, incidentally, to pay for the privilege. The collection was eighteen million dollars. A few days later he met a small selected group and collected five million more. When I came to collect my money I was given a long and circumstantial spiel on the history of Zionism and the problems of absorption and immigration facing the young State, and a promise of one and a half million dollars. In the end we got something like $500,000. To show its goodwill, the Government of Israel did give us the grounds and buildings of the Agricultural Research Station which nestled at the entrance to the Weizmann Institute. I accepted it as part of the debt and began to plan the integration of this little compound into the Institute just as soon as the agricultural research scientists moved out. The Faculty of Agriculture of the Hebrew University and the Agricultural Research Station began to build a new campus across the way from the Institute. They are still building. Need I add that in addition to their fine new campus and numerous annexes at Beit Dagan, nearer to Tel Aviv, they still occupy the grounds and buildings which nestle at the entrance to the Weizmann Institute?

During that visit of Weizmann's to the States, which was his last, Israel celebrated its first Independence Day. In New York a rally was held at Madison Square Garden and as Keeper of the Keys I had promised that Weizmann would make an appearance. When I informed Weizmann that he was expected to turn up there, he informed me that he was not going. After all the exhilaration and personal triumph with the Jews of America he retreated into moodiness. He hadn't wanted to be in New York on Israel's Independence Day. He told me point blank: 'For once I am going to make a liar of you.' I went down to the Garden taking Yehoshua Harlap along. Yehoshua was Weizmann's bodyguard, driver, confidant and devoted companion. He remains to this day the guardian of the Weizmann residence in Rehovot. If I couldn't persuade Weizmann at least I could persuade Yehoshua, and then I could trust Yehoshua to persuade the Chief. The place was packed to exploding and some 150,000 people were milling around the streets outside, unable to get in. Dull speeches were being relayed to them over the loudspeaker system but they stood there, stubbornly expectant. 'What are you waiting for?' I asked someone in the crowd. 'Weizmann,' came the answer. And others joined in. 'It's inconceivable that the President of the State of Israel should be in New York and not come tonight.' And they stood and waited. We went back to the hotel and I told Weizmann that tailors and shopkeepers, shoemakers and just ordinary Jews were waiting for him, and had been waiting since the morning. When Yehoshua added his plea, in Hebrew of course, Weizmann relented. The Jews reached out to touch him as he passed. They cheered, they stomped, they clapped. And he was no less moved than they.

In June 1949 Shirley and I took possession of our home in Rehovot. At the same time I bequeathed my New York apartment to Aubrey Eban, Israel's Ambassador to the U.S. Subsequently, we moved most of our furniture and belongings to Rehovot and established a small pied-à-terre in New York on Central Park South, which we still use.

When the house in Rehovot was being built, back in 1947, as part of the Institute housing estate, I had a very interesting discussion with the architects and builders. It was mid summer, the temperature around a hundred and air-conditioning had not yet penetrated the Middle East. During the course of the discussion I naively asked what kind of central heating units were being installed in the houses. My question was received with a kind of open-mouthed astonishment. Nobody said outright: 'Are you in your right mind?' But that was the general feeling. Being a man of imagination I was not put off by this show of incredulity. 'I know, gentlemen, that it is hot now, but what about winter?' I was informed that a) Israel is a subtropical country, b) Rehovot is one of the warmest places in the country, c) central heating would be an unheard of extravagance, etc., etc., etc. I let the subject drop, but before the meeting broke up I called over Aryeh el-Hanani, the architect, to me and said: 'Look here, I may be wrong, I may be right. But I don't want to take any chances. Put central heating into this house. I'll probably be living in it on and off. Put it in in such a way that if we don't need it, no one will know it's there.' The scientists, it turned out, were less robust than the builders when the temperature dropped and the general outcry assured the installation of central heating in all new houses. Just to make sure, I held further planning sessions in the dead of winter.

My home in Rehovot, to which I knew I would come again and again, was my bond with the new State and I was fairly certain that my time in the future would be in part devoted to the new Institute. I say in part because my mind was already casting about for some new mission. With the inauguration of the Institute, which was set for November 2, 1949, my major involvement with it would cease. There was a promising nucleus of scientists and administrators, led by Bergmann and by Dr. Benjamin Bloch, the former administrator of the Sieff Institute, and beyond them the authority and resources of a state machinery. I could be of help—in America, in England. I might act as adviser here and there but by and large, I could say, in Lessing's words, 'the Moor has done his work, the Moor can go.' The first building was completed; the housing estate was finished; the area was attractively landscaped. I was satisfied and Weizmann had every good reason to be.

I should have known my Chief better.

For him the birth of the State was the bitter-sweet culmination of his life struggle and the beginning of the end. For me, it turned out to be a kind of half-way mark, the resting post, a pause before the final plunge: the events being plotted on the graph of my life would circumscribe it from that point on. November 2, 1949 marks the beginning of a twenty-year sentence at unremitting labor. I discovered this in the early hours of the evening; until that moment I still considered it the epilogue to the five years of work and planning which had gone before.

The inauguration was planned to perfection. I sweated over every detail of the proceedings, the timing, the entrances and the exits, the selection of the speakers, the decor. Weizmann insisted that I be one of the speakers. I didn't want it. This was his day and I was determined that as little as possible should detract from him. I explained to him that my place was behind the scenes, directing the action. He was surprisingly firm, and in the end I acquiesced, but I kept my remarks very short and to the point.

It was a beautiful day. Thousands of people had assembled from all over the country, hundreds had come from abroad. The stage was positively cluttered with Nobel Laureates from all over the world in their colorful academic dress. And the principal speaker for the occasion was David Ben Gurion, the Prime Minister of Israel. Ben Gurion on this occasion was magnificent. He had stripped himself of all his prejudices, and discarded his real or imagined differences with Weizmann. He spoke what I believe was his true feeling when he said: 'Weizmann wears two crowns, the crown of statehood and the crown of learning.' It was an old and bowed head that wore them.

Weizmann was the last to speak. When he stood up before the audience the sun was at a point where it flashed directly in his eyes. After a few words he stopped and said, almost inaudibly: 'The sun is in my eyes. I can't go on.' But the microphones picked up these words and carried them to every corner of the assembly. A throb went through the audience. Here was one who had used up his entire life in the service of his people, and there was not a man or woman or child in the audience who did not feel the anguish of that moment. But immediately after, there was a thunder of applause as Weizmann pushed aside his notes and began to speak, as usual, without them:

. . . here in Rehovot we are also engaged in a peculiar kind of pioneer work—we are pioneering in Science. There are many problems to be solved in our land, many difficulties to be overcome. There are also many dangers still to be met. But to meet them, we must not rely only or chiefly on physical force. We have a mighty weapon which we must utilize with ingenuity and skill, with every means available to us. Science is that weapon, our vessel of strength and our source of defense.

When the speeches were over Weizmann walked arm in arm with Ben Gurion, flanked by Dewey Stone and Harry Levine, two of his most trusted and devoted supporters in the U.S., to the ceremonial ribbon cutting. Prof. Leo Ruzicka, the Nobel Laureate from Zurich, and Rebecca Sieff cut the ribbon. The Institute was opened. There was a lot of milling around for a few more hours. People walked in and out of the buildings, inspecting the equipment and the grounds. Dr. Weizmann, exhausted by the proceedings, went home immediately after.

I myself, exhilarated though weary, returned to what eventually became my home for the next twenty-one years. It stood at the top of an incline in the housing area. It was late afternoon and though I wanted desperately to sleep I was too agitated to relax. What now? I asked myself repeatedly, what now? I thought of the years I had spent running back and forth between New York and Rehovot. This day had been the climax to those years. But what next? I was in the prime of life and although my heart had long been set on making at least a part-time home in Israel, I really did not know which way to turn. Very few people voluntarily pull up stakes and move from one country to another. It will happen under compulsion, because of persecution or the search for a livelihood. In my own case, there was no strong motivation. I had lived the greater part of my life in America, had married there and raised a family. True, my daughter had decided to make Israel her home, but there were two other children, Mendy and David. There was my wife, my family, and friends. Everything that I was or had created was the result of the opportunities given to me in the United States, and my ties to that country were indissoluble. All these thoughts kept running through my mind and robbed me of any rest I had hoped to get. Then in the midst of my restless meditations the phone rang. 'The Chief wants to see you.' It was about 5:30 and the tone of the summons was urgent. Within fifteen minutes I was in his presence.

Dr. Weizmann was sitting in the half-darkened library, opposite the fireplace, his head tilted to one side, resting on his palm. After a few pleasantries about the events of the day, he sat silently and it was difficult to tell if he was contemplating something or just dozing. Then he motioned to me to come and sit next to him and his first words to me, in Yiddish, were: 'Meyer, *gib mir t'kias kaf.*' Literally this means: give me your hand. But its true meaning is 'give me your word, your promise.' My answer was: '*Vos plutzling?* Why all of a sudden?' He repeated: '*Gib mir t'kias kaf.* I want you to promise me never to leave the Institute. If you think that a scientific institute has been created today you are mistaken. It has only been born. It still has to be nurtured and brought up into manhood. Promise me that you will never abandon this place, that you will devote the rest of your life to it.'

My reply was: 'Chief, I am not a scientist. How can I take over in the way you mean?' Weizmann's answer was: 'You don't have to be a scientist to know what I want. All you need to remember is that Israel's future will rest on three pillars: science, security and education—above all education. The Institute must become the strongest pillar in scientific education and I want to entrust it to you. *Gib mir t'kias kaf.*' I gave him my hand and I felt we were both on the verge of tears. It was a moment of solemn decision both for him and for me. He wept because he realized that his life was spent, and though his mind was as alert as ever, his physical scaffolding was disintegrating; I because of the confidence he reposed in me, and because I was frightened by the responsibility, not only for the Institute but for myself, my wife and family. But the reader will understand that this—for me—fateful scene would never have occurred but for the long series of events that led to the opening of the Institute.

Dr. Weizmann's trust in me was absolute. Whatever disagreements we had—and we did not always see eye to eye—we used to argue out. The reader by this time should also know something about my temperament; yet difficult as it may be to imagine, my discussions with Weizmann were always held in subdued tones. He never liked my high octaves and used to say: 'I have heard of the walls of Jericho being brought down by shouts but I never heard of walls going up to shouts.' More often than not, he would convince me that he was right and I would defer to him. At other times he would concede: 'Maybe you've got something there. Let me sleep on it.' And if I had convinced him I always heard about it the next morning.

Never during our long, long association did a word of recrimination pass between us. His trajectory was from extreme exhilaration to the lowest depths of despair. But never did he vent his moodiness on me. On the contrary, he looked to me for relief and release.

So much for background. For the rest, it had always been assumed that Weizmann's scientific mantle would fall on Ernst Bergmann. The Chief had relied upon him implicitly and unreservedly for many years. Bergmann once told me that during his frequent talks with Weizmann —and these were held almost daily—he would be fascinated by the latter's theories. No matter how late at night—Bergmann sometimes worked around the clock—whether in London, New York or Rehovot, he would rush to the laboratory and put Weizmann's theory to the test. Invariably it was provable. Later, when Weizmann's eyesight began to fail him, he relied almost completely on Bergmann's experiments. Just as he needed me for other purposes, he needed Bergmann for his science. However deeply involved in Zionist and political problems, he could always find an hour or two to relax with Bergmann.

This close and intimate relationship with Bergmann was intensified a hundredfold after the death of Weizmann's younger son Michael in the R.A.F. Weizmann used to call Bergmann 'my *ben yochid*, my only son.' It was a relationship not like that of David and Jonathan but rather like that of Saul and David; and I choose the second parallel because of later developments. In 1947 a black cat crossed their paths, as the old saying goes. What actually happened was made up of many small and a few big things, personal and scientific. I inevitably became involved in these unpleasant intramural affairs. I did what I could in the role of catalyst to smooth the way to their continued cooperation. And I succeeded to some extent because I could understand their mutual dissatisfactions, though some of my arguments did not convince Weizmann. 'After all,' I would say to him, 'for the past three years we planned and built an Institute on the assumption that Dr. Bergmann was your heir apparent. How can we now, almost on the eve of the dedication of the Institute, reject the very person on whose shoulders the Institute was to rest?' There is a long correspondence on the subject but it would make very dreary reading.

In those days Mrs. Weizmann was deeply under the spell of Bergmann's magnetic personality, and she defended him ardently. He served her in many ways and he became for her, too, a substitute for her lost son. It was all understandable, but it did not make things easier. At any rate nothing untoward happened to mar the preparations for the opening. Outwardly Bergmann was more or less in the good graces of Dr. Weizmann. He was still the '*ben yochid*,' but all along I felt dissatisfaction mounting, something gnawing at Weizmann, from which he could not free himself. From time to time he would drop a few words to me when we were alone. He felt that the altar of pure science was being turned into a citadel. He understood the pressures but he did not want military necessity and involvement to influence permanently the character of the Institute. And this fear, I believe, was rooted in Bergmann's relationship with Ben Gurion. He acted as Ben Gurion's scientific adviser, which, consciously or unconsciously, Weizmann sensed as alienating. There were other, collateral issues, and the intimacy, the genuine rapport, the complete reliance that had existed for so many years between them dimmed, and then disappeared. It was torture for everyone concerned and perhaps most of all for me.

When Weizmann uttered those words, *Gib mir t'kias kaf*, I felt it was a *cri du coeur*. I knew instinctively that what he wanted of me was not merely to raise the walls of a scientific compound but to preserve within them his cherished ideals. He was helpless to influence the affairs of state. He fervently hoped that the Institute would become, and remain, even beyond the grave, the embodiment of his conception: that Zion would be redeemed, not by fire and the sword, but in humility and learning.

Six months before that evening's talk, Weizmann had already entrusted to me a different kind of legacy. He wrote me from Rehovot asking me to be responsible for the collection and eventual publication of all his letters and papers:

Feb. 20, 1949

Dear Meyer,

Now that 'Trial and Error' is published and is in process of being translated into 'shivim leshonot,' I have been thinking about the many unpublished documents and letters of the past forty years and more that might be of some public interest. These letters and documents are scattered all over the world and in many hands. The main sources, however, are London, Jerusalem, Rehovot and New York. I should very much like to see them collected in one place and prepared for proper editing and publication. Would you be willing to undertake this task? I know it is quite a job and will involve a great deal of collaboration and probably several years of work.

I cannot think of anyone other than yourself to whom I would entrust this work with the feeling that it will be done with responsibility and fidelity . . .

Affectionately,
Chaim Weizmann

And now, the Institute.

From that time I became, as it were, an instrument of Weizmann's will, the repository of his dreams, and the carrier of his tradition—responsibilities which were to determine the course of my life from that point on. In retrospect it appears that November 2, 1949 *was* the turning point in my life, as I said above. All my energies, all my powers, all my diverse and diffused activities were now channeled toward a clearly defined end. The objective had been decided upon by someone else, by Weizmann, and I had accepted. But of course it was not a change of direction; it was, rather, the only possible conclusion to everything that had gone before. It was the last and the longest chapter.

Early in 1950 Mendy and Mary-Jo presented me with my first grandchild, Alexandra. At the end of 1951, Helen and Shmuel presented me with my first grandson, Aminadav Chaim. I try not to play favorites with my grandchildren, but I have cause to remember his birth more clearly because the Chief was then critically ill.

Since the opening of the Institute, I had been commuting regularly between New York and Rehovot, first on the affairs of the Institute and then, at the request of the Israel Government, in order to help Henry Montor set up Bonds for Israel, and prepare for Ben Gurion's trip to the United States. At all events, Shirley and I returned to Israel on December 6, 1951, to be with Helen during her confinement. Soon after our arrival I learned that it was a matter of hours, or at most days, for the Chief. I went straight to see him, but only for a few minutes. He clutched my hand and said softly and with great difficulty: 'My heart overflows with gratitude to all my friends. I don't deserve it.' He asked after Shirley and the children, and went off into what I thought was a deep sleep. At a gesture from the doctors I slipped out of the room. Later I heard that when he opened his eyes and the doctors told him that I was gone, he said: 'This Meyer is a peculiar person. He can't sit still for five minutes.'

The next day Shirley went down to Kibbutz Shuval in the Negev to see Helen and arrived just in time to drive her into the hospital in Beersheba. Considering that we had made the calculation six thousand miles away from the scene without either telephone or computer, the timing was remarkable. The following morning, naturally, that is, unaided by modern contrivance, Helen brought forth a seven-pound boy.

When I went down I told her that the Chief was dying, and I asked her to call the boy Chaim. They had already decided on a name but agreed to give him a second name. And so it was. A few days later she returned to her sumptuous quarters in the kibbutz and, in rain and mud, the young man was duly admitted into the Covenant of Abraham. The ceremony was held in the tiny foyer of the kibbutz baby house and I of course was the proud godfather.

On my way back to Rehovot I kept thinking: *dor holech v'dor ba*, one generation goes and another generation comes, or perhaps the order is reversed.

I saw Weizmann again twice in the next two weeks. Once he started to say something but could not. He simply kept repeating the name Meyer. Then I was told to remove myself.

Within a few days there was a miraculous change. The doctors were bewildered. He seemed to be defying every law of nature. Except for the immediate family, no one was permitted to see him, but from time to time he would call for Sprinzak and Meyer.

One day I was attending a meeting presided over by Harold Goldenberg. Harold and Zelda were then living on the campus and helping to make life tolerable, even fun, in that social desert. Suddenly an urgent summons came from the 'White House.' I was sure it was all over with the Chief. When I arrived, I found him sitting in a chair, the first time for many weeks. The doctors and his wife were there purring over him. He wanted to see me and I was left alone with him for half an hour. I was asked to tell him funny stories and cheer him up. That is not so easy, when it comes as an order, and under such circumstances. Every five minutes the nurse came in for a look, without saying anything. The third time she said: 'When you want to leave you can call me. I am outside the door.' This was a sort of *kapulier unziherenish*, a hint with a hammer, to be off. I said to him: 'Chief, I guess I must go now, otherwise my life will not be worth two cents.' He held on to my hand, and with his customary gesture of dismissal with the other, said '*Bleib, bleib, ich vel dich oislesen.*' This phrase, in Yiddish, carries with it a profound folk meaning. '*Oislesen*' means, simply, redemption. Throughout the Jewish exile entire Jewish communities had to be redeemed from imminent danger by stripping themselves and the community of all their worldly goods in order to save their lives from a greedy overlord. Weizmann used the phrase jocularly in relation to the nurse but as he talked I understood the spiritual implications as well.

He did most of the talking during the whole time, haltingly, weakly, to be sure, but with remarkable clarity, and no lapse of memory. He spoke only Yiddish—not a word in English or any other language.

Afterwards when I came home I dictated the whole conversation, or as much of it as I could remember, half in English, half in Yiddish to to my wife in the form of a letter to Moish Samuel. It has always been easier for me to write to a particular person than to make notes. The burden of it was:

'My greatest difficulty in lying here in this helpless condition is to watch and see all the mistakes that are being made in this country. You see, the Jews are a small people, a very small people quantitatively, but also a great people qualitatively. An ugly people, but also a beautiful people, a people that builds and destroys. A people of genius and, at the same time, a people of enormous stupidity. With their obstinacy they will drive through a wall, but the breach in the wall [or as he put it *der loch in der vant*] always remains gaping at you. Those who strive consciously to reach the mountain top remain chained to the bottom of the hill.' As if to illustrate this point, he suddenly turned to science and said: 'Those who set out to achieve something specific in science, never achieve it. But those who work *lishmoh* [for its own sake] usually reach the top of the mountain. Take for example,' he said, 'the science of microbiology. With the exception of Pasteur, it is almost entirely a Jewish science. Jewish scientists everywhere worked on it in dark dismal laboratories, abandoned it, took it up again (*gelozt lign in a vinkl a lange tseit*), and now it has been taken out and enthroned as one of the chief instruments of human healing.' He spoke of the Jewish people and then paused, and after a few seconds said: 'I want to tell you something about Ben Gurion.' I made a gesture with my hand, as if to say, this is not the time. I was afraid that the subject would over-excite him. But he continued: 'No, no, listen,' and he went on. 'Ben Gurion did something which I could never have done, no matter what the circumstances. He sent Jewish boys and girls to the front to die for the State of Israel. It was probably necessary and history will accord him his place for this. But,' he added after a long, long pause, 'I would not like to be around when he himself will try to destroy the very things he helped to create.'

Then he turned to me and in an almost pleading voice said: 'Meyer, you have been a loyal friend all the years I have known you. I have other loyal friends, perhaps many more than I deserve. Tell them not to permit the destruction of the thing we have labored over for years.' I tried to comfort him and say a few words to the effect that things were not as bad as he thought. Then he gave me a big *krechts* [groan] and said '*Alevai*' [I hope so].

In the letter to Maurice I recorded my conversation with Weizmann verbatim except for his remarks about Ben Gurion. Those I have kept locked in my bosom, or rather in my safe, for these many years. I have often been tempted to unlock them when he embarked on one of his rampages, especially when it ended in the destruction of someone who had been loyal to him, and whom I admired and respected.

In 1960, almost ten years later, I revealed Weizmann's remarks to Levi Eshkol. Richard Crossman had quoted part of my conversation with Weizmann in his book, *A Nation Reborn*. Eshkol, then Prime Minister, wrote a charming and thoughtful note telling me how impressed he was with Weizmann's words. In my reply I told him, 'I did not quote everything,' and gave him the full account.

A few days later I met Eshkol at the opening of the Sheraton Hotel in Tel Aviv. As I passed him in the lobby he shouted after me: '*Mir velln ihm nisht lozn,* we won't let him.' I was immediately besieged by hordes of newspapermen to find out what secret message Eshkol had relayed to me in those few words. I said it had to do with a financial transaction involving several million dollars. The newspapermen were not convinced but that's all they got. In the years that followed, burdened as they were with one Ben Gurion 'affair' after another, I always reminded Eshkol of '*mir velln ihm nisht lozn.*' Some years ago there appeared a cartoon in one of the Hebrew papers showing Ben Gurion hacking away relentlessly at a statue of himself. What a pity! More than anyone else he has been the one to tarnish his own image.

For the greater part of 1952, until his death in November, Weizmann was bedridden. He died on November 9, 1952 at 6:03 a.m. I was in New York when the telephone informed me. A few hours later I was on a plane. For two days his body lay in state on the lawn in front of the Weizmann House and some quarter of a million people passed by to pay homage, to pray, to grieve over a man whom most of them had never seen in person. It was an anonymous multitude, the humble and the great mingling indiscriminately in a unifying democracy of grief and lament for the departed leader. I had never before personally experienced an emotional outpouring of this kind; a popular outburst of genuine sorrow touched by that sublime pathos which Chaim Weizmann, had he known of it, would have deprecated and endeavored to minimize in his characteristic aversion to dramatic gesture. Yet for all that, it would have moved him to the soul as all such demonstrations did, because they were his people, the masses, *amcho*.

Among the mourners there was one, strange to say who was more perplexed than grieved. That was Benjy Weizmann, the only surviving son. 'What was he to these people that he never was to me?'—the tragic question of an alienated son.

He was buried in the garden in the back of his house at Rehovot and the words on the simple marble slab are: 'Chaim Weizmann. 1874–1952.'

21　The Institute Takes Shape

Although during the year or so before his death I had seen Weizmann all too infrequently and I had known that the end was near, the blow was shattering. It was as if my father had died again—as if I had been deprived again of a protective buttress between me and the rest of the world, and I stood alone in the midst of the storm.

These were intimate, private feelings, and strangely mirrored in the changed public attitude. It had been bruited about for some time that Weizmann's death would signal if not the end of the Weizmann Institute at least a perceptible decline in its fortunes, and with it the eclipse of Mr. Weisgal—that once Weizmann went it was *finis* for Weisgal; this was repeated in an infinite variety of forms which came back to me, embellished, augmented and embroidered in lively colors.

In a perverse way I am indebted to those prophets of doom; they spurred me to the determination that Meyer Weisgal, Weizmann's 'shadow,' would have the last word.

When I first set out to nurture the infant Institute in 1949, I was guided by instinct rather than knowledge. But Weizmann had repeated to me over and over again two things: 'Take your standards elsewhere, from Princeton, Cambridge, Oxford, M.I.T., Copenhagen. These are the centers of learning we must emulate.' 'You must wear blinkers. Look only ahead, never to the left or right.' These were the two principles that I laid on my forehead.

Rehovot was at the time a small, insignificant provincial town, almost on the edge of the desert, thousands of miles away from the centers of scientific thought. We had to attract gifted scientists and create conditions to make them stay. I often thought of Herzl's dictum about the Jewish State: '*Wir mussen die Dinge und Bedingungen schaffen*—We must create the things and the conditions.'

Fortunately, from the very beginning there was a group of people in the United States and Great Britain deeply devoted to Dr. Weizmann. In Britain were the Sieffs, the Marks and the Sachers, known to all as The Family, the Rothschilds, Sigmund and Henny Gestetner, Abraham and Michael Wix, and Isaac Wolfson; in America, Dewey Stone and Harry Levine, Albert K. Epstein, Benjamin Harris, Lewis Ruskin, Edmund Kaufmann, Sam Zacks, Samuel Zemurray, Harry Frankel, Teddy Racoosin, Abraham Feinberg, Gottlieb Hammer, Maurice Boukstein and scores of others. They were prepared to underwrite any idea of the Chief's, and they even transferred to me part of the affection they had nourished for him. Support for the Institute came from many people in many places, but it is to this handful that the Weizmann Institute owes the fact that like Athene it sprang fully armed into the world.

But it was the 'blinkers' that really preserved the idea of the Weizmann Institute as it was originally conceived. And the will-power required to withstand the external pressures took a toll inside me, for the situation in Israel was then appalling. In 1949 the country received hundreds of thousands of refugees from the camps of Europe and hundreds of thousands more from the hovels of North Africa and Asia. Half the population was living in tents and tin huts. During the winter of 1949–50 floods were worse than usual. Everywhere a struggle went on for the bare necessities of life, and a severe austerity regime was imposed. Everything was temporary and makeshift. The Hebrew University, deprived of Mount Scopus, carried on wherever an empty building could be adapted. And meanwhile we in Rehovot were building in 'marble and glass'! We became the target of a wide campaign of abuse. I was accused of doing things that the country could in no way afford. My answer was always the same: 'True, the State of Israel cannot afford the Weizmann Institute, but the Jewish people can.' At the same time I believed that the Jewish people and the State of Israel could not afford to have a mediocre scientific institute, and to my mind the twin principles of internal content and external beauty were of one piece and could not be tampered with. Had I succumbed—not to the vilifications of my foes but to the supplications of my friends—the picture today would be entirely different. I am prepared to say something which may even sound treasonable. Had the idea of the Weizmann Institute been projected *after* the birth of the State of Israel, there would have been no Weizmann Institute. Fortunately, at the beginning there was no Jewish government and the British couldn't have cared less. Our vision had free range and by the time the State came into existence it was too firmly lodged to be abandoned.

The one person in the government who showed any sympathy for what we were doing (and certainly from an unexpected quarter) was Israel's Minister of Finance, Levi Eshkol. When he was invited to speak at one of our early anniversaries, he said: 'We are a poor country. We cannot afford many beautiful and worthwhile things. But if we have to have one beautiful and worthwhile thing to serve as an example for the rest of the country, an example for the future, it should bear the name of Weizmann.'

Although to many our concept of building seemed extravagant and wasteful, I insisted that nothing but the best would do. What others criticized as being too luxurious for a poor country, I saw as enduring, both aesthetically and functionally. My principal insurance was that the Jewish people would not go bankrupt. It hasn't yet.

Even before Weizmann's death, the Institute was something of a show-place. We had certain natural advantages, such as the lush citrus groves which complemented the landscape gardening around the houses and laboratories. Yosef Sprinzak, the Speaker of the Knesset, used to come and visit his son Yair, a scientist, every Friday and afterwards would drop in on me for a drink and chat. Once, as he rose to leave, I said: 'What's your rush? Stay a while longer.' Sprinzak replied: 'If I stay here much longer I will forget that I am in Eretz Yisrael.' Sprinzak meant it as a compliment. Others were less generous.

The bulk of criticism and unfriendly gossip came from the Hebrew University. Their resentment was understandable. Stripped of their beautiful campus on Mount Scopus, it was hard for them to enjoy our progress and prosperity. Instead of expressing their envy in greater exertions, they bemoaned their helplessness and envied our success. Such, alas, is part of the nature of the species.

The implication that without Weizmann I was nothing might have annoyed me had I not known myself well enough not to take it to heart. During my long career as editor, theatrical producer, organizer, etc. I had been driven by temperament and by ideals to undertake all sorts of enterprises. All, or at least most, of them had a central motivation: the survival of the Jewish people, its civilization, its culture and its life in the Diaspora and in Israel. And whatever I did, it was with enthusiasm to the end. I myself am impressed by the manner in which I drove myself, and others—and to drive others successfully is no mean skill—to achieve things which seemed if not quite impossible on conception at least highly improbable. My successes, *and* my failures, all had the merit of quality. I could never stomach mediocrity or its blood-brother pomposity. I have been accused of many things—rudeness, impatience, extravagance, overheated imagination, indecorousness—a long list—but never of pomposity. My distaste for self-glorification led me not to self-ab-negation—that would be going too far—but to a certain reticence in singing or even humming my own praises. I always took my work seriously, but never myself. I never really cared for the aggrandizements of office or position, nor even, sometimes to the detriment of my family, for the material compensations. I was almost shy of them at times. With *The New Palestine*, for example, I slaved for years putting out a good weekly—that was what counted. Only after ten years, in 1928, did my name appear regularly on the masthead as editor. With *The Eternal Road* I pawned all I had and all my family had rather than take money out of the kitty which I controlled. I doubt that another few hundred dollars a week would have made any difference to our enormous deficit but I could not bring myself to 'live off' what I considered a public cause. With the Weizmann Institute it was much the same at the beginning. I held no official office and took no salary for several years. It was my intention to withdraw from the enterprise in 1949, once it had been launch-ed. And even after I had pledged to Weizmann to remain and see it through, I gave less than a tinker's dam for either the emoluments or the title on my stationery.

Louis Lipsky wrote a sketch of me some years before his death which he intended for inclusion in a sort of Rogue's Gallery of Famous Zionists. I dissuaded him from printing it. It eventually appeared in a book of tributes on my seventieth birthday. He wrote: 'It would be timely for Meyer W. Weisgal to abandon the prompter's box and appear in person . . . Meyer is known by his *unsigned* works. He has almost always been like the invisible stage manager in his productions, wearing muffled shoes, never to be caught on stage while the curtain is up. What he has put together—light and color and story—speaks for him, and he dares not intrude in person with his natural voice.'

Lipsky was my first mentor and teacher, Reinhardt my second and Weizmann my second and third. None of them were ever my patrons. It was not in my nature to solicit patronage nor in theirs to offer it. I was drawn to these people and they to me out of a community of interest which transcended the private and personal while encompassing it. If my efforts contributed to their prestige or whatever you want to call it, it was entirely incidental—to them and to me—as long as the work continued and flourished. It was only after Weizmann's death that I was forced, publicly, to abandon the prompter's box and speak, as it were, in my natural voice. If the Weizmann Institute and its imminent decline were to be identified with Meyer Weisgal, so be it. I would give them a good run for their money.

I had not the slightest doubt that the Institute would grow and prosper. But like the proverbial war horse I responded to the sounds of gunfire. Early in 1952 I discussed Weizmann's condition with the doctors. They told me it was a matter of days, of weeks, maybe months, they could not be sure, but time was running out. I know it sounds callous to say that I had my plans ready in anticipation of Weizmann's death, but it was not in my power to prolong or shorten his agony. I could only prepare for an eventuality, and if I did it with deliberation and foresight it was out of reverence for a man I loved, and in the sure knowledge that I was furthering his own cherished dreams.

It was not difficult to envisage Yad Weizmann, the Weizmann Memorial; lack of imagination is not one of my failings. It was to be basically an extension of the Weizmann Institute into a larger educational and cultural center. Even in those days I knew instinctively that eventually the Weizmann Institute, like the Rockefeller Institute, would become a university. It could not be otherwise. But envisaging was not enough. Weizmann was the President of the State of Israel. The Government of Israel had to initiate the memorial. The first step was to persuade the government that the memorial it wanted to establish was what I had in mind.

On May 23, 1952, six months before Weizmann's death, Sir Simon Marks, in consultation with Sigmund Gestetner and Israel Sieff, wrote to Prime Minister Ben Gurion the following confidential proposal:

In my opinion, a monument erected on some hilltop to Dr. Weizmann's memory would not truly express what he has meant to so many Jews. The shrine we will create for him must be such as will renew itself from time to time by its inherent character of being a living focal point in the Jewish State for succeeding generations. This shrine can only be founded in the place where Weizmann lived, worked and dreamed—in his home—in the Institute and surroundings—namely Rehovot. We know it is his expressed wish and that of his wife, that his final resting place should be there.

We would therefore like to propose that the Government acquire, or take steps to acquire and restrict, the whole area and approaches from Weizmann's house to, and including, the Institute, such development as may be determined by a Commission that will be appointed by the Government at a later date.

He further suggested that the Commission be composed of Levi Eshkol, for the Government, Dr. A. Granot, for the Jewish National Fund (which owned tracts of land in the area), Meyer Weisgal, for the Institute, and Ben Zion Horowitz, the Mayor of Rehovot.

On June 4, 1952 I myself wrote to Ben Gurion:

Sir Simon Marks was good enough to send me a copy of his letter of May 23 addressed to you and your cabled reply to him. Needless to say, I am deeply interested in the subject matter raised in his letter and very happy to know your positive reaction to the proposal made.

The subterfuge is admittedly transparent. Ben Gurion certainly knew that I knew of Sir Simon Marks' letter long before he himself had received it. He may even have guessed the truth: that I had prepared the original draft. But formally or otherwise, Marks, Sieff, and Gestetner had certain persuasive powers which I lacked. It was not only the money which they generously poured into the young state for every conceivable need; they were veteran stalwarts of the Zionist movement and men of enormous influence, publicly and politically, in Great Britain. Ben Gurion, of course, realized the importance of the Institute and its potential for the young state. In all probability, if I am to judge from his previous and subsequent attitudes towards Weizmann, he was torn between conflicting emotions. But his ambivalence towards Weizmann did not, in this instance, warp his outlook. Much later, on two separate occasions, he refused to accept an Honorary Fellowship of the Institute.

The Commission was called into being and one of our first meetings took place on the roof of the Weizmann House, which is perched on a hill commanding the entire area. As we stood there, Eshkol turned to me and asked in his characteristic easy-going fashion: '*Nu, mein kind, vos vilst du?* Well, my child, what do you want?' I made a broad circle with my arm reminiscent of the circle made by the rabbi in Ansky's *Dybbuk* around the bride who is inhabited by the spirit of her former lover. Eshkol said: 'Good! We'll leave the details to Weitz.' Yosef Weitz was the head of the Land Purchasing Department of the Jewish National Fund.

By August 25, the plan for Yad Weizmann was adopted by the Commission. The National Memorial zone of five hundred acres 'will have the character of a scientific and cultural center, interspersed with woodlands, parks, walks and green open spaces . . . so arranged as to attract visitors from all over the world. The motto must be Beauty, Utility, Permanence, and bear the character and style of the man whose name it will perpetuate.' It was to include the President's home, as a national shrine, the Weizmann Institute and the Agricultural Station, a national library, an amphitheatre, a school of art, parks, avenues and shady walks and a garden hotel. If I compare today the conception with the realization, I have little to complain of. The art school never materialized but everything else, and more, did.

The idea of the memorial was kept secret for five months, a miracle in the State of Israel, never since repeated. There were perhaps a score of people who knew about it, including some members of the Cabinet (it was approved at a secret session), the architects, and the committee. It was revealed only on the eighth day after Weizmann's death.

A week after the funeral, following the seven days of mourning, Ben Gurion, on behalf of the Government and the Jewish Agency, announced at the graveside, in the presence of Mrs. Weizmann, her son Benjamin and the entire Cabinet and the Executive of the Jewish Agency, the establishment of Yad Chaim Weizmann. The next day the bulldozers moved in. Every single detail had been planned in advance and within twenty-four hours the place was transformed into a shambles. Trees were uprooted, roads opened where there had been none, plazas planned where it seemed impossible, mountains split in two,—much to the chagrin of the unimaginative people who couldn't see further than their noses. I find it hard to remember now what the place looked like before the transformation.

We had our troubles: there were the citrus-growers in the area, and there were the politicians. But the worst headaches came from Mrs. Weizmann. I was destroying the house! That was when we broke a road through to the grave. Her Roman wall—whatever that was—was ruined! I told her, 'Wait, you will see, the trees will grow, flowers will bloom, this is going to be more beautiful than it ever was before.' She didn't believe me; in her opinion I was destroying all that Chaim loved.

Somewhere Vera Weizmann wrote that she got to know me only in 1952 after her husband's death. There is an element of truth in this. Not that she didn't know me before. She had known me only too well since 1921. I was just never her cup of tea, nor she mine for that matter. After the Chief's death she had no alternative but to know me, and slowly she learned that her preconceived notions were slightly out of focus.

Vera Weizmann was undoubtedly a great personality. She possessed regal qualities. When I made this observation to a friend of mine—a notorious wit—he replied: 'Indeed, she does. Like the Hapsburgs she has unlimited ingratitude; like the Romanoffs suspicion of friend and foe; like the Hohenzollerns a contempt for servants; and like the Bourbons the ability neither to forgive nor forget.'

I do not subscribe to this assessment, but it contains a small grain
of truth. She did not make friends easily unless they belonged—or she
thought they belonged—to the higher strata of society, a duke, a duchess,
or at least a lord. The lowest rung of the ladder was lordship.

In 1921, when I was organizing Weizmann's reception in New York,
I was one of a half dozen young secretaries moving in and out of their
suite at the Commodore Hotel. Mrs. Weizmann must have seen me at
least a hundred times. She never deigned to say good morning or good
afternoon, either to me or to any of my fellows. Many of Weizmann's
enmities in the Zionist movement grew out of her aloofness and her
social disdain. More than one hand would be lifted against him at a
Zionist Congress because of her refusal to be part of its society. When
I came to London in 1926, I rushed, as usual, to Zionist headquarters, on
Great Russell Street. Weizmann received me joyfully and in a moment
of recklessness invited me to tea at Addison Crescent, his home. Mrs.
W. was not at home. About a half an hour before I was to leave she
arrived. Weizmann, with bubbling warmth, said in Russian: 'Verachke,
you know Meyer, don't you?' She froze like a turnip and replied: '*Ya
yevo nye soznayu*, I don't recognize him.' Weizmann could only flinch.

Withal, she served a great purpose in Weizmann's life. She saved
him from many pitfalls. He might have become another Zionist *Luft-
mensch*, as happened with many young talents in those days. Her snobbery
—if you will—kept him away from the captivating Romanische café
atmosphere which flourished in Geneva, Vienna, Berlin or wherever
Russian students and intellectual émigrés met. Weizmann was by nature
warm, affectionate, *folksmenschlich*, and he loved to talk Yiddish. Somebody once described Weizmann with great insight: his singular quality, so
rare among mortals, was his ability to speak to Balfour, Churchill, Lloyd
George and Smuts and the other great of those days with the same effectiveness as to a Jew from Mottele, or for that matter Kikl, and still feel
at home. Mrs. Weizmann spoke only to God when she deigned to speak
at all.

She was an accomplished hostess, and had been, for many years, a
practising pediatrician. She was able to endure hardship and carried the
burden of their poverty with the same grace as she did their later affluence.
Her Zionism, until her husband died, was rather thin. Despite her pro-
testations, I don't think she understood very much about politics. It was
only after his death that she cast off the shadow of her husband and emerged
as her own self. She became a patriot, defending every Israeli action, good
or bad, and continued to maintain a court without the slightest diminution

of days gone by. She remained, for as long as she lived, the First Lady of the Land.

Although we had many disputes during the fourteen years she survived her husband, our mutual regard grew. I think she finally came to understand that whatever I did in Rehovot or elsewhere was in memory of the person she had adored. Moreover, she was very fond of my wife. They met almost daily, they traveled together, and Shirley had a deep affection and great admiration for the lady. Whenever I uttered a rude word about Mrs. Weizmann, which was often, I was promptly slapped down. Vera Weizmann died in London in the fall of 1966.

I must add that she died the death of a *zaddik*, a saint, since only *zaddikim* die on *Shabbos* or Yom Kippur. She died on Kol Nidre night, Erev Yom Kippur, which was also Saturday, what is called in Hebrew a sort of triple Sabbath of Sabbaths. Flora Solomon, the close friend with whom she had been staying in London, started burning up the telephone wires to inform me. She finally located me at four in the afternoon at the home of Gita and Miles Sherover in Jerusalem where I was observing the Fast. I called my friend Shlomo Arazi, the chief custodian of government property and chief expert on ceremonies, processions and burials and told him that I thought Vera Weizmann merited a state funeral. By seven in the evening Arazi informed me that a state funeral was out—Mr. Eliahu Sasson, the Minister of Police, had vetoed the idea. There remained only one person who could veto the veto, Levi Eshkol. When I spoke to Eshkol, he asked for a half hour to consider my request. After half an hour he called and told me his assistant, Addi Yaffe, would take care of everything and would get in touch with me. Within the hour he turned up at Sherover's. I was just about to introduce the subject with a volume of invective beginning: 'Your lousy Minister of Police . . .' when Gita gave me an urgent kick in the leg and pulled me aside to tell me that Addi Yaffe was Sasson's son-in-law. I skipped the introduction and told him only of Eshkol's decision. Thus a state funeral was held, and Vera Weizmann was buried next to her husband in Rehovot. The only eminent figure in the State of Israel to absent himself from the funeral, and to express no condolences either publicly or privately, was David Ben Gurion.

I must return now to Flora Solomon. Her reputation does not rest on the fact that she was a close friend of Vera Weizmann and of Dr. Weizmann. She is herself a kind of social institution as well as the creator of social institutions. Flora was the daughter of a St. Petersburg millionaire who escaped from Russia at the time of the Revolution with the help of a Bolshevik, indebted to him from his student days when Benenson, the guild merchant, extricated the young man from his debts at the Casino in Monte Carlo. In London Flora, who to this day considers herself a socialist, put her energies to designing the social welfare program of Marks & Spencer, probably the most notable of its kind in the world. My name for Flora is Mrs. Fix-it. I don't think there is anything or anybody she doesn't know, either in London or in Tel Aviv, and she spends her spare time and energies fixing things up. Give her any problem and she will solve it and be grateful for the opportunity.

To return to the beginnings of Yad Weizmann, we had literally to dis-embowel the earth in order to proceed with construction of the Memorial Plaza. A road had to be laid from the main area of the Institute up to the proposed site of the Plaza which bordered the grounds of the Weizmann Estate. From the Plaza a way would lead to the grave in the garden behind the house, thus delineating, more or less, the broad area of Yad Weizmann. Up to then there had been three separate zones: the Institute, the housing estate and the Weizmann Estate. They were connected, or disconnected, by vast tracts of citrus groves, a few dirt roads leading here and there and often nowhere, and the usual rubbish heaps and sand dunes.

If Mrs. Weizmann made trouble for reasons which she believed to be aesthetic, the owners of the orange groves had pains in their pockets. In Israel at that time, and to a lesser extent even now, a tree, any tree, was sacred, like the cow in India. We were accused of profanation in uprooting trees for the road—despite the fact that for every tree we uprooted for the boulevard of Yad Weizmann we planted five others. What really bothered them was the fact that the entire area had been 'frozen' by the government as a horticultural district, to maintain the green belt, and the grove owners were prevented from carrying out the parcellation of their agricultural property for urban building.

Fortunately, or unfortunately, depending on your point of view, the memorial required the expropriation of certain tracts of land. As in any civilized country, such expropriation required due process, and wheels were set in motion to compensate the orange growers who would be affected. To prepare the public, I held a press conference and presented the entire development program. In the question period I was told that a certain member of Knesset had announced that we would get the land 'over his dead body.' My diplomatic reply was: 'That's a very small price to pay,' which got more headlines than the development plans. A minor civil war was sparked. Sprinzak called me to Jerusalem. He was addicted to cigars, so I took a box of Havanas to soothe his ruffled nerves. 'Are you crazy?' he wanted to know. I told him I didn't mean it; it had just slipped out; I was ready to apologize, publicly and privately. And I I did. The poor victim of my retort actually died six months later but, I hasten to add, through no fault of mine. The incident confirmed my view that dispossessed capitalists lose their sense of humor during the process of dispossession.

One of the afternoon dailies took up the case of the orange growers with a charming feature about me spread over six columns and entitled 'The Man Behind the Scenes.' I quote:

Suddenly he launched a complete industry in America to immortalize the dead President in Rehovot, and the overseas public was requested to contribute $20 million for the purpose. In order to encourage it to do so, Weisgal himself flew to all the countries where those who revered Weizmann's memory resided—bowl in hand. And of course the bowl began to fill. It was also essential to look after the personal representative, himself, may he be spared for long life, as, otherwise, who among us would look after the deceased?! That this was Mr. Weisgal's view too we may see from his having agreed to receive a most respectable percentage from the millions—some say 15% and some say even 18%. As this has never been revealed, all that is known is that the percentage is a handsome one.

No one has ever been able to explain to me who *decided* on this whole program; who determined there was a need for a special Rehovot campaign, who decided that Weisgal should be the one to head it, who discussed the rate of percentage accruing to Weisgal for his efforts and why he is entitled to percentages several times greater than those given to all the other *schnorrers* of Israel in our time.

Above all, as I labor over these various perplexities, Weisgal wallows in almost legendary wealth. The unsuccessful producer suddenly became a Croesus. He did not bring his wealth from Kikl, nor from his short-lived secretaryship, and certainly not from his writings, or from his productions in America. Thus it follows that he himself was not impoverished by the perpetuation of his friend, to our great joy—and as a millionaire all doors were opened to him, because this 'left-wing' country loves millionaires. When Ministers wish to relax from their labors, where should they go? To Meyer Wolf in his mansion in the south. When Weisgal telephones to one of our Olympians, his friends doff their hats at the other end of the telephone. And Weisgal, too, knows his power in the State and rules through it. Through the State machinery which is subject to him, he governs in his Rehovot as a kind of Oriental satrap, and disports himself holding all the orange growers of the place in the palm of his hand, expropriating from them anything his heart desires.

As a defense of the dispossessed and impoverished orange growers of Israel it was not very good. As for my control over the machinery of the 'left' government, would it were true. I would have had considerably fewer headaches. And as a piece of savory journalism it revealed that Israel had no libel laws worth mentioning, although a libel suit was the last thing on my agenda. I was not so much worried by the mythical fifteen or eighteen percent as were my children who swooped down on me and wanted to know where my millions were. I could only tell them that I had a salaried income, appreciably lower than those of some of our fund-raising emissaries who raised less money in a year than I did in a month. They could not even expect to inherit my mansion which was Institute property for which I paid rent.

The cumulative effect of these exertions on behalf of the Jewish people was that in June, 1953, for the first time in my life, I collapsed. Doctors hovered around me like moths around a flame, and finally ordered six weeks of uninterrupted rest, or else. It was a most unfortunate time. The Memorial Plaza and the road had to be completed by November and nothing but my high octaves appeared to have any effect on the inefficiency and red-tape. The walls of Jericho fell to the sound of trumpets and shouting; the road and Plaza were being erected on the same engineering principle despite Dr. Weizmann's admonition to the contrary. There was nothing to do but leave matters in the hands of God, which is exactly where they remained until I returned.

Apropos of high octaves, there is a story which has circulated about mine for many years, often embellished in the retelling but essentially true: I was once seated with Dr. Weizmann in the Dorchester in London discussing a variety of subjects. Aubrey Eban had an appointment with Dr. Weizmann and I removed myself to the next room and engaged in making several telephone calls. I must have raised my voice somewhat, because Weizmann asked: 'What's all this noise?' Eban replied: 'Meyer is speaking to Palestine.' Weizmann: 'Why in hell doesn't he use the telephone?'

With a despairing backward glance I was shipped off to La Croix, in the south of France, to the home of Dr. Josef Blumenfeld, Vera Weizmann's brother-in-law, to rest and regain my health. Vera's sister, Rayatchka, and her husband, Ossie, were the most hospitable people imaginable. Raya was as outgoing and warm as Vera was reserved and cold.

The weeks in La Croix were memorable for two reasons. First, it was there that I started dictating my memoirs to my wife. Contemplating my imminent end I was naturally distressed that I would leave this world without having said my piece. Aside from that I had nothing to do. I was alone with my wife, chained to my bed, deprived even of visitors. I began where most people end, with a touching dedication to my long-suffering wife, and a lengthy acknowledgment to a host of friends without whose help the book would never have been written. Having thus dispensed with essentials, I managed the beginning of a first chapter. The

above Discussing finances of the Weizmann Institute with Dewey Stone, Isaac Wolfson and Harry Levine. *below* In the beginning was the Daniel Sieff Research Institute, nucleus of the Weizmann Institute of Science

Bird's eye view of part of the Institute today
below Science Square, hub of the Institute

above, left Sigmund Gestetner, who set me free (see page 293). *below, left* With Niels Bohr, father of modern physics. *right* Shirley with Marcus Sieff

With Nobel Laureate Felix Bloch

above, left With Nobel Laureate Isidor Rabi, my eminence grise. *above, right*
J. Robert Oppenheimer in Rehovot, 1958
below, left With Yaki Sheibe, my sabra jewel. *below, right* With U.S.
Ambassador to Israel, Walworth Barbour

With Amos de-Shalit, whose untimely death deprived the Institute of one of its outstanding scientists and leaders
below With Dewey Stone, William Paley and Victor, Lord Rothschild at a Weizmann Dinner in New York at which Paley said: 'Anyone who has dealt with Meyer knows that it's both an enriching and impoverishing experience'(see page 137)

'The Family'—with Becky and Israel Sieff (above), Simon and Miriam Marks (below), and Harry and Miriam Sacher (opposite, above)

below Mr. and Mrs. Arthur Krim. He stole the
Institute's most beautiful scientist (see page 314)

With Charles Clore

below Planting a sapling on the grounds of Me'onot Edith Wolfson with advice and encouragement from my son David, Shirley and neighbor Edith Wolfson

effort revived me completely and I abandoned the entire thing for another fifteen years. (There are still some yellowing pages around—living evidence of those immortal words dictated in La Croix.)

The second reason for remembering La Croix is more substantial. Sigmund Gestetner called from London: 'Hello Meyer. I hear you're kicking the bucket, is that true?' This naturally braced me up considerably. 'Sigmund,' I said, 'don't be a damn fool.' He went on: 'I'm very serious, Meyer. I don't want Shirley to remain a Zionist *almonah*, a Zionist widow.' The phrase has special significance in Zionist tradition. There were many women whose husbands had died for the cause and they used to make the rounds hat in hand. Pensions were not part of the Zionist constitution; a place in history was, however, assured: that is, a side street in Tel Aviv with one's name on it. (Even here the Jews were thoughtless. Why call a street or a village by someone's full name when it is cheaper for the sign painter to write only the first half? How many people in Kfar Shmaryahu know that Shmarya Levin was the inspiration? Or that the two trees and bench in the middle of Tel Aviv glorified as Gan Meir, Meyer's Park, is homage not to me, not even to Golda Meir, nor even Rabbi Meyer Berlin, but to the first Mayor of Tel Aviv, Meir Dizengoff? This, by the way, is why I insisted that the Memorial in Rehovot be called Yad Chaim Weizmann, and not Yad Chaim as was proposed.) A place in history was assured, but a roof over one's head, bread for one's children —that was another matter altogether.

I told Sigmund that to begin with I wasn't kicking the bucket; secondly, that I had three children, and lastly, that I would take care of her myself. He answered, 'To begin with, don't rely on children. Secondly, the fabulous wealth of a guy working in the Zionist vineyard is well known to me.' That ended our conversation.

Sigmund passed away prematurely a few years later; only then did I learn that shortly after that conversation he had established a trust fund of considerable dimensions for my wife and family in case I should be whisked off into the beyond. Throughout our frequent meetings he never uttered a word to me of his intentions.

Sigmund Gestetner was otherwise remarkable. He and his wife Henny were deeply devoted to Weizmann and I first met him during the war when Weizmann sent him to me in New York. He was an immensely successful businessman as anyone who has ever rolled off a stencil must know. But he spent most of his time in the Zionist cause. No enterprise was too large, no task too menial. He had the courage to challenge any laws or conventions that ran counter to British public opinion on the Zionist issue. He was from the outset one of the firm pillars upon which the Institute rested; and he was a very great personal friend, a rarity among Zionists. When he died, we dedicated the large gardens at the entrance of the Institute to his memory and the inscription which Henny insisted upon reveals more about the character of the Gestetners than it does about their identity. It reads: 'Aviezer Gardens, to the memory of a devoted friend of Dr. Weizmann.' Anyone interested in the immortality of the deceased would have to make certain inquiries in order to discover that Aviezer was Sigmund's Hebrew name.

The modesty of the Gestetners was in proportion to their generosity and their generosity was unlimited—is, I should say, because Henny has continued the family tradition. Once when she was in Rehovot, she learned that it was my sixty-eighth birthday and that morning she came to me with a cheque for £68,000 for the Institute. I told her that there must be a mistake: I felt like eighty-eight. Her reply was: 'That much I can't afford.' It was a typical Gestetner gesture. There was a rare quality to their generosity. It is much more common for people to take pride in their good deeds and I am the last person on earth to begrudge them their share of immortality—even while they are alive. As a matter of fact, most of the Institute has been built around the principle that people should be encouraged to establish their immortality while they are still around to enjoy it. One enterprising journalist even dubbed me 'The Merchant of Immortality.'

When I left La Croix I was not only alive and kicking but, without knowing it, a man of potential financial independence. But quest for wealth had never been particularly powerful in my makeup. If I had money I spent it; if I didn't I usually found someone who was prepared to finance my *meshugass*. Not, God forbid, that I didn't enjoy my comforts. I certainly did, and what's more, I was entitled to them, especially since our home had by that time become the center for the ingathering of various Jews from exile.

My attitude towards money is this: when something of importance is involved, expense does not count. I have never left anything undone for lack of money, mine or anyone else's—usually both. I don't spend money for the sake of spending it —although my wife may have contrary views on the subject. I do sometimes scatter it around but I scatter it much as a farmer scatters seed on a ploughed field, so that it will germinate—in kind or in marketable good will. Having what I would call a private slush fund enabled me in later life to do unto others what others had done unto me, that is, finance other people's insanities. As a result of all this I have gained a reputation for being one of the greatest spend-thrifts on record. To illustrate:

During the war there was a standing agreement between Weizmann and me that I would call him each week, on Saturday, whether he was in England, Switzerland, or Palestine. This I did, but one weekend nothing of particular importance had happened and I decided to save the expense. The next day I got a cable from the Chief asking why I didn't call. So I called and explained to him that there was nothing worth reporting and I had been put off by the unnecessary expense. A few days later I received a charming letter from him in which he wrote that he didn't mind so much my not calling 'but your sudden attack of economy frightened me.'

When I descended on Rehovot at the end of August, I discovered, not at all to my surprise but much to my chagrin, that nothing had been done in my absence. The entrance road into Yad Weizmann and to the Plaza was a heap of fine red earth and the mile or so of road had to be completed by November, the first anniversary of Weizmann's death. It was only through the personal intervention and cooperation of Golda Meir, then Minister of Labor, that the public works department started moving. I invited Golda to my home and not to my office—there was a road to the office—and asked the driver who was going to pick her up to accelerate the journey once he hit the sand. As she entered she complained energetically about the rough trip. 'Ah, my dear,' I answered, 'that's what I need you for.' I don't think the bumps were strictly necessary, but they helped. The road was miraculously finished for November 2 and was probably a record in the history of road construction. The Plaza was only partially ready, but usable.

The first Weizmann Memorial Assembly and the activities which were planned to coincide with it initiated a new era in the development of the Institute. The Institute was only four years old, young by any measure, but the quality of its promise was high, and had to be kept that way. I remember that every time I would set out on one of my fund-raising jaunts to the four corners of the earth I would call the scientists together and tell them: 'I am going out to tell a lot of lies about the Institute. When I come back I want them all to be true.' It was a paraphrase of Shmarya Levin's quip about Palestine: 'All the lies we tell about Eretz Yisrael are true.'

That first memorial was an auspicious beginning. It included Professors Niels Bohr, Ernst Chain, Herman Mark, Linus Pauling, Sir Robert Robinson and Dr. Francis Peyton Rous. All of them were awarded—and accepted—Honorary Fellowships of the Weizmann Institute. We instituted the Weizmann Memorial Lectures which were delivered by Sir Robert. The others lectured at the Institute and were invited to lecture at Israel's other institutions of higher learning.

We dedicated the Department of Experimental Biology financed by Isaac Wolfson, and Niels Bohr laid the cornerstone for the Institute of Nuclear Physics. It was on this occasion that I was finally confirmed in my brand of 'appreciation' of science. Following the cornerstone ceremony, Professor Bohr lectured on the Philosophy of Physics. I was in the Chair. I strained every brain-cell trying to follow what he was saying. I soon gave up and just sat there with a bright look on my face. When it was all over I approached separately several of the eminent gentlemen in the audience and asked what it was all about. Their replies were comforting. The chemists understood about thirty percent, the biologists even less. And their obvious discomfort indicated to me that even so they were exaggerating.

The following morning there was another symposium, not physics this time. It was held in an old Arab house in Rehovot which had been converted to look like the Waldorf Astoria—our own Wix Auditorium had not yet been built. On my way there I met Niels Bohr, who was strolling around the gardens of the Institute, leisurely examining the flowers. 'Professor Bohr,' I said, 'can I give you a lift?' 'I'm not going,' he said. I reproached him: 'But they all came to hear you yesterday. Don't you think you should reciprocate?' 'I'll tell you the truth,' he answered, 'I don't know what they are talking about.' My subsequent modesty about my grasp of scientific matters derives, therefore, from the father of modern physics.

The Memorial Assembly itself was the biggest innovation of all. It lasted exactly one hour. It started at five and ended at six. The gates were closed at 4:45. It was to be shock treatment for all the Jews who either misread what was printed on the invitation or refused to take it seriously. There were two speeches, one by Nahum Goldmann who had by this time succeeded Weizmann as President of the World Zionist Organization, the other by David Ben Gurion. Neither speech exceeded ten minutes. For the rest there was a soloist, the Metropolitan Opera tenor Jan Peerce, choir and a procession to the tomb, at which the police and the armed forces mounted a guard of honor.

The first effect was one of disbelief. Jews are strangers to the art of brevity, and they left the grounds bewildered. Was this all? But afterwards they gathered a lasting impression: it had been short, striking and to the point. Influenced by my experience in the theatre and especially with

Reinhardt, I established a pattern in our public events which was envied but not easily imitated. A public affair has all the elements of a theatrical presentation and it has to be treated as such. Everything had to be rehearsed. If you tell a speaker that he has ten minutes and leave it at that you are done for. He will go on for forty-five minutes and then remain convinced that he made a great sacrifice in stopping so short. I never relied on chance. I insisted on seeing the texts of speeches beforehand and mercilessly whittled them down when necessary. People often wondered how I managed. Shmarya Levin used to tell about a meeting of the Bnei Moshe Society in Odessa. Ahad Ha-Am presided and Menachem Mendel Shenkin, a famous old-time Zionist, was given the floor. He was supposed to speak for three minutes. But he went on and on and on. Finally Ahad Ha-Am, the great Zionist philosopher, leaned over, pulled at his coat-tails and hissed: 'Shenkin! Stop talking.' Whereupon Shenkin turned around with a furious look and hissed back: '*Eych iz leycht tsu zogn, ober ich ken nit,* It's easy for you to say that, but I can't.'

Once a modern Demosthenes was invited to speak at the Plaza. He came armed with a forty-five minute speech and I must admit it was a good one. I was obliged to inform him, however, that the whole program lasted only an hour and that he would have to reduce his golden words to ten minutes. Mortally wounded, he could only appeal to my sentiments: 'You mean to tell me that Weizmann doesn't deserve more than ten minutes?' I answered: 'What Weizmann deserves leave to me.' We settled for twelve minutes and some precious musical number of which I was very fond was sacrificed for these two extra minutes. An old hand at editing manuscripts, I took it upon myself to reduce the forty-five minutes to twelve. Good as the forty-five minutes were the twelve were better—even the speaker admitted it.

In the old vaudeville shows in the U.S. there was a saying: 'Keep 'em hungry,' meaning, get off the stage while you're still ahead of the audience. This should be an inviolable rule for actors, singers, speakers. Disappear while the disappearing is good. When I hear of some of our master orators milking audiences for two and three hours I shudder.

The following year the Memorial Plaza was finished and we invited five thousand people. They came on time in an orderly fashion and departed, satisfied, after an hour. The press talked for days of the spectacle of so many people in one place without rioting, without shoving, without shouting.

In 1954 the Government officially designated November 2 as Weizmann Day, tying it to the anniversary of the Balfour Declaration. It was the first and unfortunately the last time the Israel Government showed flexibility and intelligence as regards the calendar. For some reason I can't understand—perhaps because the Institute was never run on a coalition basis with religious parties—official days in Israel are celebrated according to the mysterious cycles of the Hebrew (lunar) calendar. This tradition may be valid for some of the Jewish holidays but I cannot, for the life of me, understand why Israel's Independence Day, for example, must fall one year on May 15, the next on April 30, the next on May 7 and so on. November 2 became the climactic point in the yearly affairs of the Institute. It saw the opening of new buildings and departments, the laying of cornerstones, the awarding of fellowships and the presentation of the Weizmann Memorial Lectures, not to mention a spate of social events to honor our important contributors and encourage potential ones.

One of the most constant visitors to Rehovot during those early years was Isaac Wolfson, later Sir Isaac. He and his wife Edith would come, lay a multi-million dollar cornerstone, go home again, come back, lay another cornerstone, and so on. Finally he got tired of lugging his suitcases back and forth, and told me that he would like to have a house on the grounds of the Institute. I didn't have anything suitable to offer him but next door to our house was a prefabricated Swedish bungalow which had housed the offices of Yad Weizmann. Isaac and Edith decided that the 'shack,' as we called it, would do very well, and after a few 'minor' transformations moved in and became our neighbors. It became, so to speak, their weekend or country home. The Wolfsons never had one in England. 'Because you see,' he explained, 'a country house is for weekends. But how can I build a house in the country that will be near enough for me to walk to *shul*? Here in London, my *shul* is right around the corner.' And he was serious. The penalty I paid for having Isaac Wolfson as my neighbor is that every Sabbath morning the two of us left, at dawn, to walk to the synagogue in Rehovot.

Once established at their *pied-à-terre*, the Wolfsons made their trips to Israel longer and more frequent. Isaac would tell new visitors, pointing to our house, 'We have a wonderful neighbor over there. Whenever we need milk or bread or onions, we go over to Weisgal's and get them. Whenever he needs money, he comes over here.' Since then, they have built a more spacious house, still practically in my backyard. I offered them a more capacious site to build on, but they were hankering, like the Jews who left Egypt, for the onions, and remained.

If I had to single out the individual outside of The Family—i.e. the Sieffs, Marks and Sachers—to whom the Institute owes the most, I would have to name Isaac. Whenever we were in deep water I turned to him, and I assure you deep water was my natural element. He never let me go empty-handed, whether in loans or in outright gifts. He was, and still is, generous, understanding and helpful, aided and abetted by Edith and their son Leonard.

I first met Isaac in London in 1945, by chance, and it was of no significance at the time. The first time I approached him for money for the Institute I asked him for £100,000. He somberly informed me that when Weizmann had approached him it had been for £500 and both considered it a generous and weighty sum. I told him that Weizmann and I had different conceptions of money. He said: 'I must consult my son.' My heart sank into my shoes. Children are not sympathetic about giving away their parents' hard-earned money, and I had not yet met Leonard. Just as we were talking Leonard walked in from the next room. Isaac said: 'Leonard, what do you think of this guy? He has the nerve to ask me for £100,000.' Leonard answered: 'Why don't you give it to him? You can afford it.' He did. Many years later I discovered in a letter from Weizmann to Isaac that the first £500 was £10,000. Isaac would sacrifice £9,500 for a good story!

When I first set out to write these memoirs, I made up my mind that I would not write a history of the Weizmann Institute. It will be written, I am sure, by other hands. Despite all our troubles and headaches, the story of the Institute is a success story and there is nothing quite as dreary as cataloguing success. We grew from year to year, expanded the scientific staff, added new buildings, new housing estates; the trees grew, the gardens bloomed, the campus became the envy of scientific institutions throughout the world, and our scientific reputation, like our deficit, became enormous.

In the main, two categories of scientists were involved in determining both the framework and the content of the Weizmann Institute. There were those who had won their first laurels abroad and were now drawn to the idea of a new center of scientific research in a new country. And then there were the 'natives'—young men and women either born in Israel or brought to the country as very small children.

I know I am treading on dangerous ground by mentioning names. I can never mention them all—all three hundred and fifty of them—or even catalogue them properly as Leporello catalogued his master's amorous exploits. I must limit myself to those I knew intimately, and may our other worthy men and women have mercy on my soul.

Prominent in the first group were men such as Chaim Leib Pekeris, a distinguished mathematician who had received his Ph.D. from the Massachusetts Institute of Technology, worked at Cambridge and Columbia and who, in 1940, had joined the Institute for Advanced Study in Princeton. He came to Rehovot in 1948 and organized a Department of Applied Mathematics—which designed and built Israel's first handmade electronic computers. Joseph Gillis, although much younger, belonged to the same category. They were joined later by Smil Ruhman who became the main builder of our 'Golem' (a computer which, in addition to making calculations, also plays 'Hatikvah').

Similarly, Isaac Berenblum, already famous in the field of cancer research, came to Rehovot from Oxford and founded the Institute's Department of Experimental Biology—which was to father at least two other departments that concern themselves with biology: the Department of Cell Biology today headed by Michael Feldman and the Department of Genetics which is directed by Leo Sachs. Then there was Gerhard Schmidt, the renowned organic chemist, born in Germany, educated in Great Britain and one of the few scientists willing and able, when the call came, to combine scientific research with heavy administrative responsibilities as Scientific Director.

Among the most prominent of the Israelis who were to set scientific standards at the Institute and acquire considerable reputations among their peers elsewhere were such scientists as Aharon and Ephraim Katchalski— Ephraim probably the most outstanding scientist at the Institute; Israel Dostrovsky, who for years headed the Department of Isotope Research and who built the Institute's plant for the production of heavy oxygen, for years one of our few self-supporting units; David Samuel, today one of the Institute's pioneers in the new field of chemistry of memory, whose links with the Institute date back to apprenticeship as a boy of fourteen in the workshop which Dr. Weizmann set up at the Sieff Institute; Michael Sela, initially a member of Katchalski's Biophysics Department, whose reputation as an immunologist is international; Shneior Lifson, who came to us via a kibbutz, fought in the War of Liberation and joined the Army Scientific Corps, which brought him eventually to the Weizmann Institute; and of course the late Amos de-Shalit, a nuclear physicist, and his colleagues Igal Talmi and Harry Lipkin.

There were and are dozens of others; physicists, chemists, biochemists, molecular biologists, electronics experts, and mathematicians. Together, they created what one of my writer friends called 'an independent republic of science,' a 'republic' which now comprises nineteen separate departments with a staff of more than three hundred—among them just to mention a few who joined us in the early days or were left overs from the days of the Sieff Research Institute: David Shapiro, Ernst Simon, Arieh Berger, David Lavie, Heine Eisenberg, the Taubs (father and son), David Danon, David Vofsi and Ora Kedem. These and hundreds of others, too numerous to mention, together with technicians, administrative workers, gardeners and post-graduate students at the Feinberg Graduate School, made up a total population of over two thousand people.

I am quite aware that if history chooses to accord me a place of honor in its crowded annals, it will probably be because of my role in the conception and realization of the Institute. But this volume is the story of Meyer Weisgal which, believe it or not, did not end with the Weizmann Institute, as it did not begin with it. Nor even, which is more relevant, did my twenty-five years' association with the Institute limit or call a halt to other activities and interests. Indeed, it was a springboard from which I pursued life—and vice versa—relentlessly.

22 After Office Hours

The fact that under one title or another I was the head of the Weizmann Institute, an onerous and exacting position, never deterred people from claiming my attention daily for a thousand different purposes. I had come to Israel with a reputation—some of it merited—for all sorts of achievements: I had been a writer and an editor, so I was besieged in Israel by newspapers and magazines to write, to sponsor, to publish, to edit; and occasionally I yielded. Again, I was known as an organizer, and that meant anything and everything. In 1951, for example, the Government of Israel asked me to take a leave of absence from the Weizmann Institute and help Henry Montor set up the Israel Bonds Organization, and take charge of Ben Gurion's trip to the United States, especially New York. A few years later I helped reorganize the Government Information Services. Then there was my experience in the theatre and the movies, by now legendary though it had been real enough—beginning with *The Romance* and ending with Reinhardt in Hollywood—not to mention catastrophic. The famous Weizmann Memorial Day was a notable addition to my successes in that field. The theatres in Israel sought my patronage; every insane Hollywood producer who wanted to make a film in Israel knew that I was the man to help him do it. I appeared to know everyone in the establishment worth knowing.

My activities outside the Institute usually began after four in the afternoon, when everyone in the Middle East goes home for a siesta. In a way they were a form of relaxation from the rigors of running a scientific institute. My temperament, my nervous energy, set the pattern of my life; and I could never resist all those calls—I was an easy target for people with projects that appealed to my imagination, whether they wanted my help to get money, my advice, or my patronage. Flattered, like that girl who couldn't say no, I invariably said yes.

There was, indeed, an inescapable relationship between one activity and the other. Every success or seeming success bred new invitations and challenges. The only escape was to fail, like in a poker game; if you go on winning, there is no end to it. Over the years, I became the address for every conceivable kind of *nudnik*, missionary or artist—if one cares to distinguish among the three—with a cause, private or public. If a Yiddish writer wanted to publish a book, he came to me. If a young Israeli singer with the exotic name of Sheherazade wanted to become another Maria Callas and had to have her studies in Rome financed for seven years, who was I to refuse her? Actually she could have been a great singer: she had the voice, the temperament, the '*centrale latte*,' but she lacked the necessary discipline. If a young scholar, sent to me by Golda Meir, wanted to make a study of the influence of the Bible on Shakespeare, or of Shakespeare on the Bible—I don't remember the sequence—could I resist? And if Rehovot needed a home for the aged, wasn't I just the man to help them get it?

I once calculated that on the average I collected several hundred thousand Israeli pounds a year for various causes outside the Institute. At first I operated as a sort of hand-to-mouth foundation, or intermediary. I knew someone who needed money and I knew someone who had some to spare. As time went on and the requests piled up, I institutionalized this side-line into something called 'The Chairman's Fund.' It was very simple. I would approach a Jew for a quarter of a million or a million for the Institute. If his answer was: 'Sorry, I don't belong in that category,' I would ask: 'In what category do you belong?' If he claimed to belong in the five or ten thousand class and I had reason to believe he was telling the truth, I would explain that the Institute was not really interested in such trifling sums but that I ran a small retail business called the Chairman's Fund whose monies I distributed to worthy supplicants. I made it clear that these funds were distributed solely at my own discretion without any public or private interference. In most cases they were glad to get rid of me so cheaply. Since the Fund was established I have disposed of over one million dollars for artistic, social, educational and charitable causes in Israel. Not that my real millionaires were absolved of responsibility to the Chairman's Fund. If I interested them in some particular small project, they looked on it as a fringe benefit they paid for along with their massive contributions to the Institute.

The financial immaculacy of the Fund was guaranteed by Dr. Hans Karger, the Institute's comptroller. Dr. Karger possessed qualities of meticulousness and fidelity to the letter of the law which made him the ideal manager of my often free-wheeling financial openhandedness. Once

I turned over to him a check for 41,000 Swiss francs given to me by someone for a project costing $10,000. He informed me that I had been 'cheated': there were ninety Francs missing for the exact dollar count. Every penny that came my way passed through Dr. Karger's scrutinizing accounts. (I needed him as insurance against 'The Man Behind the Scenes' sort of thing.)

That $10,000 project was one of the most unusual to come my way. I was sitting one evening with Gershon Plotkin and Shayke Weinberg of the Cameri Theatre. Avraham Shlonsky, probably Israel's greatest living poet and translator, was there and he told us the story of a young Georgian Jewish poet, in Russia, Boris Gaponov, who had produced a remarkable Hebrew translation of a great Georgian epic by Roshtavili. The young man wanted to come to Israel to publish his work, but that appeared to be impossible. His manuscript, however, was in Shlonsky's hands and he was trying to get money to finance the publication. I was impressed by the fact that this young Georgian had taught himself enough Hebrew to do what according to Shlonsky—who should know—was a masterpiece of creative translation. I saw the original, in beautiful Hebrew script. I could not judge its literary merits but I certainly could appreciate the dedication of this Soviet Jew seeking expression in the language of his people. It was a massive piece of work.

The following evening I was at the home of Lou Simonson, one of the gifted people working at the Institute in public relations, i.e. receiving visiting firemen. His job was, among other things, to be gracious to all and sundry—something I did not have the time to do. Whenever he spotted what Sam Rothberg, Chairman of the Board of Governors of the Hebrew University and very active on behalf of the State of Israel, called a 'live one,' he would bring him to me for the rest. That evening he was entertaining the late Mr. John Simons, a very 'live one,' a devoted friend of mine and of the Institute. I told them the story of my encounter of the night before. I did not direct my words to Mr. Simons especially, as I had absolutely no ulterior motive, as God is my witness. I simply wanted to share my experience with them. Simons made no comment but the next morning I found an envelope on my desk with a check from him for 41,000 Swiss francs.

The book was eventually published and I received a copy inscribed by Shlonsky. None of the sponsors of the book—including the American Paper Mills in Hadera who had donated the paper—were acknowledged. Shlonsky explained that all names were omitted to protect Gaponov from the possible accusation of complicity with 'western imperialists.'

Shayke Weinberg, the Director General of the Cameri Theatre, Gershon Plotkin, its dramatic director and Orna Porat, the distinguished actress, were part of an entourage which loomed large on my extra-curricular horizon for long, long years. My association with the Cameri— it was more like seduction—began as a temporary obligation from which I was to be released after two years. That was in the fifties. It has been going on ever since.

That I should be drawn to the Israel theatre is, given my past, hardly a surprise. Actually the beginnings of the affair go back all the way to 1927, when Sol Hurok brought the Habimah to New York under the patronage of Weizmann and Louis Lipsky. Artistically, they were a sensation, financially a catastrophe. Already in those early years the salvaging of the wreck fell to me. I believe it was something like $3,000, a small fortune in those days, but I somehow produced the money. I think it was Morris Eisenman and a few friends of his who ponied up. It was then that I got to know Chana Rovina and Aaron Meskin and Nahum Zemach and the others. Whenever I came to Palestine I went to see the Habimah and if I did not appreciate all the nuances of their Oxonian, or, better, Muscovite Hebrew, we made up for it afterwards till the early hours of the morning, singing and reminiscing.

With the Cameri Theatre, which grew out of the Second World War as the native Israeli challenge to the Russian-born Habimah, I came into contact with a host of dedicated artists, among them the incomparable Hanna Marron, and the ebullient Yossi Yadin. Yosef Millo, probably the most talented of the theatrical directors in Israel and one of the founders of the Cameri, fell out with the management in 1955, and I was called in to mediate. Like the man who came to dinner, I stayed on. I became the President of their various public committees, their patron saint and their father confessor. A repertory theatre is like any other closed institution. When the principals are not working, they are complaining about each other. I remained the white-haired arbiter of their internecine disputes. The relationship, however, has always been symbiotic. I helped them get their theatre, which they have outgrown and we are now jointly engaged with the Mayor of Tel Aviv, Yehoshua Rabinowitz, in plan-ning for a new theatre which will bear the name of Max Reinhardt. Gershon Plotkin has, since 1954, been the directing hand behind all the Weizmann Memorial Days and has brought into my orbit Dani Karavan, a stage designer and one of Israel's most talented young artists and sculptors. Whenever I have to hang a plaque or choose a site for an imposing work of art, and the professorial pundits of the Institute stand about issuing opinions and directives, I end the discussions with 'Get Dani in, let him decide.'

My own weakness for injecting art and drama into science was abetted by Margalit Sela from the staff of the Institute. Margalit, the wife of Professor Michael Sela—he is the Institute's and probably the world's foremost authority on immunology—was my right hand, special assistant and secretary of the governing bodies of the Institute and of Yad Weizmann, initiator and executor of special events and chief liaison with representatives of the world of art. Margalit, whose flaming red hair is no doubt the clue to her temperament, has always managed to wed art with practical efficiency; at any event she turned to either with equal effect.

There are certain incidental benefits I look forward to reaping from my association with the Cameri. When I give up the ghost, I shall have given them instructions for the staging of my exit.

My most formidable encounter with the combined forces of art, music, theatre, public relations and the Jewish people came with what I later—when it was all over—called 'Israel's Triumphant Tenth,' the tenth anniversary of our independence. For Jews to last ten years more or less in concert, and under one roof, was no small achievement. Charles Malik, UN delegate from Lebanon, had this observation to make when the Jewish State was declared: 'It's comparatively easy to proclaim a state but to have it endure is quite another thing. The Jews have no sticktoitiveness.' The ten years that gave the lie to Mr. Malik deserved a celebration.

Early in 1957 Teddy Kollek, then Director General of the Prime Minister's Office in Jerusalem and later Mayor of Jerusalem, appeared in my office in New York. Of all the sabras or half-sabras or Young Turks of Israel who have come into my orbit it was Teddy who struck the most responsive chord with me. He was a *kibbutznik* from Ein Gev (he eventually turned it into a national music center) and one of the up-and-coming Mapainiks. Although part of the political establishment, he was always slightly outside it. He was not really a political animal. He often tried to liberate himself from the Procrustean bed in which the party system puts people in Israel. He was easy-going and independent, he radiated Viennese charm, and he found it hard to submit to the dictates of party discipline. I first met him when he was breezing in and out of New York in the days before the State. He was a refreshing new face among the Palestinian emissaries, with all of their dedication but none of their brashness. He took his job seriously but not himself—the greatest compliment

I can pay him. After the establishment of the State he became Minister at the Israel Embassy in Washington. He was not very happy there and at one point thought of throwing it up in order to take courses at Harvard. He never quite made it and was sucked back into politics. When he became the Director General of the Prime Minister's Office, under Ben Gurion, I liked to think of him as 'my friend in the White House.' Every time I had a conversation with B.G. I would call Teddy in to act as my witness before God.

Then, in 1957, he came to me bearing a message from Ben Gurion: I was to assume the World Chairmanship of the Tenth Anniversary Celebrations of the State of Israel. The legend of my organizational genius had penetrated the Prime Minister's Office! I was reluctant and gave many reasons: my responsibilities at the Institute, my white hair, my decreasing strength, to name only three. But the real reason was my deep-seated aversion to working with a government bureaucracy which was as familiar to me as any of the Zionist bureaucracies with which I had had to contend.

If the scope of the 1958 celebrations was to be as all-embracing as the Prime Minister saw it, the middle of 1957 was a little late in the day for a proper start. Such a program called for at least two years of preparation. Actually they had set up a Public Council for the Tenth Anniversary in Israel. Its Chairman, Mr. Ishar Harari, a member of the Knesset, was hard at work in New York with the Israel delegation to the United Nations; the burden of his work for the Tenth Anniversary lay in persuading me to take over. When I asked him why he wanted to get out he told me: 'I've tried to hold on for six months. If *you* last that long, you'll be lucky.'

By the time I returned to Rehovot, I was beleaguered as if the fate of the Jewish State depended upon my acceptance. I knew it was all exaggerated, but as usual, the easiest way out was to accept; I must confess that I too had my plans: I would get some people who knew the ropes and let them break their necks.

That wasn't exactly what happened. I began by making one condition: I would operate from an office in Rehovot and not from Tel Aviv or Jerusalem, and the Government would erect that new office for me. (I have a penchant for offices. During the past twenty-five years I've had four or five different offices in the Institute. First, at the Daniel Sieff Research Institute. Then at the old Club-House. Then at the San Martin Faculty Club. And finally a sumptuous office in the beautiful Administration Building built by Anne and Dewey Stone as a permanent monument to their love for the Institute from the very beginning. Like that Jew on the desert island who built two synagogues because there had to be one he didn't go to, I rarely, if ever, occupied any of these offices; I preferred to work at home where I also had two offices, neither of which I ever used. I conducted my affairs from one end of the dining room table or from a card table in the corner of our immense reception room, known locally as the 'schnoratorium.' It could and often did hold one hundred or more guests for Passover or some other notable occasion. The card table was often moved outside to the garden which was in fact my favorite office.) They accepted the condition although they knew it was impossible to run the show from Rehovot. What was more, they themselves insisted it would take six months to build the new office. I said I needed less than half that time and I called to me the Rehovot representative of Solel Boneh, the building colossus of Israel. His name was Shabtai. I asked him what his name was before it was Shabtai and he answered 'Sonnabend.' 'Sonnabend, Sonnabend.' It rang a bell. 'Where do you come from?' He answered: 'Kikl.' 'Kikl!', I said, 'why haven't I seen you before?' He confessed that he had not had the *chutzpe* to call on me. I told him that according to the Government it would take six months to put up the building. He said: 'Six months? I'll do it in six weeks. Everything is possible with a *landsman* from Kikl.' He did it.

Then I settled down with Julian Meltzer, my old friend and for long years my valuable co-worker, and got to work on how to celebrate the Tenth Anniversary in Israel and throughout the world. We worked feverishly in three shifts and the more I was sucked into it the more I realized that it was a limitless enterprise, and with time so short it would require the boldest kind of plans to produce results. Israel is very good at bold military action, less talented on the civilian side. A crash program would mean unorthodox methods and conflict with the bureaucratic rigidity of my colleagues. I was nearly strangled by red tape. Originally I had been wooed with promises that I would have full authority to do what I thought had to be done. But at every step I was faced with para-military organization and civil service passivity. And the top-echelon men who were my deputies, advisers and chief operators spent half their time leaking juicy tidbits to the scandal-hungry press about 'Weisgal's Folly.'

When the slander became so vicious that I offered to 'disembarrass' the Government by resigning, my offer was rejected; Ben Gurion expressed surprise that I, a newspaperman, should take account of what some journalists write. One friend of mine pointed out to me that Israel's parliamentary elections were just around the corner. If the Tenth Anniversary program succeeded and achieved its objectives, Mapai would take the credit; if it failed, I would be thrown to the wolves. Having , been thrown to the wolves many times before and having survived, I decided as usual: the hell with them all, let's get the whole business moving.

The business, as I saw it, was not merely to enlarge the scope of celebration of Israel's Independence Day. There were major objectives of greater scope. The first was to attract tourists and establish Israel as a tourist center. To this end, and also as an end in itself, it was necessary to clean up the country. After a press conference one journalist wrote that the job I most longed for in Israel was apparently that of chief street cleaner. There was much truth in the observation—if offered the job with proper authority I might have considered it. I could not stomach the public filth and neglect which was always apologetically defended with 'We are a pioneering country.' A second objective was to restore Israel's image throughout the world. We had just indulged in the Sinai Campaign and Israel was 'a combative nation.' I deeply believe today, after the Six-Day War and all that has followed, as I did then, that the overwhelming majority of the people of Israel seek only peace. (I don't deny that we have been blessed with a highly vocal fringe of extremists, but they are a fringe.) Thirdly we wanted to reenforce the bond between the State of Israel and the Jews of the world.

When the smoke cleared a year or so later, the objectives had by and large been achieved. The number of tourists broke all former records and if we didn't reach our goal of 100,000 that year, we were well on our way up the graph. Thousands of outstanding people came to the country to visit, to take part in artistic events, in scientific programs (I did not take a leave of absence from the Institute during the Tenth), in international conventions, exhibitions, and the like. Dimitri Mitropoulos and Richard Tucker performed to jammed concert halls. Miss Katherine Cornell came with a superlative company to perform Christopher Fry's *The Firstborn*. The play was produced in New York under the auspices of the Tenth. My son Mendy, known in the theatre as Michael Wager, played the part of Rameses. Niels Bohr, Isidor Rabi, Felix Bloch, J. Robert Oppenheimer and Harold Urey came to open the Nuclear Research Institute in Rehovot. There were gala festivals, concerts, shows all over the country—all the year round. What had been affectionately nicknamed by the press as the 'Ten Plagues,' electrified the country. What is more, throughout the world millions of words were written about the country, countless TV and radio programs accented Israel's peaceful achievements, hundreds of editorials and supplements glowed with admiration and friendship, and of course Jewish communities all over the world joined in the celebrations and, incidentally, increased their contributions to the United Jewish Appeal. Once, during the initial stages, I asked for a visit from Dr. Shmuel Z. Kahane, the Director General of the Ministry of Religious Affairs, a very affable and learned Jew with a shrewd head on his shoulders. I said to him: 'I need 365 *psukim*, quotes from the Scriptures, commanding the Jews to visit the Holy Land.' According to Jewish tradition the Jews are supposed to visit the Holy Land three times a year. He said: 'This is quite an enterprise but it can be managed. Do you have a budget for it?' I told him: 'You bring the *psukim*, I'll provide the budget.' His conception of a budget was IL500 but he didn't call it a budget; he called it a *budgetl*, the Yiddish diminutive thereof. He produced not 365 but enough to go around, not only from the Bible but from the Talmud, the Midrash, and other sacred sources. They were very useful for speeches and general propaganda purposes.

In preparation for the onrush of tourists who would 'go up' to Jerusalem, I planned a special program of local improvement. My friend Gershon Agronsky, who was by now Gershon Agron and the Lord Mayor of the Holy City, pitched in, and we decided to put a new face on the entrance to the city. My idea was a boulevard of olive trees, *old* olive trees. Gershon thought it was a grand idea providing it could be done. The experts were divided and in the end I resorted to Herzl's dictum: 'If you will it, it is no legend.' The olive trees were replanted and in defiance of nature took root. As an additional touch we christened the avenue: Chaim Weizmann Boulevard. Whether the sign is still there I don't know but it was there during the Tenth.

Applications for landscape face-lifts at our expense were numerous and widespread. The village committee of Ein Hod, among others, approached us. This former Arab village had been turned into an artists' colony, and located as it was on the slopes of the Carmel, its picturesqueness and pictures were assumed to be a reasonable tourist attraction; they were thus entitled to some consideration. They had a hall which served as a gallery for the work of the local geniuses. Unfortunately, as they explained to me, this hall had no roof. Well, with a little money and the cooperation of Solel Boneh, the roof materialized and the pictures were hung. Ten years later, my nephew Freddie Weisgal, a distinguished civil-rights lawyer and jazz pianist from Baltimore, who at the age of fifty settled in Israel, was visiting the country and my daughter took him on an all-round tour, including the artists' colony at Ein Hod. When they returned they told me how enchanted they were to discover that all the master-pieces of Ein Hod were hung in a place called the Meyer Weisgal Hall. They had therefore tried to get in as freeloaders—without success. I had to confess that I was unaware of the existence of this monument. The surprise was one of my fringe benefits.

I remember that somewhere in the middle of the excitement, around Rosh Hashana 1958, I decided that too much of a good thing is no good at all and I flew into exile for a rest. I betook myself to a quiet mountain resort in New York. I might just as well have stayed home. Grossinger's was celebrating the Tenth.

During the preparations for the big year I sought the cooperation of Mike Todd for a mammoth event in New York. Mike was then at the height of his glory and powers. We met at the office of United Artists and before I could open my mouth, he took over. Mike not only became the great theatrical producer, director and impresario—which he indeed was, he also claimed mastery of Jewish law and tradition. When I challenged his knowledge, let alone authority in these matters, he answered curtly: 'My father was a rabbi.' The truth of the matter is that his father was not a rabbi but a *shammes* (the nearest thing to a janitor in the House of the Lord). Then I claimed descent from a long line of rabbis including my father who had a rabbinical certificate but turned cantor. With Mike Todd these credentials didn't carry any weight. He knew better—about everything.

When we finished our business, he announced that he wanted to meet the Chairman of the American Committee for Israel's Tenth Anniversary. We had established such committees all over the world. Not without mis-givings I picked up the phone and called Senator Herbert H. Lehman to warn him. I think I heard a sigh on the telephone. From the moment we reached the tenth floor of 820 Park Avenue, a painful change came over the equable, the patient Herbert Lehman. Mike strutted around holding forth on what Israel's Tenth Anniversary meant to American Jews, and I could see our Chairman slowly slipping through our fingers. Mike went on and on, interrupting himself only to put through long-distance calls to Liz Taylor, 'How are you darling,' every half hour. During one of these transcontinental love fests Lehman turned to me: 'Get him out of here, I can't take it any longer.' I managed just in time for Lehman to survive the chairmanship.

On our way back with my customary presence of mind, I informed Mr. Todd of my interest in the Cameri Theatre, and the new building going up. He offered us the Israeli royalties on *Around the World in 80 Days* for for the benefit of the Cameri. He even offered to fly me to Israel in his private plane for the opening of the new theatre and to bring Liz with him. In a word he offered everything. Nothing was too difficult or too much for him. He was a remarkable character and a warm-hearted Jew under his brash exterior. We arranged to meet in Paris on an appointed day and thence to Israel in his private plane. He never arrived. I was cooling my heels in the Plaza Athenée when I received the tragic news of his crash.

Postscript: a few months later I remembered his promise, which had never been put in writing or recorded, and I went to Hollywood to see Liz Taylor. With the help of Bob Blumoff, the United Artists representative in Hollywood, I met her at her home where she had just returned from a visit to her former husband Michael Wilding. She had either just married or was about to marry Eddie Fisher who was fluttering around the wings. She told me her mission to Wilding had been to ask for permission to bring his children up as Jews. Jestingly I asked: 'Why do you want to impose that burden on your children?' She replied: 'I want an integrated family.' I told her of Mike's promise and she said she would honor it. She further offered a very handsome contribution for a plaque at the theatre in memory of Michael Todd and promised to come to the opening. She was as good as her word—up to but excluding her own appearance. At the last minute Eddie Fisher called from Rome and informed me that Liz was in the middle of *Cleopatra* but that he was prepared to substitute for her. (Richard Burton was substituting for him by that time.) I turned down his well-meant offer. Either Liz or nobody. It was nobody.

When the sun rose on Israel's Eleventh Independence Day, everyone reluctantly admitted that the Tenth was over. The Government presented me with a handsome plaque in tribute to my dedication of spirit and flesh. Some misanthrope in the crowd proposed that now we could start the round of festivities all over again by celebrating the First Anniversary of the Tenth Anniversary. I commented, in an interview in *The Jewish Observer and Middle East Review* about my plans for Israel's twentieth anniversary: 'If I am still among the living, I plan to spend it under a palm tree in some secluded spot, counting the brick-bats that will be hurled at the World Chairman of the Twentieth Anniversary. He will have my sympathy—and I'll be wondering why he volunteered to preside at his own destruction.' I never make the same mistake twice. Hard as it may be to believe—it is not only fact, it's the truth, as the Yiddish saying goes—on May 24, 1970, I was summoned to the Prime Minister's Office. Her Excellency, Golda Meir, the greatest woman Israel, Milwaukee, and Russia together have produced, had just had a brainstorm. In 1973, Israel would celebrate its Twenty-fifth Anniversary, and I the eve of my eightieth. Would I agree to assume the World Chairmanship of the celebrations? I said no. I was tempted to say yes on one condition: that she produce a document signed and sealed by the Almighty guaranteeing that I would still be alive. Golda asked that I secure a similar document for her. (At this writing my 'no' has not yet been accepted; the Director General of the Prime Minister's Office, Dr. Ya'acov Herzog, is still pursuing me.)

With the Triumphant Tenth fading into history I again became absorbed with the Institute. The time was the summer of 1959, the place my home in Rehovot, when, like a bolt from the blue, a call from Hollywood was announced. After a dozen interruptions the booming voice of Otto Preminger, a friend from Reinhardt days, came through. He had acquired the film rights of *Exodus* by Leon Uris, and wanted my cooperation to make the picture in Israel. At that time I had neither seen the book nor heard of it. Publication date was some months off. Within about ten days, four 'telephone' books arrived; the postage stamps represented a king's ransom. I began to wade through them, but then turned them over to my son Mendy who happened to be in the country at the time and wanted to take them with him to Jerusalem. A few days later he called me and when I asked him what he thought of it, 'Daddy,' he said, 'it is unadulterated ★★★★, but I can't stop crying.'

Preminger wanted to know my opinion—not that he gave a damn for anybody's opinion. I told him that I thought it would make a good picture, providing he put his directorial genius into it. In due course he arrived on the scene, and Israel has not been the same since.

In those days the government machinery for helping a producer make a film in Israel was not what I would call ideal. We operated in a wilderness, but both the director and distributor were determined to do it in Israel as their contribution to the nascent Jewish State. The distributor was United Artists and the President of this prestigious firm Arthur Krim. Still a young man, Arthur had been almost a youngster in the days of *The Eternal Road*, when he and Robert Benjamin were partners in Louis Nizer's law firm. This triumvirate had been responsible for disentangling all the legal knots into which I had so successfully tied that production. For the same fee that they never got they fed and housed me into the bargain. Arthur and Benjamin took over the bankrupt United Artists, which had fallen on evil days since the Charlie Chaplin, Mary Pickford and Douglas Fairbanks years, and restored it to its former glory. Arthur became a globetrotter in U.A. affairs. I met him by chance one summer in Rome and he confided that after he finished his business he intended to take a long vacation. 'Why don't you come to Israel?' I asked. This idea had never occurred to him, but he took it up and after spending two weeks at a seaside resort near Nahariya, he landed in Rehovot. In return for my hospitality, Arthur—at the time still a confirmed bachelor—stripped the Institute of its most beautiful female scientist, Dr. Mathilde Danon. He came to me one morning for breakfast and like a shy eighteen-year-old said: 'Meyer, I want to reveal a secret.' I answered: 'Don't tell me, I already know.' The *shidduch* was not altogether a loss for the Institute. Arthur became the Chairman of the Institute's Committee for Affairs in New York, and Mrs. Arthur Krim, while transferring her talents to the Sloan-Kettering Institute, responded to every request of ours to speak on behalf of the Institute. They also built a house for themselves in Rehovot for sentimental vacations at the scene of the crime. Otto Preminger, too, gave me a role in his marriage. When he came to film *Exodus* he brought with him, in addition to a big crew, his intended, Hope Price. For some reason, Otto was determined to wed in the Holy Land and gave not a second thought to the fact that marriages between Jews and non-Jews in Israel, while not unknown, are almost impossible. But to Preminger nothing is impossible. He corralled into the service of this ambition a trio consisting of Abba Khoushy, the late Mayor of Haifa (where he was doing much of the shooting), Khoushy's secretary, Milka (who was also appearing in the film) and me, as coordinator. We had to convince the rabbinate of the urgency of the marriage without revealing too many unnecessary details about Hopie's ancestry. The rabbinate proved amenable and understanding and the wedding took place. *Mazel Tov!* My services to Otto Preminger and United Artists were not entirely selfless. I was promised the Israel royalties from *Exodus* and income from all world premières for the Institute. It meant approximately $1,000,000 for scientific and a wide variety of cultural and artistic purposes.

I was in effect the liaison between Mr. Preminger and the Government. They didn't speak exactly the same language, and I am not referring to Hebrew. Preminger is very demanding, and usually in the right; but his manner of asking sends a shudder down the spine of government officials and bureaucrats who are prone to think that the sun rises and sets with them. The shouting continued for a considerable time until everything was set—or until we thought that everything was set. Israel was converted into one huge film lot, and finally the actors arrived: Paul Newman, Eve-Marie Saint, Sol Mineo, Lee J. Cobb, and last but not least my son, who was given the part of David, the young Israeli officer in charge of the Cyprus refugee camp. After the shouting, the shooting began.

I thought I had done my share and left for London where I was booked for a conference with a group of scientists. In the midst of it came the familiar booming voice over the telephone: 'Meyer, this is Otto.' 'Yes, Otto, what's wrong now?' 'We have an agreement, remember?' Of course I remembered, or so I thought; I helped him, he helps us. Otto: 'On June 23 (this was June 17) you will be in Jerusalem to appear in the balcony scene.' Me: 'What the hell is that?' Then I vaguely remembered that in the course of one of our conversations he said that he would give us the royalties if I would be in it. At the time I had taken it as a joke. But Mr. Preminger does not joke. Differing from other directors and producers I have known, when Otto makes a gesture it is equivalent to a promise, and unlike those other directors and producers, he keeps it. And when he extracts a promise, he expects it to be kept. I pleaded: 'Otto, I'm up to my neck in work. What do you need me for?' He replied: 'No appearance, no million. Come to Jerusalem. It will be only a matter of five or ten minutes. You'll be on the screen for approximately two seconds.'

I concluded my conference, packed my bags, flew to Zurich where I had other duties, and from there to the Holy City, where like a good actor, I reported for duty. I was at the Russian Compound at exactly 5 p.m. My exacting role consisted of jumping up like a rabbit and embracing 'Golda Meir' at the announcement of the Jewish State. Golda was played by Milka, my fellow conspirator at Preminger's wedding. I didn't think that it was too great a sacrifice for a million dollars, and I I was by far the highest paid actor in that production. The main role on this brilliant occasion was played by the superb Lee J. Cobb.

I had been told that it was a matter of five or ten minutes but, being skeptical, I didn't make any other appointments until 7 o'clock that evening.

The five minutes stretched into an hour, then two, three, four and finally twelve—to 5 *a.m.* The scene was repeated about once an hour. I adore Golda but I don't remember ever having kissed her that often.

No scene in a Preminger film, I've been told, ends without a scene, and the great moment in the Russian Compound was no exception. Forty thousand extras had been gathered from all parts of the country to rejoice at the click of Klieg lights. Lee Cobb was made to repeat the scene at least ten times. Preminger was sitting on a crane at the other side of the square, giving directions through a megaphone, fortunately not within reach of any of the actors on the balcony. On the eleventh call, Mr. Cobb revolted in the midst of general pandemonium, rushed to the balcony and delivered himself of a speech which was not part of the script but highly dramatic nonetheless. Preminger's only response to the outburst was 'You're an idiot!' Preminger's various assistants made themselves inconspicuous in corners. I thought it was time for me to take charge. 'Boys,' I said, 'you can't do this. In this kind of crisis you have to stay on the job.' The response came back in a mighty chorus: 'You keep out of this. You're not at the Weizmann Institute. Our union will protect us.'

Not more than a handful remained. Finally Preminger emerged from the crane and I tried to calm him down. We went to the King David Hotel for 'breakfast.' As the car started he turned to me and said: 'That son of a bitch. I pay him $75,000 and he doesn't even know his lines.' That morning Lee Cobb ate no breakfast. He was lucky enough to get a few hours sleep in a bed he had to vacate: Preminger had canceled his accommodation at the hotel. Later that day Cobb turned up at Rehovot to cry on my shoulder and return the compliments which Mr. Preminger paid him. Thus ended my first and only appearance as an actor.

On Mr. Preminger's insistence that I appear in the balcony scene proclaiming the Jewish State hangs a tale, nay, one of the real ironies of history. For decades I have been the poor man's Ben Gurion. I have been dogged for years by a physical resemblance which I personally find hard to account for since it rests largely on coiffure. My hair, though equally undisciplined, is the more luxuriant; to the unobservant, its upward flow has been enough to mislead the eye and stir the imagination. My problem has been whether or not to destroy the illusions of those taxi-drivers and tourists, both in Israel and abroad, who, spotting me, are thrilled by the sight of B.G. in person. Should I tell them? Should I sign the outstretched autograph book? For the most part, honesty has triumphed over complacency, and I have told the cruel truth. Once, in Paris, on the way to Orly, the cab driver thrust pencil and paper at me for my signature. He could not get over my denials. All the way to the airport he kept turning around and muttering: '*Formidable. Formidable.*'

After Weizmann died I urged Ben Gurion to become Israel's next President. 'Expand the office,' I said. 'Increase the President's powers.' B.G. pushed my suggestions aside with his usual mixture of offhandedness and bluster. I tried another tack. 'Look here, B.G.,' I said. 'Think of it this way. You are the most famous Jew in the world.' He flung his hands out in a gesture of vast distrust. 'Beh!' he said scornfully. 'But I can prove it,' I continued, and told him something that happened to me only a week before in London. Walking toward the Dorchester at midnight I was accosted by a young lady who more or less offered to show me her etchings. My response was not encouraging but she persisted and fell into step beside me. Suddenly she blurted out: 'I know who you are. I saw you in the flicks.' I told her it was a case of mistaken identity. She was not convinced and further offered to protect my incognito. When we reached the threshold of the Dorchester, she turned to me wistfully: 'I would so love to go to bed with a Prime Minister.' I ended the story dramatically: 'Everyone knows you, B.G. Even the people who have only seen me!' B.G. listened, still unconvinced, but obviously interested in the story asked: 'Was she Jewish?'

Another time I was outside the Jewish Agency building in New York on Park Avenue trying to find a cab. A cabbie passed at top speed. Suddenly he braked sharply and turned his head to look at me. He must have turned his head in indecision ten times. Finally, he reversed and drew up alongside me. The vision coupled with the location convinced him that I was B.G. No amount of denial helped. He even produced a Yiddish paper to prove to me that he was a good Jew. Finally, resigned to the bitter truth, he said: 'If you were Ben Gurion I would tell you something.' I rejoined: 'Assume I am, and tell me.' He said: '*Vos treibt ihr die odern dem oremen Eshkol?*' A literal translation is impossible; the nearest I can come to the meaning calls for a world of comment. The gist was: 'Why do you continue to torture poor Eshkol? He was your loyal follower; you yourself gave him the mantle. What do you want from him? Let him alone.' When I reached home, the meter showed ninety cents. I felt that this cabbie deserved an extra tip, and I gave him two dollars. He turned again: 'You must be an important man too.' 'No,' I said, 'I'm just a simple Jew.' 'No, tell me who you are.' Finally I gave him my visiting card and his eyes bulged. 'You know,' he said, 'my son is a physicist. Maybe you can use him over there.' 'Tell him to write to us,' I answered. As he pulled away, he leaned out of the window: 'Don't forget my message to Ben Gurion.' In any case, it took Otto Preminger to immortalize the resemblance on film.

There came, shortly after, another call which led me into a round of activity, but the voice from which it emanated was infinitely more alluring than Otto's. Erev Shavuot, the eve of the Feast of Pentecost, is everywhere, and not only in Israel, a day of repose to celebrate the giving of the Ten Commandments, and to enjoy the special dishes associated with the festival. To be sure I have never understood the connection between cheese blintzes and the Ten Commandments unless as a general compensation for adhering to them. On that serene afternoon in Rehovot of June, 1960—almost time to go to *shul*, which I had no intention of doing—a telephone call from Paris was announced. At the other end of the line I heard the sulphurous voice and in my mind's eye saw the incomparable legs of Marlene Dietrich. 'Meyer, dear, I'm dying to come to Israel and I have only ten days until my next engagement. Can you arrange something?' My reaction was instantaneous: 'Marlene, today is a holiday in Israel but you will hear from me within twenty-four hours.'

I searched my mind for somebody to handle the lady's visit and decided on the impresario Giora Godik. He simply danced when I mentioned the idea. 'I will fly to Paris immediately,' he said, 'leave everything to me. You just arrange to get us the Mann Auditorium.' And off he went to Paris and Marlene. This is neither the time nor the place to give my opinion of the management of the Mann Auditorium. They agreed, they disagreed, they agreed again, and then disagreed again, all because of the fact that Marlene Dietrich *might* sing in German. It was disgraceful. Finally we were able to secure the Tel Aviv Cinema which seats two thousand, but Godik had to make the condition that she sing no German songs. She agreed, and she made it clear that she wanted no fees, only the expenses to cover her trip. All income she would turn over to any project I would choose.

On Opening Night, the Tel Aviv Cinema was jam-packed and Marlene was at her best. There were fourteen curtain calls. The house was ablaze. All the *Yeckes* (our nickname for German Jews) began to shout, '*Die Fesche Lola*,' '*Ich bin vom Kopf bis Fuss*,' and in the end Marlene was compelled to sing in German at the request of the Israeli audience. Nostalgia took over from foolishness. Was the German language responsible for Hitler? At the fifteenth curtain call she came out breathless and said: '*Ich kann nicht mehr*.' Dahn Ben Amotz, the *enfant terrible* of Israeli humorists and literati, called out: 'Then show us your legs.' Instead Marlene sat at the edge of the stage and made a little speech. 'We have suffered, you and I during those terrible years. If there is any consolation or comfort for the incalculable suffering of your people and my people, your warmth and affection has restored in me my faith in human beings, in humanity. I love you dearly.' After the show—and long past midnight—Marlene asked me and Shirley to go to her hotel and wait for her there. She had an important mission. There was an old Jewish woman living in Tel Aviv, a survivor of the concentration camps, who had been her neighbor in Berlin. Marlene had promised to go to see her. When she returned to the hotel, her eyes were red.

I have made it abundantly clear that with all due respect to Hebrew, Yiddish was always my favorite language. As a young man in New York, in my efforts to learn English I thought foolishly that it was necessary to try and forget Yiddish. One can as easily forget one's mother and father. I soon realized that it was possible to enjoy *Hamlet* without giving up the pleasures of Sholem Aleichem, Peretz, Mendele Mocher Sforim or Sholem Asch. When I reached this enlightened stage, I began to resent the 'war' which was being waged in the Zionist movement in its early days and in Palestine against the Yiddish language. People were expected to speak Hebrew and if not Hebrew, at least Russian. The slogan in those days was 'Ivrit or Russit.' Yiddish was too strong competition for Hebrew. There is the story of Bialik, walking down a street in Tel Aviv in the twenties with Ahad Ha-Am. Naturally they were talking Yiddish. A young sabra upbraided them with 'Jew, speak Hebrew.' Bialik's response was: '*Gey avek sheygetz, es is zu heis, mir hoben nisht kein zeit*, Leave us alone *sheygetz*. We have no time. Besides, it's too hot.' The fact is that the giants of Hebrew loved to relax in Yiddish. There is no language on earth so colorful, so intimate, so succulent.

In time, of course, Yiddish stopped being a 'threat' to Hebrew and the war petered out, or so I thought.

Before the twentieth anniversary of the State I proposed to the Establishment that one of the Israel Prizes be awarded to the lyric poet Itzik Manger for his contributions to Yiddish literature. The prizes, awarded on Independence Day, are the closest thing Israel has to a Legion of Honour or F.R.S. They are awarded for various academic, scientific and literary achievements. Itzik Manger was the Yiddish Heinrich Heine. When you read Manger you feel like singing and dancing. At the time Manger was desperately ill.

The committee which determined the issue was on the verge of agreeing when the secretary, supported, I am sorry to say, by some very distinguished Hebrew writers, threatened to resign and make a public scandal. The war was on again. Manger was not awarded a prize.

Many of my creative urges are generated by anger. This was one of them. I rushed to the President, Zalman Shazar and told him, in Yiddish, that this was indecent, an outrage, provincial, etc. Shazar, it must be remembered, is a scholar in Yiddish, in Hebrew, in Russian, in German, etc. He is one of the most charming writers on the Jewish scene and the burden of of the presidency has not obstructed the flow of his pen. I told him that I was prepared, on my own, to establish a Manger Prize for Yiddish Literature if he would accept the honorary chairmanship of the Committee.

He did so, promptly. From the presidential palace—a somewhat embellished prefabricated Swedish bungalow—I went to S.J. Agnon and told my story. He had just been awarded the Nobel Prize. As he wrote in Hebrew, his reply was interesting: Don't you think it would be strange for me now to join a committee for Yiddish literature?' Between one brandy and another and a few 'l'chaims,' he became less rigid. I said to him: 'Mr. Agnon, there's nobody here now but you and me. You know that what you write is Yiddish. Only on paper it comes out Hebrew.' His only reply was: 'If you took the trouble to come from Rehovot to Jerusalem to ask me, how can I refuse you?' I added to the committee Levi Eshkol, Golda Meir, Zalman Aranne (the Minister of Education), Reuven Rubin, the artist, Shalom Rosenfeld (one of the editors of the Hebrew daily *Ma'ariv* and a friend of Manger who had devoted years to helping the neglected and destitute poet) and Eliezer Rubinstein (Agnon's translator from Hebrew to Yiddish) who became the Secretary of the Committee. By the time the first prizes were awarded Manger had passed away. The first recipients were Abraham Sutzkever, a Yiddish poet and the editor of the distinguished Yiddish literary magazine '*Die Goldene Keyt*,' *The Golden Chain* (it is on the level of America's *Commentary*) and Aaron Zeitlin of New York, a Yiddish writer and scholar, and son of the famous Hillel Zeitlin who, defying the Nazis, marched in dignity to his death wearing a *tallis*. A special award of IL 10,000 was made to Mrs. Manger, who turned it over to the Hebrew University for the establishment of a Manger Archive.

It is known that one transgression leads to another, and I was soon declared, unofficially, the Maecenas of Yiddish writers. These stepchildren of Israel's intellectual society are debarred from entering the golden portals of the Israel Writer's Union. Just to make sure, it calls itself the Hebrew Writers' Union thereby shielding its immaculacy from any Israeli using another language, incidentally excluding Israeli Arab writers too. Had Sholem Aleichem lived in Tel Aviv, I wonder if they would have changed their rules. Anyway, one day a delegation of these 'downtrodden' appeared on my doorstep proposing that in memory of H. Levick, the Yiddish poet, playwright and essayist, a center be established over whose destiny I should preside. I didn't fall for the presiding but I promised to help them. Up to then they had been using a bedraggled cellar for their meetings. There they would sit and reminisce about the good old days when people still stuttered in Hebrew. A fortunate coincidence made the enterprise possible. Yehoshua Bertonoff, a ninety-year-old actor from Habimah, was prepared to sell his house for a song or, to be more exact, a ballad, and I told my writers to take it; I would find the IL 50,000. When the building was ready for its new occupants, I was invited to take part in the ceremony. Everything was perfect except the timing. I had to give away my tickets to Jascha Heifetz's first recital in Israel after an absence of seventeen years. I was surprised and delighted to discover that the main auditorium of Levick House was named Weisgal Hall. It is odd to note how, within the last few generations, Hebrew and Yiddish have changed places. For centuries Hebrew was the holy tongue, Yiddish the profane. Today, especially after the six million, Yiddish has become, as it were, the *loshn kodesh* of the Jewish people, revered for its past glories but exiled from daily life. It was so designated following the holocaust by Dr. Moshe Sneh, himself a Yiddish writer and speaker. Probably only in parts of the Soviet Union does Yiddish still have an organic existence and Hebrew the aura of the forbidden tongue.

There are a few more peculiar 'extra-curricular' episodes which I would like to record. I refer to my numerous encounters with representatives of the 'eastern' world, the tiny handful who slipped through the cracks of Russia's shifting foreign policy and found themselves face to face with the imperialist satrap of Rehovot. Perforce, most of them were Jews.

We have on the grounds of the Institute a hall called the Wix Auditorium. It has only one-sixth the seating capacity of the Mann Auditorium but what our local audiences lack in quantity they make up in quality and enthusiasm. As a result, when the great ones leave Tel Aviv for the provinces they sooner or later end up at the Wix. And so it was with the Russian pianist Lev Vlasenko and the Russian-Jewish violinist Jakov Wyman. (There was actually a third, Wyman's woman accompanist, but she got lost in the shuffle.) This was long before the Six-Day War after which Israel was denied diplomatic relations with the Soviet bloc—the only 'running dog' of imperialism so honored. Many innocent people wanted to know why the Soviet Union didn't break off relations with the United States, the chief imperialist itself. When the concert was over, my wife and I gave a garden party and invited the elite of Rehovot and Tel Aviv to bask in one of the zigs of zig-zagging Soviet-Israel friendship. The evening was a great success, in spite of the officials of the Soviet Embassy being there to watch over the proceedings. But what interested me more than anything was a study in the comparative behavior of the two artists.

Vlasenko, a young, handsome and spirited fellow, was winging his way around like a free bird, jumping from table to table, telling jokes, singing

Hebrew songs, running through the house and emerging every few min-
utes to tell me what a wonderful house it was, how he liked this picture
and that; in short, utterly uninhibited. When he finally sat down for a few
quiet moments, he said to me, 'You know, you have a *lichtig ponim.*'
This is a good Yiddish-Hebrew idiom for 'you have a radiant face.'
'Where the hell did you pick that up?' I asked. 'From my mother-in-law.'
His wife was Jewish. He himself really had a *lichtig ponim* as I suppose this
Jewish mother-in-law never tired of telling him. He invited me to come to
Moscow and gave me his address. 'You must stay in my dacha. It is almost
an island.' And then he was off again. Mr. Wyman, on the other hand,
came into the house, sat down in a corner, and remained there for the
duration. He never uttered a single word, never moved from his place. He
was Elie Wiesel's 'The Jews of Silence' in microcosm.

But the terrified tribe of Israel is not only confined to the Soviet Union.
It is found elsewhere. Some years ago in Paris I was invited by a dis-
tinguished Jewish violinist to his home for a reception in honor of David
Oistrakh after the concert. I was warned by my host not to press my
Jewishness too hard or become too lyrical about Israel or Jewish music.
My son Mendy was with me and seemed to acquiesce in the interests of
artistic co-existence. The guest of honor, as usual in such cases, came late.
Meanwhile we lesser mortals were allowed to act natural and we sat
around the piano singing Yiddish songs while a young Canadian girl
with a beautiful voice accompanied us. When the guest of honor arrived
she was in the middle of a particularly nostalgic Jewish song, '*Mai ko
mashma lon,*' and I was there with my distinguished basso profundo. Our
Jewish host signaled us to discontinue. But Oistrakh took over: 'Why
the abrupt interruption?' he asked. 'Continue. It is one of my favorite
songs.' And so the singing continued for some time. I turned to my host
and said: '*Nu?*' It was the most profound sentiment I could muster.

Why do I tell this story? To show that Oistrakh is a man of freedom by
nature and Wyman a cogenital bore? Not at all. I merely want to point
out that if you are a Jew in the Soviet Union you have to be a colossus
before you can be a Jew as well. If you are simply a good violinist, silence
is preferable.

I suppose it is one of the ironies of history that the Jews, in Russia and
outside, were always among the foremost admirers and adherents of the
Russian Revolution. It wasn't only the revolution, although that too
played an important part. It was also a real Russian patriotism or nostalgia.
Russian songs, Russian music, the fascinating Russian language all
combined with the dream of a better world on the ruins of the old; the

dream was nurtured in the bosoms of the Jews and handed down to their children. I once observed that if the Russians had concentrated on spreading Russian music they might have conquered the world much more readily and certainly less painfully than with their brand of communism.

The nostalgia for things Russian was a salient feature of American-Jewish life in the twenties and thirties and through the Second World War, and very pronounced in Palestine. The *chalutzim* wore Russian shirts, danced Russian dances and sang Russian songs (sometimes with Hebrew words) and maintained an emotional, and frequently political loyalty to the Soviet 'motherland.' Disillusionment set in slowly, for some sooner, for others later. One thing became clear: whatever the virtues or defects of the Russian Revolution, it was not made for the sake of the Jewish people. The ancient socialist slogan that with the liberation of mankind will come the liberation of the Jewish people was blotted out over and over again. Every generation had to learn it anew and the Russians were very generous in repeating the lesson.

The first wave of disillusionment which set in in the early twenties was followed by the works of the *Yevseksiya*, the so-called Jewish Sector of the communist faithful, then by the removal of the Jews from the foreign service (except where it was specifically in the Russian interest to keep them on), then the gradual, progressive and inexorable disappearance of every vestige of Jewish life in the Soviet Union, and concomitantly the trumped up charges against Jews for 'factionalism,' 'cosmopolitanism,' 'economic crimes,' etc., the destruction of the synagogues, the outlawing of Hebrew studies, the Doctors' Trial and so on endlessly. These acts were not merely the side effects of an atheism even-handed in its repression of all religious manifestations. It was, if not exclusively, at least deliberately and emphatically, directed against the Jews and Judaism in the Soviet Union. When the apologists for the Soviet Union (since the Six-Day War their numbers have dwindled) point to the high proportion of Jews in science, education, law, etc., they neglect to mention the consistent effort to displace them at the earliest opportunity. Until the Russians can provide their own professionals, the Jews will do. Three million Jews—a solid ethnic group, deserving as little or as much consideration as a few hundred thousand Volga Germans—have been condemned to spiritual death.

I once asked Moshe Sneh, why, if the Jews are such a thorn in the side of Russia, they are not let out. He is one of the few communists I know with a sense of humor. He replied: 'If the Soviet Union were to open the doors to the Jews they would be faced with a mass conversion to Judaism.'

Every now and then, as I have remarked, there were occasional openings in the curtain and Russians came to Israel. At the first Molecular Conference at the Institute in 1956 there came, surprisingly, a rather large delegation of Soviet scientists. Everything went along swimmingly until one day the chemist, Annushka Weizmann, Dr. Weizmann's sister, recognized the head of the delegation from the laboratories of Petersburg many years before. The meeting was effusively emotional. There was a real and genuine *embrazzo*. From that moment on, the NKVD took over. There was no more mixing with the scientists, no socializing. They came and went as a flock, shepherded by a few NKVDs posing as members of the Russian Embassy staff. It was tragicomical.

In 1959 the first and, as far as I can recall, the last organized group of Jewish tourists from the Soviet Union, artists, writers and distinguished professionals, arrived to spy out the land.

The Foreign Office asked me to show these people the Institute, entertain them for lunch, and in general put out the red carpet. There were thirteen of them. They could not get over the wonders of this Institute in the desert oasis. Then we sat down to a festive luncheon. I made a little speech beginning with the Hebrew phrase: *Ma tov' u'ma na'im shevet achim gam yachad* (How good and pleasant for brothers to sit together). I then told them in Yiddish—which was our only common language—that when two *goyim* are slugging it out, it is best for the Jew to keep out, lest he get hurt. There was one member in the group, apparently the guardian, the *apparatchik*, who didn't quite understand my Yiddish. He jumped to his feet and began to protest. 'We are Russians. We do not know the difference between Jews and Gentiles. We are all equal'—the whole litany. A Russian-speaking member of our staff explained to the guardian of the Revolution that he had misunderstood—that all I meant was that the State of Israel had to be friendly to all powers, east and west, and tend to its own vineyard. This was, in fact, the point I was trying to make. If he understood me differently, it was his own fault for being so perspicacious.

Following this intermezzo, one of the women members of the group rose and made a fiery speech about the Soviet Union, how wonderfully the Jews were treated—witness the high position she held; for good measure she threw in a few complimentary remarks about the future of socialism in Israel.

The lucheon over, Mr. Plotkin, the head of the group, heartily shook my hand, embraced and kissed me and made a gesture as if crossing a knife over his throat, 'They can slit my throat but I will tell the truth about Israel.' It sounded quite genuine.

As I accompanied the visitors to their cars, I noticed that the woman who had made the fiery speech was dragging her feet as if she wanted to be the last to descend the stairs. We paralleled our steps going down. She clutched my hand and said, *sotto voce*, '*Ihr farshteyt doch az ich hab gemust azoy reden,* You understand that I had to say what I did.' That was all, and I understood.

As for Plotkin, I waited for the axe to fall upon him on the altar of Jewish patriotism. Fortunately I didn't hold my breath. A squalid and unspeakably base picture of Israel emerged from under his pen in a small book entitled 'Visit to Israel,' published by *Literaturnoy Gazette*. The book ends with an open letter, in rhyme, addressed to me, Professor M. Weisgal. The gist of it is that all Jews are not brothers; and some Jews he, Gregory Plotkin, would not even deign to call distant cousins. That category includes Jews who weave threads of untruth, who drink 'Bruderschaft' with Bonn, who welcome those who would lynch Paul Robeson, and who dream of invading his country. The poem concludes with a declaration of identity: 'I am a beloved native son of my beloved Ukraine; the Soviet land is dearer to me than life itself; I am its son and there is no other title that I can be called by.'

There were other encounters with the Russians, none of them calculated to inspire admiration. The Weizmann Institute fellowships and tenures for visiting scientists are open to scientists of all nationalities. The Russian Embassy in Ramat Gan asked us to allow a Russian scientist to come to the Institute. 'By all means,' I said to the Embassy secretary. 'Let him apply.' But the Russians don't leave such things as scientific exchange to chance. They would apply for him. The name they offered was unknown to the scientists on the campus. Anyone familiar with scientific intercourse knows how international it is. People working in any specific field, no matter how obscure, are known to each other through their papers or through participation in congresses, whether they live in Kamchatka or in Boston. This particular Russian was nothing but a question mark. I told the secretary, after the preliminary investigations, that he wouldn't do. He protested. I added: 'The man must have some scientific reputation to be accepted.' The Russian continued to press me. Finally I told him what I really thought. 'If you want to send us a scientist, we'll be very happy to have him. We will even lean over backwards to make it possible. But we're not interested in stooges.'

The Institute's mathematicians and geophysicists were very much involved in the International Geophysical Year (1957–8). Joseph Kaplan of UCLA was chairman of the United States committee. Chaim Pekeris, one of our pilgrim scientists and my neighbor, one house removed, attended a meeting in Moscow where the proposal to hold the next conference in Rehovot was unanimously accepted—a mark of tribute to the Institute for its contribution. The Soviet Union was supposed to send five delegates. As is usual in such affairs all countries send in the names of their delegates in advance and barring a major crisis, the delegates show up on schedule. With the Russians, however, it was one day yes, one day no. The day before the conference opened one of them actually turned up. His name was Professor Kolos Ubrakim. Pekeris arranged a reception and the Russian was the beau of the ball. Naturally I went over to greet him with 'Shalom.' His reply was: 'Leshanah haba b'Yerushalayim.' He explained that with proper pronunciation his name, obscured by the Russified spelling, was no more and no less than good Hebrew for 'thunder and lightning.' His father had been a Hebraist as well as a good socialist, and when he was born in the midst of the Russian Revolution which was to bring to mankind the new Ten Commandments, his father recalled the 'thunder and lightning' which accompanied Moses on his trip up the mountain. He has borne the name ever since. As is our custom, the conference ended with a banquet at which each head of delegation said a few words, either in English or his own language. Kolos Ubrakim elected to speak English. He said the following: 'This is a country of miracles [which he pronounced mirahkels]. The first is that you exist. The second is that you have an institute of this standard here. It really belongs either in the U.S. or the USSR or perhaps England. In all my scientific experience I have never encountered such an institute in so small a country. The third miracle is that I'm here.' With that he walked off the platform. I gathered that like Oistrakh he was a colossus and could afford to take chances.

Being an eternal optimist, I never let these minor skirmishes becloud my senses. In 1966, Lillie Shultz, one of my associates in New York, met Yevgeny Yevtushenko, the young Russian poet, during one of his international poetry-reading tours. Lillie, aware of my—by now—somewhat dormant impresario instincts, proposed that I invite him to appear at Yad Weizmann. I did. That was all I dared offer, but I knew that others would get into the act and provide him with a platform. He accepted enthusiastically. I believed it would have been a great experience both for the young poet and for a whole legion of Russia-nostalgic Israelis. Alas, it never came to pass. The Six-Day War intervened. A week or two after I received a letter from Yevtushenko:

Dear Mr. Meyer Weisgal,

Unfortunately by difficult international situations I cannot now accept your invitation to Israel, it must be clear to you. But I hope it will be possible in the future.

Thanks for your invitation.

If there will be a possibility to realize your proposition, will inform you IMMEDIATELY.

Many greetings,
Yevgeny Yevtushenko

As of this writing, the possibility has not yet presented itself. The clouds over our relations with Russia have become, if anything, much darker. But Israel has managed so far to survive the wrath of Soviet power; there is hope that the Russian people will do likewise.

23 In Memoriam: Sharett and Eshkol

I have repeatedly pointed out that though I have been a Zionist all my life, I have never been embroiled in the Zionist political game. I *was* involved organizationally with the ZOA as editor of the journal, National Secretary, and Lipsky's trouble shooter; but my experiences had blotted out any miniscule hankering I might have had for political stardom.

My subsequent association with Weizmann led me again to the fringe of politics, but only to the fringe. I could never work up the necessary loyalty to party—the fundamental stuff of politics. 'I wore the badge of no party and the livery of no faction.' I had friends and foes in all the parties and my sympathies veered from left to center. The Hashomer Hatzair kibbutz movement, in its early puritan days, before it became Mapam, was my ideal. I was a liberal, against extremism either left or right, religious or secular.

This does not mean that politics did not interest me. On the contrary, it fascinated me—from a distance. When I came to settle in Israel, I had no intention of shifting from Zionist politics to Israeli politics. The infighting, the intrigue and the power game in Israel was too much like that of the Zionist movement. Zionist politicians used to go home after Congresses to their jobs as rabbis, newspapermen or businessmen, or just plain intellectuals. In Israel they went home to party meetings.

In Israel too I was never identified with any one party. Indeed I thought the Weizmann Institute would shield me from involvement altogether. I was mistaken. When Weizmann was alive my proximity to him and the widespread illusion that I could get him to do anything I wanted turned me into a sort of buffer. Everybody wanted my support, from Moshe Sneh on the left to Itche Meir Levin on the religious right. Then the Institute itself inevitably involved me with the Establishment in financial, educational, political, and security matters. Finally, I had known them all for so long, and in so many circumstances, during my own and their political transmigrations, that there was hardly a member of the Israel hierarchy who didn't let his hair down—if he had any—over a glass of tea with me. Whether I wanted to or not, I knew much of what was going on in the inner sanctum. Most of the Israel leadership felt free to unburden themselves of their troubles, internal feuds, political shenanigans, intrigues and all the human impulses from which no one, not even the highest, is immune. The smaller the country, the more dense the political environment, the more ferocious the personal feuds. Our home became a kind of Wailing Wall.

During the first fifteen years of Israel's statehood, the scene was dominated by David Ben Gurion for good and for bad. His iron will was the cause of one crisis after another, major, minor, and trivial. It is not surprising, then, that he should have been the major subject of all these lamentations. But it is revealing that the tears were shed not by his opponents from other parties, but by the members of his own party, his dedicated associates and supporters. They include people who are part of Israel's history: Israel Galili, Moshe Sharett, Pinchas Lavon, Levi Eshkol, people who not only helped him to power, but helped preserve him in it.

So it is more in sorrow than in anger that I put pen to paper on this subject, sorrow over the fates of three people, two of whom I loved and admired, and who suffered at his hands: Moshe Sharett and Levi Eshkol, and the third, Ben Gurion himself.

A case can be made for doing as Weizmann did, in the interest of peace and unity and good feeling—omit the unpleasantness. There are rooms full of files, bulging with the juicy tidbits, which, in the course of human events, will become available 'for scholarly purposes.' *De mortuis nil nisi bonum* is no longer practised—it is not until after a person's death (usually at least twenty-five years) that we have access to records and facts that begin to show us both his *bonum* and his *malum*, in short, his wholeness. So *mortuis* now becomes *senioribus;* and I am moved by J.K. Galbraith's generosity to Krishna Menon ('now an old man') in declining to open old wounds, and deleting the angry references and comments which appeared in the *Journal* he was writing in the heat of events.

But this is my autobiography. It is not intended as a scholarly work (though the facts in it can be checked in records when the time comes). But I too lived these events, and they made my life different from what it would otherwise have been, and I intend to tell them truthfully and without rancor. So I have concluded that they must be included, albeit with restraint.

In 1966, for B.G.'s eightieth birthday the Hadassah Organization of America, for unfathomable reasons, asked me to write a piece for the *Hadassah Magazine*. The letter requesting the article began as usual: 'You are the only one . . . ' I was really the *last* one. True, I had just read a delectable little book by my friend Mordecai Tsanin 'celebrating' the event. It was called 'The Decadence of a Messiah' and its motto was an old Yiddish saying: 'Long for the Messiah but pray that he never comes.' I called my article 'Ben Gurion . . . Without Tears.' I made the condition that they exercise no censorship—a condition that they accepted as readily as they broke. But that is neither here nor there. What appeared in print was true, only not everything appeared. I wrote, *inter alia*:

Most great men are simple men, and their essential character is understandable. But David Ben Gurion is certainly not one of them. He is, has always been, a most complicated man, with complicated drives, and complicated methods of functioning.

The character of leadership is not a monolithic entity which lends itself to easy analysis or examination. Throughout history, the men who have come to the forefront of the masses have followed no set patterns; each has been spurred by his own particular drives.

Perhaps one approach to Ben Gurion is to see him in the Zionist context and try to compare him with the two other giants of the movement. Out of the ranks of the devoted and the dedicated, there tower, I think, only those three—Herzl, Weizmann and B.G. And of these, it is B.G. who differs most. Seen against the long perspective of time, perhaps Herzl was farthest from the cause itself; the least Jewish, the most sophisticated, and paradoxically, also the most naive. I have often wondered to what extent he himself understood the implications of his own massive idea. Weizmann, to whom of course I myself was closest, was, I think, the most Jewish, the most subtle; the man who, in himself, bridged East and West most perfectly, and bridging them, bridged also the distance between a personal crusade and an individual avocation. Scientist and states-man combined, he was above all else a Jew, and as such truly a cosmopolitan.

But what of B.G.? Of all of them, he was the most profoundly involved with the Land itself; the *Palestinian* Zionist, the son and the leader, at once, of the Yishuv. Never mind Plonsk [his Kikl]. It was the physical Eretz Yisrael, and later, and even more dramatically, the State of Israel, with which he will be forever identified.

If it is true that history repeats itself, sometimes, surely, this repetition is uncanny. Consider the stories of Abraham, Moses and Joshua. It was Abraham who received the Revelation; Moses who moulded a serf society into a national entity and brought it to the borders of Canaan. But it was Joshua who crossed into Canaan at its head!

And so it was Ben Gurion who realized the vision of Herzl and Weizmann, and who, at the end of the journey from Zionism to Zion, became the one to execute the final history-altering decision. By this one act his place in history is assured.

. . . In the years that followed our first meeting, in the 20s and early 30s, B.G. was primarily a Palestinian leader concerned with the country itself, the specific problems of a working population in a country governed by an alien administration. In those days he was not among the foremost of Mapai's theoreticians. Labor's intellectual leader was Berl Katzenelson: B.G. was his loyal and energetic disciple. Katzenelson, a shrewd observer of men and character, once remarked: B.G. is at his best when he is challenged. Called to the platform to speak, he looks about the hall for his target. When he finds one, he is superb, even if one disagrees with him—but occasionally no target is to be found . . .

Then time, place, the man, and the need converged, as they have a way of doing. By the late 30s and the 40s, with the onrush of the cataclysm, when the battle lines were drawn, it was, of course, B.G. who became the leader *par excellence* of the *Yishuv*. Like Churchill, his personality had equipped him for the moment: so did his intimacy with the country, his innate belligerence, his ability to make his mind up quickly, his defiance of other people's opinions, his lack of objectivity—and his courage.

When emphasis shifted ultimately from the Zionist endeavor in the *Galut* to the actual fight for national survival in *Palestine*, when 1948 arrived at last, Ben Gurion took his rightful place. He became *the* leader of the collective Jewish will to statehood—and to survival.

When Churchill was ousted from power on the very eve of victory, he took it very hard. His wife said to him at the time: 'Who knows, maybe this is a blessing in disguise.' It was. Churchill remained the grand old man of Britain. Had Ben Gurion been ousted or had he withdrawn within a reasonable time after the consolidation of the young state, his place in history would also have been untarnished. It is idle to speculate what developments in Israel would have been without him. Our relations with the Arabs might have taken a different turn; internal developments might have been better or worse. But B.G. clung to his power, intensified it, hung on for fifteen years as a one-man arbiter until he was definitely rejected by the electorate, by his party and by his closest supporters. And in those fifteen years, alongside the good he did—and he did a great deal of good—he also did a great deal of damage, to his country, his colleagues, and mostly to himself.

I said that my home (and my shoulder) was a Wailing Wall in the early days. Israel Galili, the leader of the Palmach, the pre-state military force, was unceremoniously deposed when the Israeli Army was created. He spent a night in Rehovot, bitterly regaling me with the details. My own personal opinion is that B.G.'s disbanding the various military groups which had grown up to resist the British and in their place creating a unified, nonpolitical army was a statesmanlike performance. The history of the development of the defense forces since then has proved that he was right. But his treatment of Galili was crude.

He was unable to share power or even delegate authority to his equals or near equals. Instead of cultivating capable partners in the exercise of government, he pruned them out. Moshe Sneh is another example. Sneh was no doubt the best of the younger leaders, and served as pre-State C.-in-C. of the Haganah. Intellectually he was superior to all of B.G.'s other aides. He began his career as a radical Zionist in Poland, a young disciple of Yitzhak Gruenbaum, the venerable leader of Polish Zionism. He had a degree in medicine, but he practiced politics. In many respects he resembled B. G. but he possessed a charm and sense of humor which B.G. lacked, and he was steeped in *Yiddishkeit*. Their occasional disagreements soon led to a break: Sneh had violated the first commandment.

When B.G. dismissed him he reacted by moving into the opposition, first to Mapam and then to the extreme left and from there to the Communists. His public activities as a member of the Knesset, a writer and speaker, while always brilliant and trenchant, have the overtones of tragedy. Had he remained in the fold, he might have become Prime Minister and he certainly would have had a lot less recanting to do when he returned, as he finally did, to his Jewish loyalties.

Eliezer Kaplan was a case apart. He was never a follower of Ben Gurion. He was the economic and financial brain of the Zionist movement; subsequently he became Israel's first Finance Minister. By the time he reached his pinnacle he was already exhausted, and spent, and suffering from a heart condition. Nevertheless he continued to labor unremittingly, traveling endlessly throughout the world on his mission. When he was finally laid low he said wryly to a friend who had come to comfort him, 'I will survive my heart attack, but,' pointing to a picture on the wall, 'I doubt if I'll survive his attacks.' (These were not the words Kaplan used. I cannot bring myself to quote the original.)

Ben Gurion's bitterest thrusts were against the two people closest to him in Mapai (the Labor Party): Moshe Sharett and Levi Eshkol. Sharett was his Foreign Minister, and for a brief period Prime Minister when B.G. retired from politics to become a farmer in the Negev. But B.G. soon unretired himself, and Sharett was let go. Eshkol succeeded Kaplan as B.G.'s Finance Minister, and was his choice for Prime Minister when he retired a second time.

What is baffling is that for many years these men complained and beat their breasts privately about his ill treatment, and endured it publicly. Eshkol said to me, not long after B.G. returned from Sde Boker to the Prime Ministry, 'At least here we know more or less what he's up to.' Perhaps, but Sharett was off in India, sent by B.G. to persuade Nehru to moderate between Israel and the Arabs, when the Israel Army moved into Sinai (half an hour before the time appointed for the interview), and he felt it as 'a knife in the back.'

I had known Sharett since 1925. We were colleagues of a sort when, in 1927, he was editing the English edition of the Palestine daily, *Davar*, and

With President Zalman Shazar, presenting Manger Prize for Yiddish Literature 1970 to poet Joseph Kerler, new immigrant from the USSR. *below* With Yosef Sprinzak, first Speaker of the Knesset

above Escorting Abba Eban and David Ben Gurion to Weizmann Memorial Assembly with Lola Beer-Ebner looking on. *below* With Zippora and Moshe Sharett in New York

above With Levi Eshkol. *below* With Golda Meir

above With Finance Minister Pinhas Sapir and his Deputy Zevi Dinstein:
'Money I didn't get, but the organization in there is terrific' (see page 351).
below Baron Edmund de Rothschild on one of his visits to the Institute,
with Chani Bergmann and Teddy Kollek

I was producing a Zionist journal in New York; and we met and corresponded. His newspaper training was even less academic than mine. He had been studying at the London School of Economics when he was called back to Palestine and *Davar*. Before returning he spent twenty-four hours in the offices of a London daily. Sharett had an obsession about Hebrew, but not, as some have said, a pedantic one. He was simply a purist about everything he touched, and had a profound feeling for form. Hebrew had to be transformed from a sacred to a profane language, capable of describing the sewage system of Tel Aviv, and he insisted that the Hebrew rendition of sewers be precise in form and pure in derivation. When he became Israel's first Foreign Minister, he led in the practice of Hebraizing Jewish names, changing his own to Sharett, meaning 'servant.' He attempted many times to persuade me to Hebraize my name and finally we agreed on Gal-Lavan. After a while it became clear that the hyphen would get lost and I would end up an Irishman. We therefore dropped the matter.

He did not take easily his ousting from the Premiership; but did not sulk and protest. Instead he took upon himself the onerous and thankless job of Chairman of the Jewish Agency and the World Zionist Organization. In the Israeli hierarchy, one rises from the 'lowliness' of the Zionist Organization to the higher levels of government; to move from the Premiership of a country back to the Zionist Organization is considered a retreat. Sharett, in all humility, accepted the demotion as a challenge to revitalize the ties between the State and the Diaspora. I do not link Ben Gurion's subsequent onslaughts on the World Zionist Organization to his rancor against Sharett. They may indeed have sprung from deep conviction. But his scathing remarks on the movement as useless, antiquated, and impotent were certainly not designed to enhance Sharett's position. I myself have written more than one lengthy treatise on the functions of the world movement and the need for streamlining its apparatus. But I never dismissed it as a dead loss. It was the connective tissue between the State and the Jews of the world. The fact that millions of Jews could not or would not settle in Israel but, nevertheless, felt a close affinity to the country, and a warm desire to further its growth, was meaningless to B.G. There was one blast from him in 1961 on who is and who is not a Jew which stunned the whole Jewish, not to mention the gentile, world. The burden was: If you are a Jew you have to be a Zionist, and if you are a Zionist you have to settle in Israel, period. I remember one devoted American Zionist saying to me: 'What does B.G. want? Does he expect me to embrace Catholicism? If mass conversion will save Israel,

we'll accommodate him.' B.G. almost, but not quite, succeeded in alienating some of the Jews from Israel.

Sharett had been for many years devoted to Ben Gurion and even during
the period of 'demotion' he kept his peace, continuing at his work,
meticulously, trying to repair the movement's institutions and breathe
new vigor into it. It was only when he became convinced that B.G. was
destroying the labor movement in the country that he spoke out, and
unburdened himself of the doubts which had been gnawing for years.
Sharett had devoted most of his life to Mapai, which was the pillar of
Israel's labor movement, and when he saw its principles being trampled
on he rose to its defense. He came to regard B.G. as the single most de-
structive force threatening the cohesiveness of the young State and when
he finally spoke out against him, he became, quite literally, the moral
conscience of the State of Israel. During the tragic years that transformed
Sharett into a prophetic figure, he was fighting his last battle against a fatal
disease. And there was tragic symbolism in the figure of a man in a wheel-
chair, mounting the rostrum of the Mapai Convention in 1964 to speak
out against the man he served for so many years. A few days before his
death, Sharett wrote a letter to *Davar* in which he said:

In his speech yesterday Ben Gurion advocated loyalty to the truth, the pursuit of justice,
the maintenance of comradely relations, and the preservation of the moral values of
the labor movement. I see it as my duty to state that I am amongst those who, on the
basis of their experience, cannot—with all their appreciation of Ben Gurion's great
achievements—see in him the model of a man of truth, pursuer of justice, one who
maintains comradely relations or one who exemplifies the moral values of our movement.

Sharett's funeral became one of the greatest demonstrations of public love
and admiration and identification that Israel had ever seen.

In my reading of history, it was the frustration of the Sinai period which
heralded the downfall of B.G. I was on the scene and in the thick of battle
during the three Israeli wars of 1948, 1956 and 1967. Each had its own
character. The first was not really a 'war.' It was a 'do or die' struggle
without the means to do and with the certainty of death if we failed to do.
In 1956 it was quite different. It was preceded by a reign of Arab terrorism,
with incessant *fedayeen* attacks from the south. Rehovot, being in the
proximity of the Gaza Strip, was highly exposed. There were daily
casualties, even in the long prelude which was more wearing than the
war itself.

I knew little about the political maneuvering of Israel, France and

England in that war, nor was I very much interested. But I was in Rehovot when the fighting broke out.

The war, while giving us respite from the *fedayeen* attacks for a number of years, was considered by some, though not all, a waste of human lives. Strategically, it was a perfect plan. Politically, diplomatically, it was a considerable failure. World public opinion had not been prepared for it; the dangers to which we were exposed were not sufficiently known. Our 'partners,' England and France, had no interest in Israel, and looked only to their own imperial interests. A tyro, I refrained from expressing my views about the conduct of the war; but a few days after B.G.'s statement to the Knesset announcing Israel's withdrawal from the Sinai Paula called me from their Tel Aviv home where B.G. was in bed with a severe cold. She asked me to bring him what he euphemistically called 'The Weisgal pills.' These were a brand of sleeping pills which he liked and with which I had been supplying him for many years. He was lying in his little room next to the kitchen under many blankets with papers and maps all over the place. He was in very bad humor, and stories were never his strong point; nevertheless I insisted on trying to cheer him up with one. Apropos of our retreat, I told him the story of the Jew who comes home at midnight and, sure that his wife is sleeping soundly upstairs, decides to visit the maid. Proceeding carefully on tiptoe through the kitchen, he suddenly upsets a tray of dishes. As the racket subsides his wife's voice comes booming down: '*Mishugener, wie gehs du?* Lunatic, where are you going?' He shouts back: *Shoin, ich geh shoin nisht,* Forget it, I'm not going anymore.' B.G. made a broad gesture with his hand as if to say 'don't act the buffoon this time, it is too serious a business.' I told him then: 'Mr. Ben Gurion, it is written "*lo b'koach ela, b'ruchi,* not by might but by My spirit," and my spirit includes a sense of humor. It is the greatest weapon in our arsenal—the ability to laugh at our own mistakes, our setbacks, even our defeats.' But B.G. laughed at nothing.

During that period Israel was in a state of confusion, with sharp internal conflicts, squalid bickering, personal vendettas, and all the rest. It was as if the old man, then close to eighty, had decided: *Après moi, le deluge,* or, like Samson, 'Let me die with the Philistines.' Over the whole period hovered the infamous 'Lavon Affair.' But before I descend into that morass I will go back a few rungs and tell you about B.G.'s better half, Paula.

Paula Ben Gurion was an authentic 'character.' If I had to sum her up in one sentence I would say: 'Take Vera Weizmann, imagine her very opposite and you have Paula.' She was open, warm hearted, informal to a

fault, an outrageous gossip and, to complete the contrast, likeable. She
was deeply devoted to B.G.—he could do no wrong, although privately,
from time to time, she would be concerned about his abrasiveness. In
most cases, the people he disliked she liked, or feigned to like. Her defense
of them always ended with the phrase: 'What does *he* know about people?'
She never took seriously her position as wife of the Prime Minister. In
fact, she made a point of denigrating the job, or, as she would put it:
'Anybody can become Prime Minister, nobody can be B.G.' How true!
She was the most outspoken person in my experience. Whenever I
brought a distinguished person to her I would warn him in advance:
'Don't be shocked by her. She can, and probably will, say anything.'
And she usually did. Once I took the Duchess of Westminster to meet her.
All the way from Rehovot to Tel Aviv, I primed the aristocratic visitor.
'At all events,' I summarized, 'don't expect much formality.' When I
presented the Lady, Paula had nothing more fitting to say than 'What kind
of *duchess* are you?' When *Exodus* was shooting in Israel, my son Mendy
told me the cast would like to meet Ben Gurion. Of course no one could
get through to him without running Paula's gauntlet, and since she herself
was anxious to meet Paul Newman it was arranged. Mendy presented him
to her. 'You're Paul Newman?' she said. 'You're not even so good looking.' Paul blushed; Mendy wanted to scream.

Maybe she really wanted to be a person in her own right, separate and
apart, not living in the shadow of B.G. In the early days in New York,
where she trained as a nurse, she saw herself as the representative of the
Russian revolutionaries. But it didn't come off. Later, she had to assert
herself by making a career of her irreverence. Any stray thought that
flitted through her mind came immediately to her tongue; and gossip
ran from her tongue faster than her mind could frame it.

Paula's big social hour was at seven in the morning. She was always up at
that hour preparing B.G.'s breakfast. Nobody else could be trusted with
it. She would call me and her first question was always: 'What are you
doing up so early?' Once after a robbery at our house in Rehovot, she
called: 'Meyer, I hear they stole your silver.' 'Yes,' I replied. She: 'What
did you need so much silver for?' When she read in the early morning
papers that I had returned from some trip abroad she would pick up the
phone: 'Meyer, what did you bring me?' She meant it, and always turned
up to collect. Once I turned the tables on her, and called at seven the night
after she arrived from New York, and asked, 'Paula, what did you bring
me?' Her answer was quick: 'Regards from your wife.'

Knowing Paula as I did, I can just hear her, when B.G. was embarked on some of his anti-Eshkol rhetoric: '*Meshugener,* what do you need it for?' Had he been endowed with one-tenth of her humor, he would have saved himself and Israel a good deal of agony.

The 'Lavon Affair' will go down in history, in Israel's history at least, for one reason: it blew the halo off Mr. Ben Gurion's head and revitalized Israel's democratic processes, which had been deteriorating in a cult of personality. It proved what everybody knows, but what many tend to forget: no one is unexpendable.

Pinchas Lavon had been Defense Minister in B.G.'s cabinet until B.G. took over the job himself. A member of a kibbutz, Lavon later became the General Secretary of the all-powerful Histadrut, Israel's labor federation. The 'Affair' centered about what is delicately known as a security mishap. Since I have little taste for cloak-and-dagger adventures, I never bothered to go into it. It was one of those undercover operations which misfired and which make up the hidden weave of espionage and counter-espionage. But it became a *cause célèbre,* on the minutiae of which the destiny of Israel hinged: In the last analysis, according to B.G., the fate of the country was in the hands of a court of inquiry which should establish the guilt of the culprit. That the issue was raised five or six years after the event indicates its irrelevance. Who wrote the letter? Who signed the forgery? Who said what?—and when and why? What was so-and-so's secretary doing in the office when she should have been at the hairdresser's?—these exciting questions agitated the country. The Knesset finally established a commission of inquiry, headed by the Minister of Justice Mr. Pinchas Rosen, one of the most revered men in Israel, whose integrity was unquestioned. Its verdict did not find favor in the eyes of B.G.; he accused the commission of being party to a travesty of justice, and demanded further inquiry and a new commission dedicated to the truth, the whole truth and nothing but the truth. In his opinion, anyone—and that meant practically everyone—who disagreed with him was either a liar, a fool or guilty of moral turpitude. All his speeches and pronouncements—and there were many—were studded with the most pious phrases about justice, truth and righteousness.

One day in 1961 or thereabouts I was in Washington for the Weizmann Institute, and had occasion to meet with a highly placed government official, a non-Jew. Among other things, he asked me what all the shouting in Israel was about, referring to the 'Affair.' I tried my best to explain it to him. When I got through with my recitation he said to me: 'You Jews are supposed to be a smart people, you advise governments all over the world; but when it comes to your own affairs you seem to act rather foolishly. If we in Washington were to concern ourselves, as you do, with every intelligence mishap, we would be doing nothing else. No country, no leadership with any responsibility probes too deeply or even tries to uncover such mishaps. They are usually swept under the carpet. In the whole history of the United States, there was only one incident in which a President, in my opinion, foolishly, owned up to an intelligence mishap, with tragic results.' He was referring to Eisenhower and the U-2. What could I tell him? I sighed.

Finally the country got fed up with the business, but B.G. continued to storm. In 1962 he resigned from the premiership and made Eshkol Prime Minister. Eshkol had played the role of moderator during the 'Affair,' trying to soothe ruffled tempers and prevent what soon became inevitable: a split in Mapai. The basic issue ceased to be the 'Affair'—it was merely the catalyst—the basic issue was unquestioned loyalty to Ben Gurion. Once that became clear, everything proceeded logically and inevitably. B.G. denounced the Mapai leadership, including Eshkol, and called on his loyal stalwarts to abandon the 'party of iniquity and deceit.' About thirty percent of the membership—notable among them Moshe Dayan and Shimon Peres—followed him out of Mapai to establish a new party, Rafi. All this was done in time for the 1964 elections and the main plank in the platform of B.G.'s Rafi was 'Down with Eshkol.' In 1962 he himself had passed the mantle of leadership to Eshkol; by 1964 he proclaimed that Eshkol was 'unfit' to be Prime Minister. Perhaps it rankled that Eshkol had decided to be his own Prime Minister, had made successful visits to the United States, and did not come often enough to Sde Boker to seek advice.

According to Jewish lore, the burial place of Moses is unknown. The Sages have it that his final resting place is unmarked because Jewish tradition does not encourage the cult of personality and God frowned on the notion of the grave of a dead leader elevated to a place of worship. I myself, coming from a long line of rabbis, have my own instinct about what happened. After leading the Jews out of bondage in Egypt and suffering their misbehavior in the desert for forty years, Moses brought them to the edge of the Promised Land. One day he woke up and realized that he was not getting any younger. He looked about the camp and called Joshua. 'Joshua, my son,' he said, 'I am getting old. I have led our people through the desert but now my strength is running out. I want you to take over the job and bring these Jews into the Promised Land.' Joshua agreed. After some reflection, Moses regretted his decision. After all, he had done so much, why not finish the job? So he betook himself to God and said: 'Look, Pop, I've changed my mind. I would like to lead the Jews into the Promised Land.' God looked at him and said: 'My dear Moses, you have rendered high service to the Jews but you have not always obeyed me. I told you to talk to the rock and it would produce water. But no. You had to strike the rock. Now you must be punished. You may not go into the Promised Land. Besides, you've already handed over the leadership to Joshua. You can't push him out now.' Moses was crestfallen but he understood. Nevertheless as a politician he could compromise. 'I'll tell you what. I agree to stay behind but let me at least see the Jews entering the Promised Land. That won't hurt anybody, will it?' Now, the God of Israel is a God of mercy and he said: 'All right. I don't mind your watching.' And he took Moses to Mount Nebo from where he could get a good view. Moses watched Joshua leading the people from victory to victory and the sight of someone else leading the Jews so successfully was too much. In agony he cried to God: 'I don't care what you do with me, but get me out of here. I can't stand it any longer.' God took him at his word, and that is why nobody knows where Moses is buried.

As with Weizmann, B.G.'s differences with Eshkol were not mainly ideological or political. That is not to say there were no such differences; there were very serious ones; but they were of temperament, character, and method.

Eshkol was known as the great compromiser, which got him a reputation for indecision. It is true he lacked fire and eloquence, or, as Abba Eban, after the Six-Day War, put it so well: 'The difference between B.G. and Eshkol is: the one speaks loudly and effectively, pounds on the table and retreats. The other stammers and goes forward.' There is, of course, more to it than this, but the quote is irresistible. It must also be said that B.G. depoliticized the schools; that, with all the tempestuous rhetoric, he acted with statesmanlike caution against the Brass (in his *Diary*, Dayan says, 'The war is over,' and B.G. says, 'That is just the thing you cannot stand'); that he was acutely aware of the limits of Israel's power (as when he ordered Allon back from El Arish, under U.S. and British pressure, knowing that without allies he could not go alone).

That Eshkol always tried to keep peace in his own camp is not to his discredit—it was he, after all, who achieved what B.G. only shouted for: the unity of the fragmented labor parties. Even when his own creation, Rafi, decided to return to the fold, B.G. refused to go along and established himself as a one-man faction in the Knesset. No, Eshkol was not eloquent;

he did not provide *Zukunftsmusik*, but he was wise, he was human, and he got things done.

In one of my early encounters with him, when he was Finance Minister, I had what appeared to be a thorny legal problem: a friend of the Institute had given me £100,000 for the Institute with the proviso that I give ten percent of it to some other needy institution in this country. When I passed these instruction on to Dr. Benjamin Bloch, our Administrator, he told me such a transaction could not be recorded. I said, 'OK, I'll go to Eshkol.' I told him: 'My Rehovot *chochem* says it's not legal, the comptroller will object, we cannot accept money given this way etc.' Eshkol listened, and told me a story. 'When I was a young man in Degania my job was that of a kind of traveling agent for the kibbutz. I used to go out in the morning, sell crops, buy equipment, get loans, purchase feeds, make mortgages. In the evening I would return to the kibbutz secretary and dump a batch of papers on his desk, IOU's, slips, receipts, notes. One day he said to me: "Shkolnik [his original name], this can't go on any longer. It is impossible to make head or tail of your doings." My answer was "Just because you don't know how to write you want me to stop doing business?" Go back to Rehovot and tell your *chochem* to learn how to write.'

The greatest compliment that I can give Eshkol is that he was a Kikl Jew—warm-hearted, full of humor, kind and generous. His generosity was not the generosity of affluence, it was of the spirit: he never had a private penny to his name. He was always a kibbutznik: he considered Degania his home. When B.G. started his violent-rhetoric campaign against him during the elections in 1964, I was indignant enough to take advantage of an opportunity to vent my feelings. My friend, Jon Kimche, editor of the *Jewish Observer and Middle East Review*, wanted an interview with me on the election issues. One of his questions was 'What do you consider to be the fundamental differences between Mr. Ben Gurion and Mr. Eshkol? Do you see it as a personal or as a political issue that has its roots further back in Zionist politics? (Please use only language fit to print.)'

I answered in accordance with my views—and in language which would meet with the approval of the Pope—but was naive enough to think that Kimche was really interested in my views. Otherwise why ask me for them? Moreover, he himself had stipulated 'statesmanlike fireworks.' So I gave them to him.

In a letter informing me that it 'would be a mistake for us to publish it' and 'an even greater mistake for you to appear in print with this' he ended: 'I had hoped that your interview would be on a more Olympian plane but instead you have reduced virtually every question to one of personalities.' I composed a letter to Mr. Kimche, which, like the interview, remained locked away in his files. But I too keep files. And though my wrath and interest in the whole sordid affair has long passed, I was very much tempted to disinter the questions and answers as well as the lethal correspondence that followed the editor's refusal to publish the requested interview. But when I came face to face with such delectable phrases (my own) as 'power-hungry coterie,' 'depths of iniquity,' 'supergods and little gods,' I decided this time to follow Galbraith's example and leave these morsels to future generations.

Eshkol was returned to power with a thumping victory. The country was seventeen years old and reaching maturity. It didn't need a strong man.

One of the more interesting accusations B.G. continued to make against Eshkol, before and after the elections, was that Eshkol was not paying proper attention to the military needs of the country. Eshkol needs no testimony from me here. The Six-Day War is testimony enough. It is interesting that when the war was over and a foreign journalist asked B.G. what he thought of the Government's conduct of it, he replied: 'The Government didn't fight the war, the Army did.'

Eshkol died in office in February, 1969. I was at the time in Caracas, Venezuela. My health was not good and my 'advisors' withheld the news from me, knowing I would fly to the funeral, leaving the Weizmann Institute campaign in the lurch and perhaps doing myself physical harm. They told me only when it was too late for me to leave. I asked that the dinner scheduled for that evening be, instead, a memorial service, and I made this eulogy:

I am here today, representing no organization and no institution, only myself, to bid farewell to Levi Eshkol, a friend and colleague with whom I shared for decades the joys and sorrows in the building of the Jewish National Homeland and the State of Israel. Circumstances beyond my control made it impossible for me to be in Jerusalem today, where I should have been, and where with all my heart I wanted to be.

It is too soon to assess the role played by Eshkol in the past forty years and more, from very humble beginnings to the pinnacle of power. I trust it will not be considered impertinent of me to paraphrase Abraham Lincoln: The world will little note nor long remember what I say here, but it can never forget what he did there. All Israel is dotted with his achievements, from Degania on the Sea of Galilee to the depths of the Negev.

We bid farewell to this man, deeply suffused with Jewish wisdom and rich in humility. Levi Eshkol died of a heart attack, but also of a broken heart. 'Ingratitude' (to continue my 'impertinence') 'more strong than traitors' arms/Quite vanquished him.' Farewell, dear friend. Shalom, shalom.

Ben Gurion made no eulogy for Eshkol, as he made none for Sharett.

Shimon Peres, one of B.G.'s staunch supporters, made a special trip to Sde Boker to plead with him unsuccessfully to attend Eshkol's funeral. B.G. clinched the argument with, 'He needn't go to mine either.'

At this writing he goes on, restless and tumultous, still playing his role as fiery prophet, defender of the truth, conveyor of the Word. In 1966 when I wrote that article for his eightieth birthday I concluded with a wish (deleted from the printed text) which I repeat now:

'Koneh olamo b'sha'a achat,' says the Talmud. One can achieve one's immortality within an hour. Perhaps one can lose it as quickly. My own birthday wish for Ben Gurion is that, in the quiet of his desert study, he ponder a lovely verse from the Psalms:

'So teach us to number our days
That we may apply our hearts to wisdom.'

24 Summing-up at Seventy

I was seventy in 1964 and my birthday, in November, coincided with the twentieth anniversary of the founding of the Weizmann Institute. This happy coincidence naturally produced a spate of combined festivities in various parts of the world, in which I was alternately venerated as an old man about ready for burial and admonished as irresponsible for contemplating retirement. One day, in the midst of it all, I received a visitor from the World Zionist Organization. 'Mr. Weisgal,' he said to me with appropriate reverence, 'I have come to ask your permission to submit your name to the next Actions Committee as a 'virilist.' In Zionist parlance, when you lose your virility you become a virilist. It is a title reserved for nice Jews and good Zionists who stay alive too long. Having just recently agreed to stay on the job a little longer, I told the man to go home and come back when I was eighty.

There is an old saying borrowed from the French Senate: 'Zionists sometimes die, they never resign.' I wanted to prove an exception, and if I succeeded only five years later, when I was seventy-five, it was not from want of trying.

I had once planned to retire in anticipation of my sixty-fifth birthday. I felt that my promise to Weizmann had been fulfilled: the Institute had grown to maturity with an international reputation as a scientific center; the Yad Weizmann Memorial had been firmly established; Mrs. Weizmann had almost forgotten my injuries to her 'Roman Wall'; the flowers were blooming and the trees were growing. I began to confide to friends and members of the family that the day was about to arrive when I would become a free man. It was not to be. Dewey Stone and Harry Levine stopped me before I began. 'Are you crazy? You're at the height of your powers. Sixty-five is no time to retire [etc., etc.].' I submitted, but for a reason I understood better than they: I had not yet produced a successor.

The complications of my involvement with and responsibility for the Institute were manifold. I combined many functions, some willingly, others reluctantly. When I wondered aloud whence I drew my stamina, my wife would reply, 'You love every minute of it.' Of course, I could not otherwise have withstood the strain.

After assembling scientists, my primary concern was raising money. Anyone familiar with a scientific institute knows that in addition to its enormous daily consumption it must provide for investment in building and expansion. Dr. Weizmann once said to me: 'Meyer, when you see a scientist strolling around the grounds, apparently doing nothing, let him be. He is thinking. If you see him with a pretty girl on his lap, leave him alone. He is getting inspiration. Let them be free and never, never interfere with their work. But one thing I want to warn you about. Don't let them get near the *shissel*, the cash box. If you do you are a ruined man. Scientists don't spend money, they burn it.'

In the years that followed, they (and I too) burned quite a lot of money. But we weren't ruined. In 1956 in my report to the Board of Governors I said:

For one thing, I have discarded the generally accepted belief that scientists are nervous, naive and fragile beings, inclined to be loosely coordinated in mind—the syndrome commonly called absentmindedness. Good scientists, I have come to learn, are usually men of dynamic energy and a wealth of imagination over which they have effective control. Their absentmindedness, if any, becomes perceptible only when financial matters are broached, that is, when the issue at stake relates to our financial resources versus their scientific needs. I have learned to compromise on such occasions—by accepting the scientists' views. As a result, I think I am fair in saying that by and large they have given us a more difficult time than vice versa. But they have given us something much more enduring: an institute of science standing on a par with, if not higher than any comparable institution anywhere in the world. If I never tire of repeating this it is because we have come to take the eminent position of the Institute for granted, forgetting sometimes that this is an attainment perhaps unique, and certainly extraordinary, for a scientific institution functioning in a tiny country, somewhat removed from the mainstream of intellectual endeavor—and this within the space of only a few years.

I never had cause to change my views on this subject and never had any regrets, even when the *shissel* was not merely empty but full of IOU's.

The New York Times reporter Alfred Friendly Jr. once asked me what measuring rods I used for assessing the reputation of the Weizmann Institute. I told him that there were several standards. One, the number of scientists from abroad who visited us regularly either to learn or teach or do research; two, the number of papers by our scientists published in recognized journals throughout the world; three, the number of inter-

national scientific conferences held at Rehovot; four, the number of
invitations extended to our scientists by other institutions of higher
learning; and five, the size of our deficit. Mr. Friendly eliminated the
first four yardsticks and said, of the last, by that criterion our reputation
was enormous.

Actually I learned very early that scientists were not interested primarily
in high salaries (at least until recent years). They wanted good equipment,
good working conditions and decent homes and surroundings. Above
all they didn't want to be harassed by their wives on the wherewithal
to buy milk for the children. We must have succeeded in creating attractive
conditions—we have remained immune to the 'brain drain.' At most
a sprinkling of scientists have left the Institute for greener pastures, or
what they hoped would be greener pastures, all through our own fault.
Some returned.

Weizmann, of course, thoroughly understood science and scientists;
he was less perspicacious when it came to money. Once when I told him
I was departing from Rehovot because the *shissel* needed refilling he
said: 'Before we had a State I understand it was necessary for you to go
around the world begging. But now we have not only a State, we have
a post office. Why don't you sit still and let your clients send in their
cheques through the mail?'

There may come a day when the head of the Institute will sit in an
office opening envelopes, but I doubt it. Heads of academic institutions
usually have to work very hard for their money. I know I did.

Popular legend has it that I have a closely guarded secret formula
for getting money. The truth is less exciting and more exhausting. I
was never what is called a professional fund raiser. A fund raiser is someone
who can raise money for anything, from soap bubbles to the Brooklyn
Bridge. My only talent in this field was infecting people with my own
enthusiasm. Neither soap bubbles, nor even the stocks and bonds of William
Rosenblatt could have spurred me to collect a penny. Believing
as I did in the Weizmann Institute, I was able to infuse others with my
belief. I traveled long routes seeking out people who, having made their
millions, were wondering why. Nicholas Murray Butler, President of
Columbia, used to regale my brother Josh with stories when he bought
his morning paper. I was nibbling courses in journalism at Columbia
in those days, and I never suspected that these stories would one day be
an inspiration to me. Butler used to say that a man passes three stages
in life: the first is the stage of accumulation. At this point you leave him
alone. The second stage is contemplation. Now is the time to flutter

about him. The third stage is distribution. Now is the time to be on the spot, and deliver the kill. There were substantial numbers of Jews all over the world who had arrived at stage three. I used to seek them out at dinner parties, country clubs, private gatherings, public banquets, yachting trips (for which I was not particularly suited), and the like. Others sought me out, in New York, in Rehovot, in Europe. These millionaires I used to call 'my customers.' I was selling something that they wanted to buy: some a piece of immortality, their names on a building; some the privilege of being associated with a renowned scientific institution in Israel. Some wanted to impress their alienated intellectual children; others wanted to buy off a bad conscience. A very few didn't know what they wanted, they only knew that they should want something.

There were times when I felt like a prostitute, decking myself in my tinsel—that is my tuxedo—to woo some Jew overburdened by his possessions. But for the most I played it straight and ended up not only with money for the Institute but with people—friends. One such was Siegfried Ullmann.

Siegfried Ullmann came from an orthodox Jewish family in a small town in Germany. Usually when a German Jew is orthodox there is no limit to his piety. Every custom is elevated to dogma. Siegfried, who left Germany as a young man, managed to liberate himself from strict orthodoxy but he remained a traditional Jew. His equally orthodox partner, Ludwig Jesselson, never removed his orthodox blinkers. The two men ran a vast international business in iron, steel and copper. Ullmann came to visit the Institute and it was a case of love at first sight. He was brought to me by Leo Sachs. Ullmann wanted to contribute then and there an enormous sum of money. One of my theories is that it is not good to take money from people who are guests at your home; it is neither good manners nor good business. I told Mr. Ullmann that I would be in New York shortly, where we could meet; he would have time to sort out his impressions and emotions and I would look into the present needs of the Institute and come to him with a concrete suggestion. When I arrived in New York Ullmann called me, not I him, and we met many times thereafter. His wife and his son Jacob also became good friends. His original gift of a million dollars grew to three and half million for the Ullmann Institute of Life Sciences.

A year or so before he died he asked to see me. He was an art collector and an amateur painter, and wanted me to have his art collection appropriately housed at the Institute. Then he made another request. He wanted to be buried in Rehovot. He must have had a premonition, for shortly after he died, and I found myself in a wretched predicament. He had not set this wish down in his will, it had been a confidential request. I was afraid of looking like a body snatcher. Fortunately he had also confided in Jesselson, and Jesselson's testimony, like his orthodoxy, was respected by Siegfried's family. If our friendship grew out of his generous impulse toward the Institute, it quickly transcended it. There were others with whom the pattern was similar. I met them first as 'customers' and in the course of time discovered them to be friends. A lot of money passed between us but none ever came between us.

John Simons, the man who gave me 41,000 Swiss francs for the publication of the Georgian Jew's masterpiece, was another example. From the moment we met, he latched on to me and my wife. He would confide private affairs to me: his successes, his failures, his ambitions—and his infatuation with a very charming lady whom he wanted to marry. He was divorced and lived in Lausanne. A visit to Lausanne was imperative whenever we passed through Switzerland. One evening we were having dinner at the Beau Rivage with this lady friend, and he produced an elegant diamond ring, saying to her, 'This is for you, darling.' She demurred, but after much pleading on his part she relented, on one condition: that it eventually become the property of the Weizmann Institute. Not long after, we received a legal document stating that in the event etc., the ring is the rightful property of the Institute. It was worth $55,000.

When the American Committee for the Weizmann Institute celebrated my seventieth birthday at a New York banquet, Simons brought a cheque for $100,000 in honor of Shirley and Meyer, accompanied by a letter full of sentiment for 'the man who' and 'without his life's companion' and so on. He also intimated to me that there was much more where that came from, and he would reveal the catch to me only if I visited him at St. Moritz on one of his skiing and tobagganing jaunts. He was in his sixties and had a 'heart condition,' which did not prevent his living it up to the hilt. On my way back to Israel I stopped off in Switzerland (I had only one evening to spare) after requesting Josef Cohn's assistant, Renate Bamberg, a capable woman and scion of a great Zionist family, to make the arrangements, and include herself in them. I fancied that her charms would not hurt any transaction that lay ahead of me.

During the evening Simons began to unfold his fanciful idea to me. He was interested in cancer research. As the Weizmann Institute had an international reputation in that field through Isaac Berenblum, the head of the Department, he was prepared to raise a hundred million dollars,

including, of course, his own fortune, for cancer research to be implement-
ed in Rehovot. He would write to the Pope, Nasser, Tito, Adenauer,
Kennedy, Rockefeller, Melon, every head of state, East and West, travel
to all these places at his own expense and 'come back with the bacon.'
I was fascinated by the naiveté of the proposal; it reminded me of Dr.
Jacob's 'cure' which was to gain us the Jewish State. I pointed out to
him all the difficulties, but nothing fazed him. 'Just let me have a letter
authorizing me to do this and make me the Chairman of the project.'
I knew that nothing could possibly come of it except the loss of his own
fortune but I yielded to his compulsion. He made one more condition.
He had just built a new apartment and in it was a suite especially for me
and Shirley, which we were to use whenever we were in Switzerland.

A few months later Mr. E. Spier of Amsterdam, one of his trustees,
informed me of his death. Except for specific legacies to members of
his family, I, i.e. the Weizmann Institute, was his sole heir. Like Ullmann,
his final request was that he be buried in Rehovot. With him in the grave
is his hundred-million-dollar project.

The effect of this 'talent' for collecting people was that my home in
Rehovot became open house, and it was difficult to distinguish between
work and play. My social life and my money-making jaunts were peculiarly intertwined. Shirley was probably the only other person in a roomful
of fifty who knew whether I was discussing art for art's sake with a jewel-
bedecked woman of eighty or leading her on to the ultimate seduction
of her bank account. I myself sometimes lost track of my intentions.
What it all finally added up to was that I was a fixed asset for the Institute.
My style or stratagems on this front were highly personal. They could
not be easily transferred, like an office or a title, to a successor.

My quest for funds for the Institute was not limited to a circle of millionaires. This would have been shortsighted and finally self-defeating. If
I wanted to retire, eventually, I had to secure a sound financial base for
the Institute, independent of my personal appeal.

As the reader may have gathered by now, I work in waves and flashes
of inspiration. They are not uniformly good but sometimes they yield
results. One day, in 1959, in New York, an emissary of John Foster Dulles
called to discuss something important with me. The United States had
seven or eight million surplus pounds in Israel (among millions more)
which they wanted to distribute to various institutions as gifts. Very
nice. What would I advise him to do? I gave him what I thought was good
advice. 'Don't fritter away the money on a hundred and one different

projects. Pick five or six big things. It will be good for Israel and for the United States.' I mentioned the Hebrew University, the Technion, the Weizmann Institute, the contemplated Israel Museum in Jerusalem, and one religious project. He was 'overjoyed' with my advice and a few weeks later, ensconced at the Dan Hotel in Tel Aviv, he began to distribute American largesse in small doses in all directions. The Weizmann Institute received a generous gift of a few hundred thousand pounds which I promptly returned to the gentleman. I went to Mr. Ogden Reid, then the American Ambassador, and told him in my purest diplomatese what I thought of the business. A good ambassador, he remained unperturbed, saying only, 'I suppose you would have been happier if the entire amount had been given to the Weizmann Institute?' I protested. I wasn't thinking that at all. As a taxpayer in the United States, I simply hated to see American money being wasted in this manner. Then in one of my flashes from the blue I said, 'As a matter of fact, I don't want any gifts from the U.S. Government. I want a long-term loan, and what's more, I will take all your unused Israeli pounds and will return to you good American dollars.' Reid's interest was excited. 'Are you serious?' he asked. 'Of course I am serious. I was never more serious in my life.' 'Do you know,' he asked, 'that you have to get permission from the Israeli Government?' I didn't know but assured him that it was only a technicality.

By the time I was knocking on Eshkol's door in Jerusalem, the entire plan had crystallized in my mind. The American Government would lend us twenty-five million dollars payable in their surplus Israeli pounds. The Institute would return the loan over a long period of time with the dollars it collected abroad. It would give us the ready cash to build, expand and complete the Institute and maintain the new laboratories. My 'customers' could build in haste and repay at leisure. After such a *coup* I would be able to retire and rest under my fig tree.

Eshkol was not enthusiastic but he was not opposed. He did ask, however, who would guarantee the loan. I said I would. He smiled as if to say: Look who's talking? Finally he said, 'Go see Zevi Dinstein (Eshkol's Deputy Minister of Finance). If you can convince him of the soundness of the idea, I will go along.'

To make a very, very long story as short as possible, Dinstein agreed with certain modifications, namely that the loan be given in three and a half-million-dollar installments over seven years. A few days later I was on my way to Washington. I went to see my friend, the highly respected David Ginsburg, at one time a Supreme Court law clerk to one of those nine legal geniuses on the Bench. He advised me to see C. Douglas Dillon,

the Secretary of the Treasury. My audience with him lasted about five
minutes, and he handed me over to a man named John Leddy. I didn't
know then, but I know now that he was one of the more brilliant minds
in the Treasury. 'I see what you're after,' he said. 'You want to establish
immortality on the installment plan at two percent interest.' 'Mr. Leddy,'
I answered, 'you hit the nail on the head.' With a sigh that could be heard
all the way to India and Pakistan he added, 'If only you could bring me
similar propositions from a few dozen other countries where billions
are involved, I would accept them all.'

From then on in, it was just a question of stamina. A.I.D., the Agency
for International Development, was intent on getting the guarantee of
the Israel Government. I knew this was impossible. I said the American
Committee for the Weizmann Institute would guarantee the loan. This
was a novel idea. Governments like to deal with governments. With
great dexterity and an unrivaled knowledge of the wheels within
the wheels of the government hierarchy in Washington, David Ginsburg
navigated all shoals and the agreement was eventually signed. While
all this was going on, the Israeli pound was devalued and so what would
have been forty-five million pounds became seventy-five million pounds.
What is more, in case the story seems drawn out, 1959 had meanwhile
become 1961.

By this time, when the first ten and a half million pounds were about
to be handed over to the Institute, there was a new (and excellent) Ambas-
sador, Walworth Barbour, a new President of the United States, John
F. Kennedy, and a new (and formidable) Finance Minister of Israel,
Pinhas Sapir. Eshkol was Prime Minister. When I came to the American
Embassy, it was clear that all the paraphernalia of publicity had been
alerted. Half the senior staff was present, reporters and photographers
were all over the place. I whispered to Mr. Barbour, 'Mr. Ambassador,
I don't want any publicity on this thing.' 'Why?' he asked in amazement.
I told him that once the Jews got wind of the business he would have no
peace. He was perceptive enough and quick enough on the trigger to
say, 'I get your point.' And so the secret lasted three years, after which
everybody who had a cause started to move in. Especially our religious
establishment and their representatives in the United States. (The American
Government seems to have a weakness for these characters, who hang
around the Senators and Congressmen and promise the delivery of votes
on election day.)

I claimed a 'patent' on the idea, and with the decisive help and sympathy
of Sapir and Dinstein, and a good deal of storming around in Washington

and Jerusalem, we got the twenty-five million, plus another three and a half million as a bonus for my copyright.

We were thus able to spend some eighty-seven million pounds to consolidate the Institute. The happiest man on campus was Gershon Dror, the administrator and man in charge of the building program. He dealt like Croesus with contractors, paying money in advance and skinning them alive in the process. The entire program was completed at two or three percent (Dror denies even this discrepancy) above the original estimate, an unheard-of achievement in Israel, or anywhere else for that matter. Thirty or forty percent is the customary 'discrepancy.'

Before leaving the 'Washington-Rehovot Axis' I return to Sapir and Dinstein. Pinhas Sapir is a man of enormous energy and financial astuteness. Indeed he has managed at times to mesmerize even me into believing that he had given the Institute money when in fact he was only transferring through the Treasury some of my own hard-won dollars. Most of my trips to Jerusalem, or to his little house in Kfar Saba, to enlist help for the Institute were not in vain. He at least had a real understanding of the importance of scientific research, which cannot be said of many of those in the government who considered the Weizmann Institute a white elephant, or at best an extravagance.

Once, however, my labors were in vain. I had spent weeks and months preparing, with innumerable meetings and interminable memoranda, a statement for his poverty-stricken Finance Ministry; it should have, but did not, loosen the pursestrings of his Director General. Walking out with Sapir, through the long corridors of the Treasury, I told him the story of the two panhandlers at the gates of the House of Rothschild arguing about what strategy they would employ to extract money from the old Baron Edmund. They decided that only one of them would go up, the other would wait on the sidewalk. The first one went up to the third-floor elegant office of the great Baron. He told the flunkey at the top of the stairs that he had come for a donation for his widow and orphans, whereupon he was promptly and unsympathetically kicked downstairs. On the second floor a second flunkey delivered him in the same manner to the first floor, where he was picked up by a third and tossed out on his ear. When the first panhandler asked him eagerly, 'How much did you get?' he replied, 'Money I didn't get, but the organization in there is terrific.' Sapir said, 'I get the point. How come we never get any accolades from you about our organization?'

But when I actually resigned from the Presidency of the Institute, Sapir made a most becoming gesture of largesse in the presence of his Deputy

Finance Minister, Zevi Dinstein, Honorary Treasurer of the Institute. Dinstein was actively interested in the Institute, and took seriously his 'honorary' job. With a show of deep emotion, as if he had been personally orphaned by my departure from the Elysian Fields of Science, Sapir told me he would recommend to the Prime Minister that a substantial grant be made outside the regular budget in my honor for past services to the State of Israel and my role in the creation of the Weizmann Institute. My only response was a hearty embrace.

My involvement with the Institute did not, of course, end with the balance sheet; nor even with the endless round of entertaining, which followed as the night the day on the heels of every cornerstone-laying, dedication, new plaque, or other intimation of immortality. My main purpose was to create a living image of Weizmann's dreams and ideals.

I was among other things the Institute's caretaker. Whenever I returned from one of my sojourns abroad the first thing I would do—literally, before going home—was to take a drive around the grounds of the Institute. Before there were roads I would get out and walk—which is why we soon had paved roads leading everywhere. I simply don't like walking. It wasn't to check up on the scientists to see if they were working. They knew better what they were doing than I could even guess. I was inspecting the physical appearance of the campus. The architecture I left to the architects and the landscaping to the gardeners but I was the chief and self-appointed custodian of the way it looked. It was an obsession with me. I had the peculiar notion that the exterior and what went on inside were inextricably linked. For a long time this was not an accepted principle in Israel. Sloppiness was always excused by some mystical reference to the 'pioneering spirit.' Laundry on a front porch, any litter, bicycles cluttering up the entrances to buildings or houses, would send me into a rage. I didn't find it picturesque. I would shout and storm and stomp. The people around me and within hearing distance—and my voice in its fuller octaves carries rather far—would tremble. Simon Legree was back! I didn't care. I wanted the place clean. And I made no class distinctions. I used the same tones on the lowliest gardeners that I used on the wives of the scientists. 'Get that **** out of here' was my battle cry. And it worked. Wives began to hang their laundry in the back yards. Bicycle racks were put up inside the entrances. Construction foremen discovered that it was possible to restrict and even camouflage the areas of disarray. People began to care, and the war was over. A local legend had it that Mrs. Heine Eisenberg, the wife of one of our chemists, was bawling out her young son. After she finished her *gevalden*, the little brat turned on his mother, 'Who do you think you are—Weisgal?'

The families at the Institute didn't have much cause for complaint. There was plenty of playground for the children—trees, lawns, bicycle paths and, eventually, a swimming pool and recreation park. The pool and park were built by Miriam Sacher and bear the name of 'The Shirley and Meyer Weisgal Recreation Centre.' It was characteristic of Miriam to make this kind of gesture. The rest of The Family, the Marks and the Sieffs, went in for science and culture; Miriam went in for things that gave people a kick. She likes what she likes and makes no bones about it. Every summer she turns up in Rehovot with six swimming trophies for the youngsters who win the meets at the pool. Of all the members of that illustrious family, Miriam is the one I am closest to. She is the most reticent of the lot, the least conspicuous publicly, adhering faithfully to the biblical injunction 'Let her works praise her in the gates.' It is to her charming estate, Berrydown, near Basingstoke, England, that I retreat when the going gets rough, which is frequently. She has that rare quality of utter goodness unadulterated by foolishness. She feigns a complete lack of sentimentality, with her direct, clipped, no-nonsense talk. But her actions, her generosity and her concern give her away. One of the most pleasurable things I ever did—my last official act as President of the Institute in 1969—was to make Miriam an Honorary Fellow of the Institute.

As I said a few paragraphs back, I shouted at the gardeners with the same enthusiasm as at the scientists and their wives. This direct confrontation had a peculiar effect. It made me accessible to everybody. You can't shout at people and then ignore them. You shout and then open half an ear to their explanations. The explanations are long and drawn out so you end up with 'All right, come and see me about it.' The 'it' in most cases of course had nothing to do with the original shouting. What happened, good or bad, was that everyone at the Institute—the scientists, their wives, sometimes their children, the administrators, the technicians, the charwomen, the gardeners—came to look upon me as an ear for their problems, dispenser of justice, purveyor of needs, settler of disputes, advisor to the lovelorn, etc., etc., etc.—and three etceteras would still not cover the field. I am told this is not the way to run an institute, it produces a type of paternalism which is inimical to efficiency. But I still believe a touch of humanity is worth more than a bushel of efficiency. It may confuse areas of authority and complicate decision making. What of it? In twenty years we built a great scientific institute and in addition made a lot of people happy. At the beginning we were a small compound;

there were no established hierarchies; there was an atmosphere of egalitarianism; if so-and-so had a baby it was obvious that he needed a larger flat; if I could help Chaim Yankel, the driver, get his mother-in-law to a heart specialist, it was a *mitzvah*; if the biologist was having an affair with the chemist's wife, couldn't I talk to him—after all, I knew his parents; and so forth and so on. The Institute grew, the staff expanded, the pattern remained unchanged. It caused me considerable headache and ate up a lot of valuable time but I served as an informal court of appeals against the crasser forms of bureaucracy which inevitably appear in any burgeoning establishment. And I knew what was going on onstage and behind the scenes. The scientists came to me with their troubles, cried on my shoulder. Sometimes I could help, sometimes I couldn't, so I cried with them, which also helped. I knew many of them intimately. On the whole there was more mutual affection than there was animosity, although animosity reared its head from time to time. And in the long run I think I did more good than harm.

This kind of multiple involvement created the myth that I was irreplaceable. The fact that I derived great satisfaction from my work and, because of my temperament, could not be other than totally immersed in what I was doing, convinced many who should have known better that I too considered myself unexpendable. This was not the case. *Sui generis* I was, but not devoid of common sense. As far back as 1956 I proposed to the Board of Governors a restructuring—as they call it nowadays— of the Institute's institutions. We had no President. Since Weizmann's death that office had remained empty. I felt that as a mark of tribute to him it should remain empty for a time. But in 1956 the time had come to fill it. My proposals included a President and a number of Vice Presidents to share the responsibilities and functions; a committee would look into the situation and come up with suitable candidates. After listening to my exposition, Sir Robert Robinson, the Nobel chemist and our elder scientist, so to speak, said to the Board: 'Why must you look for a president? You've got one already and he's sitting here. He already functions as one.' This was quite true but not everybody was as enthusiastic as Sir Robert, and frankly I was perfectly willing to continue as Chief Executive—I had a strange feeling about assuming Weizmann's title. And so the search began.

There were rumors floating around at the time that Aubrey Eban was about to retire from the Israel Embassy in Washington and from his post as Israel Ambassador to the United Nations. His reputation was at its zenith. He was the Voice of Israel spoken in pure Oxbridgian; at the

UN they heard a new Churchill. My search was violently interrupted by the Tenth Anniversary celebrations, but on one of my visits to New York I attended an event at the Polo Grounds together with Aubrey, during which I tried out the idea on him. It was agreed between us to keep it secret until he had a chance to make up his mind. As is usual in diplomatic circles we arranged a code. I would invite him to speak at the Weizmann Memorial Assembly on November 2, 1959. If the answer was affirmative it meant he was ready to accept.

I played the whole thing very close, never revealing even to the Chairman of the Board, Dewey Stone, or the President of the American Committee, Abraham Feinberg, what I had up my sleeve. In the meantime, our friends in England headed by Marcus Sieff, the Deputy Chairman of the Board, also had a brilliant idea in the form of a retiring ambassador, Eliahu Elath, Israel's Ambassador to the Court of St. James's. This information was conveyed secretly to Dewey. Now Dewey and Anne Stone were intimate friends of Aubrey and Suzy Eban and at the first opportunity Dewey sounded Aubrey out on the London suggestion. Eban listened very attentively. It was probably the first time in his life that he was at a loss for words. He finally said: 'I think you had better consult Meyer.' The following morning Eban got stuck in Boston because of fog and called me in New York telling me what had occurred the night before. I immediately called Dewey and asked him to come to New York the following day and when I told him the whole story he exclaimed: 'Now I understand why Aubrey was speechless.' There was subsequently some embarrassment in my relations with Eliahu Elath, who eventually became the President of the Hebrew University. But over the years friendly relations developed again.

Lillie Shultz was at that time working for me as Director of the Tenth Anniversary celebrations in New York. Lillie had been secretary of the American Jewish Congress for many years, after which she joined Freda Kirchway, the editor of *The Nation*. When Eban's affirmative answer arrived, I engaged Lillie to do some thinking on how to launch Eban's inauguration as President of the Institute. As usual she gave birth to a brilliant idea, and thus was born the International Conference on Science in the Advancement of New States, over the first of which Mr. Eban would preside as the new President.

The Board of Governors was overjoyed at Eban's acceptance. Even Mrs. Weizmann thought it a good idea. But it soon became clear that Eban's presidency was essentially titular. He was interested primarily, if not exclusively, in politics. The Institute became for him a temporary

abode until he was invited into the Government. He joined with
alacrity.

For some time he rode both horses. As a dignified spokesman for the
Institute, he was certainly *ne plus ultra*. But he had no inclination to get
involved in the daily affairs of the Institute. I remained the chief executive
and continued to carry the burden. Eban was more and more sucked into
the vortex of political life, and his career makes an interesting study.
He had been a staunch follower of Weizmann and one of his brilliant
and eloquent young associates after the war. Weizmann sent him to the
United Nations during the crucial days of partition and he stayed on there
as Israel's representative after the State was established. By nature he was a
man of moderate views, highly educated, fluent in a half a dozen languages,
nonparochial, a born diplomat.

There is a story, probably apochryphal, but with elements of truth,
that at the time of the Suez Campaign of 1956 Eban spoke out very
sharply against the action at a closed meeting of the Israel contingent
in New York. The same day instructions came through from Ben Gurion
laying down the line. That afternoon Eban made such a compelling speech
at the UN defending the Israeli action that when a transcript reached
Ben Gurion, the old man was reported as saying, 'I had some doubts
about the wisdom of the thing but Eban's speech has convinced me that
I was right.'

When Eban returned to Israel after ten years at the UN, his political
proclivities did not make him a natural candidate for position in B.G.'s
roost, where Moshe Dayan and Shimon Peres were the young heirs-
apparent. A rather perceptible adjustment in Eban's views began to take
place and he was soon invited to join the Government. When the storm
broke over the Lavon Affair, Eban was again back with the moderate
majority. The Israeli electorate, while highly appreciative of his talents
as spokesman to the world, was never quite sure exactly where he stood.
The hawks distrusted him as a dove and the doves were wary of his
tendency to stick to whatever political line was in the ascendency. Eban's
weakness is no greater and no smaller than the weakness of all men tempted
by political office. My own opinion is that after his diplomatic success, he
should have steered clear of politics. With his talents he could have carved
a handsome niche for himself in any public field and exerted great influence
over the destinies of Israel as an independent thinker. While he was still
Minister of Education and part-time president of the Institute, I had a
number of conversations with him after which I wrote him the following
letter:

Dear Aubrey:

As I told you, it is my firm conviction that you would be acting in your own highest personal interest, and certainly in the interest of the Weizmann Institute, if you were now at this juncture of events in Israel to bow out gracefully from all governmental and parliamentary office and activity.

You were the first to admit in our conversations that the experience of political and governmental life which you have had these past eighteen or twenty months has not been exactly pleasant or exhilarating. Politics is a rough-and-tumble game at the best and invariably deteriorates into a rat race; and you have endured no exception to that rule of public political life.

Much as I regret to repeat this, and as I regretted saying it to you, your prestige in Israel has suffered considerably following your acceptance of government office. Were it not for the fact that you hold the title of President of the Weizmann Institute, and in that capacity convened the highly successful International Conference on Science in the Advancement of New States, I honestly believe that your prestige in Israel would have been even lower. It is sad, but, I think you will agree, an inevitable conclusion as things are these days in this country.

I have not altered in any whit my opinion concerning your brilliant gifts and talents that equip you to fill the active, full-time Presidency of the Institute to high purpose and distinction. I explained to you the character of the organizational structure which I propose to recommend to the Board of Governors in substitution for the present cumbersome set-up. It is my firm conviction that you would be doing both the Institute and yourself the greatest possible service if you were to decide and announce now, without delay, your intention to devote yourself to the active Presidency of the Institute for at least the next five years.

I am equally convinced that such a dramatic step at this time would electrify public opinion and draw attention to your own high moral stature, without in the least damaging your prospects for a brilliant and successful political career in the future. On the contrary. It would considerably enhance them...

Soon after, before he left for the United States on a speaking tour, he left a note under my door: 'I am thinking audacious thoughts'—a typical Ebanesque phrase. I was happy. I thought he had taken my advice. I was mistaken. A little while later he asked to be relieved of the presidency and went on to become Israel's Foreign Minister.

As a world tribune for Israel he has no peer. But I still think that had he stayed on as an active President of the Institute, his position today inside the country would be even stronger. One of his great assets is his wife, Suzy—young, beautiful, intelligent, and, like her husband, a linguist. She is not, like him, a Demosthenes, but she is a speaker of charm. And her looks are by no means an impediment.

With Eban's departure, we were back where we started. Or to be more exact since we had not gone forward, we did not have to go back. Nothing had changed at the Institute. We still needed a President and I was still getting older, not only from Zionism but from years. After Eban my first choice for president of the Institute was Victor, Lord Rothschild. I wooed him for a number of years. The answer was always 'Perhaps, give me time to think it over.' It was never a yes or a no. I eventually put Marcus Sieff on his trail with similar unsuccess. Victor Rothschild had all the qualifications, and more. First, he's a Rothschild. Second, he's a distinguished scientist. Third, he is an administrator. Fourth, he has charm and wisdom enough to distribute to half a dozen presidents of universities. Fifth, he is deeply devoted to Israel. Sixth, he was a friend and follower of Dr. Weizmann from way back. Seventh, Tess, Lady Rothschild is his charming, lovable, educated wife. She is a niece of Richard Meinertzhagen, himself a friend of Weizmann and devoted Zionist. Last, but least, he has command of vast sums of money in various family foundations of which the Institute has been the recipient many times over—and there is more where this comes from. These funds are devoted primarily, if not exclusively, to Israeli purposes. The tradition has been handed down from the days of the first Baron Edmund, *Hanadiv*, who in his relations with Palestine almost a hundred years ago was not only a philanthropist but a gifted and far-sighted statesman.

Victor held out some vague hope but there were always problems— children, wife, the wrench of giving up a lifetime in England. These are things, by the way, that people in Israel don't seem to realize when they glibly ask other Jews why they don't come here to live.

A few years ago when we were building the Animal Breeding Center at the Institute—a sterile mouse factory—I informed Victor, who was its patron saint, that we were going to have a big to-do over its inauguration. 'Nothing doing,' he replied. The Center does not even bear the Rothschild name. I persisted and Victor resisted. He neither wanted nor needed the publicity and fanfare attendant on such ceremonies. Finally, I summoned his ancestor, the Baron Edmund, to my aid. I told Victor a story, probably apocryphal, about the late *Nadiv*, who upon entering a famous hotel in Paris was approached by a Jew. 'Baron Edmund,' he said, 'allow me to escort you into the dining room.' 'No,' said the *Nadiv*, 'I need no help.' Replied the Jew: '*You* may not need it, but *I* do. Two of my creditors are waiting for me in the lobby. When they see me walk in, arm-in-arm with you, my credit will be vastly improved.' 'Victor,' I ended with a flourish, 'you may not need it or want it, but *I* do.' This story broke down Victor's resistance and he agreed to let me escort him and his wife to the platform.

When it became ultimately clear to me that Victor was not to be had, I turned in my search for a president in another direction.

J. Robert Oppenheimer, head of the Institute for Advanced Study in Princeton, had begun to take an interest in the Institute following his visit there in 1958, when, with Niels Bohr, he dedicated the Physics Institute. He became a member of our Board and we were in frequent touch with each other. More than once he called me from Princeton, admonishing me: 'Don't be too hard on the scientists'—this after reading some critical remarks I had made in one of my reports. He was a dedicated person, strangely alien to Jewish life and all its implications, but Rehovot and Israel fascinated him.

Long before I ever dared to dream of Oppenheimer considering this post at the Institute, before I even knew him personally, I made an appointment with him at Princeton. It was at the time of Israel's Tenth Anniversary and I wanted to invite him to attend the inauguration of the Physics Institute. The very day that I was to meet him, *The New York Times* carried a seven column news story: 'Oppenheimer Declared Security Risk.' I sat in my office in New York waiting for the appointment to be canceled. I considered it a most inopportune moment to discuss such a picayune thing as an invitation. I hadn't the foggiest notion of how to start a conversation under such circumstances. I had never met him, didn't know what kind of man he was. Should I, or could I, commiserate with him? The telephone never rang. Because of my anxiety and my anger over American official stupidity, I was literally ill on my way to Princeton. I had written him the purpose of my visit, and when I arrived his secretary immediately ushered me into his presence. There he sat with myriads of newspapers on his desk. While I was hesitating how to begin he said to me: 'You don't think for a moment that after what has happened the Government of the United States will give me a passport to go to Rehovot.' My reply was: 'Professor Oppenheimer, your invitation to visit the Institute has no statute of limitations.' This was the beginning of our personal acquaintance. He did come to Rehovot for the inauguration of the Physics Institute. During one of our conversations, he spoke to me about his impressions of Israel. I don't remember his words but I remember clearly that his voice was choked and there were tears running down his face. He had a strange, wonderful face, gaunt, saintly.

Much later, after he returned to America, when Eban had become Foreign Minister and there was no hope of getting Victor, I asked Oppenheimer if he would consider accepting the presidency of the Institute. We talked about it, alone, and then with his wife, Kitty. Shirley and I visited them a number of times and continued the conversation. Finally he said: 'I will accept the job on the following conditions. One, I must come back to the United States three months every year because I don't want to give the impression of running away after what has happened; two, I will not do any entertaining. You will have to do it for me but I will be present whenever you call me; three, I will want to continue to do some physics.' I accepted all three conditions and we made a date to meet a few months later when I would again be in New York. When I returned and called his secretary I was given the shocking news that he was dying of cancer. No one could see him. A few months later he died. His funeral was one of the saddest experiences in my life. It was simple and moving. George Kennan delivered a eulogy. Many distinguished scientists, among them Isidor I. Rabi, Nobel physicist, and very active in the affairs of the Institute, paid tribute to a great spirit, a great man and a great scientist. One of the decenter footnotes in the history of America is that some time before Oppenheimer's death the action initiated by President Kennedy to award him the Distinguished Service Award was carried out by President Johnson.

There was another candidate hovering in the wings for some time. Sir Solly Zuckerman, the scientific adviser to Her Majesty's Government, said to us more than once: 'Keep the seat warm for me.' But he never moved to occupy it.

In 1961 Professor Amos de-Shalit, one of Israel's young physicists, became the Scientific Director of the Institute. A gifted and charming sabra, Amos, still in his thirties, was too young for the presidency. But, as far as I was concerned, he was the heir-apparent and the scientific directorship was a natural training ground. At my behest Amos was elected *ad personam* to the Board of Governors, the only member of the scientific staff of the Institute so elected, but he needed more first-hand experience in the administrative and financial affairs of the Institute. He was highly versatile and a natural born leader of men, full of ideas—even if he changed some of them between morning and evening. He was bright, persuasive, and possessed of an infinite degree of charm and boyish handsomeness which is always connected with what we call in Hebrew a *mushlam*, one endowed with every desirable quality. It was my hope that when he reached the age of forty-five and his period of creative physics would be more or less over and his inner conflicts resolved, the mantle of the presidency would fall on his shoulders. This was denied us when Amos died in 1969 at the age of forty-three. It was a most grievous loss, to the Institute, to the country, and to me personally.

It wasn't until 1965, after nine years of search on three continents, that the Board of Governors finally found a suitable president. I myself was not particularly enamored of the choice. It was, at best, another stop-gap measure. In fact it was a ruse. By proposing *me* as president, the Board of Governors extricated itself from two problems at one blow: the role was filled and my departure was forestalled. I did not tingle with excitement over the honor. It was a little too late for that. I wrote to Dewey Stone at the time:

Dear Dewey:

Now that the 'Kings and Captains' etc. have departed, I have been able to do some thinking about a number of problems concerning the Institute, particularly, the subject of the Presidency.

After considerable soul-searching, I have come to the conclusion that no purpose would be served either for the Institute or for myself were I to accept the post of President. In a moment of weakness I wrote in my letter to you of February 24, that if ' . . . it is decided to have a layman, I claim that post for myself . . . I regret it now. On reconsideration I have decided, and my decision is irrevocable: I do not want the title and will not accept it. As a famous American once said: 'If nominated I will not run; if elected, I will not serve.' Let me give you my reasons:

I am by nature an aesthete. In everything I have done in my life, whether it was journalism, editing a magazine, producing plays or, in the final phase of my life, building an Institute, I was dominated by considerations of form, beauty, symmetry, etc. I always shied away from the grotesque, the ridiculous and the pompous. I have never sought directly or indirectly public acclaim or public office merely for its own sake. If it came, it came as a result of what I had done. When some ten years ago, Sir Robert Robinson suggested that I be elected President, I accepted his judgment as a logical conclusion of what he thought I had done for the creation of the Weizmann Institute. It made sense then. You and others thought differently. But there is no point now in trying to probe into the past. What happened, happened.

Now, some ten years later, when I am on the eve of my 72nd birthday, it would be extremely foolish on my part and certainly meaningless for the Institute, for me to accept this office. It would not add one iota to my prestige nor to the scientific eminence of the Institute. Moreover, aesthetically the whole thing goes against my grain.

You will tell me that I am inconsistent. Perhaps. But I'd rather be inconsistent than foolish. Consistency, it has been said, is the hobgoblin of small minds. Mine is not a very great mind, but in all modesty I can say it is not a small one, either.

I am writing this, my dear Dewey, because we ought to set our minds moving in another direction and think seriously of what the future structure of the Institute should be. I have a feeling, and I know I am right, that my election as President at this juncture will constitute a public confession of our failure to provide for the future active leadership of the Institute which is so essential. For me to assume this role now it is too late, much too late.

I am writing this to you in all candor and—I am ashamed to admit—after some sleepless hours. I want you to believe me when I say that I am thinking only of the future welfare of the Institute. Nothing else. Too much of my life-blood has been invested in the Institute to think in any other terms.

The above letter should have put an end to it but it didn't. The opponents of 1956 concluded in 1965 that the years had added sufficient dignity to me to make me eligible for the presidency. It was a sort of belated atonement. There are documents to this effect but I shall not weary the reader with these interminable exchanges except to quote one sentence from one of these letters from one of the more distinguished members of our Board: 'Just as I was opposed in 1956, I insist today that you must accept the presidency.' I felt it was too little and too late but there was no one around to agree with me. And so I was, with due pomp and ceremony, invested with the dignity of President. It effected only one change in the affairs of the Weizmann Institute as far as I was concerned: I had to order new stationery.

My election as President of the Institute came as a sort of postscript to the honors conferred upon me on my seventieth birthday. These were many and varied, and I admit I enjoyed them immensely. For one, I was awarded a Ph. D., *honoris causa*, the Institute's first, and so far only, such award. Now I was a 'doctor' among doctors. I had always been Dr. Weisgal to elevator boys and reception clerks in European hotels. My crown of luxuriant white hair coupled with my address in Rehovot were sufficient academic credentials for them, and when it wasn't 'doctor' it was 'professor.' No amount of denial ever helped. It always reminded me of a banquet I attended thirty years ago in a town called Yarmouth, in Nova Scotia. I was the guest of the Jewish community and was invited to speak on behalf of a great cause, I don't remember which. During the preliminaries to my speech (other speeches), the chairman of the banquet leaned over and asked me, *sotto voce:* 'Is it all right if I introduce you as *Dr.* Weisgal?' '*Hack mir nisht in kop.*' I answered, which means, more or less, 'Cut the comedy.' A few preliminaries later, he made another appeal: 'It would make a very nice impression if I introduced you as *Dr.* Weisgal.' 'I don't need any titles,' I answered. The third time, his plea was more to the point. 'If I introduce you as *Dr.* Weisgal I think it would be better for the campaign.' Wearied, I answered: 'Do whatever the hell you want.' When my turn finally arrived, the chairman stood up to make the introduction. Suddenly he bent down to me: 'By the way,' he whispered, 'what kind of doctor are you?'

On the evening of November 10, 1964 there was a birthday dinner for me at the Institute's San Martin Faculty Club-House, known to the cognoscenti of Rehovot—because of its high culinary standards—as 'The Suicide Club.' The chief architect of this event was my old friend and colleague Julian Meltzer, aided and abetted by Margalit Sela. There were speeches, presentations, even a birthday cake. Everybody was in good spirits, my friends because I was still around, my enemies because I was getting older. It was memorable for two reasons. First of all, Moshe Sharett was there to wish me well, and acted as chairman. It was one of the last times he appeared at any public gathering. His illness was so far advanced he could hardly speak but he made the effort and it was profoundly touching. Secondly, there were among the guests two men with whom I had been very close in the distant past and because of certain happenings completely out of touch with for long years: Ernst David Bergmann who had quit the Institute a year or two after its dedication because of serious disagreements with Weizmann although he should have been Weizmann's successor; and Harry Montor who after rendering great services to the State of Israel had been cast out of its good graces. The fact that they accepted the invitation and came meant a great deal to me.

By far the most intriguing honor was the publication of a volume of tributes called *Weisgal At Seventy*. Everybody who knew me and whose name looked good in print was invited to contribute. I know how these things are done, having done them myself more than once. The idea for the book was hatched by my two friends Joe Brainin and Julian Meltzer, who intended to produce it for my sixty-fifth birthday. I got wind of it and nipped it in the bud. By the time my seventieth began rolling around, they were at it again in dark secrecy. Between my sixty-fifth and seventieth birthdays Joe and Julian widened the circle of conspirators under vow not to divulge anything. The inner circle of editors and writers included my old friend and a journalist of no mean attainment, Lillie Shultz, Rinna Samuel, the editor of *Rehovot* and an important writer in her own right, and my own rebellious daughter, who was induced to contribute a moving poem for the volume.

When the volume was finally off the press but still unbound, I was let into the secret with the gleeful pronouncement that nothing could stop it any more. I bowed to the inevitable. I must confess I even enjoyed some of the pieces. The contributors were certainly a galaxy of international personages from the world of politics, science, art, and finance. The London publisher George Weidenfeld, who had been a friend of mine for many years, said to me in his most charming Viennese manner: 'You will have a chance to correct all the mistakes in your autobiography.' He even inserted an introduction in the book to the effect that he was publishing this worthy volume only as an inducement to me to write my own book. I knew exactly what he meant. The exaggerations, the misinformation, the apocrypha, the contradictions—delightful as most of it was—weighed on me. Nahum Goldmann, for example, claims that the first time he saw me in the twenties at a Zionist Congress, I was attired in 'a light blue suit, green socks and a provocatively yellow tie.' This is inexcusable. Dazzling I might have been to Nahum, but my sartorial fastidiousness has never been questioned. Maurice Samuel, who certainly observed me more often and at closer quarters, wrote within those same two covers: 'He reacted to jarring details like a composer to false notes. In other words, he had style . . . I was for instance disdainful of his sartorial fastidiousness, and therefore unappreciative of its symbolic and practical significance.'

The London edition was called *Meyer Weisgal at Seventy*. Not long after, an American edition, prepared by Atheneum, was in the making. It had a more imaginative title: *The Odyssey of an Optimist*. That was me again. There were new pieces by some American friends who having read the London edition were outraged that they had not been asked to contribute and forthwith penned some more immortal words. One of these was the playwright, S. N. Behrman. My acquaintance with Sam Behrman began in the days of Reinhardt and Rudolf Kommer and *The Eternal Road*. He contributed to the book I edited on Weizmann in 1944 with a piece called 'Zion Comes to Culver City,' a *tour de force*. Anyway, Sam called me. He had to see me urgently and we met at a small French restaurant. 'Meyer,' he said, 'how could you possibly have allowed that book to appear without me?' He referred to the London edition. I comforted him that he had probably been left out of nobler anthologies and added that I had had more trouble from the book than he could possibly imagine. The very title, I told him, had cost me at least ten girlfriends in various parts of the world who had been laboring under the illusion that I was a younger Lochinvar. '*Oi*,' he blurted, 'I've got a theme for an article about you. Can I still get in somewhere?' It so happens that Atheneum is his publisher and he managed to get into the American edition with a charming piece that begins and ends with my ten lost girlfriends. When it was all over I asked Joe Brainin how he had overlooked Sam for the original. Joe informed me that he had written Sam at least seven times. I wasn't surprised. Sam rarely replies to letters or even phone calls. He is, out of print, one of the shyest men in captivity. Some years ago he was staying with us in Rehovot working on a new play, based on his autobiography *The Worcester Story*. He wanted to finish it in Rehovot so that he could add Rehovot, Israel to the preface. He would sit upstairs in his room all day, working on a bridge table—a desk was out of the question

above At a meeting of the editorial board of the Weizmann Papers with Joseph Eligouloff, my secretary; Leonard Stein, editor of Volume I; and Isaiah Berlin. *below* With Richard Crossman in Rehovot

above Music and Art: Alice and Jan Peerce, Esther and Reuven Rubin.
Rubin: 'It is worth dying just to hear Peerce sing '*El Mole Rachamim.*'
below With Julian Meltzer and Otto Preminger during the filming of
Exodus

My family: the American Branch. *above* David and Ruth with Benji
and Jonathan, *below* Mendy with Marc; Alexandra

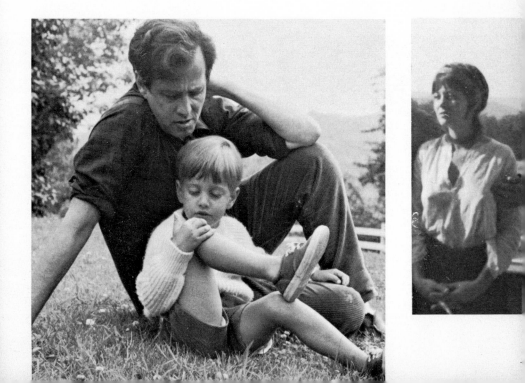

The Israeli Branch. With (sitting left to right) Helen, Shmuel, Eli, Dan, Shirley; (standing) Assaf, Aminadav

—wearing a shirt torn both back and front. That was his uniform. He would never venture downstairs if he heard a strange voice. The theatrical community of Israel was interested in meeting him and I arranged a reception at our home. Mr. Behrman came downstairs, took one look at the assembled guests, developed a high temperature and retired to his room.

With the publication of the two editions, I began to entertain the idea that I had been relieved of the necessity of writing my own autobiography. But the more I thought of it, the more I realized that the opposite was true. A book of tributes, by nature, is doubly selective. The contributors are selected for their ability to speak kindly of the victim; they in turn select their sentiments for the occasion, leaving harsher truths for their own autobiographies. Ben Gurion's little piece, for example, is as innocuous as a newborn babe. It was those unwritten or half-written autobiographies of my contemporaries which made me wary. Everybody has his own version of history, of the truth, of what really happened. Why should I suffer by default? True, I didn't create the Jewish State singlehandedly as so many of my contemporaries did. I didn't even build the Weizmann Institute by myself although some of my well-wishers credited me with this feat. But I did hover around the wings on some notable occasions; I was privy to some historic moments. Why shouldn't my testimony, my prejudices, my partialities be thrown on the scale for the final balance?

Then there was Mr. Weidenfeld, now Sir George, who never let up. Whenever we met, in London or Israel or New York, he would broach the subject. 'You have so much to tell, you've had a checkered career for more than fifty years. You're an old journalist and editor. What's the problem?' My answer was always the same: 'Time. The Jews give me no rest. The Institute gives me no rest.' 'Why don't you take a machine and dictate—at your leisure?' 'That,' I said, 'I can't do. I can talk to people but I can't talk to a machine. I need someone who answers me back.' On one of these occasions George came up with an idea: 'You talk to your daughter and she will write. Her poem in your book is a gem. I will even advance her a thousand sterling.' 'No, no,' I said, 'no advance. If and when I write I'll make my own terms, and do my own financing.' No publisher has ever said no to such a proposition.

The idea appealed to me—talking has never been my problem. The problem was to persuade my daughter, and she was not only persuadable, but enthusiastic. True, she had a full-time job, a husband, and four children, not to mention political and social causes, but she promised to find the time. That was in 1966. A single stroke of fortune brought her husband a research grant for a year in Scotland and cut her loose from her job and her causes. We got to work. I dictated to her in Torphins, a little town near Aberdeen. When I left, after four weeks, my appetite having grown with eating, Shirley became my victim. I even wrote myself—many pages which I had to redictate because I couldn't read my own hieroglyphics.

When Helen and her brood returned from Scotland we continued in Rehovot, in Tiberias, in Bat Yam where she lives, in New York, in Rome —wherever I was or wherever I went and could persuade her to join me. She even seemed to enjoy these little junkets. Her husband, Shmuel, be it said to his credit, was most cooperative. He groaned a little and continued his research on the cows of Israel, getting them to eat less and less and produce more, and more often. Frankly, I never understood his experiments and preferred to argue politics with him. But apparently he was up to some good because the U.S. Department of Agriculture gave him enormous grants. To me he was like Sholem Aleichem's Tevye, the Dairyman, who trained his 'kliatche,' hag, to eat less every day. On the third day Tevye complained that just as she reached the stage where she was eating nothing at all, she dropped dead.

I plied Helen with papers, old speeches, letters, etc., and gave her license to draw on her own memory and imagination when I was too busy elsewhere. She produced some remarkable fiction. (When Herodotus found himself short on facts, he did not hesitate to use his imagination—which may be why he is called the first historian.) I would have to say, 'Where in hell did you get that?' 'Well, then, tell me what did happen,' was her reply, and I would begin to dictate again. When she finished the first draft of half the book, we gave it to Joe Brainin to look at. Joe was merciless in his criticism. He figuratively tore it to shreds. Helen, instead of taking umbrage, was pleased as punch. She had acquired an ally. Joe forced us to sit down together for longer periods, corrected our 'facts', straightened out dates, reminded me of long-forgotten incidents, advised Helen where to go for material, and provided some of his own. More often than not at our sessions, Joe and I would begin to reminisce about some particularly picturesque character or lively event in our dim and distant past, and Helen's eyes would light up. 'Pop, you never told me. Can I put that in?'

My answer was, 'Yes, if not more,' paraphrasing Peretz's story 'If Not Higher.' She regretted the question, because it broke the dam and a Niagara Falls flooded her typewriter.

25 The Six-Day War: Reflections

The Six-Day War in June 1967 is not a subject I can pass over without some reflections, however brief. It was a traumatic experience for the Jewish people; it has proved a catalyst in the definition or redefinition of Zionism and in our relations with the Arabs; it once more revealed to us the non-Jewish world's volatile attitude toward the people of the Book.

When I try to recapture the mood of the country during those days, I recall that there was much more excitement during the tense period preceding the war than during the actual fighting, which was over so quickly one could hardly catch one's breath. Everybody was hoping for the best and preparing for the worst. Anxiety extended throughout the Jewish world coupled with an outpouring of generosity unequalled in the history of the Jewish people—and redemption in the face of possible annihilation has always been a feature of Jewish community life. Even the non-Jewish world was full of sympathy for the plight of small Israel. Some countries which had been remiss during the days of Hitler thought that they would be given an opportunity to rectify their sins, and started to collect food and money for the expected wave of refugees. The world was, in fact, preparing itself for another collective sigh. The poor Jews were about to get it again, a subject which makes excellent copy for pious sermons, and unleashes oceans of purifying tears. It was encouraging while it lasted but it didn't last long. Israel made the mistake of reversing the traditional pattern. A dead Jew is more easily taken to the bosom of mankind than a live, victorious one. . . Alas! even the dead ones are not always welcome.

It is difficult for me to write the following lines without a feeling of deep revulsion. The historian Arnold Toynbee, that paragon of Christianity, makes the calm and unequivocal statement that what happened to the Arabs in Palestine in 1948 was on a par with what Hitler did to the six million Jews and worse than what was done to the Jews at various times in the past by Nebuchadnezzar, Titus, Hadrian and Torquemada. These latter, according to Toynbee, were, at least, not sinning against the light that God had vouchsafed them. As for the National Socialist Germans, 'On the Day of Judgment the gravest crime standing to their account might be not that they had exterminated a majority of the Western Jews, but that they had caused the surviving remnant of Jews to stumble.' How did the surviving remnant stumble? The answer is very simple. Mr. Toynbee had long ago relegated the Jews to the order of 'fossils.' But the 'fossils' refused to be fossilized; they decided to live again, to create again, to reject Toynbee's verdict. This was an unforgivable sin. We said: This shall not happen again. We have the same right as any other people on earth to be ourselves, to be left alone within our four walls.

But I have digressed.

At the Institute there were twenty-four-hour vigils. Everyone not in the army was either cleaning shelters, digging trenches, or piling up sand-bags. Shirley was running around collecting money and blankets and games. The biggest man on campus during that period was undoubtedly Yoram Dafni, the fourteen-year-old son of Rinna Samuel. Yoram was put in charge of shelters and made everybody's life miserable by insisting that they go down into them for drills.

I intended to leave for Paris on Sunday, June 4. I had cabled Helen in Scotland to stand by that night for a call. I saw Eshkol Saturday afternoon and when I asked him what was happening he answered, 'Don't pull me by the tongue. But it can't go on this way much longer.' I kept my thoughts to myself but that evening I canceled my flight. Weeks later, Helen told me that she waited for my call until midnight, and when it didn't come she said to her husband: 'Either my father is sick or war is breaking out.'

On June 5, the war was on. A Talmudic dictum says, '*Im ba lehorgcha, hashkem lehorgo*, If one is coming to kill you, rise up and kill him.'

I hated air-raid shelters and had successfully forestalled our warden during all his drills. That morning, however, Yoram was so imperious that we went 'underground' (a small concrete passageway between the kitchen and the garage). We took the radio with us and spent the morning listening to the raucous voice of the Arab newscasters who said Tel Aviv was in ashes and Rehovot was burning. The Institute was, after all, a prime target. I told Shirley to go into the kitchen and see if anything was burning. The Israel station reported only that our forces were engaged in Sinai. Outside, the sky was clear and blue and silence reigned. I said to her: 'I think the war is over.' Well, it wasn't, but my instinct was right.

As could have been expected, before, during and immediately after the war Israel became the Mecca of the journalists of the world, great and small. The invasion of the press corps was almost as great as the expected invasion of the Egyptians which never materialized, despite the thousand tanks amassed on Israel's borders, the hundreds of airplanes lying in wait for the kill, and Hussein's shooting gallery from across the Holy City, not to mention the Syrian gun emplacements pointing down at us from the Golan Heights. Most of the accounts were exceptionally friendly and sympathetic to Israel for a variety of reasons: the imminent danger to us, the blood-curdling speeches of Mr. Shukeiri, Mr. Nasser, and others, the hysterical war whoops from the Arab capitals, the extraordinary skill of our Air Force, not to mention the memory of the holocaust.

Following the war there was another minor invasion of the editors themselves, come to check upon the fantastic accounts of their reporters which were being converted into a flood of books. Among the great and near great who came were the editors of *Time* magazine and as often happens one of their stops was Rehovot. One of them, Otto Feurbringer, expressed his admiration for Israel for winning the war simultaneously on three fronts. I told him that in fact we had won on four fronts—Egypt, Jordan, Syria and *Time*. He asked: 'Were we ever in the class of enemies?' 'Not exactly,' I answered, 'but you were certainly not our friends.'

It didn't take very long for all this to change. The erstwhile aggressors became the victims and vice versa. David, by the very fact of having survived, became Goliath. We 'stumbled.'

There was, following the war, a kind of euphoria in Israel. Having won the war so quickly, we would soon win the peace. Now, three years later, the euphoria is gone and with it a considerable amount of our earlier optimism. We are fighting a declared war of attrition, declared, that is, by the Egyptians, in which no side can win and both can lose. In the spring of 1970 I wrote to Richard Crossman:

The situation in this country, and for that matter in the whole Middle East, leaves me in a state of despair. We didn't come to this country to shed blood or to shoot or to be shot at. The Zionist ideal was totally different. I am neither a dove nor a hawk, certainly not a vulture—just a very simple, sad Jew who has daily been working for the Zionist cause practically all of his adult life. I ask myself all kinds of questions: When will the end come? Will there be an end? Will we ever be able to use our resources, our intelligence, our ability to work hard for the renaissance—not only of Israel itself but of the entire area? This, after all, was the essential idea of Zionism, and the motive force behind the re-establishment of the Jewish State. This was Weizmann's ideal and that of all of those who followed him.

There is a beautiful old Midrashic legend which says that God, in His infinite wisdom, covered Palestine with rocks and debris of all kinds so that strangers would not covet the Land and only those closely involved with its creation would uncover its original beauty. We have done so for the last one hundred years; now that the Land has been uncovered, it is coveted by all, including the Russians, the Egyptians, etc. The land would have remained derelict and untouched by human hands for another thousand years if not more had not the Jews rediscovered its beauty. Our umbilical cord with the land has never been severed.

Believe me, I write out out of a sense of great frustration. I have never been involved in Israeli politics or affairs of defense. All I know is that my grandchildren will be in the army soon—one is already in, one goes in August, another a year later—and only God knows what will happen to them. Only God knows, for that matter, what will happen to the character of the Jews if the stress and the peril continue. Lamentably, there is no voice in the world that can, somehow or other, bring back a sense of sanity to all those concerned—not only to the Arabs but to the Jews themselves, so that they try to see what can be done to end the bloodshed.

My dear Dick, you have long been one of our staunchest friends. Of all the politicians in England, you are the only one with enough intellectual drive to want to do something so that peace returns to this troubled and exceedingly explosive area.

I invited him to come to Rehovot but he couldn't manage:

My dear dear Meyer,

I had been hoping at one time that I should get a chance of taking a brief holiday in Israel, mainly in order to see old friends with whom I desperately want to talk things over. However it looks to me as though electionitis will keep this country at fever heat through the summer and keep me tied to the treadmill.

I too am desperately anxious and I fancy our thoughts and feelings about the future in the Middle East are not very far apart. . . There is nothing I want more than a week at Rehovot provided it is a week when you are there to walk and talk in the garden with you.

Crossman had been a friend of Israel from the time of the Anglo-American Commission for Palestine in 1946. He was an admirer and friend of Weizmann. Yet he, too, began to doubt the wisdom of some of Israel's policies.

I do not always see eye to eye with the government but I am certain that in the flood of Arab propaganda since the war the true essence of Zionism has become obfuscated.

I have lived in this country spiritually all my life, physically for more than a generation. For almost sixty years I have been involved in Zionist activities from the most menial affairs to the highest ranks of intellectual endeavor. I have lived through every Zionist crisis, all the joys of creation as well as the many frustrations and disappointments one encounters in a life time. I have been a part of its youthful idealism, its utopian dreams, its hopes and despairs. I have always been in revolt against something— it would be futile to enter into details—I have never belonged in what is called today the Establishment. I saw the strength and weakness of all. Often I was beset by terrible doubts, but more often I saw in what we were trying to create here the pinnacle of human idealism, human sacrifice and all that is regarded best and lofty in our sinful and imperfect world. And yet today, I am troubled beyond belief by what is going on. Above and beyond the daily struggles and mistakes, I am aware of a growing misconception, even an appalling ignorance and growing enmity, in the world at large, about the relation of the Jews to Palestine or Israel. This applies to some Jews as well, to the well-fed self-satisfied Right, and even more so to the lean and hungry New Left, among them some, fortunately not many, of the young generation in Israel. One often hears, bandied about as if it were an unassailable fact, that the establishment of the Jewish State, in itself, was an injustice to the Arabs, indeed an act of aggression.

I do not think that 'establishment' is the right word; 'proclamation' is better. As an idea the State had been there for many years, from time immemorial; it was only waiting to be given a name. Let me say these things in as simple a language as I can find: The Jews perforce carried their state with them wherever they went. It is a mistake to think that Zionism began with Herzl, or Weizmann, or even with Hibat Zion in Russia in the nineteenth century, or even with the Bilu. Beginning on the day after the destruction of Jerusalem by Titus in AD 70, Jews have prayed for its restoration. All our liturgy, all our poetry, all our prayers are yearnings for the return to Jerusalem. At first it was the yearning for a messiah, forgetting that in Jewish tradition messianism has always been a hope deferred. Jewish history is full of sincere messiahs, false messiahs, pseudo-messiahs. Throughout the centuries Jews lived in the holy cities— Safed, Tiberias, Jerusalem. Jews went there—some walking hundreds and hundreds of miles—to come to the Holy Land if only to die on its soil. They lived in exile as if the Land were only waiting for them to return. Indeed, the Yemenite Jews who were flown to Israel in the early days of the State believed that they came on the wings of the messiah. When miracles and messianism began to lose their hold even on the pious, when nationalism took hold all over Europe, the Jews, too, began to take matters into their own hands. But it was not only nationalism; it was despair with the world, disillusion with all those movements and promises to the Jews.

The Jews who came to Palestine at the end of the nineteenth century,

to live and not to die, came to a wasteland. For a description of the 'flourish-
ing' civilization that existed in Palestine at that time read Mark Twain's
Innocents Abroad. His credentials are good, I believe, even among the New
Left. The country was sparsely inhabited—I cannot even say settled
because settlement implies continuity—by Arab nomads and fellahs who
used the land and then moved on. There *were* rural villages or encampments;
there *were* semi-urban communities in Jaffa, Jerusalem, Nazareth and
Bethlehem. But until the Jews came, Palestine was a land of *emigration*
for the Arabs. It could not support an expanding population. It was Jewish
settlement which brought water and land conservation to a static, even
dying, area. Arab emigration ceased, *immigration* began. Perhaps they too
were returning to the land of their fathers, but they could return only
because we had returned; ironically enough, in creating our homeland
we created, at the same time, the force that would eventually seek to
destroy us.

That's why it seems to me that the idea of doing the Arabs an 'injustice'
merely by coming to Palestine is really a malevolent distortion of the
facts. There is a Talmudic injunction, 'Two are holding one *tallis.* One
says it is all mine; the other says it is all mine. Divide it.' This is what
happened in 1948. The country was divided into a Jewish State and an
Arab State. The Jews accepted the division; the Palestinian Arabs did
not even have an option on accepting; their 'big brothers' from the
surrounding Arab states declared war on us and in the aftermath what
was to have been a Palestinian State was absorbed partly by Trans-Jordan,
partly by Egypt. Seven or eight hundred thousand, some say a million,
Arabs fled the country, many in fear, but many, many more in answer
to the call of Arab leaders: 'Leave your homes and villages now. Soon
we will return and cast the infidels into the sea.' It is common knowledge
that the leaders of the Yishuv pleaded with the Arabs of Haifa to remain
but they left, in anticipation of the great day of reckoning.

I am not callous about the Arab refugees. But the crocodile tears of their
Arab brethren who left them to waste in pitiful camps for twenty years
leave me cold. They could have been absorbed easily into the neighboring
countries, as Israel absorbed hundreds of thousands of Jewish refugees
from the Arab countries who, too, left, or were forced to leave, their homes,
land, and property. The refugee problem festered like an untended wound
and soon the world called us to task for our hardheartedness: Jews, you
are acting in an un-Christian manner. I would like somebody to define
for me what *is* the Christian manner.

There were tens of millions of refugees in the world after the Second

World War. Who cares? Not a whisper about them. Millions of people were moved over rivers, pushed hither and yon, borders were 'adjusted,' gigantic territories annexed. The Russians alone took over alien territories comprising one hundred and twenty million people which never belonged to them. Did they give back an inch? Not at all; they are striving for more. Even the United States, which certainly needs no territory, has not returned to the Japanese the islands they hold. But no explanations are required in these cases. '*C'est la guerre.*' This is punishment for the sin of unleashing war. But it is permitted only to Christians. The Jews of Israel did not even unleash a war. A thousand tanks were poised on the borders of Israel, hundreds of planes were awaiting the signal. And the message of Mr. Nasser and Mr. Shukeiri and hundreds of others in the Arab world could not be mistaken: 'We will murder you; we will throw you into the sea; you shall never emerge alive after this onslaught; you will be slaughtered, finished.'

Universal rules do not apply to the Jews. We are a class apart. We are the traditional accursed of the world. Treatment to us must be meted out according to that tradition. It seems to me almost impossible sometimes not to see in this deliberate, almost single-minded indifference to Jewish plight an echo of ancient, ingrained prejudices. I have occasionally had the impression that even Gentiles with genuine goodwill cannot free themselves from the heritage of all those centuries when it was taken for granted that it was natural, it was *right* for Jews to be a wandering people: it was their Destiny; they were living on sufferance.

After all, just as they had refused to depart from the religion of their fathers, so they went on refusing to become wholly integrated with the life of their neighbors. They went on persisting in remaining themselves. This was their great sin, both to Christians and Moslems. Sometimes it was impossible to acknowledge this ancient feeling even in private; it had to take countless forms of apologia, of rationalization, of argumentation.

Yet the fundamental attitude remains the same—a rooted, though unavowed conviction that the Jews remain an accursed people, accursed because of their determination to remain themselves and thus to remain different.

When I read, for instance, that the peace settlement must not reflect the 'weight of conquest,' it's all I can do to keep my blood-pressure under control.

Weight of conquest!

This delectable phrase has been invented especially for us. I would like to know how many conquering countries ever gave back anything, unless there was at least a *quid pro quo*. But let us forget this futile verbiage. Do we really want 'their' territories? The answer is 'No.' A state is not measured by its size. It is measured by the quality of life within its borders. We want peace, but a peace based on equity and security. Another thing which is so often forgotten but must be repeated over and over is the promise made to the Jewish people fifty-three years ago, approved and confirmed by all the powers of the world, the Balfour Declaration. What is left of that promise? Exactly one-twelfth of the area granted to us then.

The Arab leadership, after harassing the Israelis for twenty years, beginning with the attack on the infant State at its birth, and through the establishment of a vast Soviet-supplied armory in the Sinai in 1956 and 1967, now brazenly asks for the Israelis to withdraw before they will even *discuss* peace!

In those moments of despair that sometimes lead to cynicism I have even found myself reflecting on the motives of those humane Gentiles who bewailed the catastrophe of the Holocaust. It's hard to forget an odd fact about fairly recent relations between Jews and Gentiles: I was recently reminded that countless millions of dollars have been spent on converting Jews to Christianity, to be sure without much to show for it. A mathematician once calculated that it cost the Christian world hundreds of thousands of dollars for every Jewish soul that could be laid claim to on behalf of Christianity; most such converts, of course, generally sought some material advantage. Heinrich Heine's conversion—to digress for a moment—is classical: while studying for the Bar he became a Christian in order to acquire a license to practice. Later in life he returned to Jewish practices and when asked how he could switch back with so little ceremony he replied: 'I never left. Did you ever know one Jew to believe in the divinity of another?' In a more sober moment he wrote:

> *Vier tausend Jahre schon und länger*
> *Dulden wir uns, brüderlich*
> *Du, Du duldest, dass ich atme,*
> *Dass Du rasest, dulde ich.*

June 1967 was an agonizing defeat for the Arabs. It has proved an agonizing victory for the Jews. We have been clamped into a vise from which liberation is more easily expatiated on than achieved. The occupied territories hang like a weight around our necks. To abandon them without the guarantee of peace would be suicidal. To defend them is to sentence our children and grandchildren to the battlefield, some to death, others to crippling injury, all to a never-ending nightmare of uncertainty.

There are those like my friend Nahum Goldmann who sharply criticize the Israel leadership for its lack of flexibility. I myself at times feel inclined to question the sagacity of some of their actions and statements, but I lack Nahum's assurance that there really are clear-cut alternatives. And I hold my tongue, in public at least, out of modesty. I have never, thank God, had the responsibility of making political decisions which determine the life and death of others.

When Eshkol died in February 1969 the burden of Prime Minister was thrust on Golda Meir, and it was indeed a terrible burden.

I have known Golda from the days of her and my youth. I don't think there is a single facet of Palestinian or Israeli life in which she didn't take a part. She was a kibbutz member, a labor leader, an ambassador, Foreign Minister, Prime Minister. She raised a family under sometimes incredibly difficult circumstances. She has always possessed a determination that seems to know no obstacle. She has been called hard and inflexible, but I have seen her shed bitter tears. When she was asked to take Sharett's place as Foreign Minister, she was shattered and heartbroken.

Golda had more or less retired from public life—she was close to seventy—when she was urged to return as Prime Minister. When the news of her election reached me in Caracas I wrote her:

> Though I am far, far away from the scene I have been thinking of you constantly and reflecting on how foreordained Destiny orders your life and actions irrespective of your own wishes and desires. I remember 1956, with what heavy heart you were compelled to take over the burden of the Foreign Ministry and especially the circumstances that led to the decision.
>
> And now, thirteen years later, when you have earned the right for a bit of peace and tranquility, and under circumstances far more tragic than 1956—the death of a dear friend—you are being forced to assume the terrible burden of Prime Minister. My dear Golda, you will need all the strength and wisdom which you so abundantly possess to lead our people out of the unbearable morass in which we find ourselves today. I wish you with all my heart good fortune in the conduct of this high office and stay with it until real and genuine peace reigns in our land. The power lies in your hands. Take counsel with yourself and only with yourself—and think of our children and grandchildren and their grandchildren who will inherit the land.

26 Meyer Weisgal . . . So Far

My recorded odyssey will—hopefully—come to an end in this chapter with my resignation from the Weizmann Institute, concomitant with my seventy-fifth birthday. Although the line is arbitrary, it is appropriate; my association with the Weizmann Institute was the apex of my career. It can have no sequel.

My decision to resign (this time—unlike my numerous previous decisions—irrevocably) was made on June 10, 1967, the last day of the Six-Day War. I announced my intention to the Board of Governors on December 5, 1968 and I gave them one year to find a successor. My resignation became effective on December 31, 1969.

This last chapter is being written now, seven months later, in July of 1970, in the small Swiss village of Celerina on the edge of St. Moritz. Ostensibly I am vacationing here with Shirley at the home of Karl Kahane (of Vienna, Geneva, Jerusalem, and other points East and West; but the Viennese charm is still dominant). In fact, I have pledged myself to the completion of this book. It has already become a burden. And just like the yellow pages of 1953 moldering somewhere in my files, these lines are taken down in longhand by my lor ɣ suffering wife. It is even appropriate to end in the same fashion as I be　　ᴗeventeen years ago in another small village, La Croix.

As I mentioned, June 10, 1967 was the last day of the Six-Day War. It was also my forty-fourth wedding anniversary. The 'gift' I gave my wife, more precious than rubies, would have been unthinkable a week before—a visit to the Wailing Wall in the Old City of Jerusalem. The city had been reunited only two days before. The public was not yet permitted to visit the Wall because the entire area was mined, there was sniping from rooftops and, formally, there was still a war on. These weighty considerations notwithstanding, through General Uzi Narkiss, the Commander of Jerusalem, we made the journey. A few weeks before, Narkiss had come to me with a request from Pinhas Sapir, the Minister of Finance, for a contribution of IL 25,000 for a monument to the Negev Brigade and its deeds in the War of Independence. I asked him how much Sapir was giving and he told me IL 50,000. I said, 'If he gives you IL 50,000, I should give you IL 5,' but I sent him a check for IL 10,000. He thanked me for the 'first installment.' I replied that it was the first, second, third, and last installment; but during the first days of the war I made a silent pledge that if the Old City was restored to us I would give him the other IL 15,000. (Narkiss was unaware of my silent pledge until I reached New York some weeks later.)

It was a memorable pilgrimage. Soldiers were standing there, ammunition belts over their shoulders in lieu of *tallisim*. Old Chassidim were dancing ecstatically. They apparently needed no dispensation from anyone. The painter Reuven Rubin and his wife Esther were with us, and we joined the dance, with our old bones. Out of this experience came his painting 'The Shechinah Returns to Jerusalem.' Also with us were Julian and Ruchama Meltzer and Dolphie and Lola Beer-Ebner, all dear friends who had come to celebrate our anniversary in Rehovot and joined us with alacrity when we announced the change of the new to the old city.

While at the Wall, I said to Shirley, 'I have another present for you. I am at the end of my rope. Next year I will be seventy-four, and on that birthday I will give notice. I will give them one year to find a successor.' A vow made at the Wailing Wall must be kept. And this one was kept.

During that year and a half I planned my resignation, or retirement (or whatever it is I'm doing), and had very much on my mind the promise to Weizmann about the publication of his Papers. I felt that I had fulfilled my first promise, to build this Institute in his image—not that any such institution is ever finished, but it was finished as far as I was concerned. I had no more to contribute. Now it had to be taken up by younger and sturdier hands. The second promise was still awaiting fulfillment.

After almost fifteen years, only Volume I was out, published in 1968 by the Oxford University Press, a superb scholarly job, worthy to serve as the standard for all the volumes to follow. The Hebrew edition, by Mossad Bialik, was also ready for publication. But some eighteen or twenty volumes were projected, and I was impatient and, let me confess, worried about lasting long enough to finish the job. When the task of producing the Weizmann Letters had to be taken by the horns, my ignorance of how to go about it (despite my editorial and journalistic experience) was equalled only by my instinctive drive to surround myself with masters of the trade. My directive or authority came from Weizmann's letter to me in 1949: 'I cannot think of anyone other than yourself to whom I would entrust this work with the feeling that it will be done with responsibility and fidelity. Will you undertake it? If so, let this be your authority to begin gathering the material and to approach any and all persons and organizations in whose possession these letters and documents may be.' (I still have, among my souvenirs, a few dozen of his 'blank cheques': pieces of Presidential stationery with his signatures, some Hebrew, some English, at the bottom.)

In 1950 we began to build the Weizmann Archive. In 1940 Weizmann had taken the first steps to assemble the records of his forty years' work and after 1950 the work was continued and completed in 1958. Thanks to the generosity of Mr. and Mrs. Abraham Wix of London, the Archive was transferred to its permanent home as part of the Central Library on the grounds of the Institute. There were some 23,000 letters in addition to diaries, photographs, press cuttings, biographical material, scientific lectures, writings and patents, in Hebrew, Yiddish, Russian, German, English and French. Not only could Weizmann express himself freely in these languages but he was widely read in all of them. His familiarity with so many diverse literatures to which was added a more than superficial interest in the arts, especially music, considerably complicated the job of rendering them authentically.

In 1957, after the preliminary research and collection of material had been more or less completed, I conferred with leading scholars and friends of Weizmann, notably Isaiah Berlin, Leonard Stein, and the late Lewis B. Namier and Charles Webster, who came to be known as the 'Implementation Committee.' They were giants in their fields.

Sir Charles was an historian and professor of international relations, a barrister and writer who had been an admirer of Weizmann since the days of the Peace Conference in Paris in 1919 after World War One. He once delivered the annual 'Oration' at the London School of Economics on the 'Art of Diplomacy' and he used Weizmann as his first example.

Leonard Stein was a man of exactitude and vast erudition, and, had been very close to Dr. Weizmann, his political secretary and personal assistant for many years. He wrote a monumental work on the Balfour Declaration.

Lewis B. Namier, one of England's great historians and an influential figure in modern historiography, was to my mind the strangest of the lot. He was an East European Jew who never lost his foreign accent, though he mastered an English style in writing almost peerless in its lucidity and terseness. I don't think he ever came to terms with the fact that he was a Jew; some claim that he was even anti-Semitic. Weizmann could not forgive him for converting from Judaism in order to marry. I do know that he could be arrogant, and was one of the most humorless men I ever met. He had been a close associate of Weizmann's for many years, but they became quite estranged. Nevertheless he joined us eagerly on the Letters. During our meetings in London he asked to see me privately. As he came into my room he said: 'I would like to apologize to you.' 'Why the apology?' I asked innocently. 'I once called you Dr. Weizmann's court jester.' I replied: 'I was not offended. Even a court jester has his uses.' 'No,' he insisted, 'I meant it in a derogatory way. I have since discovered that you are a serious person.' I appreciated his good intentions, feeling at the same time something in common with those old-guard Bolsheviks generously rehabilitated after thirty years in Siberia or in the cemetery.

Isaiah Berlin, whom I had known for more than twenty years, was a category unto himself. When I met him in Washington during the war, it was love at first sight. His stature is so universally acknowledged that I can add nothing, but that wasn't what captivated me. It was much more his wisdom, his charm, his humor, his warmth. I often visited him and his lovely wife, Aline, at Oxford. Once he asked me if I could bring his mother along with me on a visit to his home. All the way from London to Oxford we talked—in Yiddish with a slight mixture of English. She was so full of fascinating wisdom that for once I wished that the distance between London and Oxford were longer. She spoke a Weizmann Yiddish or better still a Shmarya Levin Yiddish, rich, musical and overladen with an abundance of sagacity. When we arrived, Isaiah was standing on the steps to welcome her. I said to him: 'Yishayahu, now I know whence came your strength and wisdom.'

The Implementation Committe held its meetings at the Reform Club in London, one of those hushed, sedate, deferential monuments of Victorian England. Isaiah, who was the youngest, managed to introduce from time to time a touch of humor but the others, ancient and overburdened with erudition, maintained an austerity of tone and thinking which was somewhat stuffy for my tastes—as was the decor, actually arsenic and old lace—but entirely befitting the project at hand.

At about the same time we established a larger editorial board which was later merged with the Board of Trustees and consisted of Mrs. Weizmann, Isaiah Berlin, Aubrey Eban, Nahum Goldmann, Aryeh Pincus, Leon Dultzin, Israel Sieff, Yigal Allon, Boris Guriel, for a time the Archivist, Berl Locker, Julian Meltzer, Lewis B. Namier, Maurice Samuel, Zalman Shazar, Leonard Stein and Yigal Yadin. Later Jacob Katz, Joshua Prawer, Jacob Talmon and Nathan Rotenstreich, all of the Hebrew University, were appointed as an Editorial Committee, to supervise the work of the researchers headed by Gedalia Yogev. I was Chairman of the Editorial Board and General Editor. Subsequently, when progress was faster (I was eager to have it ready for Weizmann's hundredth birthday, in 1974), I appointed Joel Carmichael as Deputy General Editor and Julian Meltzer Managing Editor.

The first volume covered the years 1885 to 1902. Both before and after its publication there was endless discussion as to whether or not the Letters should be all-inclusive or selected. It was extremely interesting to hear the views of those that favored selectivity. Fundamentally they all wanted to protect Weizmann from himself as an historical figure. There were references to Lord Acton's dictum: 'There has never been an historical figure whose reputation will stand the scrutiny of his personal correspondence.' What was most revealing for me during these discussions was the fact that the politicians, or shall I say those involved in politics, were in favor of censorship, obviously thinking of their own personal correspondence. The professional historians and philosophers, with whom I agreed, wanted to present Weizmann altogether, leaving history to judge whether or not he needed protection. Webster, Namier and Isaiah, and later Talmon, had taken the line that the editors had no moral right to select, and this had been our approach from the beginning.

Much could be quoted from these learned discussions both *pro* and *con*, especially Isaiah Berlin and Jacob Talmon—the 'pros'—and Nahum Goldmann and Aryeh Pincus, the President and Chairman respectively of the Jewish Agency—the 'cons.' But just as I must overcome my temptation to quote, I cannot resist quoting the illuminating remarks made by Zalman Shazar, who is both a scholar and a political figure. He had not participated in the discussion, and spoke *ex tempore* when I asked him to close the meeting:

A man who is in the public eye addresses the public directly whenever he writes an article or delivers a speech, but the publication by someone else of his private letters would clearly be an inadmissible violation of his privacy. Yet when such a man has become a historic person, his private secrets need no longer be kept secret. The Scriptural verse tells us: '*Ve'hayu einecha ro'ot et morecha*—Thine eyes shall see thy teachers.' Rightly to see one's teachers means knowing and understanding them fully and without reservations.

Some of the participants in this morning's discussion have advocated adopting what they called the principle of 'selectivity.' It would seem to me that when a man becomes a subject for scholarly research, he must be studied completely, in every aspect of his being. The editor must convey the whole picture; he should be the liaison, not the barrier, between the subject and the reader.

What Isaiah Berlin has said this morning about Karl Marx seems to me a remarkable contribution to clarification of our problem. By knowing Marx completely, knowing even a hidden, private chapter in his life, historians have been enabled to understand more completely both his development and the history of Socialism. To this argument against selectivity in the publication of Weizmann's letters, let me add another parallel which I consider close and instructive: the case of the letters of Ferdinand Lassalle. An artist, as well as a politician and a Socialist, Lassalle made statements in early life that he later regretted. Like Weizmann, he was temperamental, impulsive, effervescent, self-centered. In his diary he once wrote: '*Ich habe heute noch nicht geglänzt*'—reminiscent in a way of Weizmann's careful preparations before delivering an address to the Zionist Congress. It was Edouard Bernstein and then Gustav Meyer, leaders of German Socialism, who published the complete letters of Lassalle, and they were both highly responsible, very moral personalities. Moreover, they loved and honored Lassalle deeply. Yet they published all the letters in their entirety, including those concerned with Lassalle's romantic involvement with the Gräfin Hatzfeld. They drew aside the curtain and revealed all Lassalle's weaknesses, faults, hesitancies—the complete man portrayed through the contradictions within his personality.

The moral to be drawn from this is that a movement which respects itself must know and reveal its leaders in their entirety. That is the significant role played by Yad Weizmann in establishing this fine monument to Weizmann—the Complete Letters and Papers. Selectivity can come later, in the form of Selected Letters after the publication of the complete texts. And there is no need to be afraid of a large number of volumes, for these volumes will preserve the heritage Weizmann left us.

The only possible argument for selectivity was that it would have shortened the job considerably and cost less money, hardly a scholarly approach, and certainly unworthy of the subject. So, during the year and a half of preparation for my retirement, I enlarged the staff of scholars, researchers, and editors, hoping (against hope) to complete the job in five years' time. Some forty people were gathered from various parts of the world, and, of course, much effort went into providing the finances, which, alas, are not completed at this writing. But God will help us.

During the summer of 1968, while I was in New York attending to these financial and literary matters, I complained to my doctor, Isaac Chomski, of a pain in my leg. Chomski, who is the doctor of all my friends and all my enemies, and who insists on lightening the misery of his patients by telling old Yiddish jokes, put me through the usual tests. When it was over he told me that he had observed something which alarmed him and insisted that I have an immediate biopsy. I told him: 'Nothing doing.' I had gone through that once before and suffered five days of agony while my children stood around practicing *Kaddish*. When it was over, the doctor came in with a broad smile: 'Sorry, Sir, we'll have to shoot you.' I told Chomski that if it were serious, I certainly *had* to go first to Israel to settle my accounts and wind up my affairs. If it weren't, I simply could not go through that torture again. Chomski reluctantly prescribed something for the interim. Meanwhile I cabled my Israeli doctor, Chaim Sheba, and told him to expect me as soon as I arrived, armed with all the damaging evidence. As I came off the plane I found Dr. Sheba waiting for me on the tarmac with his car. (I wonder how many doctors of Dr. Sheba's standing taxi their patients from airports. But then Sheba is Sheba and doesn't fit into ordinary categories.) We had a philosophical discussion on the whys and wherefores of life and I made an appointment to come to the hospital the next day. After tests and x-rays galore, he said, 'What Chomski prescribed for the interim will do for the present. You don't need any biopsy.' 'Why?' I asked, and here is a stenographic record of what he said: 'As you know, I am not an idiot. I think I am a fairly good doctor. I believe in letting sleeping dogs lie. My personal opinion is that you're O.K. If, God forbid, something should show up later, we'll always have time to monkey around with you. Moreover, by the time something happens you'll be dead anyway. Why should I hasten the process?' With this encouraging prospect, I returned home. Unbeknownst to me, Chomski had alerted my children to my imminent demise. I had no idea why suddenly they all turned up in Rehovot, including my granddaughter Alexandra, who arrived fresh from the barricades of the Paris revolution. They secretly cornered Dr. Sheba who, I later discovered, gave them one piece of medical advice: 'Try and persuade the old man not to resign from the Institute. That will keep him alive.'

To me, of course, Dr. Sheba is one of the greatest human beings ever to wear a white coat—at least the Jewish Shweitzer. He sits in his little two by nothing office at the Tel Hashomer Government Hospital, which he created and heads, receiving any patient who comes and sits on the wooden bench outside. There is no screen of nurses or impossible answering service between him and the ill.

On December 5, 1968, bolstered by a variety of green and white pills, mystifying liquids, and Dr. Sheba's prophetic optimism (I'm still here), I opened my report to the Board of Governors of the Weizmann Institute as follows:

We are meeting on the eve of the 25th Anniversary of the establishment of the Weizmann Institute of Science. I think that I need not elaborate on the obvious; clearly this is a most appropriate moment for us to glance at all that has transpired over the past quarter of a century, and even more importantly, to chart our course, if not for the next 25 years, then at least for the foreseeable future, for the next five to ten years.

It is with a certain degree of nostalgia, that I permit myself to quote my own report to this Board, presented in 1961:

'In view of my retirement from the active service of the Weizmann Institute on December 31, 1961, I deem it my duty to lay down before the Board of Governors a number of recommendations on what, after much reflection, I consider to be the best possible organizational structure for the Institute, both administrative and scientific [etc. etc.].

It seems almost impossible that seven years have passed since that report was made. It is even more astonishing to reflect that I made similar statements several times before. I am going to indulge in the same exercise now, but with a slight difference. I say to you categorically: '*Ich bin nicht mehr zu haben.*'

'Next year I shall be 75. There was a time when I thought that 65 was a good age for retirement. I was cheated out of that; perhaps it was my own fault. But be that as it may, there is no reason to prolong my agony any further—or yours. *You* need a new and younger President, and *I* shall consider my task undone if I do not attend to certain matters which still press on me. . . I am impatient for time in which to read, and to write, and in some way to place the body of all that I have learnt myself at the disposal of others—for whatever it may be worth.

And lastly, I crave time for my family, from whom I have both demanded and received so much, and to whom I have been able to give so little.

If I deserve anything from this Board and from the colleagues with whom I have worked for so long, it is not praise nor honor, but rather that I be enabled to retire before I can no longer hope to achieve these goals.

In the body of my report I recommended that the Board appoint a committee of five or seven urgently charged with seeking a successor and that they report back no later than April 1969. By the end of that year the new President would take office.

Whether it was rumor about the state of my health or the conviction that I really meant business this time, or simple common sense which recognized that the Institute required younger leadership, my proposal was accepted and a Committee of Seven established. With all sorts of *ex officios*, the members of the Committee came to eleven. I took no part in their deliberations or decisions, except, regrettably, for a foolish cablegram I sent to Dewey Stone, the Chairman of our Board.

On April 27, 1969, in accordance with the timetable I had proposed, the Board of Governors, at an Extraordinary General Meeting convened in Rehovot, announced the election of a new president, Dr. Albert B. Sabin, who would assume office on January 1, 1970.

I would be lying through my teeth if I said that I enjoyed that meeting. Despite my eagerness to retire and my profound conviction that it was in the best interests of the Institute for me to do so, there was a wrench.

After all my life blood was imbedded in every square inch of the beautiful campus. But there was something else: I had expected, I thought it was only natural to expect, that the Chairman of the Committee, reporting on the selection of the new President, would, at this point, address a word or two to me. But no. Not a word—I was already the forgotten man. It was careless, heartless, inexcusable—and painful. The Board of Governors sat for two days. They elected the new President, discussed the Endowment Fund, heard the financial report. A vote was taken and the business concluded. The Chairman of the Board, Dewey Stone, was about to adjourn the meeting when Professor Gerhard Schmidt asked for the floor. Gerhard was not a member of the Board of Governors. He was there by invitation as the Scientific Director-elect. Gerhard is a big man, tall and robust, self-possessed and little given to small talk. He is usually short-worded, even abrupt. At this particular moment, he   l lost control. Trembling, he said:

The newspapers this morning carried the results of our vote yesterday; it is common knowledge in Israel, particularly at the Weizmann Institute, that we have elected a new President who will take office some time next year.

I think that I speak for the staff, for Professor Avron [the incumbent Scientific Director], for the people I have discussed this with, and certainly for myself, when I say that it would be appropriate if I just told Meyer Weisgal how the staff feel about this particular moment in the history of the Institute.

I am not good at making speeches, particularly at moments when I feel very strongly. I would just like Meyer to know that, without anticipating anything that his seventy-fifth birthday will inspire, without anticipating any future festivities, we would like to say to you Meyer, how we feel about what you have done for the Institute. We know that but for you the place wouldn't look the way it looks. We know that but for you some of us, most of us, wouldn't have the standing that we have achieved. We know that you have built up something in this country which is unique and we know that it is going to be very difficult for the next man to carry his job.

And finally, we would like you to know that we will always regard you as the senior member of our staff. We look upon you as the father of the Institute, even though you have decided to resign—and I know how hard it has been for you to decide to withdraw from the affairs of the Institute.

The entire staff wishes you many more years in which to achieve the things that you want to do, to write your memoirs, to bring out Weizmann's letters. We hope that this part of your life's work will be achieved as magnificently as everything you have done for the Weizmann Institute.

Gerhard was crying when he finished. So was I and many others in the room, especially my friend Yosele Rosensaft, whose audible sobs reached my ears. They touched me deeply. Since his days in Bergen-Belsen, he been fighting 'forgetfulness.' Poor Dewey! He looked as if he had been struck by lightning. He was never reconciled to my leaving, hence he didn't think any words were necessary. He probably was the unhappiest man in the room.

There were a few other 'incidents' at the time of my retirement which did not add to the gaiety of the nations, nor to my own gaiety, but I shall not burden the reader with them.

Anyway, at the end of 1969, we packed our accumulated treasures of seventy-five years—books, pictures, silverware, sheets, towels, and memories—and moved from the 'presidential' residence to the Wolfson 'shack' next door, where I could continue with the Weizmann Papers. But it was necessary to get off the campus as soon as possible to give my successor a free hand, without embarrassment; and our friend Ida Kimche, an art dealer, generously offered the use of her unoccupied house in Herzlia for as long as we wanted it. We were there for a few months until we found a spacious and well-appointed flat in the north part of Tel Aviv. Had it been less well-appointed and less spacious, I still would have taken it for sentimental reasons: it was located, I discovered, between Chaim Weizmann Street, one half block east, and Louis Lipsky Street, one half block west, a location impossible to resist.

My withdrawal from the Institute was accompanied by more joy than heartache. The minor wrenches and wounds were amply offset by a flow of generous affection and appreciation. Literally thousands of friends and acquaintances from all parts of the world, the great and the small, the known and the unknown, poured out love and gratitude. I was showered with honors. First came the coveted Rothschild Prize bestowed upon me at a magnificent function at the Knesset in Jerusalem in the presence of Victor, Lord Rothschild. Victor and Tess were at their most charming. My wife and daughter, her husband and my grandchildren were all there rejoicing in the 'greatness' of their father and grandfather. Unfortunately, the American branch, Mendy and David, with their wives and children, were not with us. I was awarded an Honorary Doctorate of Philosophy from the Hebrew University presented on the recreated campus on Mount Scopus. This occasion was made more meaningful by the fact that Mrs. James de Rothschild, one of our great patronesses, received a similar honor that day. As we approached the twenty-fifth anniversary of the Institute and my own seventy-fifth birthday, there were functions and tributes in New York, Washington, London, Rehovot and Tel Aviv. My friends at the Cameri Theatre, pleased with the fact that I was resigning from the Institute—their great competitor—and not from *their* affairs, conspired with my wife and daughter, and arranged a delightful show on the eve of my birthday: 'Portrait of the Man as a Young Artist.' They dug up pictures and songs from my childhood and youth, scenes and stories from *The Romance* and *The Eternal Road* and staged it with professional elegance, Gary Bertini conducting the orchestra and choir and their own captive actors reading the narration. They concluded the story of my 'life' with *The Eternal Road*, adding only that after this phenomenal artistic success 'there has been no trace of him. But there are certain rumors abroad in theatrical circles that he established —secretly—a scientific institute in some developing country.' They at least appreciated my long apprenticeship. There was only one speech— by Golda Meir; it was charming, affectionate, and deeply moving. The next day, my birthday, the staff of the Institute gave a party for me in the Gestetner Gardens. It was warm and happy; and, of course, especially meaningful to me. The entire staff, the gardeners, the technicians, the charwomen, the secretaries, the scientists all came with their children and grandchildren. It was like a country fair. These were the people with whom I had worked for twenty-five years, these were the people who made the Institute.

The Israeli press made much of me. A Zionist who actually resigned while he was still alive! One day during the festivities my daughter Helen asked me after reading a richly illustrated article in *Maariv* by Raphael Bashan, Israel's well-known interviewer, 'Daddy, aren't you fed up with all these celebrations and encomia?' Unblushing, I answered, 'No. I've had enough slaps, why not a few bouquets?' And remembering something Adlai Stevenson once said, I added, 'Flattery is not bad, providing you don't inhale. And I don't.'

In New York my son David had been for a few years Executive Director of the American Committee, and he and the entire New York staff worked day and night for weeks to make the Twenty-fifth Annual Weizmann Dinner the exciting and meaningful climax it turned out to be. Martha Loewenstein heads the staff there, and is still the 'conscience' of the American Committee, the Keeper of the Keys, managing to keep our meager finances, not to mention my own, in some sort of order. With Reva (Ziff) Stern, the incomparable Lillie Shultz, Evelyn Scapier, she— they all—have executed my impossible and insane demands with love and faith and dedication.

The architect of the London affair was Marcus Sieff, and everybody who was anybody was there. The principal speaker was The Honorable Richard H.S. Crossman, then a member of the Labour Government, who threw protocol and caution to the winds, paid tribute, and reminisced.

On May 4, 1970, I transferred Dr. Weizmann's legacy to me, the verbal part of it, to the new President, Dr. Sabin. 'Treat those who work here imaginatively and with affection. Make no distinction between the highest and the lowliest. . . All are Jews, all are human beings; all have come here from different climes and different conditions—many of them, alas, plucked from the burning. . .'

That's about it. My retirement is upon me. I am a free man, free to decide what to do with my next seventy-five years. Because, judging from the offers I've had, I am apparently—green pills notwithstanding—in the first flush of youth. Everybody from the Prime Minister down is trying to hang something on me, thinks I am unemployed, and need something 'to crown my career.' The Weizmann Letters don't count, nor does the proposed Max Reinhardt Center for the Performing Arts, commitments I made long ago. So far I have admirably resisted all temptation. I have said no to everybody. Well, to practically everybody. I couldn't very well refuse Teddy Kollek's request that I become the presiding genius of a new committee, or commission, to enhance the spiritual, intellectual, and aesthetic character of the Holy City. Jerusalem is, after all, something special and apart. Nor could I with a clear conscience refuse Nahum Golmann's request that I become Chairman, if only provisionally, of *Beit Hatefutzot* at Tel Aviv University. Jewish history deserves some consideration. And my Yiddish writers—I can't orphan them. The *Mishnah* says: 'It is not your duty to finish the work; neither are you free to desist from it.'

I could not have chosen a more approrpiate place than this—Celerina—in which to end the book. I began with Kikl and I end with Celerina. They have something in common. When I speak now of Kikl I refer not to the Kikl of Chapter One, the *shtetl* itself, but to the rim of Kikl—the forests, the meadows, the river, the brooks. True, there were no mountains as there are here, but there were elevations which we used to climb, especially near the orchards, steep walks up to forbidden places where dogs would bark at us and chase us and sometimes even bite us and pull at our trousers. Here in Celerina, too, we are surrounded by meadows, forests, brooks, and a lake. And through the streets, which—as in Kikl—are not really streets, the peasants pass in their carts. Nor are there real sidewalks—just narrow strips above the cobblestones, little ancient houses and a church right under my window somewhat reminiscent of Kikl's surrounding 'grandeur.'

In Kikl there was a church too and when the bells rang calling the faithful to prayer, the Jews of Kikl trembled: after the prayers the more devout would make themselves merry and beat up a couple of Jews who happened to be in the vicinity of the holy place. It very often happened. I remember the first two lines of a Yiddish song: '*Hert shoin of ihr kirchen glocken—Tzu lang hot ihr unz geshroken,* Let the church bells cease to ring —Much too long we've felt their sting.' But the church bells don't frighten me any more; I welcome them. They remind me not only of where I come from but of how far I have come. We Jews, too, called our faithful to prayer; at dawn the sexton would timidly knock on the window of each Jewish household: '*Shteyt uf zo avodas haboreh,* Rise and give thanks to the Creator.' It was done modestly, surreptitiously so as not to arouse the wrath of our Gentile neighbors. And then quietly, one by one, the Jews would gather, not in the 'great' synagogue which was reserved for the Sabbath only, where my father performed, but in the small annex of the Beit Hamidrash where the Jews studied the Torah.

Poor Kikl. Where is it now? Gone, I suppose, but never, I trust, to be forgotten. We Jews are strong on memory. For two thousand years, sitting in the Kikls of Babylon, Spain, Eastern and Central Europe and the New World, we remembered Jerusalem. And now in Jerusalem, let us not forget all the Kikls that nourished us spiritually, intellectually, and religiously, that gave birth to giants of Jewish and universal thought. If memories of them and their deeds continue to live within us, our two millenia of wandering will not have been in vain.

Celerina, July, 1970

Index